The Longman Handbook of Modern European History 1763–1985

The Longman Handbook of Modern European History 1763–1985

Chris Cook and John Stevenson

Longman

London and New York

Longman Group UK Limited,
Longman House, Burnt Mill, Harlow,
Essex CM20 2JE, England
and Associated Companies throughout the world.

Published in the United States of America
by Longman Inc., New York

First published 1987

British Library Cataloguing in Publication Data
Cook, Chris
    The Longman handbook of modern European
    history 1763–1985.
    1. Europe – History – 18th century
    2. Europe – History – 19th century
    3. Europe – History 20th century
    I. Title   II. Stevenson, John, *1946–*
    940.2   D208

    ISBN 0-582-48585-1   CSD

    ISBN 0-582-48584-3   PPR

Library of Congress Cataloguing in Publication Data
Cook, Chris, 1945–
    The Longman handbook of modern European history,
    1763–1985.

    (Longman handbooks to history)
    Bibliography: p.
    Includes index.
    1. Europe – History – Handbooks, manuals, etc.
I. Stevenson, John, 1946–   II. Title.
III. Series.
D299.C627   1987   940.2   86–18618
ISBN 0-582-48585-1
ISBN 0-582-48584-3 (pbk.)

Set in Linotron 202 9/10pt Univers

Produced by Longman Singapore Publishers (Pte) Ltd
Printed in Singapore

Contents

List of maps

Preface and acknowledgements

This handbook attempts to provide a convenient reference work for both teachers and students of modern European history from 1763 to the present day. It is a much condensed work, bringing together chronological, statistical and tabular information which is not to be found elsewhere within the confines of a single volume. The handbook covers not only political and diplomatic events but also the broader fields of social and economic history. It includes biographies of important individuals, a glossary of commonly used historical terms and a topic bibliography. No book of this type can be entirely comprehensive, nor is it intended to substitute for textbooks and more detailed reading, but we have attempted to include those facts and figures which we believe are most useful for understanding courses in later modern European history. The coverage of the volume is European-wide in its broadest sense, including events in Russia, the Balkans and Scandinavia where they are of importance. Some material on Irish history is included in this volume, but a fuller treatment can be found in *The Longman Handbook of Modern British History, 1714–1980* (Longman 1983).

Both authors would like to acknowledge the considerable help and advice in the preparation of this book of Lawrence Butler, Bob Moore, Stephen Salter, and John Young. We are also grateful to Lynda Harrison and Pat Holland for the typing.

The publishers would like to acknowledge the following for permission to use copyright material: Macmillan, London and Basingstoke for the use of tables from B. R. Mitchell, *European Historical Statistics 1750–1970* (2nd edn), 1980; and Fontana/Collins for the use of tables from C. M. Cipolla (ed.), *The Fontana Economic History of Europe*, vol. iv, 1975.

Chris Cook, Polytechnic of North London

John Stevenson, University of Sheffield

January 1987

Section I
Principal rulers and ministers

Austria

Maria Theresa	1740–65 (sole ruler)
Maria Theresa and Joseph II	1765–80 (co-rulers)
Joseph II*	1780–90 (sole ruler)
Leopold II	1790–92
Francis II	1792–1804 (when he became Francis II, Emperor of Austria)

* Joseph II was also Holy Roman Emperor (see Holy Roman Empire Sect. I).

On 11 August 1804, the Habsburg rulers took the title Emperor of Austria. Francis II renounced the title of Holy Roman Emperor (see Holy Roman Empire, Sect. I, p. 15) on 6 August 1806.

Emperors of Austria

Francis I	1804–35
Ferdinand I	1835–48
Francis Joseph	1848–1916 (after 1867 Emperor of Austria–Hungary)
Charles	1916–18 (abdicated)

Principal ministers, 1804–1918
The following individuals (extracted from a long list) wielded effective power:

Prince C. Metternich	1809–48
F. von Kalowrat	1848
Prince F. von Schwarzenberg	1848–52
A. Bach	1852–59
A. von Schmerling	1861–65
Count F. Beust	1867–70
Count E. von Taaffe	1870–71
Prince C. von Auersperg	1871–78
Count Taaffe	1879–93
Field Marshal A. Windischgrätz	1893–95
Count C. Badeni	1895–97
M. W. von Beck	1906–08
Count R. von Biernerth	1908–11
Count C. von Sturgkh	1912–16

Presidents (after the proclamation of the Republic on 12 November 1918):

Presidents

Dr X. Seits	1918–20 (stood in for Head of State)
Dr M. Hainisch	1920–28
Dr W. Miklas	1928–38

From 1938 to 1945, Austria was part of the German Reich.

Prime ministers/Chancellors (prior to the Anschluss)

E. Dollfuss	May 1932–July 1934
K. Schuschnigg	July 1934–Mar 1938
A. Seyss Inquart	Mar 1938–45

Presidents after 1945

K. Renner	1945–50
T. Körner	1951–57
A. Schárf	1957–65
F. Jonas	1965–74
B. Kreisky	1974 (April–July)
R. Kirchschläger	1974–

Bavaria

Electors

Maximilian III	1745–77
Charles Theodore I	1777–99
Maximilian IV (King Maximilian I after 1806)	1799–1825

Kings

Maximilian I	1806–25
Ludwig I	1825–48
Maximilian II	1848–64
Ludwig II	1864–86 (became insane)
Otto I	1886–1913 (insane; regents in charge)
Ludwig III	1913–18

In 1918 a Republic was proclaimed.

Belgium

Independence from Holland was proclaimed on 18 November 1830.

Kings

Leopold I	1831–65
Leopold II	1865–1909
Albert I	1909–34
Leopold III	1934–51*
Prince Charles (Regent)	1944–50
Leopold III	1950 (20 July–10 August)
Baudouin, Prince Royal	(after 11 August 1950)
Baudouin I	1951–

* Leopold III was a prisoner of war, May 1940–5. There was a Regency (1944–50) after which Leopold briefly resumed his duties (1950), Baudouin then took over, and Leopold formally abdicated in July 1951.

Czechoslovakia

Founded as an independent state, 14 November 1918.

Presidents

T. Masaryk	1918–35
E. Beneš*	1935–38
E. Hácha	1938–45

* Beneš was President of the Czech government-in-exile after the proclamation of a German Protectorate in March 1939. Beneš returned to Czechoslovakia in 1945.

E. Beneš	1945–48
K. Gottwald	1948–53
A. Zápotecký	1953–57
A. Novotný	1957–68
L. Svoboda	1968–75
G. Husák	1975–

Denmark

Sovereigns (Norway as well as Denmark until 1814)

Frederick V	1746–66
Christian VII	1766–1808
Frederick (Crown Prince Regent)	1784–1808
Frederick VI	1808–39 (not King of Norway after 1814)
Christian VIII	1839–48
Frederick VII	1848–63
Christian IX	1863–1906
Frederick VIII	1906–12
Christian X	1912–47
Frederick IX	1947–72
Margaret II	1972–

Finland

Finland proclaimed independence on 6 December 1917 (having previously been part of Czarist Russia). The following were presidents of the Republic:

Prof. K. J. Ståhlberg	1919–25
Dr L. Relander	1925–31
Dr P. E. Svinhufvud	1931–37
K. Kallio	1937–40
Dr R. Ryti	1940–44
Field-Marshal C. Mannerheim	1944–45
J. Paasikivi	1945–56
Dr U. Kekkonen	1956–82
Dr M. Koivisto	1982–

France

Kings

Louis XV	1715–74
Louis XVI	1774–93 (deposed, Sept. 1792; executed Jan. 1793).

First Republic, 1792–95

Maximilien Robespierre – dominant figure from July 1793–July 1794

The Directory, 1795–99

The Directory: the following filled the five Directorships, 1795–9: Paul, Count de Barras; Jean François Rewbell; Louis-Marc de Larevellière-Lépeauz; Charles Le Tourneur; Lazare Carnot; François de Barthélemy; Nicolas François; Philippe de Douai; Jean Baptiste Treilhard; Louis Gohier; Jean François Moulin; Roger Ducos; Emmanuel Sieyès.

The Consulate, 1799–1802

The Directory was overthrown by Napoleon on 9 November 1799. Napoleon set up the Consulate, in which he filled the post of First Consul from 9 November 1799 until 18 May 1804 (alone from 4 August 1802). His fellow-consuls from 9 November 1799 until 27 December 1799 were Emmanuel Sieyès and Roger Ducos; from 27 December 1799 until 4 August 1802 Jean Jacques de Cambacérès and Charles Lebrun.

The Empire, 1804–14, 1815 (Mar.–Jun.)

Napoleon became Emperor on 18 May 1804, abdicating on 6 April 1814. He returned briefly as Emperor, 10 March 1815 until his second abdication on 22 June 1815.

Kings, 1814–48

Louis XVIII	1814–24 (but see above)
Charles X	1824–30 (abdicated)
Louis Philippe	1830–48 (Feb.) (abdicated)

Prime ministers, 1815–48

Duc de Talleyrand	1815 (July–Sept.)
Duc de Richelieu	1815–18
Marquis Dessolles	1818–19
Comte de Décazes	1819–20
Duc de Richelieu	1820–21
Duc Villèle	1821–28
Vicomte de Martignac	1828–29
Prince de Polignac	1829–30
Duc de Mortemart	1830 (July)
Marquis de Lafayette	1830 (July)
Duc de Broglie	1830 (Aug.)

Jacques Lafitte	1830–31
Casimir Périer	1831–32
Duc de Dalmatie	1832–34
Admiral de Rigny	1834 (Mar.–July)
Comte Gérard	1834 (Jul.–Oct.)
Duc de Broglie	1834 (Oct.–Nov.)
H. B. Maret	1834 (Nov.)
Duc de Trevise	1834–35
Duc de Broglie	1835–36
Adolphe Thiers	1836 (Feb.–Sept.)
Comte Molé	1836–39
Duc de Dalmatie	1839–40
Adolphe Thiers	1840 (Mar.–Oct.)
Duc de Dalmatie	1840–47
Guillaume Guizot	1847–48

Second Republic

Louis Bonaparte (President)	1848–52

Second Empire

Napoleon III (the title adopted by Louis Bonaparte on the proclamation of the Second Empire)	1852–70 (abdicated)

The Third Republic (presidents)

A. Thiers	1871–73
Marshal MacMahon	1873–79
J. Grévy	1879–87
S. Carnot	1887–94 (assassinated)
J. Casimir-Périer	1894–95
F. F. Faure	1895–99
E. Loubet	1899–1906
A. Fallières	1906–13
R. Poincaré	1913–20
P. Deschanel	1920 (Jan.–Sept.)
A. Millerand	1920–24

G. Doumergue	1924–31
P. Doumer	1931–32
A. Lebrun	1932–40

Marshal Pétain on 11 July 1940 took over the powers of President and added them to his own as Prime Minister. He then appointed a chief of state.

Chief of state

| Adm. Darlan | Feb. 1941–Nov. 1942 |
| P. Laval | Nov. 1942–May 1945 |

A government of National Unity was formed on 1 December 1945 with General Charles de Gaulle as head of state. He resigned on 2 February 1946. A new constitution came into force on 24 December 1946 (Fourth Republic).

Prime ministers: Inter-war France

G. Clemenceau	1917–20
A. Millerand	1920 (Jan.–Oct.)
M. Leygues	1920–21
M. A. Briand	1921–22
R. Poincaré	1922–24
F. Marsal	1924 (June only)
E. Herriot	1924–25
M. Painlevé	1925 (May–Nov.)
M. A. Briand	1925–26
R. Poincaré	1926–29
A. Briand	1929 (July–Nov.)
A. Tardieu	1929–30
M. Steeg	1930–31
P. Laval	1931–32
A. Tardieu	1932 (Feb.–June)
E. Herriot	1932 (June–Dec.)
J. Paul-Boncour	1932–33
E. Daladier	1933 (Jan.–Oct.)
A. Sarraut	1933 (Oct.–Nov.)
C. Chautemps	1933–34
E. Daladier	1934 (Jan.–Feb.)
G. Doumergue	1934 (Feb.–Nov.)

P.-E. Flandin	1934–35
F. Bouisson	1935 (June only)
P. Laval	1935–36
A. Sarrault	1936 (Jan.–June)
L. Blum	1936–37 (June–June)
C. Chautemps	1937–38 (June–Mar.)
L. Blum	1938 (Mar.–Apr.)
E. Daladier	1938–40
P. Reynaud	1940 (Mar.–June)
Marshal P. Pétain	1940–42

(Fourth Republic)

President of the Republic

| V. Auriol | 1947–53 |
| R. Coty | 1953–58 |

A new constitution came into force on 5 October 1958 (Fifth Republic).

(Fifth Republic)

President of the Republic

Gen. C. de Gaulle	1958–69
G. Pompidou	1969–74
A. Poher	1974 (Apr.–May, interim)
V. Giscard d'Estaing	1974–81
F. Mitterrand	1981–

Prime ministers (after 1946)

F. Gouin	1946 (Jan.–June)
G. Bidault	1946 (June–Dec.)
L. Blum	1946–47 (Jan.)
P. Ramadier	1947 (Jan.–Nov.)
R. Schuman	1947–48 (July)
A. Marie	1948 (July–Sept.)
R. Schuman	1948 (Sept.)
H. Queuille	1948–49
G. Bidault	1949–50

H. Queuille	1950 (July)
R. Pleven	1950–51
H. Queuille	1951 (Mar.–Aug.)
R. Pleven	1951–52
E. Fauré	1952 (Jan.–Mar.)
A. Pinay	1952–53
R. Mayer	1953 (Jan.–June)
J. Laniel	1953–54
P. Mendès-France	1954–55
E. Fauré	1955–56
G. Mollet	1956–57
F. Gaillard	1957–59
M. Debré	1959–62
G. Pompidou	1962–68
M. Couve de Murville	1968–69
J. Chaban-Delmas	1969–72
P. Messmer	1972–74
J. Chirac	1974–76
R. Barre	1976–81
P. Mauroy	1981–84
L. Fabius	1984–86
J. Chirac	1986–

Germany

The German Empire was established on 18 January 1871. Henceforth, until 1918, the Kings of Prussia were Emperors of Germany.

Emperors

William I	1871–88
Frederick III	1888
William II	1888–1918 (abdicated)

Chancellors

O. von Bismarck-Schönhausen	1871–90
L. von Caprivi	1890–94
Prince von Hohenlohe-Schillingsfürst	1894–1900

Baron von Bülow	1900–9
T. Bethmann-Hollweg	1909–17
G. Michaelis	1917
G. von Herling	1917–18
Prince Max of Baden	1918
Friedrich Ebert	1918

The Republic was proclaimed on the abdication of Kaiser William II, on 9 November 1918.

President

| Friedrich Ebert | Feb. 1919–Feb. 1925 |
| P. von Hindenburg | Apr. 1925–Aug. 1934 |

Reich chancellors, 1919–33

P. Scheidemann	1919 (Feb.–June)
G. Bauer	1919–20
H. Müller	1920 (Mar.–June)
C. Fehrenbach	1920–21
J. Wirth	1921–22
W. Cuno	1922–23
G. Stresemann	1923 (Aug.–Nov.)
W. Marx	1923–24
H. Luther	1925–26
W. Marx	1926–28
H. Müller	1928–30
H. Brüning	1930–32
F. von Papen	1932 (May–Nov.)
K. von Schleicher	1932–33 (Jan.)

Chancellors and Führer

| Adolf Hitler | Aug. 1934–Apr. 1945 |
| Adm. C. Dönitz | Apr. 1945–June 1945 |

After the Allied administration of Germany after 1945, the Federal Republic of Germany (i.e. West Germany) came into being in September 1949.

(1) Heads of state (presidents)

| T. Heuss | 1949–59 |
| H. Lübke | 1959–69 |

G. Heinemann	1969–74
W. Scheel	1974–79
K. Carstens	1979–

(2) Chancellors

K. Adenauer	1949–63
L. Erhard	1963–66
K. Kiesinger	1966–69
W. Brandt	1969–74
H. Schmidt	1974–82
H. Kohl	1982–

In the German Democratic Republic (East Germany), the position was:
Head of State (President until 1960, Chairman of the Council of State thereafter)

W. Pieck	1949–60
W. Ulbricht	1960–73
W. Stoph	1973–76
E. Honecker	1976–

Great Britain

Sovereigns

George III	1760–1820
George IV	1820–30 (Prince Regent since 1811)
William IV	1830–37
Victoria	1837–1901
Edward VII	1901–10
George V	1910–36
Edward VIII	1936 (abdicated, never crowned)
George VI	1936–52
Elizabeth II	1952–

Prime ministers

George Grenville	1763–65
Marquess of Rockingham	1765–66
Earl of Chatham	1766–68
Duke of Grafton	1768–70

Lord North	1770–82
Marquess of Rockingham	1782 (Mar.–July)
Earl of Shelburne	1782–83
Duke of Portland	1783 (Apr.–Dec.)
William Pitt	1783–1801
Henry Addington	1801–4
William Pitt	1804–6
Lord Grenville	1806–7
Duke of Portland	1807–9
Spencer Perceval	1809–12
Earl of Liverpool	1812–27
George Canning	1827 (Apr.–Aug.)
Viscount Goderich	1827–28
Duke of Wellington	1828–30
Earl Grey	1830–34
Viscount Melbourne	1834 (July–Nov.)
Duke of Wellington	1834 (Nov.–Dec.)
Sir Robert Peel	1834–35
Viscount Melbourne	1835–41
Sir Robert Peel	1841–46
Lord John Russell (Earl Russell)	1846–52
Earl of Derby	1852 (Feb.–Dec.)
Earl of Aberdeen	1852–55
Viscount Palmerston	1855–58
Earl of Derby	1858–59
Viscount Palmerston	1859–65
Earl Russell	1865–66
Earl of Derby	1866–68
Benjamin Disraeli	1868 (Feb.–Dec.)
W. E. Gladstone	1868–74
Benjamin Disraeli	1874–80
W. E. Gladstone	1880–85
Marquess of Salisbury	1885–86
W. E. Gladstone	1886 (Feb.–July)
Marquess of Salisbury	1886–92

W. E. Gladstone	1892–94
Earl of Rosebery	1894–95
Marquess of Salisbury	1895–1902
A. J. Balfour	1902–5
Sir Henry Campbell-Bannerman	1905–8
H. H. Asquith	1908–16
David Lloyd George	1916–22
A. Bonar Law	1922–23
Stanley Baldwin	1923–24 (Jan.)
J. Ramsay MacDonald	1924 (Jan.–Nov.)
Stanley Baldwin	1924–29
J. Ramsay MacDonald	1929–35
Stanley Baldwin	1935–37
Neville Chamberlain	1937–40
Winston Churchill	1940–45
Clement Attlee	1945–51
Winston Churchill	1951–55
Anthony Eden	1955–57
Harold Macmillan	1957–63
Sir Alec Douglas-Home	1963–64
Harold Wilson	1964–70
Edward Heath	1970–74
Harold Wilson	1974–76
James Callaghan	1976–79
Margaret Thatcher	1979–

Greece

Greece proclaimed independence from the Ottoman Empire, which recognised her independence on 14 September 1829.

Kings

Otto (of Bavaria)	1833–62
George I	1863–1913
Constantine I	1913–17
Alexander	1917–20
Constantine I (again)	1920–22

George II	1922–23

A Republic was in existence, 1924–35.

George II (again)	1935–44
Regency	1944–46
George II (again)	1946–47
Paul I	1947–64
Constantine II	1964–74*

* When the monarchy was formally voted out.

Presidents (after 1973)

G. Papadopoulos	1973 (June–Nov., Provisional President)
P. Ghizikis	1973–74
M. Stassinopoulos	1974–75
K. Tsatsos	1975–80
K. Karamanlis	1980–

Holy Roman Empire*

Francis I (of Lorraine)	1745–65
Joseph II	1765–90
Leopold II	1790–92
Francis II	1792–1806

* Until 1806, when the Holy Roman Empire became extinct.

Hungary

Hungary became an independent Republic on 16 November 1918

Count Karolyi	Nov. 1918–Mar. 1919 (Provisional President)

In January 1920, Hungary was proclaimed a monarchy, but Admiral M. von Horthy was Regent, 1920–1945. The absent Charles (*see* Austria) never assumed the throne. A Republic was proclaimed in 1945 and a republican constitution came into effect in 1946.

Presidents (Chairman of Praesidium after 1952, Chairman of the Presiding Council after 1967)

Z. Tildy	1946–48
A. Szakasits	1948–50

S. Rónai   1950–52
I. M. Dobi   1952–67
P. Losonczi   1967–

Ireland

Heads of state

After 1922, although Ireland was a self-governing Dominion, the British
sovereign was still recognised as head of state. After December 1937,
when the constitution of the Irish Free State as an independent sovereign
state came into force, the following have been Presidents:

Douglas Hyde   1938–45

Sean T. O'Kelly   1945–59

Eamon de Valera   1959–73

Erskine Childers   1973–74

Cearbhall O. Dalaigh   1974–76

Patrick Hillery   1976–

Prime ministers (after 1922)

Michael Collins   1922 (Finance and General Minister
                                  in the Provisional Government)

W. Cosgrave   1922–32

E. de Valera   1932–48

J. A. Costello   1948–51

E. de Valera   1951–54

J. A. Costello   1954–57

E. de Valera   1957–59

S. Lemass   1959–66

J. Lynch   1966–73

L. Cosgrave   1973–77

J. Lynch   1977–79

C. Haughey   1979–81

G. FitzGerald   1981–82

C. Haughey   1982 (Mar.–Dec.)

G. FitzGerald   1982–87

C. Haughey   1987–

Italy

For Italy prior to unification, see under Sardinia, the Two Sicilies and the Papacy.
    The Kingdom of Italy was formed on 17 March 1861.

Kings

Victor Emmanuel	1861–78
Umberto I	1878–1900
Victor Emmanuel III	1900–46 (abdicated)
Umberto II	1946 (abdicated)

A Republic was proclaimed on 18 June 1946.

Presidents

L. Einaudi	1948–55
G. Gronchi	1955–62
A. Segni	1962–64
G. Saragat	1964–71
G. Leone	1971–78
A. Fanfani	1978 (June–July)
A. Pertini	1979–

The Netherlands

Known as the United Provinces until 1795, it was ruled by William V of Orange-Nassau, hereditary Stadtholder from 1751 to 1795. Under French occupation after 1795, the Southern Provinces were annexed to France, the Northern Provinces becoming the Batavian Republic. Louis Bonaparte ruled as King of Holland, 1806–10. From 1810 to 1813, Holland was annexed to France. Independence was confirmed in 1815, when Belgium was added to Holland to form the Netherlands.

Kings

William I	1813–40
William II	1840–49
William III	1849–90
Wilhelmina	1890–1948 (abdicated)
Juliana	1948–80 (abdicated)
Beatrix	1980–

Norway

For the period up to 1814, see under Denmark. For the period 1814–1905 see under Sweden.

Kings (of independent Norway after 1905)

Haakon VII	1905–57
Olaf V	1957–

The Papacy

Popes (since 1763)

Pope	Family name	
Clement XIII	Carlo della Torre Rezzonico	1758–69
Clement XIV	Giovanni Vicenzo Antonio Ganganelli	1769–74
Pius VI	Giovanni Angelo Braschi	1775–99
Pius VII	Luigi Barnabo Chiaramonti	1800–23
Leo XII	Annibale della Genga	1823–29
Pius VIII	Francesco Xaverio Castiglione	1829–30
Gregory XVI	Bartolommeo Capellare	1831–46
Pius IX	Count Giovanni Maria Mastai-Ferreti	1846–78
Leo XIII	Gioacchino Vincenzo Rafaele Luigi Pecci	1878–1903
Pius X	Giuseppe Sarto	1903–14
Benedict XV	Giacomo della Chiesa	1914–22
Pius XI	Achille Ratti	1922–39
Pius XII	Eugenio Pacelli	1939–58
John XXIII	Angelo Giuseppe Roncalli	1958–63
Paul VI	Giovanni Battista Montini	1963–78
John Paul I	Albino Luciani	1978
John Paul II	Karol Wojtyla	1978–

Poland

Kings (until 1795)

Augustus III	1733–63
Stanislaw Poniatowski	1764–94

In 1795, the Third Partition of Poland took place. From 1806 to 1815, a Grand Duchy of Warsaw existed, the creation of Napoleon. The Congress of Vienna created a Kingdom of Poland (under the Russian Crown). After the 1830 rising this was suppressed. Not until 1918 did Poland regain independence, when an independent state was proclaimed on 5 November 1918.

Presidents

J. Piłsudski	1918–22
Gabriel Narutowicz	1922 (assassinated)
S. Wojciechowski	1922–26
I. Mościcki	1926–39

On 29 September 1939 the German occupation of Poland began. The Polish Government was in exile until the end of the war.

Prime Ministers of the Government in Exile

General Wladyslaw Sikorski	1939–43
Stanislaw Mikolajczyk	1943–45

In July 1945 a Provisional Government of National Unity was set up, composed of the London government in exile and the Russian-backed Committee of National Liberation. Its task was to run Poland until free elections could take place. The elections were held in 1947, resulting in an overwhelming victory for the Communist-Socialist candidates.

President

Bolesław Bierut	1945–52

On 22 July 1952 a new constitution replaced the office of President with a Council of State.

President of the Council of State

A. Zawadski	1952–64
E. Ochab	1964–68
Marshal M. Spychalski	1968–70
J. Cyrankiewicz	1970–72
H. Jabloński	1972–

From 1956 to 1970, Gomulka was the most powerful figure in Poland, when he was succeeded by Gierek. Since 1981, General Jaruzelski has been Poland's strong man.

Portugal

Monarchs (Braganza dynasty) (to 1910)

Joseph	1750–77
Pedro III	1777–86

Maria I	1777–1816
John VI	1816–26
Pedro IV	1826
Maria II	1826–28
Miguel	1828–34
Maria II (again)	1834–53
Pedro V	1853–61
Luiz I	1861–89
Carlos I	1889–1908
Manuel II	1908–10

A Republic was proclaimed in 1910.

Prussia

Kings

Frederick II (the Great)	1740–86
Frederick William II	1786–97
Frederick William III	1797–1840
Frederick William IV	1840–58 (insane)
Regency	1858–61
William I	1861–88
Frederick III	1888
William II	1888–1918 (abdicated)

NB. The creation of the German Empire was in 1871, after which the Kings of Prussia became German Emperors.

Romania

Kings 1881–1947

Carol I	1881–1914
Ferdinand	1914–27
Michael	1927–30
Carol II	1930–40 (abdicated)
Michael I	1940–47 (abdicated)

As a result of a plebiscite a Republic was established and the King abdicated.

Presidents of the Praesidium

C. I. Parhon	1948–52
Dr. P. Groza	1952–58
I. G. Maurer	1958–61
G. Gheorghiu-Dej	1961–65
C. Stoica	1965–67
N. Ceauçescu	1967–

Russia

Tsars

Catherine II (the Great)	1762–96
Paul I	1796–1801
Alexander I	1801–25
Nicholas I	1825–55
Alexander II	1855–81
Alexander III	1881–94
Nicholas II	1894–1917 (abdicated)

Prime ministers (under Nicholas II, 1894–1917)

J. N. Durnovo	1895–1903
S. J. Witte	1903–6
I. L. Goremykin	1906 (May–July)
P. A. Stolypin	1906–11
W. N. Kokovtsov	1911–14
I. L. Goremykin	1914–16
B. W. Stürmer	1916 (Feb.–Nov.)
A. F. Trepov	1916 (Nov.)–1917 (Jan.)
N. D. Golitsin	1917 (Jan.–Mar.)

Under the provisional government

G. J. Lvov	1917 (Mar.–July)
A. F. Kerensky	1917 (July–

A constitution for the Federal Republic was adopted on 10 July 1918, by a government which had taken office on 8 November 1917.

President of the Council of People's Commissars

V. I. Ulianov-Lenin	1917–22

A new constitution of 30 December 1922 replaced this office by a Central Executive Committee with four chairmen. A new constitution came into force on 5 December 1936 establishing the office of Chairman of the Presidium of the Supreme Soviet of the USSR, as head of state.

Chairmen

M. I. Kalinin	1936–46
N. M. Shvernik	1946–53
Marshal K. E. Voroshilov	1953–60
L. I. Brezhnev	1960–64
A. I. Mikoyan	1964–65
N. V. Podgorny	1965–77
L. I. Brezhnev	1977–82
Y. V. Andropov	1983–84
K. V. Chernenko	1984–85
M. Gorbachev	1985–

Effective rulers (1917–86)

V. I. Lenin	1917–22
J. Stalin	1922–53
N. Khrushchev	1953–64 (deposed)
L. I. Brezhnev	1964–82
Y. V. Andropov	1982–84
K. V. Chernenko	1984–85
M. Gorbachev	1985–

Sardinia

(Sardinia–Piedmont–Savoy)

Kings

Victor Amadeus III	1773–96
Charles Emmanuel IV	1796–1802

(Sardinia annexed to France, December 1798; subsequently occupied by Russian and Austrian forces, June 1799–June 1800; French rule restored; Charles Emmanuel abdicated in 1802, in favour of his brother)

Victor Emmanuel I	1802–21 (abdicated)

(Charles Felix ruled as Regent; returned to Sardinia, 1821)

Charles Felix I	1821–24

| Charles Albert I | 1824–49 |
| Victor Emmanuel II | 1849–78 (after 1861, King of Italy *q.v.*) |

Serbia

An independent kingdom after 1878.

Kings

Milan Obrenovitch	1882–89 (abdicated)
Alexander Obrenovitch	1889–1903
Peter	1903–21*

* See also reference to Yugoslavia in this section.

Two Sicilies

(Naples and Sicily)

Kings

Ferdinand I	1759–1825*
Francis I	1825–30
Ferdinand II	1830–59
Francis II	1859–60

* Joseph Bonaparte declared King, 1806. He renounced the throne in 1808. Joachim Murat was declared King, 1808, and deposed in 1815.

Spain

Kings

Charles III	1759–88
Charles IV	1788–1808 (abdicated)
Ferdinand VII	1808

(From 1808 to 1812, when he abdicated, Spain was ruled by Joseph Bonaparte).

| Ferdinand VII (again) | 1813–33 |
| Isabella II | 1833–68 (fled) |

(Interregnum from 1868 to 1874).

Alfonso XII	1874–85
Alfonso XIII	1886–1931 (abdicated)

A Republic proclaimed on 14 April 1931.

Presidents

N. A. Zamora y Torres	1931–36
M. Azana	1936–39

Chief of the state

Gen. Francisco Franco	1939–75

King

Juan Carlos I	1975–

Sweden

Kings

Adolphus Frederick	1751–71
Gustavus III	1771–92
Gustavus IV Adolphus	1792–1809
Charles XIII	1809–18 (also King of Norway after 1814)
Charles XIV John (Bernadotte)	1818–44
Oscar I	1844–59
Charles XV	1859–72
Oscar II	1872–1907 (renounced Norwegian throne 1905)
Gustavus V	1907–50
Gustavus VI, Adolphus	1950–73
Charles XVI, Gustavus	1973–

Turkey

Sultans

Mustafa III	1757–74
Abdul Hamid I	1774–89
Selim III	1789–1807

Mustafa IV	1807–8
Mahmud II	1808–39
Abdul Mejid I	1839–61
Abdul Aziz	1861–76
Murad V	1876
Abdul Hamid II	1876–1909
Mohammed V	1909–18
Mohammed VI	1918–22

The office of Sultan was abolished, November 1922. Prince Abdul Mejid was Caliph from 1922 to 1924. A Republic was proclaimed on 29 October 1923.

Presidents

M. Kemal Atatürk	1923–38
I. Inönü	1938–50
C. Bayar	1950–60
C. Gursel	1961–66
C. Sunay	1966–73
F. Korutürk	1973–80
I. S. Caglayangil	1980 (Apr.–Sept.)
K. Evren	1980–

United Provinces

See under: **Netherlands**

USSR

See under: **Russia**

Yugoslavia

The independent Serb, Croat and Slovene State was formed in December 1918. The name was changed in October 1929 to Yugoslavia.

Kings

| Peter I | 1903–21 (formerly King of Serbia) |
| Alexander I | 1921–34 |

Peter II   1934–45 (abdicated)

A Republic was proclaimed in 1945.

President of the Praesidium

Dr I. Ribar   1945–53

President of the Republic

Marshal I. Broz-Tito   1953–80

After 1980, a 'Collective Presidency' was established.

The Bonaparte family

(† = died.)

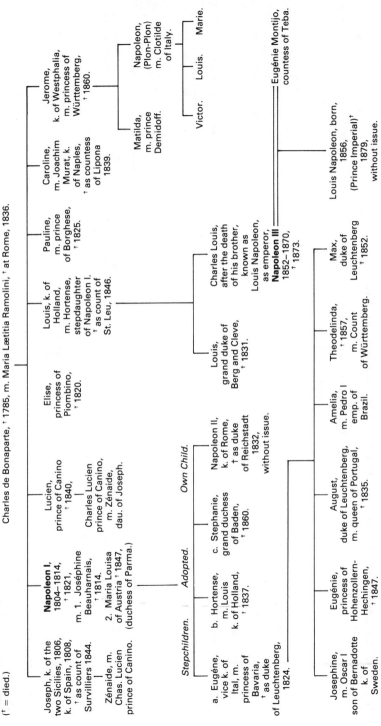

House of Bourbon in the older and younger (Orléans) line.

(† = died.)

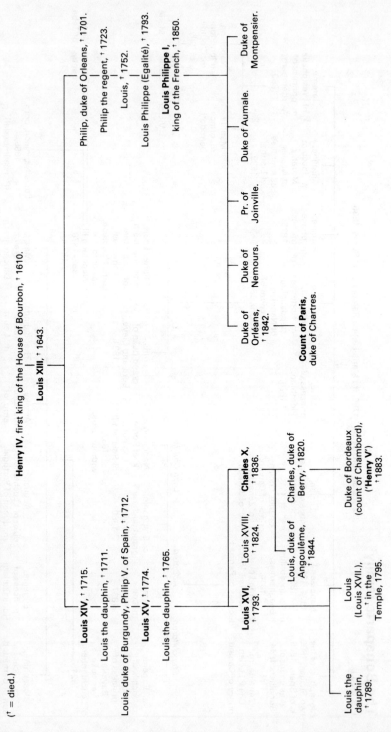

Political events

Europe at the end of the Ancien Regime

1762 Catherine the Great becomes Czarina of Russia.   Publication of
Rousseau's *Social Contract* and *Emile*.

1763 Peace of Paris ends Seven Years War; Britain makes extensive
colonial gains in North America and India from France.   Peace
of Hubertusburg between Prussia and Austria; Prussia retains
Silesia but evacuates Saxony.

1764 Stanilaw Poniatowski, protégé of Catherine the Great and
Frederick the Great, becomes King of Poland.

1765 Beginning of Stamp Act crisis between Britain and her American
Colonies.   Joseph II becomes Emperor of Austria and joint-
ruler with Maria Theresa, his mother, of the Austrian states.

1766 Russian influence in Poland forces Polish Diet to agree to equal
rights for non-Catholics and administrative reform.

1767 Catherine appoints Great Commission. Alliance of Russia and
Prussia to protect Polish non-Catholics.

1768 Polish Confederation of Bar wages war against King Stanilas who
is supported by Russia.

1771 Conflict between French Chancellor Maupeou and Parlement of
Paris; it is abolished and replaced by the Conseil du Roi.

1772 First Partition of Poland between Russia, Prussia and Austria.
Gustavus III of Sweden by a bloodless coup d'état becomes
absolute ruler and introduces enlightened reforms.

1773 Pugachev Revolt begins in Russia.

1774 Treaty of Kutchuk-Kainarji between Turkey and Russia.
Accession of Louis XVI; Parlement of Paris restored. Turgot
becomes Comptroller-General.

1775 First armed conflict between American Colonists and British at
Lexington. Conciliation attempts fail and open warfare develops.

1776 American Declaration of Independence.   Adam Smith's *Wealth
of Nations* published.   Turgot begins overhaul of French
finances, but is dismissed. Necker becomes Comptroller.

1778 France allies with the American colonists; war declared between
Britain and France.

1779 Spain declares war on Britain, Franco–Spanish fleet besieges
Gibraltar. Congress of Teschen terminates war of Bavarian
Succession.

1780 Joseph II assumes sole power in Austria; abolishes serfdom in
Bohemia, Hungary, and southern provinces.   Armed Neutrality
of Northern Powers against British interference with shipping.

1781   Joseph II introduces religious toleration and abolishes serfdom in Austria.   Necker publishes his 'Compte rendu' a first statement of French finances, but is dismissed from office.   Capitulation of British army under Cornwallis at Yorktown virtually seals fate of war in America.

1783   Treaty of Versailles recognises the independence of the United States.   Calonne becomes French finance minister.   Pitt the Younger becomes Prime Minister in Britain.

1784   Joseph II outrages national sentiment in Hungary by removing the crown of Hungary to Vienna and making German the official language.

1785   Diamond necklace scandal in France discredits the Court and Marie Antoinette.

1786   Calonne proposes sweeping reforms in France, including the revival of provincial assemblies, a land-tax without exemptions, free trade in corn, and the abolition of forced labour (corvée). The King agrees to summon an Assembly of Notables.   In Holland, the 'Patriot' Party restricts the power of the stadtholder, William V.

1787   Assembly of Notables meets in France and rejects proposals of Calonne. The Notables are dissolved and de Brienne succeeds Calonne. The Parlement of Paris demands the convocation of the States-General but is banished, only to be recalled a few weeks later.   Prussian army defeat the Dutch 'Patriots' and restores the Prince of Orange.

1788   Brienne announces national bankruptcy and is dismissed; Necker recalled and States-General summoned for 1 May 1789.
Charles IV becomes King of Spain, but power falls into the hands of his Queen, Marie Louise, and her favourite Godoy.
England, Holland and Prussia form Triple Alliance to maintain the peace of Europe.

1789   Meeting of States-General in France (see pp. 32–4)   Revolt in the Belgian Netherlands against Joseph II.

The French Revolution

1783 Dec.	The Queen's favourite, Calonne, appointed as Minister of Finance.
1786 Aug.	Calonne proposes a land tax and a stamp tax. These would be assessed by Provincial Estates. He persuades the King to summon an Assembly of Notables as he knows parliament will resist his proposals.
1787 Feb. 22	The Assembly of Notables meets and declares against Calonne.
Apr. 17	Calonne driven from office.
May	Lorriene de Brienne, Archbishop of Toulouse becomes Chief of the Council of Finance. The Assembly of Notables grants his request for a new loan of 60,000,000 livres.
May 25	Dissolution of the Assembly of Notables which has refused to agree to new taxes. There is conflict with the Parlement of Paris which refuses to accept the proposed land and stamp taxes. It asserts the States General has the sole right to levy taxes.
Aug. 6	The decrees on taxation are passed by a 'lit de justice'.
Aug. 7	The Parlement gains great popularity by challenging the validity of a 'lit de justice'.
Aug. 14	Parlement exiled to Troyes by the King.
Sept. 24	The King and Brienne agree to drop their demand for new taxes and the Parlement returns to Paris.
1788 May 8	**The May Edicts**
	Louis persuaded to hold a 'lit de justice' suppressing the Parlements and establishing new Courts of Appeal.
June/July	The Revolt of the Nobility.
July 21	At a meeting of the Estates of Dauphiné the nobility condemn the May Edicts and demand a convocation of the States General and Provincial Estates. They also speak in support of the Third Estate.
Aug. 16	Brienne announces a national bankruptcy.
Aug. 25	Brienne dismissed by the King.
	The States General summoned to meet on 1 May 1789.
Aug. 27	Necker recalled as Minister of Finance.
Sept.	Recall of the Paris Parlement which recommends the States General be held as in 1614.
Nov. 6	Meeting of the second Assembly of Notables.
Dec. 27	Decision by the Royal Council on the doubling of the Third Estate.
1789 Feb.–Apr.	Election of States-General. *Cahiers* drafted.
Apr. 27–28	The Reveillon Riots in Paris.
May 5	Meeting of the States General opened by the King at Versailles.

June 17	The Third Estate assumes the title of National Assembly, ignoring the existence of the other Estates and securing the leadership of the nation.
June 19	By a majority of one the Clergy vote to join the Third Estate.
June 20	The Tennis Court Oath taken by the Third Estate. They swear not to disband until a constitution is established and confirmed on solid foundations.
June 23	At a Royal Séance the King makes important concessions, but declares the edicts of 17 June illegal, insisting that the Estates should meet separately and that the Assembly should be dissolved.
June 27	The clergy and nobility join the Third Estate for fear that opposition could endanger the King's life.
July 6	A Committee appointed to frame a new constitution.
July 11	The electors of the Third Estate of Paris form a Civic Guard to maintain order in Paris. Under the influence of Court extremists Louis dismisses Necker.
July 12	The Parisian mob seizes arms, fearing the dismissal of Necker was the signal for a royal coup d'état. The electors refuse to sanction the mob's action.
July 14	**The fall of the Bastille** Louis is told by close adviser 'it is not a revolt, it is a revolution'. Troops withdrawn from Paris.
July 15	The adoption of the Tricolour; Bailly appointed Mayor of Paris; Lafayette appointed Commander of the Civic Guard which becomes the National Guard. The King recalls Necker
July 16	Necker returns; flight of Artois, Condé and Broglie, first of the émigrés.
July 17	Louis visits Paris where he accepts the Tricolour and confirms Bailly and Lafayette in their posts.
July 20	The beginning of the worst stage of the 'Grand Peur' (Great Fear) in the countryside.
July 22	The murder of Fouillon and Berthier in Paris.
Aug. 4	The abolition of tithes worth 120,000,000 francs.
Aug. 4–11	Decrees of the National Assembly abolishing feudal rights and many privileges in French society. Representatives of the Nobles make a voluntary surrender of all feudal rights and privileges.
Aug. 26	**Declaration of the Rights of Man and Citizens**: makes all equal before the law.
Sept. 10	The Assembly rejects the proposal of a second chamber nominated by the King as contrary to democratic sentiment.
Sept. 11	The Assembly accepts a suspensory veto for the King.
Oct. 1	The Queen and Dauphin attend a banquet at Versailles where loyal toasts are made and anti-Republican sentiments expressed.
Oct. 5	The March of the Women to Versailles. Lafayette prevents the violence getting out of hand.

Oct. 6	The Royal family return to Paris at Lafayette's insistence.
Oct. 10	Talleyrand proposes the confiscation of church lands to pay state debts. Louis XVI decreed 'King of the French'.
Oct. 12	The National Assembly follows the King to Paris.

The Remaking of France 1789–91

Oct. 19	The National Assembly meets in Paris.
Oct. 21	A decree on Public Order provides for the use of martial law.
Oct. 29	Decree on electoral regulations distinguishes 'active' and 'passive' citizens. Only certain taxpayers are entitled to vote.
Oct. 31	Decree passed providing for a uniform tariff covering all France.
Nov. 2	Nationalisation of ecclesiastical estates to relieve financial difficulties.
Nov. 6	Mirabeau defeated over the question of whether the King's ministers should be allowed to sit in the Assembly.
Nov. 7	Decree excluding Deputies from ministerial posts.
Nov. 9	The National Assembly moves into the Manège.
Nov. 10	Church property confiscated and the state makes provision for the clergy.
Dec. 12–14	Decrees passed to reorganise local government.
Dec. 12	The first issue of assignats – government notes backed by public lands, the value of which is not to be exceeded by the issue of notes.
Dec. 22	Local administration reorganised. 83 new Departments and 374 Cantons created.
1790 Jan. 28	The removal of civic disabilities for Jews.
Feb. 13	The suppression of religious orders except for those involved in teaching or charitable work. Monastic vows abolished; monks and nuns were to receive state pensions.
March 15	Decree passed concerned with the terms of the redemption of seigneurial dues.
Apr. 13	The Assembly passes a decree giving absolute toleration to every form of religion.
Apr.	Assignats declared legal tender.
May 21	Paris reorganised into sections.
May 22	Wars of conquest renounced. The King given sole right to decide whether France should go to war or stay at peace.
June 11	The inhabitants of Avignon declare their wish to become part of France.
June 19	The Nobility's status and titles abolished.
July 12	The Civil Constitution of the Clergy suppresses all cathedral chapters, and intervenes in other church questions. The Pope is not consulted and foreign bishops are forbidden to interfere in the French church.

July 14	First Fête de la Fédération. The King accepts the constitution.
Aug. 16	The reorganisation of the judiciary. Debate on the mutiny at Nancy.
Aug. 27	Louis XVI reluctantly agrees to the Civil Constitution of the Clergy.
Sept. 4	Necker resigns.
Oct. 26	For the first time Louis authorises overtures to foreign courts concerning possible intervention in France.
Oct. 29	Rebellion in San Domingo.
Nov. 27	Decree to enforce the Civic Oath on the clergy passed.
Dec. 26	The King compelled to sign the decree on the Civil Constitution of the Clergy.
1791 Jan. 4	Large-scale refusal to take the oath leads to division in France and the King more willing to gain foreign aid.
Feb. 9	The first Bishops of the Constitutional Church elected.
Mar. 2	Abolition of guilds and monopolies.
Mar. 10	The Pope's pastoral letter condemns the Civil Constitution and the Declaration of the Rights of Man.
Apr. 2	The death of Mirabeau; the breach between King and Assembly widens.
Apr. 13	The Civil Constitution is condemned by the Papal Bull *Charitas*.
Apr. 18	The mob prevents Louis from spending a day hunting at St Cloud.
May 15	Blacks living in the French colonies and of free parentage are declared equal with whites in civic rights.
May 16	The 'Self-Denying Ordinance' excludes deputies of the National Assembly from membership of the Legislative Assembly.
June 14	The 'Loi Chapelier' – The Combination Law.
June 20	The flight to Varennes; the King and Royal family are prevented from escaping from France.
June 25	The King is suspended and forced to return under duress to Paris. Louis remains under suspension until he accepts the Constitution (14 September)
July 14	Second Fête de la Fédération.
July 16	A Decree provides for the reinstatement of the King on completion of the constitution.
July 17	The Massacre of the Champ de Mars.
Aug. 27	The Declaration of Pilnitz. The King of Prussia and the Emperor of Austria threaten intervention in France.
Sept.	France annexes Avignon.
Sept. 3	The new Constitution becomes law; the National Assembly becomes known as the Constituent Assembly.
Sept. 14	Louis accepts the Constitution.
Sept. 30	Dissolution of the National Assembly.
Oct. 1	Meeting of the Legislative Assembly.
Oct. 20	Brissot calls for military action to disperse the émigrés.
Nov. 9	Decree made against émigrés suspected of conspiracy ordering their return on pain of death.

Nov. 12	The King vetoes the decree against the émigrés.
Nov. 29	The decree against non-juring priests forbids them to officiate in public and deprives them of their pensions.
Dec. 12	Brissot threatens the King with insurrection.
Dec. 14	Louis tells the Assembly that an army of 150,000 men has been sent to the frontiers.
Dec. 19	Louis vetoes decree against non-juring priests.
Dec. 30	Robespierre opposes Brissot at the Jacobin Club.
1792 Jan. 2	The declaration that 1 January 1789 should be the first day of the 'Era of Liberty'.
Jan. 25	The Assembly demands Leopold II should renounce his recent treaty with Russia and ensure the dispersal of the émigré army.
Feb. 2	The property of the émigrés was declared forfeit to the nation.
Mar. 10	Formation of Dumouriez's 'Patriot Ministry'.
Apr. 5–6	Decree suppressing the Sorbonne and all religious congregations.
Apr. 20	Declaration of war on Austria.
May	The King's bodyguard of 12,000 men disbanded.
May 27	Decree against non-juring priests (vetoed on 19 June).
June 8	Decree providing for a military camp at Paris (vetoed on 19 June).
June 13	Dismissal of the 'Patriot Ministry' by the King.
June 20	The first invasion of the Tuileries by Parisians. Louis XVI crowned with the 'Cap of Liberty'.
June 28	Brissot returns to the Jacobins.
June 29	Lafayette attempts to close the Jacobin Club.
July 1	Petition of 20,000 signatures against the events of 20 June.
July 11	Decree provides for the proclamation of 'La Patrie en danger'.
July 14	Third Féte de la Fédération.
July 22	Permanence of the Sections recognised. Proclamation of 'La Patrie en danger'.
July 28	The Brunswick Manifesto (threatening the destruction of Paris should any harm come to the Royal Family) reaches Paris.
July 30	The Theatre Français Section admits 'passive' citizens. The Marseilles Battalion arrives in Paris.
July 31	The Maunconseil Section of Paris repudiates its allegiance to the throne and commits other sections to join in its demonstration demanding the deposition of the King.
Aug. 1	Passive as well as active citizens admitted to the National Guard.
Aug. 3	Petition of the Sections demands that the King be deposed.
Aug. 4	Vergniand condemns the Maunconseil Section for its republicanism.
Aug. 8	The Assembly exculpates Lafayette rejecting Robespierre's demand that he should be impeached for supporting the King in June.

Aug. 9	The Assembly postpones consideration of any republican petitions.
Aug. 10	**The Revolution of 10 August** The Tuileries is stormed by Parisian sansculottes and Marseilles Federals. The Monarchy is suspended. The Patriot Ministers are reinstated.
Aug. 11	The Commune terrorises the Assembly into authorising the arrest of people suspected of 'crimes against the state'.
Aug. 17	The Commune forces the Assembly to create the extra-ordinary tribunal of 17 August elected by the Sections and possessing final powers to try prisoners arrested under the proviso of 11 August.
Aug. 19	Defection of Lafayette to the Austrians and a Prussian army crosses the frontier.
Aug. 20	Fall of the fortress of Longwy.
Aug. 21	The guillotine claims its first political victim. A noble is executed for raising irregular troops for Royal service.
Aug. 25	Redemption charges for seignurial dues abolished.
Aug. 30	The Assembly tries to dissolve the Commune.
Sept.	The French seize Nice and Savoy from Sardinia.
Sept. 2	Fall of the fortress of Verdun to the Prussians.
Sept. 2–6	The 'September Massacres': prisoners murdered in Paris prisons.
Sept. 18	The Assembly attempts to provide an armed guard for the Convention.
Sept. 20	France defeats Prussia at Valmy. The Prussian retreat begins.
Sept. 21	**First Session of the Convention** The monarchy is abolished. Year I of the Republic begins.
Sept. 24–25	The Brissotins lead an attack on the power of Paris.
Sept. 29	The French occupy the Sardinian territory of Nice.
Oct. 10	Brissot expelled from the Jacobin Club.
Oct. 11	The Constitutional Committee created.
Oct. 19	The Sections protest against the attacks on Paris.
Oct. 29	The Brissotins' second attack on the power of Paris.
Nov. 5	Robespierre defends Paris and the Montagnards.
Nov. 6	Battle of Jemappes. Commencement of the French invasion of Belgium.
Nov. 19	Declaration of Fraternity: the French offer aid to all peoples striving to recover their freedom. The strategically sensitive Scheldt declared an open river.
Nov. 20	Discovery of the secret cupboard in the Tuileries.
Nov. 28	Savoy, formally Sardinian territory, is declared the eighty-fourth French department.
Dec. 3	The Convention makes the decision to try the King.
Dec. 11	Louis interrogated by the Convention.
Dec. 15	Decree on the treatment and government of occupied territories.
Dec. 27	Buzot and Salle call for a referendum on the King's fate.

1793	Jan. 14–17	The Convention votes to decide Louis' fate.
	Jan.	Trial of Louis XVI.
	Jan. 21	Execution of the King on the Place de la Révolution.
	Jan. 24	The British government orders the French ambassador to leave.
	Feb. 1	Declaration of war upon Great Britain and Holland.
	Feb. 14	The Principality of Monaco annexed.
	Feb. 15	Condorcet's constitutional proposals.
	Feb. 23	Ballot for the army extended to include all of France.
	Feb. 24	Levy of 300,000 men decreed.
	Feb. 25	Food rioting in Paris.
	Mar. 1–7	Belgian revolt.
	Mar. 7	France declares war on Spain.
	Mar. 9	First authorization of missions by Convention members to the provinces and armies.
	Mar. 9–10	Further rioting in Paris–supposed plot against the Convention.
	Mar. 10	Revolutionary Tribunal set up by decree.
	Mar. 16	Beginning of rising in the Vendée.
	Mar. 18	The French suffer defeat at Neerwinden resulting in Dumouriez's evacuation of The Netherlands. Austria fails to follow up this victory and destroy the French army.
	Mar. 21	The creation of local revolutionary committees.
	Apr. 5	Defection of Dumouriez to the Austrians.
	Apr. 6	First Committee of Public Safety (set up on 26 March) reduced to 9 members.
	Apr. 13	The impeachment of Marat.
	Apr. 15	The Sections demand a purge of the Convention.
	May 4	The first 'maximum' on grain prices is decreed. Previously only Paris was covered by the 'maximum' (since 12 Sept. 1792).
	May 10	The Convention moves to the Tuileries.
	May 12	The Commune forces the Convention to establish a 'sansculotte' army to guard Paris.
	May 20	The Commission of Twelve is appointed to investigate plots against the Convention of Paris.
	May 30	Conservative coup d'état in Lyons.
	May 31	Unsuccessful rising in Paris. The Tuileries are surrounded by a mob who compel the Convention to abolish the Committee of Twelve. However it refuses to prescribe its own members.
	June 2	The Revolution of June the Second. The Convention is purged by the Montagnards and the Sections of Paris. Brissot and others are arrested.
	June 6–19	The Protest of the 75.
	June 6	Federalist movement against the Convention at Bordeaux and Marseilles.
	June 9	The Vendéans take Sanmur.
	June 24	The Convention accepts the Radical Constitution of 1793 which is to be brought in at the end of the war. Under the constitution all adult males are given the vote.
	July 10	Fall of the fortress of Condé.

July 13	Marat murdered. The end of the Normandy rising.
July 17	The final abolition of all feudal rights without compensation.
July 23	Fall of the fortress of Mayence.
July 26	Decree against hoarding, making it a capital crime.
July 27	Robespierre becomes a member of the Committee of Public Safety.
July 28	The fortress of Valenciennes falls. The outlawing of eighteen 'Brissotin' deputies.
Aug. 1	France adopts the metric system. The order for the arrest of all nationals of countries with which the Republic is at war, unless they were resident in France prior to 14 July 1789.
Aug. 10	Festival of Unity in honour of 1793 constitution.
Aug. 23	The decree of *levée en masse*.
Aug. 27	Toulon surrenders to the British and Sardinians.
Sept. 3	A compulsory loan of 1000 Francs enforced. The Law of the Maximum enforces prices on pain of death. Hébertist rising in Paris. Terror becomes the order of the day as the Convention makes the war effort increasingly radical.
Sept. 6	A Revolutionary Army is established to support the Committee of Public Safety.
Sept. 8	French defeat allied army threatening Dunkirk.
Sept. 11	The fortress of Lequesnoy falls.
Sept. 17	Decree of the Law of Suspects orders the arrest of all those who have shown themselves to be enemies of liberty.
Sept. 22	The first day of Year II.
Sept. 25	The Committee of Public Safety survives attack in the Convention.
Sept. 29	A new law on the general Maximum in restraint of prices and wages.
Oct. 3	Brissot and forty-four other deputies are impeached.
Oct. 5	Revolutionary Calendar established (as from 22 September).
Oct. 9	Lyons recaptured by Convention forces.
Oct. 10	'Revolutionary Government' decreed (sanctioned for the duration of the war).
Oct. 16	Battle of Wattignies, Austria defeated and Maubeuge relieved. Marie Antoinette executed.
Oct. 17	Vendéans defeated at Chollet.
Oct. 22	Creation of a Central Food Commission.
Oct. 24–31	Trial of Brissot and twenty other 'Girondin' deputies.
Oct. 31	Execution of the Brissotins.
Nov. 10	Festival of Reason in Notre Dame.
Nov. 21	Robespierre denounces atheism as aristocratic.
Nov. 22	Closure of churches in Paris by the Commune.
Dec. 4	The Law of Revolutionary Government (14 Frimaire).
Dec. 5	The first issue of the *Vieux Cordelier* which initiates a campaign against the Hébertists.
Dec. 15	The third issue of the *Vieux Cordelier* attacks 'the Terror'.

Dec. 19	The British pull out of Toulon.
Dec. 23	Vendéans defeated at Savenay.
Dec. 25	Robespierre's speech on the principles of revolutionary government.
Dec. 26	The French recapture Landau. The Prussian army routed at Weissenburg.
Dec. 30	The Festival of Victory.

1794 Jan. 12	Arrest of Fabre d'Eglantine.
Jan. 27	The Convention decrees the appointment of teachers of the French language in regions where French is not the native language.
Feb. 4	Slavery abolished in the French colonies.
Feb. 5	Robespierre speaks on the principle of political morality.
Feb. 21	Revision of the Maximum price control policy.
Feb.26– Mar. 3	The Laws of the Ventôse allowing for the division and distribution of suspects' property among poor and needy patriots.
Mar. 4	Insurrection attempt at the Cordeliers Club.
Mar. 14	Hébertist extremists attempt to organise a sansculotte rising against the Convention but are arrested.
Mar. 24	Hébertists arrested.
Mar. 30	Danton arrested.
Apr. 5	Dantonists executed.
Apr. 27	The Police Law of 27 Germinal.
May 7	Robespierre introduces the worship of the Supreme Being.
May 18	Battle of Tourcoing. The British routed in Belgium.
May 23	Admiral affair.
May 24	Renault affair. Both presumed attempts to assassinate Robespierre.
June 1	'The Glorious First of June'. Howe defeats the French fleet off Ushant.
June 8	Festival of the Supreme Being.
June 10	The Law of 22 Prairial speeds up the work of the Revolutionary Tribunal by removing prisoners' safeguards.
June 26	Battle of Fleurus. The French invade Belgium, Coburg is routed and the British withdraw.
July 23	The Commune imposes a new scale of wage regulations.
July 26	In his last speech Robespierre calls for a purge.
July 27	The '9th Thermidor'. Robespierre and his followers denounced. The Convention abolishes the Commune of Paris.
July 28	Robespierre and 115 others executed.
July 30–31	Reorganisation of the Committee of Public Safety.
Aug. 13	The Revolutionary Tribunal is reorganised and most
Aug.	people are acquitted. Repeal of the Law of 22 Prairial.
Sept. 18	The State withdraws financial support of all forms of religious worship.

1794 Oct.–Jan	Holland retaken; gains made against both Austria and Prussia.
Nov. 12	Closing of the Jacobin Club ordered by the Convention.
Dec. 21	The sale of the property of the friends of émigrés ceases.
Dec. 24	Abolition of the Maximum.
1795 Feb. 21	Decree providing for freedom of worship and the separation of church and state.
Apr. 1	Day of 12 Germinal. Parisian sansculottes invade the Convention demanding 'bread and the constitution of 1793'. Nothing concrete is achieved due to a lack of leadership.
Apr. 5	Peace Treaty with Prussia made at Basle.
Apr. 10	The National Guard reorganised as a middle-class force.
May 16	Peace with Holland. France recognises the 'Batavian Republic'.
May 20	The rising of 1 Prairial. The Paris sansculottes invade the Convention again repeating the demands of 12 Germinal.
May 23	The army disarms the Paris sections.
May–June	'White Terror' in the South during which Royalists murder many former terrorists.
June 8	The captive Louis XVII dies; the Count of France becomes Louis XVIII.
July 21	Hoche destroys the émigré force at Quiberon.
July 22	Peace made with Spain, by which France gives up conquests and Spain ceded half of San Domingo to France.
Aug. 22	The Constitution of Year III marks a return to a restricted electorate based on the payment of taxes.
Aug. 31	The decree of 13 Fructidor empowered the Convention to fill any unfilled seats in the Legislative Assembly (as a result of deputies being elected for more than one constituency).
Oct. 5	The Rising of 13 Vendémiaire. The army is used to stop the insurgents as they march on the Tuileries.

The Directory

1796 Oct. 26	The Convention dissolved and replaced by the Directory.
Mar. 11	Napoleon leaves Paris to take control of the Army of Italy.
Apr. 11	Mandats issued in place of assignats, but soon fall to 1 per cent of their face value.
Apr. 11–14	Napoleon breaks through Austrian front in Italy.
Apr. 28	Armistice of Cherasco with Sardinia.
May	Conspiracy of Babeuf.
May 10	French victory at Lodi. Napoleon crosses River Adda.
Nov. 15–17	French victory at Arcola, near Mantua.

1797 Jan. 14	French under Napoleon win victory at Rivoli.
Jan. 30	Conspiracy of the Royalist Abbé Brottier suppressed.
Apr. 12	Napoleon renews offensive in Italy.
Apr. 18	Napoleon agrees preliminaries of peace at Loeben with Austria.
Sept. 4	Coup d'état of 18 Fructidor; Legislative Assembly is purged.
Sept. 30	The 'bankruptcy of the two thirds'. This leads to two-thirds of the public debt being cancelled and bonds, which are soon to be of no value, are issued instead.
Oct. 17	Treaty of Campo Formio concluded with Austria.
1798 Feb. 15	Proclamation of the Roman Republic.
Apr. 12	Proclamation of the Helvetic Republic. The Directory decides to authorise an expedition to Egypt rather than England.
May 11	Coup d'état of 22 Floréal; results in a purge of the Legislature.
July 21	Napoleon's victory at the Battle of the Pyramids.
Aug. 1	Nelson destroys the French fleet at the Battle of the Nile (Aboukir Bay).
Sept. 5	Law on Conscription passed.
1799 Jan. 26	Proclamation of a satellite republic at Naples.
Mar. 12	France declares war on Austria.
Apr. 29	Russians enter Milan; during the summer successive Austrian and Russian victories all but end French influence in Italy except for a besieged garrison at Genoa.
June 18	Coup d'état of 30 Prairial.
Sept. 25–27	Russians defeated and retreat in Switzerland.
Nov. 9–10	'Coup d'état of Brumaire'.

The Revolutionary Calendar

After the fall of the Bastille, the year 1789 was known as the 1st Year of Liberty. When royalty was abolished in France on 21 September 1792, the 4th Year of Liberty became the 1st Year of the Republic, the two terms sometimes being used concurrently. When the Revolutionary Calendar was adopted in October 1793, its effect was retrospective to the first anniversary of the abolition of royalty, so that 22 September 1793 became the 1st day of the month of Vendémiaire of the Year II of the Republic. Thereafter the months of the Year II ran as follows:

Vendémiaire	1–30 the month of vintage	= 22nd Sept.–21 Oct.
Brumaire	1–30 the month of fog	= 22nd Oct.–20 Nov.
Frimaire	1–30 the month of frost	= 21st Nov.–20 Dec.
Nivôse	1–30 the month of snow	= 21st Dec.–19 Jan.
Pluviôse	1–30 the month of rain	= 20th Jan.–18 Feb.
Ventôse	1–30 the month of wind	= 19th Feb.–20 Mar.
Germinal	1–30 the month of budding	= 21st Mar.–19 Apr.
Floréal	1–30 the month of flowers	= 20th Apr.–19 May
Prairial	1–30 the month of meadows	= 20th May–18 June

Messidor	1–30 the month of harvest	= 19th June–18 July
Thermidor	1–30 the month of heat	= 19th July–17 Aug.
Fructidor	1–30 the month of fruit	= 18th Aug.–16 Sept.

17–21 September inclusive: Sansculottides – days of Festival. The Calendar was discarded on 1 January 1806.

Napoleon and France

1799 Nov. 9–10	Coup d'état of Brumaire. Bonaparte gains power.
Dec. 24	Constitution of Year VIII proclaimed vesting all power in Bonaparte as First Consul.
1800 Jan.	Constitution approved by plebiscite (3,011,007 for, 1,562 against, 4 million abstained).
Feb. 13	Bank of France founded; from the outset it was linked with the management of government loans and taxation.
June 15	Victory at Marengo re-established French command of North Italy.
Feb. 17	Local government re-organised in a way which marked a return to centralised government not dissimilar to the Ancien Regime.
Aug. 12	Commission appointed to begin work on a uniform Civil Code for France. 84 sessions, 36 of which Bonaparte presided over in person, were held to discuss various drafts of the Code.
Dec. 3	Moreau defeats the Austrians at Hohenlinden.
Dec. 24	Chouan plot fails to kill Napoleon and Josephine as they drive to the Opera. Bonaparte uses the plot to suppress former revolutionaries and Jacobins, despite the fact that the plot is the work of Royalists who are duly punished.
1801 Feb. 9	Peace Treaty of Lunéville concluded with Austria.
Mar. 21	Deflationary liquidation of public debt.
June–Sept.	French army in Egypt surrenders to the British.
July 15	Religious Concordat concluded with Pope Pius VII. Bonaparte sees the value of religion as a tool to strengthen his position in France. The Concordat in conjunction with Bonaparte's Organic Ordinances places the Church under strict state control, but recognises its position (see p. 247).
Aug.	Press censorship increased.
1802 Jan.	Napoleon becomes President of the Cisalpine Republic.
Mar. 25	Peace of Amiens with Britain.
Apr. 18	Legislature approves the Concordat.
Apr. 26	Amnesty for émigrés.
May 1	Beginning of education reforms with the establishment of 'lycées'.
May 19	Bonaparte creates the Legion of Honour establishing a new aristocracy.
Aug. 24	Bonaparte confirmed as Consul for life by plebiscite.
Aug. 16	Constitution of Year XII promulgated which strengthens Bonaparte's position.

1803 Apr.	Loi de Chapelier strengthened.
Apr. 14	Reorganisation of the Bank of France gives it a monopoly of note issue.
May 16–18	Britain declares war on France; all British subjects in France are gaoled.
Dec. 2	'The Army of England' concentrates 150,000 men in the Boulogne area for a cross-channel invasion.
1804 Feb. 25	Establishment of the Excise Bureau.
Mar. 21	Promulgation of the Civil Code.
May 18	Napoleon proclaimed Emperor of the French by the Senate. A Plebiscite approves the Constitution of Year XII.
Dec. 2	Pius VIII officiates at crowning of Napoleon as Emperor of the French in Notre Dame.
Dec. 21	Schoolteachers to be appointed by the State.
1805 Jan. 1	Abolition of the Revolutionary Calendar Press; censorship increased.
May 26	Napoleon becomes King of Italy.
Aug. 24	'Army of England' broken up and Imperial forces march into Germany.
Oct. 20	Austrian surrender at Ulm.
Oct. 21	Battle of Trafalgar.
Nov. 13	Napoleon enters Vienna.
Dec. 2	Austro–Russian defeat at Austerlitz. Austria sues for peace.
Dec. 26	Peace of Pressburg with Austria gives Napoleon influence over the whole of Italy.
1806 Apr. 22	Bank of France put under State control.
May	Imperial University established.
July 12	Confederation of the Rhine established.
Aug.	Senatus-consultum allows Napoleon to grant hereditary fiefs. Code of Civil Procedure, largely a re-enactment of earlier Ordinances, it maintained the principle that conciliation must be attempted before recourse to law courts.
Sept. 15	Britain and Russia joined by Prussia against France.
Oct. 14	Prussia defeated at Jena-Auerstadt.
Oct. 27	Napoleon enters Berlin.
Nov. 21	Establishment of the Continental System by the Berlin Decrees.
1807 July 7–9	Treaty of Tilsit between France, Russia and Prussia.
July	Theatres severely censored.
Dec. 17	The Milan Decrees strengthen the Continental System.
1808 Mar. 17	Formal establishment of new Imperial University.
May 2	Rising against the French in Madrid.
Aug.	British forces land in Portugal.
Sept.	Decrees of the Imperial University enforced. The Code of Criminal Procedure passed.
1809 Spring	Austria joins Britain against France.
May 13	The French occupy Vienna.

May 17	Breach in relations bctween Pius VII and Bonaparte when Papal States annexed (see p. 247).
June 11	Napoleon excommunicated.
July 6	Austrians defeated at Wagram. Orders issued for the Pope's arrest.
July 6	Pius VII imprisoned at Savona.
Oct. 14	Austria signs the Peace of Vienna by which Illyria (*i.e.* Carinthia, Trieste) was ceded to France.
Dec. 13	Napoleon seeks the Tsar's sister's hand in marriage.
Dec. 16	Napoleon divorces Josephine as they have no son.
1810 Feb. 9–18	Napoleon asks for the hand of Archduchess Marie Louise of Austria.
Apr. 2	Marriage of Napoleon and Marie Louise.
Apr.	Penal Code decreed.
July 9	Holland annexed by France.
Dec. 31	Russia breaks the Continental System by authorising trade with Britain.
	Press censorship increased.
1811 Spring	French driven out of Portugal.
Autumn	Preparations made for Russian campaign.
Sep. 17	The Press severely suppressed and the three remaining Paris newspapers confiscated.
Sept.	Austro–Prussian promise to aid Napoleon against Russia.
1812 June 24	Napoleon approves the Russian campaign.
Summer	French defeats in Peninsular battles.
Aug.–Sept.	Indecisive French victories at Smolensk and Borodino.
Sept. 14	Napoleon enters Moscow.
Oct. 19	The French retreat begins.
Dec. 14	The French campaign in Russia ends as last troops cross the Niemen.
Dec. 18	Napoleon returns to France to deal with abortive *coup d'état*.
1813 Jan. 10	Napoleon promised 350,000 more conscripts by the Senate.
Jan. 25	Pius VII forced into signing a new Concordat.
Mar. 24	The Pope withdraws his signature, though Napoleon does not recognise this action.
Apr. 25	Napoleon takes command of the French army at Erfurt.
May 2	Napoleon victorious at Lutzen.
May 21	French victory at Bautzen.
June 21	Wellington's victory at Vittoria, causing Joseph to flee to France.
Oct. 16–19	'Battle of the Nations' (Leipzig) results in French defeat and withdrawal.
Nov. 17	Dutch rising against Napoleon under the Prince of Orange.
Winter	The Allies enter France.
1814 Jan.	The Pope freed and restored.
Mar. 30–31	Fall of Paris.

Apr. 3	Napoleon deposed by the Senate.
Apr. 6	Napoleon abdicates in favour of his son.
May 3	Napoleon lands in Elba.
Nov. 1	First meeting at Vienna.

1815 Mar. 1   Napoleon begins 'The Hundred Days' when he returns to France.

Mar. 20   Napoleon reoccupies the Tuileries. He secures the support of most of his former ministers, including Davout as Minister of War, Carnot as Minister of the Interior, and Fouché as Minister of Police.

Apr. 23   'L' Acte Additionel' re-enacts the Charter established under Louis XVIII,* but makes Chamber of Peers hereditary and abolishes press censorship. Lafayette, the Liberal leader, demands a meeting of the Chambers in early June.

June 1   Napoleon takes oath of fidelity to the Constitution at the Champs de Mars.

June 12   Napoleon takes command of the French army seeking separate swift victories against Britain and Prussia in Belgium.

June 16   Napoleon defeats the Prussians at Ligny; British held at Quatre Bras.

June 18   Waterloo. Napoleon defeated.

June 21   The Chambers refuse to cooperate with Napoleon on his return to Paris.

June 22   Napoleon abdicates.

July 17   Napoleon surrenders to the British.

Oct. 17   Napoleon arrives at St Helena.

1821 May 21   Bonaparte dies.

* *Note*: Louis's Constitutional Charter was issued on 4 June 1814, establishing an elected Chamber of Deputies and a Chamber of Peers nominated by the King. Liberty of worship and the press granted, 'careers open to talent', and land sales since 1792 recognised.

The French Revolution and Europe

1789	July 14	Storming of the Bastille.
1790	Feb.	Archbishop of Alsace and local princes appeal for the protection of the Imperial Diet against loss of feudal privileges by French decree of 4 August 1789. The Electors of Cologne, Treves, and Mainz give shelter to the French émigrés.
	Oct.	France refuses to support Spain in war against Britain over the Nootka Sound incident in accordance with the Family Compact of 1761. The Assembly replaces the dynastic Family Compact by a national treaty for mutual defence.
1791	July 6	Leopold II of Austria issues circular inviting rulers of Europe to demand release of Louis XVI and to intervene if Royal Family harmed.
	Aug. 27	Leopold II and Frederick William II issue Declaration of Pilnitz, promising armed intervention in France if other powers will co-operate.
	Sept.	The French Assembly votes for the incorporation in France of Avignon and the Venaissin. In November French troops take control of the area.
	Nov. 9	The Assembly votes that all émigrés must return to France on pain of death.
	Dec. 14	French send an army of 150,000 men to the frontier.
1792	Jan. 25	French Assembly demands that Leopold renounce the treaty with Prussia and disperse the émigré army.
	Feb. 7	Leopold II and Frederick William II sign Treaty of Berlin, each guaranteeing the other's territories and agreeing mutual support in the event of French declaration of war.
	Apr. 20	France declares war on Austria.
	July 24	Prussia declares war on France.
	Aug. 23	Prussians take Longwy and Verdun (2 Sept.).
	Sept. 20	At battle of Valmy, French revolutionary armies halt Prussian advance on Paris. French seize Nice and Savoy.
	Nov. 6	Austrians defeated at Jemappes, French enter Brussels (14th).
	Nov. 19	Declaration of Fraternity. The French Convention offers its support to assist any people against their rulers. They also proclaim the Scheldt an open river in defiance of existing treaties. Widespread alarm expressed in Britain, Austria and Russia.
1793	Jan. 21	Execution of Louis XVI.
	Jan. 23	Second Partition of Poland by Russia and Prussia.
	Jan. 26	Belgian army incorporated into that of France.

Feb. 1	France declares war on Britain and Holland.
Mar. 7	France declares war on Spain.
	First Coalition* formed including Great Britain, Prussia, Austria, Spain and Holland.
Mar. 18	Austrians defeat the French at Neerwinden in The Netherlands. The French commander, Dumouriez, goes over to the Austrians (5 Apr.).
July 23	Prussians take Mainz.
Aug. 27	Admiral Hood lands forces to support counter-revolutionaries in Toulon. French open siege of Toulon (7 September).
Sept. 8	French defeat allied army threatening Dunkirk at Hoondschoote.
	Sardinian army driven out of Savoy.
Oct. 15–16	Jourdan defeats Austrian army at Wattignies, relieving immediate threat to Paris.
Dec. 18	British evacuate Toulon which falls to the French (19th).
Dec. 26	Hoche defeats the Prussians at Weissenburg.
1794 May 18	Austrians and British defeated at Tourcoing, rendering renewed advance on Paris impossible.
June 1	Admiral Howe defeats French off Brest in engagement known as 'the Glorious First of June', but important grain convoy safely arrives at Brest.
June 25	Jourdan routs the Austrians at Fleurus, forcing the British to withdraw into Holland and the Austrians to the Rhine.
Sept.	French defeated at Clairfait, near Mainz.
Oct.	French overrun Brabant and invade Holland. Jourdan takes Cologne, Andernach, and Coblenz.
Dec. 31	Armistice signed with Austrians.
1795 Jan.	French enter Amsterdam.
Apr. 5	Treaty of Basle signed between France and Prussia. Prussia agrees to become neutral and the French agree to regard the states of northern Germany as neutral.
May 16	Treaty of Basle signed between Holland and France. The Dutch agree to abolish the Stadtholderate and set up the Batavian Republic under French domination.
June 21	Allies and émigrés land at Quiberon.
July 22	Treaty of Basle with Spain. France gives up her Spanish conquests but is ceded half of San Domingo.
Oct. 24	Third Partition of Poland by Prussia, Austria and Russia shares out last independent areas of Poland.
1796 Mar. 27	Bonaparte appointed to command of army of Italy.
Apr. 12–13	Bonaparte defeats the Sardinian army at the battles of Montenotte, Dego, and Millesimo, and advances on Turin.
Apr. 28	By Armistice of Cherasco, Victor Amadeus III of Sardinia agrees to its neutrality and surrenders

(* See note on p. 64)

	fortresses commanding the Alpine passes. By a subsequent treaty Nice and Savoy are given up.
May 10	Bonaparte, after crossing the River Po, defeats the Austrians at Lodi and enters Milan (15th).
June 6	King of Naples makes an armistice with Napoleon.
June 23	Napoleon signs an armistice with Pius VI, in return for 20,000,000 francs and many works of art.
Aug. 2	Napoleon defeats Austrians at Lonato and at Castiglione (5th).
Aug. 5	Secret treaty of Prussia and France agrees to extension of French frontier to the Rhine in return for the Bishopric of Munster.
Aug. 19	France signs Treaty of Ildefonso with Spain.
Sept. 19	Archduke Charles of Austria defeats Jourdan at Altenkirchen on the Rhine.
Oct. 8	Spain declares war on Britain.
Nov. 15–17	Bonaparte defeats Austrians at Arcola.
Nov. 16	Pro-French Tsar Paul becomes Tsar.
Dec.	Peace negotiations between Britain and France collapse.
Dec. 16	General Hoche sails with expeditionary force to Ireland, but landing at Bantry Bay fails (21–27 Dec.).
1797 Jan. 14	Napoleon defeats Austrian army at Rivoli, and defeats a relieving force sent to Mantua (16th).
Feb. 2	Mantua surrendered to Napoleon giving France control of Lombardy.
Feb. 14	At Battle of Cape St Vincent, British under Admiral Jervis defeat a Spanish fleet.
Feb. 19	At Treaty of Tolentino Pius VI agrees to cede Bologna, Ferrara and the Romagna to France and to pay 30,000,000 francs to the Directory immediately and a total of 300,000,000.
Feb. 22–24	French landing force at Fishguard in Pembrokeshire is quickly forced to surrender.
Apr. 16	British fleet at Spithead mutiny. (Ends 5 May.)
Apr. 17	Napoleon signs preliminaries of peace with Archduke Charles at Leoben by which Austria accepts the Rhine as the boundary of France, including Belgium as French. Austria gives up Milan in return for Venice. A congress to be held at Rastadt to make peace.
May 12	Beginning of mutiny amongst British fleet at the Nore; suppressed by 13 June and leaders executed.
May 16	Napoleon occupies Venice. By Treaty of Milan the Grand Council is abolished and a new democratic council established; Venice to pay 6,000,000 francs as well as surrender works of art and manuscripts.
June 15	Ligurian Republic established in Genoa and neighbourhood.
June 28	French occupy the Ionian Isles.
July 9	Cisalpine Republic established in Lombardy.
Oct. 11	Dutch fleet carrying aid and 15,000 troops to the Irish defeated by Admiral Duncan off Texel.

Oct. 16	Napoleon appointed to command the 'Army of England'.
Oct. 17	Treaty of Campo Formio between France and Austria. The treaty follows from the preliminaries signed at Leoben. The Rhine frontier of France is recognised and the independence of the Cisalpine Republic, including Milan. Austria receives Venice and Venetian territory in Istria and Dalmatia. The Stadtholder of Holland and the Duke of Modena received territory in Germany. Secret clauses provided for Austria to evacuate Mainz and Rhine fortresses and for France to support the claim of Austria to Bavaria and the Archbishopric of Salzburg.
Dec. 29	The French enter Mainz.
1798 Feb. 15	Roman Republic proclaimed and acknowledged by France.
Feb. 20	Pius VI deported to France.
Mar. 5	Directory abandons plans for invasion of England.
Mar.	French seize Berne and exact 23,000,000 million francs indemnity from Switzerland.
Apr. 12	Napoleon appointed to command the 'Army of the Orient'. Annexation of Geneva and creation of Helvetic Republic.
May–July	Irish rebellion. Main Irish force defeated in Wexford (June) and rebellion suppressed.
May 19	Napoleon sails from Toulon for Egypt.
June 12	Surrender of Malta to Napoleon.
July 1–2	Army of Orient lands in Egypt and takes Alexandria.
July 3	French occupy Turin.
July 21	Napoleon defeats Mamelukes at the Battle of the Pyramids and enters Cairo (25th).
Aug. 1–2	Nelson destroys French fleet at the Battle of the Nile in Aboukir Bay.
Aug. 23	French force under Humbert lands in North-West Ireland. Surrenders on 8 Sept.
Nov. 29	Ferdinand of Naples takes Rome with Neapolitan troops commanded by Austrian General Mack.
Dec. 4	France declares war on Kingdom of Naples.
Dec. 6–13	Mack defeated by French troops and Ferdinand flees from Rome.
Dec. 21	Royal Family flee from Naples.
Dec. 29	Second Coalition formed of Great Britain, Austria, Russia, Naples and Portugal.
1799 Jan. 23	French enter Naples and proclaim the Parthenopean Republic.
Mar. 1	War breaks out between the Second Coalition and France.
Mar. 25	Austrian Archduke defeats Jourdan's invasion of Germany at Stockach.
Apr. 5	Austrians defeat the French at Magnano in northern Italy.
Apr. 27	Russian army under Suvarov defeats the French under

	Moreau at Cassano in northern Italy and enters Milan (29th).
June 17–19	Suvarov defeats French army from Naples at Trebbia.
July 30	Mantua surrendered by the French.
Aug. 15	Suvarov defeats Joubert at Novi.
Aug. 23	Napoleon sails for France.
Aug.	British force under Abercromby lands in Holland and seizes the Dutch fleet in the Texel.
Sept. 19	Allied force of British and Russians under the Duke of York win minor victory at Alkmaar.
Sept. 26	Masséna defeats a Russian army near Zurich but Suvarov, the commander, withdraws his troops in good order from Switzerland.
Oct. 18	Duke of York and British forces evacuate Holland after the Convention of Alkmaar.
Nov. 4	Austrians defeat the French at Cenola and drive them back into France. Collapse of the Italian Republics.
Nov. 9–10	*Coup d'état* of Brumaire in Paris.
Dec. 14	Napoleon becomes First Consul.
1800 Apr.	Moreau leads French army across the Rhine and after a series of victories drives the Austrians back to Ulm.
Apr. 15	Napoleon begins crossing of the Alps by the St Bernard Pass.
Apr. 20	Genoa besieged by the Austrians.
June 4	Fall of Genoa to the Austrians.
June 14	Napoleon defeats the Austrians at Marengo.
June 19	Following their defeat at Marengo the Austrians sign the Convention of Alessandria, giving Genoa, Piedmont and Milan to France.
June 20	Austria makes a treaty with Britain to continue the war with the assistance of subsidies and the promise of part of Piedmont.
July 15	Armistice between Austria and France.
Sept. 5	The British take Malta.
Nov. 5	Austro–French hostilities resume. French under Brune take Verona and Treviso.
Dec.	French army under Macdonald invades the Tyrol. Brune and Macdonald march on Vienna.
Dec. 3	Moreau defeats Austrians at Hohenlinden and marches on Vienna.
Dec. 18	Formation of Second Armed Neutrality by the Baltic powers (Russia, Sweden and Denmark and, later, Prussia) to resist British interference with their trade.
1801 Jan. 15	Franco–Austrian Armistice at Treviso.
Jan. 15	France and Austria sign Peace of Lunéville. Austria cedes to France all territory west of the Rhine, including Belgium and Luxembourg, and recognises the independence of the Cisalpine, Ligurian, Batavian and Helvetic Republics. The Adige is to be the boundary between French and Austrian possessions in Northern Italy. The Duke of Parma is to rule Tuscany, now known as the Kingdom of Etruria. The ex-Duke of

	Tuscany and dispossessed German Princes are to receive compensation in Germany at France's discretion.
Mar. 23	Assassination of Tsar Paul I; accession of Alexander I.
Apr. 2	At Battle of Copenhagen the British fleet attacks the Danish fleet anchored off Copenhagen in an attempt to force them out of the League of Armed Neutrality.
Aug. 2	Duke of Parma proclaimed King of Etruria.
Sept.	Batavian Republic given a new constitution making it virtually a puppet state of France.
Oct. 1	Preliminaries of peace between Britain and France signed at Amiens.
1802 Jan.	Napoleon becomes President of the Cisalpine Republic.
Mar. 25	Peace of Amiens: (i) Great Britain to keep Ceylon and Trinidad, but restore other colonies to France, Spain and Holland. (ii) France agrees to evacuate Naples and the Papal States and restore all its territory to Portugal. (iii) Malta is to be restored to the Knights of St John. (iv) The Ionian Isles are recognised as a republic. (v) Egypt is to revert to Turkey.
June 29	New Genoese constitution makes city subservient to Napoleon.
Aug. 26	France annexes Elba.
Sept. 21	Napoleon incorporates Piedmont into the French Republic.
Oct. 15	Napoleon intervenes in Switzerland in civil war between the towns and the forest cantons as 'Mediator of the Helvetic League'.
1803 Feb. 19	French Act of Mediation in Switzerland sets up a new constitution, weakening the federal government and giving greater authority to the individual cantons.
May 18	Britain declares war on France. Imminence of invasion leads to the enrolment of over a quarter of a million volunteers.
June 1	French occupy Hanover.
June 15	Camp at Boulogne established for 'Army of England'.
July	Emmett's rebellion in Ireland suppressed.
Aug. 23	Further camps for the invasion of England formed at St Omer and Bruges and invasion flotillas assembled to await command of the Channel.
Oct. 9	Franco–Spanish alliance formed.
1804 Mar. 21	Duc d'Enghien kidnapped by French soldiers from the neutral state of Baden and executed.
May 10	Pitt returns as prime minister of Britain.
May 18	Napoleon assumes the title of Emperor.
Sept.	Alexander I breaks off negotiations with France in protest at occupation of Hanover and execution of the Duc d'Enghien.
Nov. 6	Francis II of Austria makes a secret treaty with Russia to resist further French aggression in Italy.

1805 Mar.	'Army of England' waits in readiness to invade, pending Villeneuve's arrival.
Apr. 11	Anglo–Russian alliance signed in St Petersburg aiming (i) to expel the French from Hanover, Northern Germany and Italy; (ii) protect the independence of Holland, Switzerland and Naples; (iii) restore Piedmont to the Kingdom of Sardinia; (iv) raise an army of half a million men against France. Britain to provide subsidies for other members of the anti-French coalition.
May 26	Napoleon crowns himself King of Italy.
June 4	France annexes Genoa.
July	Naples forced to sign new treaty with France.
Aug. 9	Third Coalition. Austria joins the Third Coalition with Britain, Russia and Sweden in return for a subsidy of £3,000,000.
Aug. 24	Bavaria signs treaty with Napoleon.
Aug. 25	Major units of the French army begin to leave the camp at Boulogne for a continental campaign against the Third Coalition.
Sept. 3	Napoleon and last elements of the 'Army of England' leave Boulogne.
Sept. 8	Austrian army under Mack invades Bavaria and takes up position near Ulm.
Sept. 26	Napoleon's *Grande Armée* crosses the Rhine.
Oct. 7	French forces cross the Danube cutting Mack off from Vienna.
Oct. 14	Marshal Ney defeats Mack's attempt to escape encirclement at Elchingen.
Oct. 20	Surrender of Mack at Ulm with 25,000 troops.
Oct. 21	Nelson defeats the Franco–Spanish fleet under Villeneuve at Trafalgar, inflicting a decisive blow to French sea-power and virtually eliminating any realistic hope of invading Britain, although the theoretical possibility remains.
Oct. 29	Archduke Charles defeats Masséna at Caldiero in northern Italy.
Nov. 3	Treaty of Potsdam between Russia and Prussia agreeing that unless Napoleon will make terms on the basis of the Treaty of Lunéville Prussia will join the Third Coalition. Prussia's action is forestalled by the Battle of Austerlitz (2 Dec.).
Nov. 14	Napoleon enters Vienna.
Dec. 2	At Battle of Austerlitz Napoleon crushingly defeats combined Austro–Russian army, shattering the Third Coalition.
Dec. 4	Austria makes an armistice with the French. Russians withdraw to their frontier. Prussia, on news of Austerlitz, refuses to join the war against Napoleon. Russian, British and Swedish forces withdraw from Pomerania. British and Russian forces leave Naples.
Dec. 15	Prussia signs Treaty of Schoenbrunn with France.

	Prussia receives Hanover, but cedes Cleves and Neuchatel to France and Ansbach to Bavaria.
Dec. 26	Peace of Pressburg signed: (i) Austria cedes Venetia to the Napoleonic Kingdom of Italy; (ii) Austria recognises the Electors of Wurttemberg and Bavaria as independent Kings and the Elector of Baden as Grand Duke; (iii) Austria cedes the Tyrol to Bavaria and its Swabian territory is divided between Baden and Wurttemberg.
Dec. 27	Napoleon deposes Ferdinand of Naples who flees to Sicily.
1806 Jan. 23	Death of William Pitt.
Mar. 30	Joseph Bonaparte created King of Naples.
Apr. 1	Murat made Grand Duke of Berg and Cleves.
May 16	British blockade of French ports begins.
June 5	Napoleon makes his brother Louis, King of Holland.
July 4	General Stuart leads a British army to victory over the French at Maida in Calabria, but then withdraws. The French conquer southern Italy.
July 12	Napoleon creates the Confederation of the Rhine with himself as 'Protector'. The leading states are the Kings of Bavaria and Wurttemberg, the Grand Duke of Baden, and the Landgrave of Hesse. Other smaller rulers are 'mediatised', passing under the authority of the Princes in whose states their lands are situated. The Confederation declares itself separated from the Empire, makes an alliance with France and agrees to supply 63,000 men to serve in the French armies.
July 18	Masséna captures Gaeta in Italy.
July	Negotiations between Britain and France reveal to Prussia that France is prepared to return Hanover to Britain.
July 20	Franco–Russian peace treaty.
Aug. 6	Abolition of the Holy Roman Empire.
Aug. 9	The Prussian army mobilises.
Aug. 24	Tsar Alexander refuses to ratify peace with France.
Sept. 26	Prussia sends an ultimatum to France demanding the immediate withdrawal of French armies across the Rhine and Napoleon's assent to a North German Confederacy under Prussian control.
Oct. 7	French troops invade Saxony.
Oct. 8	Prussia declares war.
Oct. 14	Battles of Jena and Auerstadt. In separate engagements Marshal Davout defeats a Prussian army under Brunswick at Auerstadt, while Napoleon routs an army under Hohenlohe at Jena.
Oct. 27	Napoleon enters Berlin.
Nov. 7	Lubeck stormed by the French and Blucher surrenders. By the 11th, all major Prussian fortresses, including Spandau, Stettin, Kustrin, and Magdeburg are in French hands.

Nov. 21	Promulgation of the Berlin Decrees inaugurates the Continental System. They declare the British Isles to be in a state of blockade, order the confiscation of British goods in French territory and the imprisonment of British subjects, and close all ports in French or allied territory to ships coming from Britain or British colonies.
Dec. 10	Saxony signs the Treaty of Posen with France; its Elector becomes King of Saxony and joins the Confederation of the Rhine.
Dec. 18	Napoleon enters Warsaw.
1807 Jan. 7	British promulgate an Order in Council in retaliation for the Berlin Decrees, making neutrals liable to confiscation of ships and cargo if they trade between ports from which British ships are excluded.
Jan. 25	By the Warsaw Decree Napoleon orders the seizure of all British and colonial goods in the Hanse towns. In retaliation, Britain tightens its blockade of north German ports.
Feb. 8	Battle of Eylau between Napoleon and Russian army under Bennigsen forces the Russians to retire.
Mar. 18	Danzig besieged by French.
Apr. 1	Napoleon compels Prussia to close its ports and those of Hanover to British ships.
Apr. 26	Convention of Bartenstein signed between Russia and Prussia, and later joined by Sweden and Great Britain, to continue the war against Napoleon.
May 27	Fall of Danzig to French.
June 14	Napoleon defeats Russians at Friedland and forces them back across the Nieman.
June 25	Napoleon and Alexander meet at the river Nieman.
June 27	Britain and Sweden conclude an alliance.
July 7–9	Treaty of Tilsit signed between Russia and France: (i) Prussia loses her territory west of the Elbe which is to be included in a Kingdom of Westphalia, with Napoleon's brother Jerome as King; (ii) Prussia's Polish territories are given to the King of Saxony, along with the southern part of the West Prussian duchy of Warsaw; (iii) Russia cedes to France the Ionian Isles and the district of Cattaro in Dalmatia, but receives Bialystock; (iv) Alexander promises to mediate between France and Great Britain and recognises the French puppet states in Italy, Holland and Germany; (v) Danzig is to remain a free port but Prussian ports are to be closed to British commerce; (vi) Napoleon promises not to restore the independence of Poland. By a secret treaty: (i) Napoleon agrees to support Alexander taking Finland from Sweden and Moldavia and Wallachia from Turkey; French help is promised for Russia's claim to the Danubian Principalities; (ii) if Britain refuses to come to terms, Alexander agrees to support

	Napoleon against her and force Denmark, Sweden and Portugal to make war on her.
July 7–9	Treaty of Tilsit between France and Prussia: (i) Prussia cedes to Napoleon for disposal all lands between the Rhine and the Elbe; (ii) cedes to Saxony the circle of Cottbus; (iii) cedes for the creation of a duchy of Warsaw all lands taken from Poland since 1772; (iv) Prussia recognises the sovereignty of the three brothers of Napoleon; (v) all Prussian ports and territories are closed to British ships and trade; (v) Prussia agrees to limit her army to 42,000 men. Prussia has lost half her territory.
July 12	By the Treaty of Königsberg it is agreed that Prussia's fortresses will only be evacuated and restored when Prussia has paid her arrears of war indemnities: these are set at 120 million francs by the French (raised to 140 million in 1808). Until that time, the reduced state of Prussia has to support 150,000 French troops.
July 19	Grand Duchy of Warsaw set up.
Aug. 16– Sept. 7	To forestall Denmark's entry into the war, the British send a fleet and 18,000 troops to Copenhagen, bombard the city (2–5 Sept.) and force the surrender of the Danish fleet (7 Sept.) into British hands.
Aug. 20	French take Stralsund from the Swedes.
Oct. 4	Baron von Stein becomes Minister of Home Affairs in Prussia and helps to superintend an era of civil and military reform.
Oct. 9	Edict of Emancipation in Prussia. Serfdom and feudal dues abolished, although lords retain their judicial rights over tenants. Legal caste distinctions are abolished and all occupations opened.
Oct. 27	Secret Treaty of Fontainebleau between France and Spain, allowing French troops to pass through Spain on their way to Portugal and agreeing the division of Portugal.
Nov. 11 and 25	Further British Orders in Council declare that any port from which British goods are excluded is in a state of blockade and declares unlawful all trade in articles produced by excluding countries; requires neutrals sailing to Europe to call at a British port; encourages neutral vessels to land goods in England and to re-export on favourable terms.
Nov. 30	French occupy Lisbon.
Dec. 17	Second Milan Decree by the French declares that any neutral ship diverting its course from a French to a British port should be liable to capture.
Dec.	French invade Spain.
1808 Feb. 20	Marshal Murat appointed Napoleon's 'Lieutenant' in Spain.
Feb. 29	French seize Barcelona.
Feb.	Austria accepts the Continental System.

Mar. 19	Rising in Aranjuez in Spain. Charles IV resigns in favour of his son Ferdinand who betrays popular hopes by returning to Madrid and awaiting the arrival of the French.
May 2	Rising in Madrid against the French suppressed.
May 6	Ferdinand surrenders the throne to Charles IV who abdicates.
June 6	Napoleon proclaims Joseph Bonaparte King of Spain.
June 8	Cordoba taken by French troops.
June 9	Prussia creates national *landwehr* of all citizens.
June 15	Spanish government accepts Joseph Bonaparte as King of Spain.
June 16	Siege of Saragossa.
July 13	Spanish defeat at Medina del Rio Seco.
July 20	French army under Dupont forced to surrender at Baylen. This reverse causes Joseph to flee Madrid (1 Aug.) and the French army to withdraw to the Ebro.
Aug. 1–8	Arthur Wellesley (the future Duke of Wellington) lands with 9,000 men in Portugal.
Aug. 21	Wellesley defeats French force under Junot at Vimiero.
Aug. 30	By Convention of Cintra Junot allowed to evacuate Portugal with all arms and equipment. Widespread criticism of the Convention in Britain leads to recall of commanders and appointment of Sir John Moore.
Sept. 27	Congress and Convention of Erfurt between France and Russia. Napoleon is forced to accede to Russian possession of Moldavia and Wallachia and also of Finland. Alexander agrees to make common cause with France if Austria declares war but refuses to support its dismemberment. A joint appeal is sent to George III to re-open peace negotiations, but this comes to nothing.
Nov. 5	Napoleon takes command of the Army of Spain.
Nov. 10	Soult routs Spanish army at Burgos.
Nov. 11	Army of Galicia defeated at Espinosa.
Nov. 23	Armies of Andalusia and Aragon defeated at Tudela.
Dec. 4	Napoleon recaptures Madrid for Joseph.
Dec. 24	Moore begins retreat to Corunna to embark his troops.
1809 Jan. 16	Moore defeats Soult outside Corunna, but is killed. British troops successfully embark.
Jan. 24	Napoleon leaves Spain for Paris.
Feb. 20	Saragossa surrenders to the French.
Mar. 29	Soult captures Oporto.
Apr. 9	Austria attacks Bavaria.
Apr. 10	Tyrolese rise against Bavaria under Hofer and take Innsbruck (14th).
Apr. 20	Napoleon defeats part of Archduke Charles's army at Abensberg and the main body at Eckmuhl.
Apr. 22	Archduke Ferdinand of Austria takes Warsaw.
Apr. 26	Wellesley lands at Lisbon to command British and Portuguese forces.
May 12	Wellesley crosses the Douro river and drives Soult out of northern Portugal.

May 13	Napoleon enters Vienna.
May 21–22	Austrians worst the French at the Battle of Aspern–Essling.
June 3	Archduke Ferdinand forced out of Warsaw.
July 2	Napoleon's forces joined by army of Italy under Beauharnais.
July 6	Napoleon defeats the Archduke Charles at Wagram, although the Austrians retreat in good order.
July 12	Armistice of Znaim ends fighting between French and Austrians.
July 27–28	Wellesley defeats French at Talavera in Spain, but because of failure of Spanish allies retreats into Portugal.
July 29– Sept. 30	British land 40,000 troops at Walcheren in Holland with aim of capturing Antwerp. Flushing taken (16 Aug.), but advance bogs down and the British evacuate after losing 4,000 men from disease.
Oct. 14	Treaty of Vienna or Schoenbrunn between France and Austria: (i) Austria gives up the 'Illyrian Provinces' (Trieste, Carniola, Carinthia, Croatia and Dalmatia) to France, cedes Salzburg and much of Upper Austria to Bavaria, and gives most of Western Galicia to the Grand Duchy of Warsaw; (ii) Austria recognises French authority in Italy, Portugal and Spain; (iii) Austria pays an indemnity to France.
Nov. 1	Tyrolese under Hofer defeated at Iselberg.
Nov. 19	Spanish defeated at Ocana and Andalusia overrun.
Dec. 11	Gerona surrenders to the French.
Dec. 13	Napoleon unsuccessfully seeks marriage with the Tsar's sister.
Dec. 16	Napoleon divorces Josephine.
1810 Feb. 9	Napoleon asks for the hand of Archduchess Marie Louise of Austria.
Feb. 11	French blockade Spanish fortress of Ciudad Rodrigo.
Feb. 21	Tyrolese leader Hofer shot by French at Mantua.
Mar. 16	Louis Napoleon cedes part of Holland to Napoleon.
Apr. 2	Napoleon marries Marie-Louise.
Apr. 17	Napoleon appoints Masséna to command in Portugal.
July 9	Napoleon annexes Holland; King Louis resigns.
July 10	Fall of Ciudad Rodrigo opens way to French invasion of Portugal.
Aug. 5	Trianon Tariff allows importation of British colonial produce at a tariff of 50 per cent.
Aug. 21	Bernadotte elected Crown Prince of Sweden.
Sept. 15	Masséna invades Portugal after taking Almeida.
Sept. 27	Wellesley (now Wellington) defeats the French at Busaco and retreats behind the defence lines of Torres Vedras (11 Oct.).
Oct. 18 and 25	Fontainebleau Decrees order that all British manufactured goods found in French territory should be burnt and special tribunals established to try those in breach of the decrees.
Dec. 10	Napoleon annexes the north-west coast of Germany,

	including the free city of Lubeck and the Grand Duchy of Oldenburg, territory of the brother-in-law of Alexander I.
Dec. 31	Tsar Alexander authorises trade with Britain thus breaking the Continental blockade.
1811 Mar. 5	Masséna retreats from lines of Torres Vedras to Ciudad Rodrigo (4 Apr.) losing 25,000 men in the process.
Mar. 11	Badajoz falls to Soult.
Mar. 20	Birth of son to Marie Louise; made King of Rome.
May 3–5	Wellington defeats Masséna at Fuentes d'Onoro and captures Almeida (11th).
May 7	Beresford besieges Badajoz, but has to raise siege to defeat relieving force under Soult at Albuera (16th).
May 24	Siege of Badajoz resumed by Wellington.
June 19	Wellington forced to abandon siege of Badajoz by advance of superior French army.
Aug.	Wellington besieges Ciudad Rodrigo but forced to retire by pressure of French army.
Dec. 23	Napoleon begins military preparations for war with Russia.
Dec. 31	Tsar Alexander issues decree against French trade.
1812 Jan. 8	Start of Wellington's second siege of Ciudad Rodrigo.
Jan. 10	France occupies Swedish Pomerania.
Jan 19	Fall of Ciudad Rodrigo to Wellington.
Feb. 24	Alliance between France and Prussia. Prussia undertakes to supply French armies marching to Russia and to provide 20,000 men.
Mar. 10	Alliance between France and Austria. France promises to restore the Illyrian Provinces.
Mar. 16	Wellington besieges Badajoz.
Apr. 6	Badajoz stormed and taken by Wellington.
Apr. 9	Russo–Swedish alliance at Treaty of Abo. Sweden agrees to cede Finland to Russia and to supply 30,000 men to co-operate with Russia; Russia agrees to help Sweden to secure Norway.
May 8	Spanish Cortes at Cadiz proclaims liberal constitution.
May 28	Russia makes peace with Turkey at the Treaty of Bucharest, receiving Bessarabia.
June 18	Britain and USA go to war over British interference with American shipping and press-ganging.
June 24	Napoleon crosses the Nieman and begins invasion of Russia
June 28	Napoleon enters Vilna, capital of Russian Poland.
July 18	Britain makes peace with Russia and Sweden and by the Treaty of Orebro Britain promised to subsidise Russia.
July 22	Wellington defeats French at Salamanca, allowing Wellington to occupy Madrid (12 August) and forcing Soult to evacuate southern Spain.
Aug. 18	Napoleon enters Smolensk.
Sept. 7	French and Russians fight indecisive battle of

	Borodino, but the Russian army is forced to retreat, leaving the road to Moscow open.
Sept. 14	Napoleon enters Moscow, but Alexander fails to come to terms.
Sept. 19	Start of the siege of Burgos.
Oct. 18	Murat defeated by the Russians at Vinkovo. Napoleon leaves Moscow.
Oct. 23	Conspiracy of General Malet in Paris against Napoleon.
Oct. 24	Russians defeated at Malo-Yaruslavetz, but Napoleon is forced to retreat along a more northerly route than intended.
Nov. 2	French reoccupy Madrid.
Nov. 27–29	French fight their way across the River Beresina.
Dec. 5	Napoleon leaves the *Grande Armée* on news of the Malet conspiracy.
Dec. 13	Last French troops cross the Niemen.
Dec. 18	Napoleon reaches Paris.
Dec. 30	Commander of Prussian contingent in *Grande Armée*, York, concludes Convention of Tauroggen with Russians by which he agrees to remain neutral and to take no steps to prevent the Russian pursuit of the French.
1813 Jan. 10	Senate promises Napoleon 350,000 more conscripts.
Jan. 25	Napoleon and Pope sign a second Concordat.
Jan.	Stein, on behalf of Alexander I, summons the Estates of East Prussia, who make a general levy of the population against the French.
Feb. 3	King of Prussia issues an edict calling all Prussians to arms.
Feb. 28	Treaty of Kalisch between Prussia and Russia, making an alliance against the French. Alexander promises that Prussia will receive back all the territory lost since 1806. An invitation is extended to Austria and Britain to join the alliance. Fourth Coalition begins to form.
Mar. 3	Treaty between Britain and Sweden. Britain agrees to pay a subsidy to Sweden to enable her to put an army of 30,000 men in the field under Prince Bernadotte. Britain promises not to oppose the union of Norway with Sweden.
Mar. 4	French abandon Berlin and Russians enter.
Mar. 17	Prussia declares war on France.
Mar. 24	Pope withholds his signature from new Concordat.
Mar. 27	Russians occupy Dresden; flight of the King of Saxony.
Apr. 25	Napoleon takes command of his army at Erfurt.
May 2	Napoleon defeats a Russian and Prussian army at Lutzen.
May 18	Swedish troops land in Pomerania.
May 20	Napoleon defeats the allies at Bautzen.
June 4	The allies offer Napoleon an armistice, the Armistice of Pleischwitz, to last until 28 July but renewed until 10 August.

June 12	The French evacuate Madrid.
June 15	Britain concludes a subsidy treaty with Prussia and Russia at Reichenbach.
June 21	Wellington defeats the French at Vittoria; Joseph flees to France.
June 27	Treaty of Reichenbach. Russia, Prussia and Austria agree that the Grand Duchy of Warsaw and the Confederation of the Rhine should be abolished; that Austria will receive back the Illyrian Provinces; that Prussia will receive the territory she has lost since 1806 and France restore the North German territory taken in 1810. If France refuses to accept these terms, Austria will declare war.
July 15– Aug. 10	Congress of Prague: the French representative, Culaincourt, and representatives of the allies, Metternich and von Humbold, fail to agree terms for peace.
Aug. 12	Austria declares war on France.
Aug. 23	Bernadotte defeats the French at Grossberen, saving Berlin from capture.
Aug. 25	Blucher defeats the French at Katzbach and drives French out of Silesia.
Aug. 26–27	Napoleon defeats main allied army under Schwarzenberg at Dresden.
Aug. 30	French defeated by Russians at Kulm, saving Schwarzenberg from pursuit.
Sept. 6	Ney's thrust at Berlin is defeated at Dennewitz.
Sept. 9	Austria, Prussia and Russia form an alliance at Teplitz. It agrees: (i) on a firm union and mutual guarantee for their respective territories; (ii) each party to assist each other with at least 60,000 men; (iii) and not to make a separate peace or armistice. Secret articles provide for the restoration of Austria and Prussia to their situation in 1805, including the dissolution of the Confederation of the Rhine and the recognition of the independence of the states of southern and western Germany.
Oct. 7	British army crosses from Spain into southern France.
Oct. 8	Treaty of Ried between the allies and the King of Bavaria who withdraws from the Confederation of the Rhine and agrees to give up the Tyrol to Austria and send a contingent to fight against Napoleon in return for recognition of his sovereign rights.
Oct. 16–19	The Battle of Leipzig (or 'The Battle of the Nations'). Napoleon, outnumbered and virtually surrounded by four allied armies is defeated and forced to retreat from Leipzig which is stormed on the 19th. Prince Jerome is forced to flee Westphalia and the King of Saxony is captured.
Oct. 30	Napoleon defeats Bavarian army at Hanau which has been attempting to block his retreat to France.
Nov. 2	Napoleon crosses Rhine into France at Mainz.
Nov. 9	Allies offer peace terms to Napoleon at Frankfurt

involving the surrender of all French territory beyond the Rhine, Alps and Pyrenees, but keeping Belgium, Nice and Savoy. Napoleon refuses.

Nov. 15	Dutch rise against French, expelling French officials.
Nov.–Dec.	Rest of German states of the Confederation of the Rhine join the allies. A few German cities remain in French control, notably Hamburg.
Dec. 21–25	Schwarzenberg enters Switzerland.
Dec. 31	Castlereagh, British foreign secretary, sent to Germany with full powers to give assistance to the allies. Blucher crosses the Rhine, beginning the invasion of France by the main allied armies.
1814 Jan. 14	Peace of Kiel. Following a short winter campaign by Prince Bernadotte against Denmark, Denmark renounces the possession of Norway in favour of Sweden in return for Pomerania and Rugen. Britain restores all Danish possessions except Heligoland.
Jan. 29	Napoleon defeats Blucher at Brienne.
Feb. 1	Napoleon defeated at La Rothiére, but wins engagements at Champaubert, Montmirail and Vauchamps.
Feb. 5– Mar. 19	Congress of Chatillon-sur-Seine. The Allies offer Napoleon the possession of France at her frontiers of 1791. Conference suspended on 10 Feb. – resumes on 17 Feb. Owing to his victory at Montereau (18 Feb.) Napoleon refuses to come to terms.
Mar. 1	Allies sign Treaty of Chaumont: (i) Great Britain, Austria, Prussia, and Russia each agree to provide 150,000 men to defeat Napoleon; (ii) Britain provides a subsidy of £5,000,000 to the allies; (iii) the allies each agree not to make a separate peace with Napoleon and continue the war until France is reduced to her boundaries of 1791.
Mar. 9	Napoleon defeated at Laon.
Mar. 12	Wellington occupies Bordeaux and raises Bourbon flag.
Mar. 20–21	Napoleon defeated at Arcis-sur-Aube.
Mar. 30	Defeat of French forces in suburbs of Paris. Marie Louise flees.
Mar. 31	Alexander I and Frederick William of Prussia enter Paris. The Senate declares the throne forfeited and sets up a provisional government.
Apr. 6	Napoleon abdicates in favour of his son (this is rejected on 11 Apr.).
Apr. 11	At Treaty of Fontainebleau Napoleon renounces for himself and for his son all claims to the French, Italian and Austrian crowns, though retains Imperial title. He receives the Principality of Elba and a pension of 2,000,000 francs. Marie Louise receives the duchies of Parma, Piacenza and Guastalla with sovereign power.
May 3	Louis XVIII enters Paris. Napoleon lands at Elba.

Note: The Coalitions against Revolutionary and Napoleonic France are variously enumerated by historians, as common action against France was not always marked by formal agreements. The four major coalitions between the great powers are numbered here, but some add those of 1806, at the opening of the war with Prussia – the Jena campaign, and of 1809, when Austria re-entered the war – the Wagram campaign, and renumber those following accordingly.

The Peace Settlement of 1814–1815

The First Treaty of Paris, 30 May 1814

The Treaty of Paris was made between representatives of the allies and France following the restoration of Louis XVIII. The terms towards France were relatively lenient to assist the Bourbon restoration, although provisions were made for a strengthening of the states bordering France. The main provisions were:

1. France retained her boundaries of 1792, representing 3,280 square miles more than those of 1790, including Avignon and the Venaissin, but surrendering the left bank of the Rhine, Belgium, and territory annexed or controlled in Italy, Germany, Holland and Switzerland.

2. France was allowed to retain the art treasures plundered by Napoleon and the revolutionary armies.

3. France was to be returned most of the colonies she had lost with the exception of Malta, Tobago, St Lucia and the Isle of France.

4. Switzerland was to be independent.

5. Holland and Belgium were to be united under the House of Orange as an independent state.

6. Germany was to become a federation of independent states.

7. Italy was to consist of several independent states apart from territory ceded to Austria.

8. France promised Britain to abolish the slave trade.

9. It was agreed that the final settlement of Europe was to be made at a Congress to be held shortly at Vienna.

10. *Secret clauses*. Without reference to France, the allies agreed that Austria should receive the territory of Venetia and the Kingdom of Sardinia would receive Genoa.

The Second Treaty of Paris, 20 November 1815

Following the 'Hundred Days' and the final defeat of Napoleon at Waterloo the Allies felt it necessary to enforce more rigorous terms on France because of the widespread support given to Napoleon. But although some of the Allies, notably Prussia, demanded that France cede major parts of her territory, rivalry between the powers and the continuing desire to secure the Bourbon restoration made the peace settlement less onerous than it might have been. The main provisions were:

1. France was reduced to her frontiers of 1789. While retaining Avignon and the Venaissin, she ceded Chambéry and part of Savoy to Sardinia and some territory to Switzerland.

2. France had to pay an indemnity of 700 million francs and maintain an Allied army of occupation in seventeen border fortresses for up to five years at a cost of 250 million francs a year.

3. France was to restore the art treasures plundered from Europe.

The Congress of Vienna, 1 November 1814–8 June 1815.

As agreed at the first Treaty of Paris (see p. 65), a congress met at Vienna to settle the future boundaries of Europe. Almost every state in Europe was represented. The emperors of Austria and Russia, the kings of Prussia, Denmark, Bavaria and Wurttemberg and many German princes including the Elector of Hesse, the Grand Duke of Baden and the dukes of Saxe-Weimar, Brunswick and Coburg, attended in person. The principal negotiators were: Austria, Metternich; Prussia, Hardenberg and von Humbolt; Russia, Nesselrode and Rasoumoffski; Great Britain, Castlereagh, and later, Wellington; France, Talleyrand and Dalberg. Although interrupted by the 'Hundred Days' and beset by rivalries, the Congress achieved a settlement which while altered in the next century remained in force in much of central and eastern Europe until the First World War. The main provisions were:

Prussia
1. In Germany, Prussia received half of Saxony, the Grand Duchy of Berg, part of the Duchy of Westphalia, and territory on the left bank of the Rhine between Elken and Coblenz, including Cologne, Trèves, and Aix-la-Chapelle. Prussia also received Swedish Pomerania and the King of Prussia was recognised as Prince of Neuchatel.

2. In Poland, Prussia retained the territory gained in the previous partitions, the province of Posen, and the cities of Danzig and Thorn.

Austria
1. In Italy, Austria received Venetia, Lombardy and Milan (now called the Lombardo–Venetian Kingdom), the Illyrian provinces (Carinthia, Carniola and Trieste), Dalmatia, and the seaport of Cattaro (now the kingdoms Illyria and Dalmatia).

2. In Poland, Austria kept eastern Galicia, with Cracow made a free city.

3. In Germany, Austria received the Tyrol and Salzburg.

The German states

1. By the act of Confederation, signed 8 June 1815, and supplemented by the final act of Vienna, 15 May 1820, a German Confederacy was set up to replace the old Holy Roman Empire. The number of German states was reduced from over 300 to 39. A Diet was established under the Presidency of Austria, to which states were to send delegates. The Diet consisted of the Ordinary Assembly sitting permanently at Frankfurt and a General Assembly. Each state was to be independent in internal affairs, but war between the individual states was forbidden and the consent of the Confederacy was necessary for foreign war.

2. Bavaria received Rhenish Bavaria, extending from the Prussian territory on the Rhine to Alsace, including the city of Mainz.

3. Hanover became a kingdom and received East Frisia and Hildesheim.

Russia

1. In Poland, Russia received the greater part of the grand duchy of Warsaw which was to be made into a separate kingdom of Poland. Cracow became a free city state under the protection of Russia, Austria and Prussia.

2. Russia retained Finland, conquered from Sweden in 1808.

3. Russia retained Bessarabia, taken from Turkey in 1812.

Italy

1. Ferdinand IV was recognised as King of the Two Sicilies.

2. The Pope received the Legation of Bologna and most of Ferrara, but was refused the restoration of Avignon.

3. Tuscany was assigned to the Grand Duke Ferdinand, uncle of the Emperor Francis; Modena to the Archduke François d'Este, another Habsburg prince.

4. Parma, Piacenza and Guastella were granted to the Empress Marie Louise for life.

5. Genoa was given to the Kingdom of Sardinia.

Low Countries

The formation of the kingdom of The Netherlands was ratified, comprising the former republic of Holland and Austrian Belgium, under the former hereditary stadtholder as King William I. The sovereignty of the Netherlands was given to the House of Orange, and the King of The Netherlands was made Grand Duke of Luxembourg, making him a member of the German Confederation.

Switzerland

The 19 existing cantons were increased to 22 by the addition of Geneva,

Wallis, and Neuchatel. Switzerland became a confederation of independent cantons with its neutrality guaranteed by the Great Powers.

Sweden and Denmark

Sweden retained Norway which had been ceded to her by Denmark at the Peace of Kiel (14 Jan. 1814). The Norwegians were guaranteed the possession of their Liberties and rights.

Denmark was indemnified with Lauenburg.

Spain and Portugal

Spain lost Trinidad. Portugal lost Guiana to France.

France

Apart from the provisions of the second Treaty of Paris, France received French Guiana from Portugal, Guadeloupe from Sweden, and Martinique and the Isle of Bourbon from Great Britain.

Great Britain

Great Britain retained Malta, Heligoland and the protectorate of the Ionian Isles (the latter by a treaty signed 5 Nov. 1815), as well as Mauritius, Tobago and Santa Lucia from France, Ceylon and the Cape of Good Hope from Holland, and Trinidad from Spain.

The slave trade

In February 1815, the Congress condemned the slave trade as inconsistent with civilisation and human rights.

The Holy Alliance, 26 September 1815

On the initiative of Alexander I, Russia, Austria, and Prussia signed the Holy Alliance, declaring that Christianity was the basis of good government and bound the three sovereigns to act with Christian brotherhood towards each other. It was eventually signed by most European rulers with the exception of the Prince Regent, the Pope and the Turkish sultan. The Holy Alliance had little practical effect, but came to represent the interests of the absolute powers.

The Quadruple Alliance, 20 November 1815

In order to secure the settlement of Vienna, the allies agreed to a Quadruple Alliance to guarantee each other's possessions. The principal provisions were:

1. Austria, Prussia, Russia and Britain agreed to maintain by armed force the exclusion of the Bonaparte dynasty from France for twenty years.

2. The allies agreed to hold meetings at fixed periods to discuss their 'great common interests' and to take such action as was necessary 'for the maintenance of the peace of Europe', giving rise to the 'Congress system', or 'Concert of Europe'.

The Congress System

In accordance with the Quadruple Alliance (see p. 68) the Allies met on a number of occasions after 1815 to consider major issues. The principal conferences were:

Aix-la-Chapelle, Sept.–Nov. 1818

The Allies agreed to a conference (met 27 Sept.) to consider French issues, notably the withdrawal of the army of occupation. It was agreed that the troops should be withdrawn by 30 November 1818 and France was invited to join the councils of the great powers (15 Nov.). Having paid her war indemnity promptly, there was a final adjustment of French debts.

Alexander I also proposed that all governments should agree to maintain the territorial settlements concluded at Vienna and guarantee the position of all legitimate rulers against revolutionary movements. At a time when the Spanish colonists were in revolt against Spain, both Britain and Austria opposed the use of the Quadruple Alliance to interfere with the internal affairs of another state.

On 15 November the Quadruple Alliance between Russia, Austria, Prussia and Britain was renewed in secret to safeguard against another possible revolution in France. Although the powers declared their intention to maintain their close union, Britain refused to make a formal alliance with her allies and with France.

Vienna, Nov. 1819–May 1820

Following a meeting of ministers in September at Carlsbad where repressive legislation was passed to suppress revolutionary movements in the German Confederation, further sittings at Vienna passed the Final Act of the Conference of Vienna authorising the German Confederation to interfere in the affairs of those states unable to maintain public order and the principles of despotic government.

Troppau, Oct.–Dec. 1820; Laibach, Jan.–May 1821

Against the background of revolts in Spain, Naples, and Portugal, and continuing unrest in Germany, Tsar Alexander I demanded another meeting of the major powers. The Conference met on 23 October 1820 and was attended by Austria, Russia and Prussia, and by observers from France and Britain. The Conference was adjourned on 17 December 1820 and reconvened at Laibach on 12 January 1821, concluding on 12 May.

On 19 November 1820, Russia, Austria, and Prussia agreed a Preliminary Protocol that if developments in any state threatened any other state then the powers bound themselves to expel those nations undergoing revolutions from the Concert of Europe and allowed other states to intervene to crush revolts by force if necessary. This agreement was repudiated by Britain on 16 December 1820.

After moving to Laibach, the congress heard an appeal from King Ferdinand of Naples who had been forced to grant a constitution. Ferdinand denounced the rebels and appealed for aid. Because of Austria's special interests in Italy she agreed (13 February) that she would send an army to suppress the revolt (after suppressing the revolt and abolishing the constitution an Austrian army garrisoned Naples until 1828).

No action was taken in respect of Spain and Portugal.

Verona, Oct.–Dec. 1822

Against the background of the Spanish and Greek revolts another congress was held at Verona on 20 October, attended by representatives of Austria, Prussia, France, Russia and Britain.

Britain advocated non-intervention in Spain and with the support of Metternich prevented the sending of a European army to crush the rebels. On 19 November a French plan for intervention was approved if Spain was attacked or Ferdinand VII was deposed. (In 1823 a French army of 100,000 men crossed the Pyrenees and restored Ferdinand to absolute power.)

The end of the congress system

Growing divisions between the Great Powers and the increasing isolation of Great Britain broke down the principle of regular conferences as envisaged by the Quadruple Alliance. Although *ad hoc* conferences were held, Britain soon ceased to send full representatives and refused to allow herself to be represented at conferences on Spain (1823–4) and the Eastern Question (1824). Increasingly, individual powers or groups of powers acted selectively to further their own interests.

Tsarist Russia, 1762–1914

1762   Peter III become Tsar.   In May the gentry are emancipated from state service. Peter deposed and murdered; Catherine II (the Great) ascends the throne.

1764   Final secularisation of church lands.

1766   Catherine encourages the development of self-government for towns.   The Great Commission elected from all classes and nationalities is summoned to Moscow; sitting for eighteen months it debates subjects such as serfdom and local government.

1768   War with Turkey causes the Commission to be prorogued, though various sub-committees sit until 1774.

1768–72   The confederation of Bar puts up armed resistance to Russian demands in Poland.

1772   First partition of Poland.

1773–75   Widespread discontent comes to a head in Pugachev's revolt.

1774   Peace with Turkey concluded at Kutchuk-Kainardji.

1775   Pugachev executed in Moscow.   Town justice reorganised; establishment of courts to protect orphans and widows.

1780   Further rationalisation of provincial administration.

1783   The Crimea is incorporated into Russia.

1785   Issue of the charter for towns.   The Charter of the Nobility confirms their position in society and their hereditary character.

1787–92   War with Turkey.

1788–90   War with Sweden.

1792   Russia and Turkey sign the Treaty of Jassy. Russians invade Poland.

1793–5   Second Partition of Poland. Polish insurrection under Kosciusko suppressed (Mar.–Nov. 1794). Third Partition of Poland (1795).

1796   Catherine succeeded by Tsar Paul; at his coronation proclaims law of succession which defines the succession to the throne on the basis of primogeniture.   Paul repeals the Charter of the Nobility.   Limitations on the labour a serf has to carry out.

1799   Second anti-French coalition; Suvarov campaigns in northern Italy and Switzerland.

1800   Franco–Russian alliance.

1801   Paul's increasing tyranny results in his murder by the Palace Guard.   Alexander I becomes Tsar.

1803	Landowners are given the power to free their serfs though few actually do so. However serfdom is abolished in Estonia and a few other non-Russian provinces. The sale of serfs as a substitute for army recruits is abolished.
1806	War with Turkey.
1807	Speransky appointed to draw up a comprehensive system of constitutional government. Setting up of the Grand Duchy of Warsaw and Treaty of Tilsit (see pp. 56–7).
1808	War with Sweden.
1809	Russo–Swedish conflict ends with the treaty of Frederiksham.
1810	The setting up of a Council of State, composed of ministers appointed by the Tsar to draft new laws and preside over the legality of the administration, proves to be the only proposal put forward by Speransky to survive noble opposition.
1812	Russo–Turkish war ends with the treaty of Bucharest. Napoleon's Russian campaign (see pp. 60–1).
1813–15	Grand Alliance against France.
1815	Formation of 'The Kingdom of Poland' under Russian control.
1817	Secret societies begin to form.
1820	News of mutiny in the Semenovsky regiment helps prompt Alexander to sign a treaty with Prussia and Austria renouncing liberal ideas. Increased control of Kazan university and press censorship.
1821	Outbreak of the Greek revolt.
1822	Return to high protective tariffs begins.
1825	Death of Alexander I causes confusion over the succession. In 1822 Constantine secretly renounced the throne in favour of his brother Nicholas. On Alexander's death the brothers proclaim each other Tsar and in the ensuing confusion the Decembrists (see p. 81) lead a revolt, but this is easily suppressed once Nicholas establishes himself as Tsar.
1826–28	Russo–Persian War.
1826	Nicholas re-establishes the Third Section, Russia's secret police which have been abolished by Alexander. Rigid censorship introduced on all kinds of writing. The first of six commissions to study the peasantry is set up.
1827	Destruction of the Turkish fleet at Navarino Bay.
1828–29	Russo–Turkish War.
1829	Treaty of Adrianople (see p. 191).
1830–31	Polish revolt suppressed.
1832	The question of Greek independence is settled.

1833	Treaty of Unkiar Skelessi (see p. 191).
1833	Russia, together with Austria and Prussia sign the reactionary Munchengratz agreement. Speransky instructed to tabulate the Russian law code.
1841	Auction of serfs forbidden; conditions for state serfs improved. Convention of London leads to Straits Act (see p. 192).
1849	Intervention in Hungary.
1853–56	The Crimean War (see p. 183).
1855	Alexander II succeeds to the throne.
1856 Mar.	Alexander advocates the abolition of serfdom; few nobles support him.
Sept.	Alexander issues a manifesto pardoning political prisoners; recruitment into the army is suspended for a period of three years. The collection of unpaid taxes is also suspended for three years. The Congress of Paris (see p. 192).
1857	Introduction of moderate protective tariffs.
1858 Apr.	A department is set up to deal with the emancipation question. Acquisition of Amur and the maritime provinces from China.
1859	Two committees, later dovetailed into one, begin to draft the laws necessary for emancipation of the serfs.
1860	Reform of the State Bank; the growth of financial institutions is actively encouraged.
1860–73	First railway boom.
1861	Emancipation of the serfs; seen as a landmark in the history of Russia, opening the door to western-style modernisation. The serfs gain legal, but not economic freedom. As subjects of the government they pay redemption money for the land they receive; this land is held as shares in the collective or *Mir* (village). The Mir replaces the gentry; it is responsible for collecting the redemption money. In real terms emancipation abolishes personal servitude and substitutes communal responsibility. Army reforms; the army ceases to be used as punishment for criminals; the most brutal forms of punishment are abolished as are military colonies.
1863	Polish revolt suppressed.
1863–64	Education reform: academic freedom is restored to universities which are expanded and governed by councils elected from the various faculties. Secondary education becomes available to all who pass the necessary examinations; special local authorities are established to promote education. Censorship of books decreases and grants allow students to travel abroad.
1864	Local government reorganisation: new district and

provincial assemblies (*Zemstvos*) are established; despite the electoral system favouring landowning nobles, townsmen and peasants are also represented in the zemstvos. The zemstvos are primarily concerned with public health, public works, welfare and primary education; but they have no control over the police and they can be overruled by government officials.

1864 Nov.   Legal reform: a new legal system based on western practices is introduced. The changes include making judicial proceedings public, the introduction of equality before the law, the use of juries in serious cases and the declaration that judges of the higher courts are to be independent and irremovable except by the decision of a court of law.

1865   Changes in press censorship laws: preliminary censorship replaced by a punitive system, punishment is placed in the hands of the law courts who are invested with wide-ranging powers.

1860s   Emergence of populism, a form of socialism which advocates solving the land question to the satisfaction of the peasants.

1866   Karakosov's attempt to assassinate the Tsar causes Alexander to move towards more reactionary policies over education and the press. He fears the spread of socialism and atheism.

1868   Introduction of a law restricting the sale of certain publications to regular subscribers.   Reduction in the control Zemstvos have over taxation.

1870   Municipal reforms introduced; these are along similar lines to those of local government. Self-government under councils elected by the propertied classes is set up.

1871   In an atmosphere of increasing repression magazines have to be submitted to a preliminary censor four days before publication and preliminary enquiries into state offences are transferred to the gendarmes.   Convention of London (see p. 192).

1873   The Minister of the Interior is given the power to forbid the discussion of sensitive questions for up to three months.

Apr.   Another attempt on the Tsar's life.

1874   The populists fail in an attempt to convert the peasantry to their ideals.   Ordinary courts are no longer to try political cases. Milyutin, the Minister of War, introduces universal military service: conscripts are to be drawn from all classes, the period of active service is reduced from fifteen to six years. Conditions in the service are improved and some basic education is introduced; this is of importance as it increases literacy among the lower classes.

1876   Bakunin, Lavrov and Chernyshevsky organise the 'Land and Liberty' secret society out of the failed populist movement.

'Land and Liberty' is soon suppressed by the government who fear any signs of revolution.   Plekhanov speaks at a demonstration in Kazan Cathedral Square.

1877   Russo–Turkish war, ended by the Treaty of San Stefano (see p. 193).

1878   After the acquittal by jury of a woman who spat at the Prefect of Police in St Petersburg, political cases to be dealt with by Courts Martial.   Congress of Berlin (see p. 193).

1878–79   Mass strikes in St Petersburg.

1879   Bakunin inspires the growth of nihilism, a form of anarchy which rejects traditional values and institutions. His aim is to overthrow the state through a terrorist campaign. In 1879 he forms the 'Will of the People'. Its aim is to gain concessions by assassinating government leaders.

1880   Khalturin attempts to assassinate the Tsar.   Alexander appoints the popular General Melikov in an attempt to reduce domestic unrest; becoming Minister of the Interior in August, Melikov goes on to release hundreds of political prisoners.

1881   Melikov believes that allowing the people a greater share in government will extinguish extremism and may also produce liberal support for the government.

Mar. 31   Alexander agrees to a committee to discuss change; however the same day he falls victim of a terrorist bomb. He is succeeded by Alexander III.

1882   The reactionary Delyanov appointed Minister of Education; further changes in press censorship laws.   Introduction of legislation limiting the use of child labour.

1883–86   Bunge, the Minister of Finance, abolishes the poll taxes and appoints tax inspectors in an effort to improve the taxation system.

1883–84   Plekhanov and others set up small groups to study the work of Marx.

1884   Further legislation to protect minors in industry, including some provision for their education.   A new university statute removes all autonomy granted by Alexander II. Student clubs banned. During this period there is much student unrest; only one new university is founded though technical schools of all types are encouraged.

1885   Restrictions placed on night work by women and children in textile factories.

1886   Decrees provide for the enforcement of new factory legislation; factory inspectors have wide-ranging powers. Production of pig iron increases greatly as the result of the discovery of vast resources of coal and iron in southern Russia.

1887 Bunge driven from office by a charge of 'socialism'. France grants Russia the first of several large loans. Ul'yanov and Shevynev involved in attempt to assassinate the Tsar.

1890 Employers' pressure results in provisions to grant licences for children to work at night.   French and Russian Chiefs of Staff discuss defence measures.

1891 Construction of the Trans-Siberian railway begins. Thousands of Jews evicted from Moscow and forced into ghettos; under Alexander III the Jews lose rights they have gained under Alexander II.

July   Alexander fosters Franco–Russian relations by welcoming French warships at Kronstadt.

1891–93 Severe famine in Russia for which the administration is ill-prepared.

1892 Sergei de Witte appointed Minister of Finance and Commerce; he insists on the adoption of the Gold Standard, the nationalisation of the liquor trade and is involved in the implementation of improved factory legislation.

1893 Lenin participates in the formation of a Marxist circle in Samara.

June   France and Russia sign a commercial treaty; at the end of the year the two powers sign a secret alliance. Factory rules altered in the interests of employers, this is to result in large-scale strikes in 1897 and limits are again placed on hours; however, these limits are undermined by a circular issued in the following year by the Minister of Finance which allows the addition of unlimited extra hours.

1894 Nov. 1 Alexander III dies; succeeded by Nicholas II.

1895 Lenin organises the St Petersburg 'League of Struggle for the Emancipation of the Working Class'. He is arrested later that year.

1896 Russo–Chinese treaty; concessions granted for Trans-Siberian railway through Manchuria.

1896–1902 Several commissions investigate the condition of the peasants.

1897 Lenin exiled to Siberia; Russia adopts Gold Standard.

1898 China leases Port Arthur to Russia.   The Social Democratic Labour Party, the forerunner of the Communist Party, is founded by Plekhanov and nine other representatives of Marxist groups.

1899 First national students' strike.

1900	Leninist newspaper *Iskra* (the 'Spark') founded. Russian troops move into southern Manchuria.
1901	Foundation of the Social Revolutionary Party, mainly concerned with peasant problems and advocating the nationalisation of land.
1902	Further strikes and student disturbances. Publication of Lenin's *What Is To Be Done?*.
1903 July	General strike in Baku; strikes and peasant disturbances throughout Russia.
1903	In London the Social Democratic Party splits into two groups, the Bolsheviks led by Lenin and the Mensheviks. The Bolsheviks advocate a small disciplined party which could lead a revolution.
1904	Murder of Plehve, Minister of the Interior.
Feb. 10	The Russo–Japanese war breaks out.
May	Lenin publishes *One Step Forward, Two Steps Back*. Japanese victory at the Yalu; Port Arthur besieged.
Nov.	The Zemstvo Conference requests a wider range of liberal reforms.
Dec.	The Baku oil workers strike. The Bolshevik paper *Forward*, edited by Lenin, is published in Geneva.
1905 Jan. 1	Russians surrender Port Arthur.
Jan. 22	'Bloody Sunday'. Father Gapon leads a peaceful protest of thousands of people to the Winter Palace with a Petition for the Tsar: Troops opened fire killing many protestors. The incident triggers a series of strikes and increased unrest in Russia. Russian defeats at the hands of the Japanese add to the crisis.
Apr.–May	The Third Congress of the Russian Social Democratic Labour Party meets in London.
May–July	Strike at Ivanovo–Vosnesenk; one of the first Soviets of Workers' Deputies is formed.
May	The first edition of the *Proletarian*, edited by Lenin, published in Geneva.
June	Mutiny on the battleship *Potemkin*. Armed rising at Lodz.
July	Publication of Lenin's book, *Two Tactics of Social Democracy in the Democratic Revolution*.
Aug. 6	The draft law on the establishment of the Consultative State Duma published.
Sept. 5	The Treaty of Portsmouth ends the Russo–Japanese conflict.
Oct. 7	Nationwide political strikes begin.
Oct. 13	The St Petersburg Soviet of Workers' Deputies holds its first session.
Oct. 17	Tsar issues 'October Manifesto' promising a constitution and an elected parliament with genuine legislative power. The Tsar also grants freedom of the press, free speech and religious toleration.

Oct.	The Constitutional Democratic Party (the Cadets) is formed.
Oct. 20	Political demonstrations in Moscow.
Oct.–Dec.	Formation of Workers' Soviets in major Russian cities and towns.
Oct. 24–28	Armed forces revolt at Kronstadt.
Nov.–Dec.	The Bolshevik daily newspaper *New Life*, edited by Lenin, is published in St Petersburg.
Nov. 11–15	Rising in Sevastopol.
Nov. 21	First sitting of the Moscow Soviet.
Nov.	Rise of the moderate Octobrist Party.
Dec.	Moscow Soviet stages uprising (23 Dec.); widespread armed risings in Russia.
Dec. 1905– Jan 1906	Moscow rising crushed. Punitive expeditions by Tsarist forces near Moscow, in the Baltic and Siberia.
1906 Apr.	Elections boycotted by Social Democrats and Social Revolutionaries; Constitutional Democrats ('Cadets') win largest number of seats.
May 6	Tsar issues Fundamental Law of the Empire by which the Tsar retains most of his autocratic power. Legislative power is to be divided between the Duma and the upper house, half the members of which are to be appointed by the Tsar. When the Duma is not in session the government may legislate by decree.
May 10	First Duma assembles; votes no confidence in the government.
June	Stolypin becomes prime minister.
July 21	Deadlock over the constitutional issue leads to the dissolution of the Duma. Cadet leaders issue Vyborg Manifesto calling for a refusal to pay taxes and enter military service, but no response.
July	Soldiers and sailors rise in Skeaborg and Kronstadt. The Russian economy is bolstered by a series of enormous loans negotiated by Witte.
Aug. 25	Stolypin makes large tracts of land available to the peasants.
Sept. 1	In an attempt to suppress the revolutionary movement, the government introduces Field Courts Martial; as a result over six hundred people are executed.
Oct.	Peasants are allowed to leave their village communes or to join others. Stolypin also removes the restrictions on the election of peasants to the Zemstvos. Peasants also become eligible for any rank in government service.
Nov. 22	Stolypin's Agrarian Reform Act ends communal system of landholding. Peasants are allowed to leave the commune at will and claim their share of land in private property.

1907 Mar. 5	The Second Duma meets, dominated by opposition to the autocracy.
June 16	Stolypin dissolves Duma and introduces a new electoral law, legalising arbitrary restrictions which had preceded the second election and also greatly increasing propertied representation.
Nov.	Election of the Third Duma.
1908 June	During public discussion of the budget, Guchkov blames the government for the military failures in the Russo–Japanese conflict.
1911 Sept.	Stolypin assassinated in a Kiev theatre.
1913	Election of Fourth Duma.
1914 Summer	General Strike in St Petersburg.
Aug. 1	Germany declares war on Russia.

The evolution of nationalism in Europe 1815–1848

1815 May 31   Creation of the United Provinces.
      June 9   Congress of Vienna ends. Poland divided between Russia and Prussia.
              Cracow made an independent City Republic.
      Nov. 7   Russia grants the Poles a constitution.

1816   First signs of Decembrist organisation in Russia.
      Nov.   Diet of German Confederation meets.

1817   Festival of Wartburg to celebrate 300th anniversary of the Reformation. Absolutist texts and military effigies burnt.
      June 23   In Italy the rising at Macerata collapses.
      Nov. 5   Turkey grants Serbia partial autonomy.

1818 Sept. 27   Congress of Aix-la-Chapelle.

1819   In Russia military settlers rise at Chuguev.
      Mar. 23   Kotzebue, a Russian dramatist, reactionary and secret agent murdered by German students.
      Sept.   'Carlsbad Decrees' suppressing revolutionary activity promulgated.
      Oct.   Prussian trade treaty with Schwarzburg–Sonderhausen lays foundation of the Zollverein.

1820   Disturbances among Semenov guards in St Petersburg.
      Jan.   Disturbances among troops at Cadiz forces a return to the 1812 constitution.
      Feb. 13   Duc de Berry assassinated. In France repressive action is taken against the press and freedom of elections.
      May   Final Act of Vienna signed.
      July 2   Rebellion in Naples.
      July 6   Naples promised a constitution.
      Aug.   Lombardy and Venetia declare membership of the Carbonari high treason.
      Aug.   Portuguese garrisons in Oporto and Lisbon revolt against British influences.
              A Cortes is called which produces a liberal constitution.
      Oct. 23   Congress of Troppau.

1821   Rise of the Northern and Southern Societies of Decembrists.
      Jan. 12   Congress of Laibach.
      Feb.   Austria sends aid to Ferdinand of Naples.
      Mar. 6   Revolt in Moldavia and Wallachia. Rebels appeal to the Tsar for aid against Turkey.
      Mar. 13   Constitutionalist rising in Piedmont. Victor Emmanuel

		abdicates, leaving Charles Albert as Regent; he proclaims the Spanish Constitution of 1812. Charles Felix of Modena calls on Austrian military aid.
	Mar. 23	Austrian troops enter Naples; rebels defeated and punished.
	Apr. 8	Austrian victory at Novara. Austrian forces enter Turin and Alessandria unopposed.
	Apr. 22	Greeks massacre Turks in the Morea (the Peloponnese). Turkish repression begins.
	June 19	Turks defeat Greeks at Dragashan.
	Oct. 5	Greek rebels in the Morea capture Tripolitza.
1822	Jan. 13	Greeks declare Independence.
	Apr. 22	Turks capture Chios and massacre Greeks.
	July 15	Turkish invasion of Greece.
	Oct. 20	Congress of Verona.
1823		Formation of the Society of United Slavs – the Decembrists.
		French forces intervene in Spain freeing Ferdinand VII who instigates a harsh reaction.
	Sept.	The newly elected Pope Leo XII continues the reactionary misrule of the Papal States.
	Oct. 15	Britain refuses to aid John VI of Portugal against the forces of reaction.
	Dec. 2	Establishment of Provincial Diets in Prussia.
1824	Feb.	John VI issues a decree for the recall of the Cortes. However a coup by his brother Dom Miguel causes John to flee. He is able to regain his throne by enlisting British aid.
	Apr. 24	Byron dies at Missolonghi while supporting the Greeks.
	June 13	Accession of Grand Duke Leopold II in Tuscany.
	Sept. 16	Charles X becomes King of France.
1825	Jan. 4	In the Kingdom of the Two Sicilies Ferdinand I is succeeded by the weak Francis I.
1825	Dec.	Decembrists take advantage of confusion over the succession to Alexander I to rise in St Petersburg.
	Dec. 6–Jan.	Chernigov Regiment rises in the Ukraine under Decembrist leadership. Risings suppressed.
1826		John VI is succeeded in Portugal by Dom Pedro's daughter Maria ruling by a charter providing for Parliamentary Government.
	Apr. 4	By the St Petersburg Protocol Britain and Russia agree on Greek autonomy.
	Apr. 5	Russia sends Turkey an ultimatum over Serbia and the Danubian provinces.
	Oct. 27	By the Ackerman Convention Russia gains Serbia and the Danubian lands.
1827		Student revolutionaries in Moscow.
	Apr. 30	National Guard disbanded in France.

June 5	Turkish forces enter Athens.
July 6	By the Treaty of London, Britain, Russia and France recognise Greek autonomy.
Aug. 6	Turkey rejects the powers terms.
Oct. 20	Turkish fleet annihilated at Navarino Bay.
Nov. 5	Creation of 76 new peers in France. During election riots barricades appeared in the streets and there were some deaths.
Dec. 8	Allied ambassadors leave Constantinople.
1828 Jan. 4	Martignac's ministry replaces Villèle's in France. Dom Miguel puts an end to liberalism in Portugal.
July 19	London protocol signed.
Aug. 6	Turks under Mehemet Ali agree to leave Greece.
Oct. 11	Russian forces occupy Varna.
Nov. 16	Recognition of Greece as an independent state
Dec. 10	In France Beranger gaoled for political songs.
1829	The reactionary Baron Wenklein becomes effective ruler of Parma.
Aug. 8	Polignac forms an administration in France.
Sept. 14	Treaty of Adrianople ends the Russo–Turkish conflict.
1830 Feb. 3	Greek independence guaranteed by Britain, France and Russia at the London Conference.
May 16	Dissolution of the Chamber of Deputies in France.
July 26	Ordinances of St Cloud promulgated in France.
July 27	Revolution in France. In Paris there is fighting in the streets.
July 31	Charles X abdicates.
Aug. 7	The Duke of Orléans, Louis Philippe, is persuaded to become King.
Aug. 14	Constitutional Charter of July published.
Aug. 17	Charles X retires to Britain.
Aug. 25	The Belgians revolt against union with Holland.
Sept. 22	Revolts in Hesse, Brunswick and Saxony dethrone the rulers and result in new constitutions.
Nov. 18	In Belgium a National Congress declares Independence.
Nov. 22–4	Belgium votes for a monarchy, but the House of Orange is vetoed.
Nov. 29	The Polish revolt against Russia.
Dec. 21	Polignac and other ministers gaoled indefinitely.
Dec. 30	Belgian Independence agreed on by the powers at a London Conference. Rising in Sevastapol.
1830–31	Cholera riots in Russia.
1831 Jan. 5	Hesse–Cassel granted a constitution.
Jan. 22–27	Powers protocol for the separation of Belgium accepted by the Belgians but rejected by the Dutch.
Jan. 25	Declaration of Independence by the Polish Diet.
Feb. 2	Election of Pope Gregory XVI. Rising in Modena against Francis IV, rebellion in the Papal States. Wenklein flees from Parma.

Feb. 3	To placate Britain Louis Phillipe rejects the election of the Duke of Nemours as King of Belgium. Eventually Leopold I of Saxe Coburg becomes King, ruling by a liberal constitution.
Feb. 7	Proclamation of the Belgian constitution.
Mar. 4	In response to the Pope's appeal Austrian troops invade Italy.
Mar. 21	Austrian forces enter Bologna.
May 10	The ambassadors of the Great Powers produce a memorandum on the reform of the Papal States which is largely ignored.
May 26	Polish forces suffer defeat at Ostrolenke.
June 26	The '18 Articles' proposed by the London Conference rejected by the Dutch.
Aug. 2	The Dutch invade Belgium.
Aug. 20	Facing a French army in Belgium the Dutch retreat.
Sept. 4	Constitution granted in Saxony.
Sept. 8	The Polish Revolt collapses when the Russians capture Warsaw.
Oct. 21	The '21 Articles' of the London Conference rejected by the Dutch.
Nov. 15	The powers accept a Treaty incorporating 24 articles.
Dec. 27	In France the hereditary peerage abolished after the creation of thirty-six new peers.
1831–32	Military settlers in the Novgorod province of Russia rise.
1832 Jan.	Austrian forces put down risings in Romagna. Louis Philippe sends troops to occupy Ancona. 'Young Italy' founded by Mazzini.
Feb. 26	Abolition of the Polish constitution.
Apr. 10	Turkey declares war on Mehemet Ali.
Apr. 27	Mehemet Ali takes Acre.
May 27	In Germany the Hambach festival advocates revolt against Austrian rule.
June 5–6	Republican insurrection in Paris put down.
June 28	Metternich's Six Articles.
Dec. 21	Turks defeated at Konieh.
Dec. 23	The capture of Antwerp by French forces compels the Dutch to recognize Belgian independence.
1832–35	Ukrainian peasant's movement at its height.
1833	Donna Maria restored to the Portuguese throne.
Mar. 18	Aquittal of Bergeron and Benot on a charge of trying to assassinate Louis Philippe.
Mar. 23	Establishment of the Zollverein from which Austria is excluded.
May 3	Egypt granted independence from Turkey.
May	Belgium and Holland conclude an indefinite armistice.
June	Treaty of Unkiar Skelessi between Russia and Turkey.
Sept.	Congress of Munchengratz.
Oct.	Russia, Austria and Prussia agree to maintain the integrity of the Ottoman Empire.

1835 May	Baden joins the Zollverein.
1837 June	Ernest Augustus suppresses the Hanover Constitution.
1838 Oct.	Austria evacuates the Papal States apart from Ferrara.
1839	In Italy the Scientific Congress discusses the problem of unity.
Apr.	By the Treaty of London final agreement is reached on Belgian–Dutch borders. Luxembourg is created a Grand Duchy.
	The Turks invade Syria.
June 24	Turkey defeated at Nezib.
July 1	Sultan Mahmud dies and is succeeded by Abdul Mejid.
	Turkish fleet surrenders at Alexandria.
Nov. 3	Decree of Reform throughout the Ottoman Empire.
1840	The Magyar Diet succeeds in having Magyar substituted for Latin as the official Hungarian language.
June 7	Frederick William IV crowned King of Prussia.
June 15	The Quadruple Alliance of Britain, France, Austria and Russia supports Turkey against Mehemet Ali.
Sept. 11	The Royal Navy bombards Beirut.
Nov. 3	The British take Acre. Mehemet Ali leaves Syria.
Nov. 5	By the Convention of Alexandria Mehemet Ali agrees to the Treaty of London.
1841	Russian peasants rise in Guria.
July 13	The powers guarantee the Ottoman Empire. The Straits are closed to all warships.
1843	In *The Moral and Civil Supremacy of Italy* Gioberti advocates a united Italy under Papal rule.
1844 July 25	Bondiero brothers shot for attempted revolt in Calabria.
1846 June 15	Pius IX becomes Pope and makes several liberal concessions including reduced press censorship and the establishment of a Council of State.
1847 Feb. 3	Frederick William summons a united Diet.

The 1848 Revolution in France

1845–46	Widespread agricultural distress as a result of poor harvests.
1846	International financial crisis contributes to a high level of unemployment – about a third of the working population of Paris starve or are living on charity.
1847	Reform banquets calling for measures such as universal suffrage and parliamentary reform are held throughout France.
1848 Jan. 14	Guizot bans the holding of the 71st banquet in Paris scheduled for 22 February. The opposition politicians plan a compromise to save face but events overtake them.
Feb. 21	*Le National* publishes a detailed plan for a demonstration and calls on the people of Paris to support a procession prior to the banquet. That evening the deputies meet at Thiers's House and cancel the banquet.
Feb. 22	Only a handful of the opposition including Lamartine wish to go ahead and *Le National* calls for calm behaviour. However, unaware the banquet has been cancelled, a crowd gather in the Place De La Madelaine, though this is dispersed by the Municipal Guard.
Feb. 23	Guizot is replaced. Thiers joins the new ministry. Though tension in Paris relaxes, the barricades and crowds remain. The flash point comes when demonstrators reach the Ministry of Foreign Affairs. A shot is fired and soldiers discharge a volley into the crowd leaving fifty-two dead. The parading of the dead around Paris results in the erection of many barricades and up to 100,000 Parisians take to the streets. At first Louis Philippe determines to crush the rising; however under Thiers's influence the troops are withdrawn.
Feb. 24	Louis Philippe abdicates in favour of his grandson. Lamartine sets up a provisional government in the Hôtel de Ville, a rival workers government is abandoned when Louis Blanc and two socialist colleagues join Lamartine. The Government passes a number of liberal proclamations including the abolition of slavery, universal suffrage and freedom of the press. A Republic is proclaimed.
Feb. 27	Inauguration of Louis Blanc's plan for public relief.
Feb. 28	Institution of National Workshops to provide 'a permanent commission for the workers'.
Mar. 5	Elections decreed for 9 April, later postponed to 23 April.

Mar. 16	Demonstration of 'bonnets à poil'.
Mar. 17	Left-wing counter demonstration.
Apr. 23	Elections for the Constituent Assembly.
May 4	The first meeting of the National Assembly where elections based on universal suffrage return a moderate republican majority.
May 15	Demonstration of the Clubs. Fresh risings in Paris. A mob enters the Assembly and declares it dissolved, but is dispersed by the National Guard.
June 22	Start of the 'June Days' (22–26 June). The Assembly decrees that all unmarried workers in the 'National Workshops' should join the army and that married men must go to the provinces to do public works. Barricades go up and fighting breaks out.
June 22–26	Bloody fighting in Paris as General Cavaignac suppresses the revolt.
June	Four departments and Paris elect Louis Napoleon to the Assembly.
Sept. 26	Louis Napoleon takes his seat in the Assembly.
Nov. 4	Constitution of the Second Republic.
Dec. 10	Louis Napoleon elected President by a massive majority.
1849 Jan.	The republican society 'Solidarité Républicaine' is banned. Under pressure the Assembly votes for its dissolution.
Apr.	Expedition to Rome.
Apr. 26	French forces land in the Papal States.
May	Elections to the Legislative Assembly.
June 13	Attempted rising in Paris comes to nothing. Only in Lyons is there violence as demonstrations are dispersed. The Government passes further repressive measures.
July 4	French troops enter Rome; Pius IX restored.
Oct.	Louis Napoleon dismisses the Barrot Ministry.
1850 Mar.	Loi Falloux on education gains Louis Napoleon Roman Catholic support. Left-wing victories in by-elections.
May	As a result of left-wing victories, a new law restricting the franchise to those who can prove three years' residence in the same canton is passed. The new law will also disfranchise anyone who has been found guilty in court. The overall effect is to reduce the electorate by a third.
1851 Jan. 10	Napoleon dismisses General Changarnier, commander of the Paris garrison and National Guard.
July	Napoleon fails to gain the necessary two-thirds majority required to change the constitution and extend his tenure of presidency.
Dec. 2	Louis Napoleon carries out a successful coup d'état.
Dec. 4	Little opposition in Paris; risings in the provinces crushed.
Dec. 14	A plebiscite shows that 92% of the poll ratifies Louis Napoleon's action.

Austria–Hungary in 1848

1848 Mar. 3	Kossuth demands total change in the government of Hungary.
Mar. 11	Moderate Czechs and Germans meet in Prague to urge liberal reforms, but achieve little due to internal division caused by extremists.
Mar. 12	Revolution in Vienna heralded by student demonstrations.
Mar. 13	Following demonstrations in Vienna, Metternich resigns; the middle class gain the right to form a national guard.
Mar. 15	The liberal and constitutional reforms advocated in March 1847 are accepted by the Hungarian Diet.
Apr. 11	Hungary confirmed as a separate state. Kossuth abolishes feudalism and divides land among the peasants. However his demands for Magyarisation cause dissension among other races and create willing allies for Austria.
Apr. 25	Austria granted a constitution which includes a provision for responsible Government.
May 15	Second rising in Vienna. The National Guard refuses to intervene.
May 17	The Emperor flees from Vienna to Innsbruck, afraid to trust his troops.
June 2	Meeting of the Pan Slav congress in Prague.
June 13	Czech rising in Prague.
June 17	Windischgratz crushes the Czech rising.
June	Austria supplies secret aid to Croatia for future use against Hungary.
July	Meeting of the Constituent Assembly of the western provinces in Vienna with the aim of drawing up a constitution based on universal suffrage.
Aug. 12	Emperor Ferdinand returns to Vienna.
Sept. 7	Abolition of serfdom and the 'robot' in Austria.
Sept. 11	Jellacic invades Hungary.
Sept. 24	Kossuth proclaimed President of the Committee for the National Defence of Hungary.
Oct. 3	Austria declares war on Hungary.
Oct. 6	Third rising in Vienna.
Oct. 7	Viennese court flees to Olmuk.
Oct.	Jellacic driven from Hungary.
Oct. 22	The Assembly adjourns to Kremsier in Moravia.
Oct. 31	Windischgratz aided by Jellacic and his forces bombard Vienna into surrender.
Nov.	New ministry formed under Schwarzenberg.
Dec. 2	Ferdinand abdicates to be succeeded by Francis Joseph.
1849 Mar. 1	The Austrian Reichstag completes the Kremsier

	constitution which provides for a decentralised federal type of government.
Mar. 4	Proclamation of an Austrian constitution designed to rally German and Czech support.
Mar. 7	Dissolution of the Austrian Assembly.
Apr. 6	Hungarian forces under Gorgei defeat Windischgratz at Isaszeg.
Apr. 14	Declaration of Independence by the Hungarian Diet under the leadership of Kossuth.
Apr. 21	Austria appeals to the Tsar for aid.
May	Gorgei retakes Budapest, but the Hungarians fail to take decisive action.
Aug. 13	Austria supported by Russia defeats the Hungarians at Vilagos. Kossuth flees to Turkey.
1851 Dec. 31	Austrian constitution abolished.

The 1848 revolutions in Italy

1848 Jan.   'Tobacco Riots' against Austrian influence in Lombardy.

Jan. 12   Revolt and proclamation of a provisional independent government in Sicily. The King accepts the 1812 constitution which is also extended to Naples.

Feb. 10   Ferdinand II proclaims a constitution in Naples.

Feb. 11   In Tuscany the Grand Duke allows representative government and a constitution to be declared.

Mar. 14   Pius IX reluctantly grants a constitution in Rome.

Mar. 17   Daniele Manin leads a revolt in Venice.

Mar. 18   Uprising in Milan causes Radetzky to evacuate the city.

Mar. 20   Revolt in Parma.

Mar. 22   Manin proclaims the Venetian Republic.

Mar. 23   Charles Albert issues a proclamation sympathising with Lombardy and Venetia. Piedmontese troops attack Austrian forces in Lombardy.

Apr. 8   Austrians defeated by Piedmontese forces at Gioto.

Apr. 13   Sicily declares itself independent of Naples.

Apr. 28   The Papacy joins the war against Austria.

Apr. 29   Pius IX ceases to support the Nationalist Movement.

Apr. 30   Austrians defeated at Pastrengo.

May 15   Collapse of revolt in Naples.

May 29   Austria defeats Tuscany at Curtatone.

July 22   Radetzky wins a major victory at Custozza. Sardinian troops forced out of Milan and Lombardy.

Aug. 9   Sardinia and Austria sign the Armistice of Vigevano.

Aug. 11   Venice expels Sardinian troops.

Nov. 15   Count Rossi, Premier of Papal States assassinated.

Nov. 24   Pius IX flees from Rome to Gaeta.

1849 Feb. 7   The Grand Duke of Tuscany also flees to Gaeta.

Feb. 9   Mazzini's proclamation of a Roman Republic.

Mar. 12   Sardinia terminates truce with Austria.

Mar. 23   The Austrians win a major victory at Novara. Charles Albert abdicates; succeeded by Victor Emmanuel II.

Apr. 28   The French land troops in the Papal States.

May 15   Neapolitan troops occupy Palermo.

July 4   French troops enter Rome.   Pius IX restored.

Aug. 6   End of the Austria–Sardinian conflict called by the Peace of Milan.

Aug. 28   Surrender of Venice to the Austrians.

Italian unification 1850–1870

1850 Oct. 11	Cavour appointed Minister of Agriculture, Commerce and Marine in Piedmont.
1852 May 6	Leopold II abolishes the Tuscan Constitution.
Nov. 4	Cavour becomes Prime Minister.
1855 Jan. 26	Piedmont enters the Crimean war on the allied side.
May	General La Marmora joins the allies in the Crimea.
1857 Aug. 15	Garibaldi forms the Italian National Association for Unification of Italy under Piedmontese leadership.
1858 Jan. 14	Orsini bomb plot, an abortive attempt to assassinate Napoleon III.
July 20	Cavour and Napoleon sign the Pact of Plombières.
Sept.	Victor Emmanuel's daughter Clotilde marries Napoleon III's cousin Jerome.
1859 Jan. 19	Franco-Sardinian alliance signed.
Jan.	Formalisation of the Franco-Piedmontese agreement made at Plombières.
Jan.	Victor Emmanuel uses provocative language aimed at Austria. Finance Minister La Marmora makes war loans.
Apr. 19	Austrian ultimatum issued, demanding unconditional demobilisation within three days.
Apr. 26	Austria's ultimatum is rejected.
Apr. 29	Austrian troops enter Sardinia.
May 3	France declares war on Austria.
June 4	Austria heavily defeated at Magenta.
June 24	Austria defeated at Solferino. Both armies suffer heavy losses.
July 11	Napoleon III concludes the Peace of Villafranca, the terms of which cause Cavour to resign.
Aug.	Constituent Assemblies meet in Parma, Modena, Tuscany and Romagna forming a military alliance and demanding Victor Emmanuel as King.
1860 Jan. 20	Cavour regains power.
Mar.	Almost unanimous vote by plebiscite in the central Italian states for union with Piedmont.
Mar. 24	Sardinia cedes Nice and Savoy to France.
Apr. 2	Meeting of the first 'Italian' Parliament in Turin.
May 5	Garibaldi's expedition sets sail for Sicily.
May 11	Garibaldi lands in Sicily.
May 27	Garibaldi's forces take Palermo.
Aug. 22	Garibaldi lands on the Italian mainland.
Sept. 7	Fall of Naples; Francis II flees.
Sept. 11	Sardinian troops enter the Papal States.
Sept. 18	Garibaldi defeats Papal forces at Castelfidardo.
Oct. 21	Sicily and Naples decide to unite with Sardinia.

Oct. 26	Garibaldi proclaims Victor Emmanuel King of Italy.
Nov. 4	Umbria votes to unite with Sardinia.
1861 Feb. 13	Francis II of Naples formally surrenders to Garibaldi at Gaeta.
Feb. 18	Italian Parliament proclaims Victor Emmanuel King of Italy.
Mar. 17	Formal proclamation of the Kingdom of Italy.
June 6	Cavour dies.
1862 Mar.	Ratazzi Ministry in Turin encourages Garibaldi to mount a campaign from Sicily to overthrow the Pope.
Aug. 29	Garibaldi, having made a triumphal progress through Sicily, crosses to the mainland, but is defeated and captured by Italian royal troops at Aspromonte and imprisoned at Spezzia.
1864 Sept.	By the September Convention, Napoleon III consents to the withdrawal of French troops from Rome, in return for the Italians showing their renunciation of Rome as the national capital by removing the seat of government to Florence from Turin. Proposal causes serious disorder in Turin.
1865 Apr. 26	Florence proclaimed capital of Italy. French troops gradually withdraw from Rome and Italian kingdom bound by the Convention not to attack Papal territory.
1866 Jan.	Military influence at the Austrian court causes the rejection of an Italian offer to buy Venetia.
Apr. 8	Secret offensive and defensive alliance between Italy and Prussia. La Marmora Cabinet borrows 3 million francs and places army and fleet on a war footing.
June 24	Italian forces under La Marmora's command defeated at Custozza. All Italian forces forced to retreat and Garibaldi defeated and wounded in skirmish at Monte Suello. Italian secret convention with France.
July 5	Following the defeat by the Prussians at Königgrätz (Sadowa) on 3 July Francis Joseph of Austria cedes Venetia to the Emperor Napoleon and through him to the Italians in return for the mediation of France in the Austro–Prussian War.
July 20	Italian fleet under Persano defeated by the Austrians at Lissa in the Adriatic.
Oct. 21	Venetia formally votes to unite with Italy. Italy entirely free of foreign troops.
1867 Oct.	Garibaldi raises volunteers for a march on Rome.
Oct. 27	Napoleon III sends troops back to Rome to protect the Pope.
Nov. 3	French troops defeat Garibaldi's army at Mentana. The Italian government arrests Garibaldi, while French troops remain to protect Rome. French minister Rouher declares that the Italians will 'never' enter Rome.
1870 Sept.	Defeat of France at Sedan and collapse of Napoleon

III's government leads to removal of French troops
from Rome. New French Foreign Minister Jules Favre,
indicates that France will not prevent the fall of Rome.
King Victor Emmanuel marches on Rome.

Sept. 20	Italian forces enter Rome near the Porta Pia after resistance by Papal troops. Papal troops marched out of Rome and sent away by sea.
Oct. 2	Plebiscite in the Papal States approves union with Italy and National Assembly votes to remove capital from Florence to Rome. The Pope is allowed to retain authority over the Vatican.
1871 July 2	King Victor Emmanuel takes up residence at the Quirinal Palace as the first ruler of a fully united Italy.

The unification of Germany

1848	Mar. 17	Uprising in Berlin: Frederick William IV grants a constitution.
	Mar. 31	The *Vorparlement* meets at Frankfurt.
	May 2	Prussia invades Denmark over Schleswig-Holstein question.
	May 18	German National Assembly meets in Frankfurt.
	May 22	Berlin meeting of Prussian National Assembly.
	Aug. 26	Denmark and Prussia make peace at the treaty of Malmo.
	Dec. 5	Dissolution of the Prussian National Assembly.
1849	Jan. 23	Prussia advocates a United Germany, excluding Austria.
	Mar. 27	The German National Assembly offers Frederick William IV the title 'Emperor of the Germans'.
	May 3	Prussian forces suppress revolt in Dresden.
	June 6	German National Assembly moves to Stuttgart.
	June 18	Troops carry out the dissolution of the National Assembly.
	June 23	Rebels in Baden surrender to Prussian forces.
1850	Jan. 31	Prussia grants a Liberal constitution.
	Mar. 20	Frederick William IV summons a German Parliament to Erfurt.
	Apr. 29	The Erfurt Parliament opens.
	May	Schwarzenberg revives the old Diet of Frankfurt and invites the German states to discuss the revision of the old Confederation and the establishment of an authority for Germany. Prussia did not attend.
	July 2	Under Russian pressure Prussia and Denmark sign the peace of Berlin, a treaty which favoured the Danes.
	Oct.	The Tsar promises moral support to Austria if Prussia opposes federal execution in Hesse-Cassel. Resignation of the Prussian Foreign Minister, Radowitz.
	Nov. 20	Prussia humiliated by the Convention of Olmutz imposed by Austria. Prussia agrees to abandon the Erfurt Union and to restore the confederation. The convention also includes demobilisation on terms unfavourable to Prussia.
	Dec.	The Dresden Conference; Schwarzenberg has to abandon his plan to include the Habsburg Empire in the Confederation. The only consolation for Austria was a three-year defensive alliance with Prussia.
1853		German customs union renewed for a further twelve years; Austria only gained a commercial treaty with Prussia, not the Austro–German customs union desired by Bruck, Austrian Minister for commerce.

1855 Jan.	Bismarck, as Prussian Minister at Frankfurt persuades the Diet that Germany should keep out of the Crimean war, to the annoyance of Austria.
1859 Dec. 11	Albert von Roon becomes Prussian Minister of War.
1860 Feb.	Von Roon places his proposals for military reform before the Prussian Landtag.
1861 Jan. 2	Accession of William I to the Prussian throne on the death of Frederick William IV.
Oct.	Saxony proposes a scheme for a tripartite reorganisation of the Confederation.
Dec.	Prussia rejects the scheme on the grounds that the Confederation could not be reformed and declares further that unification could only come under Prussian leadership.
1862 Feb.	Austria puts forward a modified version of the Saxon scheme; though it wins the support of several states, Prussia rejects it.
Sept. 22	Bismarck becomes Minister President of Prussia.
Sept. 30	Bismarck makes his 'Blood and Iron' speech on the question of German Unification.
Oct. 7	The Prussian Diet rejects the military budget.
Dec.	Bismarck warns Austria of the dangers of not recognising Prussia as an equal in Germany. Bismarck fails to gain a promise of French neutrality in the event of war.
1863 Jan	Austrian proposals for the Confederation finally defeated in the Diet after Prussia threatens to walk out.
Feb. 8	The Polish revolt provides the opportunity for Bismarck to sign an alliance with Russia.
Mar. 30	Schleswig incorporated into Denmark.
Aug.	Bismarck convinces William not to attend the Austrian-organised meeting of the princes.
Oct. 1	The German Diet votes for action against Denmark.
Nov. 13	Danish council of state approves the Constitution for Schleswig.
Nov. 15	Frederick VII of Denmark dies. Succeeded by Christian IX.
Dec. 24	Hanoverian and Saxon forces move into Holstein.
1864 Jan. 16	Austro–Prussian alliance committing them to joint military action against Denmark and to deciding the future of the Duchies by joint agreement.
Feb. 1	Austro–Prussian invasion of Schleswig.
Apr. 18	Danish forces defeated at Duppel.
June 25	London Conference fails to solve the Danish problem.
July	Danes defeated.
Oct. 30	The peace of Vienna. Denmark cedes Schleswig-Holstein to Austria and Prussia who are to make a private agreement over their control.
Nov.	Bismarck bullies the Diet into leaving Austro–Prussian forces in sole control of the government.

1865 Aug. 14	Convention of Gastein: Austria receives Holstein. Prussia gained Schleswig and purchased Lauenberg.
Oct. 4–11	Bismarck and Napoleon meet at Biarritz.
1866 Jan.	Austro–Prussian friction over the Duchies.
Feb. 28	Prussian Crown Council take up Austria's challenge even at the risk of war.
Apr. 8	Secret military alliance between Prussia and Italy.
Apr. 21	On hearing rumours of Italian troop movements, Austria mobilises her southern forces. Prussian mobilisation ordered.
June 7	Prussian invasion of Holstein which is subsequently annexed.
June 10	Bismarck outlines plans for a new state excluding Austria from Germany.
June 12	Austria and Prussia break off diplomatic relations.
June 14	The German Diet takes a vote to mobilise against Prussia.
June 15	Prussian ultimatum to Saxony, Hanover and Hesse-Cassel.
June 16	Prussian invasion of Saxony, Hanover and Hesse-Cassel.
June 20	Italy declares war on Austria.
June 29	Hanoverian victory over Prussia at Langensaza, but by the end of June Hanover capitulates.
July 3	Major Prussian victory over Austria at Sadowa-Königgrätz.
July 5	Austria attempts to preserve her supremacy in Germany by seeking the mediation of France, agreeing to cede Venetia to the Emperor Napoleon, and through him to the Italians, freeing 100,000 Austrian troops in Italy for the defence of Vienna. French claims to the Rhine boundary are rejected by Prussia, but France is unable to go to war because of her involvement in Mexico.
July 26	After a rapid Prussian advance on Vienna, Prussia and Austria sign preliminaries of peace at Nikolsburg, near Vienna.
Aug. 13–22	Prussia signs peace treaty with Württemberg, Baden and Bavaria.
Aug. 23	Treaty of Prague signed on the basis of the preliminaries of Nikolsburg. Austria is excluded from German affairs and the German Confederation of 1815 is dissolved. Schleswig-Holstein, Hanover, the whole of Hesse-Cassel, Nassau and the free city of Frankfurt are annexed by Prussia, adding 5 million subjects. Austria is to pay a war indemnity of 40,000 thalers and to cede Venetia to Italy. The North German Federation is formed, comprising Prussia, Saxony, the grand duchies of Oldenburg, the two Mecklenburgs, Brunswick, part of Hesse Darmstadt, the Thuringian States and the free cities of Hamburg, Bremen, and Lubeck. Elections for a North German diet prescribed

on the basis of direct manhood suffrage.   Secret understanding reached between Prussia and the south German states in the form of an offensive and defensive alliance based upon a reciprocal guarantee of territorial integrity. The southern states place their entire military force under the command of the King of Prussia in the event of war.

Sept. 3   Peace signed between Prussia and Hesse.

Oct. 21   Peace signed between Prussia and Saxony.

1867 Feb. 24   First diet of the North German Confederation agrees a constitution with the states. Presidency of the league is united with the crown of Prussia, which represents the confederation in international relations, diplomacy and matters of war and peace. The governments are represented in the Council of the Confederation (Bundesrath), in which Prussia has 17 votes and the other twenty-one members 26 votes. An Imperial diet (Reichstag) elected by universal manhood suffrage is to meet in Berlin and make laws for the states which, however, retain their local laws and customs. The federal forces are to be reorganised under the command of the king of Prussia and introduce compulsory military service. Customs, postal, and telegraph services are united. Count Bismarck becomes Chancellor of the Confederation.

May 7–11   London Conference on the Luxembourg question. Napoleon III's attempt to purchase Luxembourg from the king of Holland prevented by the opposition of Prussia, who reveals her military agreement with the south German states. Napoleon demands that the Prussian garrison should evacuate the fortress of Luxembourg. The Conference agrees that the neutrality of Luxembourg be guaranteed by the great powers in common and that the Prussian garrison be removed and the fortifications demolished.

1870 Jan. 2   Baden joins North German Confederation.

May   North German Confederation votes subsidies to support the St Gothard tunnel through the Swiss Alps, with the aim of increasing trade with Italy. Criticised by the French for diverting trade from their Mont Cenis route.

July 2   News of acceptance of Spanish throne by Leopold, Prince of Hohenzollern, becomes general, greatly increasing Franco–Prussian tension.

July 12   Leopold's candidature withdrawn.

July 13   The French ambassador seeks assurance from the King of Prussia at Ems that the Spanish candidature will not be renewed. The King refuses to discuss the matter and refers the ambassador to the regular method of communication through the foreign embassy in Berlin. The King's report of the conversations to Bismarck is doctored by him and released to the press (the 'Ems Telegram') in order to inflame Franco–Prussian relations. War fever in France.

July 15   William I enthusiastically received in Berlin on his return from Ems.

July 16   South Germans rally to Prussia after Louis II of Bavaria mobilises his army in opposition to the French threat.

July 19   Delivery of French declaration of war.

July 23   Unanimous vote of war credits by the Reichstag.

Aug. 2   King William of Prussia takes command of united German armies at Mainz.

Aug. 19   After a series of defeats, a large portion of the French army is besieged in and about Metz.

Sept. 2   Major Prussian victory at Sedan; surrender of Napoleon III to William I and the surrender of Sedan.

Sept. 19   German armies begin siege of Paris.

Oct. 27   French forces at Metz capitulate.

Nov. 15   Württemburg, followed by Bavaria (23rd), ally with North German Confederation.

Dec. 10   Following meetings in Berlin and in the south German states calling for German unity, a deputation of the North German Parliament offer William I the crown of the new German Empire, which he accepts.

1871 Jan 18   Proclamation of William I as German Emperor (Kaiser).

Jan. 28   Capitulation of Paris.

Feb. 26   Preliminaries of peace at Versailles.

Mar. 21   First Imperial Parliament meets.

Apr. 14   Imperial constitution adopted: the King of Prussia to bear the title German Emperor (Kaiser) and represent the empire in international relations and command the armed forces. The representatives of the 25 governments form a federal council (Bundesrath) under the Presidency of the Chancellor of the Empire (Bismarck). An Imperial Parliament of 382 members (Reichstag) is to be chosen by direct manhood suffrage. Centralised military system set up based on universal compulsory service of three years, plus four in reserve. Uniform postal and telegraph service set up and uniform coinage and weights and measures.

May 10   Peace Treaty of Frankfurt am Main with France. France cedes Alsace (except Belfort) and German Lorraine, including the fortresses of Metz and Strasburg. France required to pay a war indemnity of 5,000 million francs, 1,000 million in 1871.

Germany 1871–1929

1871	Jan. 18	William I of Prussia proclaimed German Emperor (Kaiser) at Versailles.
	Jan. 28	Paris capitulates and armistice with France signed.
	Apr. 10	German Empire receives Constitution remodelled from that of North German Confederation (see p. 97).
	May 10	Peace of Frankfurt between Germany and France (see p. 97).
	July	*Kulturkampf* (cultural struggle) with Catholic Church begins with suppression of Roman Catholic Department for spiritual affairs. The Bishops of Breslau and Ermeland and the Archbishop of Cologne request that the Prussian government dismiss Old Catholics (those who have resisted the doctrine of papal infallibility) from schools and Catholic theological faculties at universities. The government refuses on the grounds of religious toleration. The bishops persist in their demands, as a result of which their state subsidies are suspended.
1872		In a series of measures Bismarck seeks to subordinate the church to the State. Jesuits are forbidden to set up establishments in Germany and provision is made for the expulsion of individual Jesuits. Germany severs diplomatic relations with the Vatican.
1873	May 11–14	The first of the May Laws are passed in Prussia. They govern the education and appointment of the clergy. Bismarck relinquishes the post of Minister-President of Prussia for a short time, rapidly reassuming it when it becomes apparent that it provides the real basis of his power.
1874	Jan.	Centre Party vote doubles.
	May	Civil Marriage introduced in Prussia; all births, deaths and marriages have to be notified to the registrar, not the church authorities. States gain the power to restrict the freedom of movement of the clergy and expel offending priests.
1875		Formation of the German Social Democratic Party. The *Kulturkampf* reaches a peak with laws empowering Prussia to suspend subsidies to the Church in dioceses or parishes where the clergy resist the new legislation. All religious orders in Prussia, apart from those involved in nursing, dissolved. Pope Pius condemns this legislation and resistance is widespread. Creation of the Reichsbank. Standardisation and modernisation of the legal system.

1876	Rigid enforcement of the *Kulturkampf* results in exile or arrest of all but two Prussian bishops. However, in the face of increasing opposition, the Chancellor, fearing for the unity of the Empire, realises it is time to cut his losses and reconcile the Church and State. Formation of the Central Association of German Industrialisation as a result of the clamour for a protective tariff from landowners and industrialists.
1878	Bismarck breaks openly with the National Liberals over the question of taxing tobacco.
Feb. 7	Death of Pope Pius IX; his successor Leo XIII wishes to settle the dispute, expressed in a letter of 20 February to the Emperor. During the summer Bismarck meets a Papal envoy at Bad Kissingen in an effort to end the deadlock.
May–Oct.	Two assassination attempts on the Emperor provide Bismarck with the excuses to draft an anti-socialist Bill; his first effort is heavily defeated. However the second attempt on the Emperor's life is more serious: Bismarck dissolved the Reichstag and in the election which followed the National Liberals lose 29 seats and a new anti-socialist law is passed. Though the Bill places many restrictions on socialism and included a ban on trade union activity it does not interfere with elections.
Autumn	The campaign for tariff reform reaches a new intensity.
1879 July 12	Introduction of a general tariff bill, the passage of which produces a new 'alliance of steel and rye' as landowners and industrialists turn to conservatism on the common ground of protection. Bismarck's political support now becomes solidly conservative. Establishment of an Imperial Court of Appeal. The Exceptional Law aimed at the Social Democratic Party, society meetings and publications concerned with spreading socialist principles. The police are authorised to deport suspects and trade unions are declared illegal. Agreement is reached with the Church by which the Government is to be notified of all impending Papal appointments and the German clergy is to cease to resist the Government. In return Bismarck begins to repeal anti-clerical legislation.
1881	Bismarck informs the Reichstag that the welfare of the working classes must be actively promoted; this will be put into practice by the introduction of a comprehensive welfare system during the next decade. The rejection of the tobacco monopoly and of a proposed increase in indirect taxation by the Reichstag ruins Bismarck's plans for financial reform.
1883 May 1	Passage of an Act providing medical treatment for three million workers and their families; the cost is shared between workers and employers.

1884   Passage of an Accident Insurance Act financed by
                employers; benefits and burial grants are provided for
                incapacitated workers.

1886   Accident and sickness insurance extended to seven
                million agricultural workers.

    Nov.–Dec.   Bismarck asks the Reichstag to agree to an increase in
                military finance in the light of the changing
                international situation. Liberals demand greater
                control over military budget.

1887 Jan.   In the face of Reichstag opposition over military
                expenditure Bismarck dissolves the house. In the
                ensuing elections Bismarck exploits nationalism to
                gain a Reichstag favourable to his policies.

1888 Mar. 9   Crown Prince Frederick succeeds Emperor on his
                death.

    June 15   Frederick dies and is succeeded by Crown Prince
                William who has the intention of removing Bismarck
                from office given a suitable opportunity.   To this
                end he appoints General Waldersee as Chief of the
                General Staff on the retirement of Moltke; Waldersee
                is one of a group of conservatives who seeks to
                remove Bismarck.

1889   Bismarck and the Emperor clash over social policy.

1890 Jan.–Feb   The Reichstag rejects Bismarck's anti-socialist Bill.
                During the Reichstag elections in February Bismarck
                refuses to counter-sign William's proclamation
                promising social legislation and announcing an
                international conference on the subject of social
                questions.   A massive rise in the socialist vote
                together with large gains by the Radicals show
                Bismarck's position is weakening.   In a last-ditch
                attempt to maintain office Bismarck revises a Prussian
                cabinet order of 1852 which maintains that all Prussian
                ministers have to go through their Minister President,
                in this instance Bismarck, before communicating with
                the Emperor. The Kaiser demands the repeal of the
                order, whilst Bismarck fails in his attempt to create a
                new power base in the Reichstag.

    Mar.   William and Bismarck clash, William demanding
                repeal of the 1852 order or his Chancellor's
                resignation. Bismarck is saved the humiliation of
                resigning over a domestic dispute when William
                accuses him of dereliction of duty over foreign policy
                (in this instance it is over his failure to warn Austria of
                'ominous' Russian troop movements in the Balkans).
                Bismarck resigns on 17 March, ostensibly over the
                Emperor's anti-Russian stance.   Bismarck
                succeeded as Chancellor by a middle-aged soldier,
                General Leo von Caprivi. In his first speech to the
                Prussian Landtag he states that he is embarking on 'a
                new course'.

Oct. 1	Expiry of anti-socialist legislation of 1878. Industrial courts established to arbitrate in wage disputes.
Oct. 21	The German socialist party, now organising openly, commits itself to a Marxist policy at the Erfurt Congress. Factory inspection improved. The Reichstag passes an Act regulating working conditions; workers gain the right to form committees to negotiate with employers as to their conditions of employment.
1891–4	Caprivi signs a series of commercial treaties with Austria, Hungary, Italy, Switzerland, Spain, Romania and Russia; this stimulated the formation of the protectionist Agrarian League in 1893.
1891	Count Schlieffen succeeds Waldersee as Chief of the General Staff.
1892	The Schlieffen plan is devised (see p. 325). German strategy becomes based on the principle of dealing a swift knock-out blow in the West against France.
Nov.	Caprivi introduces an army bill which will facilitate the carrying out of the Schlieffen plan. It aims to increase the army by 84,000 men, though the period of service is reduced from three to two years. Whilst the Reichstag is to be allowed to review the army grant every two instead of seven years, the bill is rejected.
1893 July	With the defeat of the Army bill Caprivi dissolves the Reichstag and elections are held in a nationalistic atmosphere, producing a House more amenable to the army reforms, though Caprivi's bill only gains a very narrow majority. Formation of the Agrarian League. Pan-German League founded.
1894 Oct.	Caprivi stands firm against the Emperor's demands for the anti-socialist legislation. The Chancellor resigns, to be succeeded by Prince Hohenlohe. The Reichstag is asked to pass a subversion bill making it a punishable offence to incite citizens to class hatred, to make public attacks on the family, marriage or property or to denigrate the state.
1895	The Subversion Bill is defeated.
1896 Jan. 3	William sends 'Kruger Telegram', congratulating Transvaal on failure of Jameson raid. Saxony introduces a three class system effectively eliminating socialists from the Landtag.
1897 Oct. 20	Bülow becomes foreign minister. The Prussian Landtag is asked to give the police the power to dissolve all societies threatening law, order or the security of the state. However the move is opposed and defeated.
Nov.	Bülow sums up Germany's growing desire for power

when he states 'we do not wish to put anyone in the shade but we do demand our place in the sun'.
Admiral von Tirpitz appointed Secretary of State for the Navy (June) with the aim of getting a new navy bill through the Reichstag. The bill introduced in November proposes to create seventeen ships of the line during the next seven years.

1898   Tirpitz helps found the Navy League (Flotterverein) which campaigns vigorously for naval expansion. The League receives financial assistance from industrialists, such as Krupp and Stumm. The bill is greeted with enthusiasm by the middle classes and it is carried in March by 212 votes to 139.

1898–1901   Germany rejects Chamberlain's overtures for an alliance.

1899   William asks the Reichstag to pass a law to penalise workers who compel others to form trade unions or to go on strike; the defeat of the bill and the middle-class opposition mark the end of the policy of repression. Tariff changes reduce them to the 1892 levels, on the demands of the Agrarian League.

1900   Introduction and passage of the second Naval Bill. The second bill which proposes inceasing the number of ships of the line to thirty-six is passed by a large majority.   Count von Posadowsky-Wemer, secretary of state since 1897, introduces the first of a series of social reforms when he extends the scope of accident insurance. He sees no future in a repressive anti-socialist policy and actually gains socialist support for his new measures.

1901   A new law makes industrial courts compulsory in all towns with a population of more than 20,000.

1903   The period covered by sickness insurance is increased, whilst the prohibition of the use of child labour is extended.   Opposition to increased tariffs manifested in the gain of 26 seats by the socialists.

1905   The Tangier Incident (see p. 126). (see p. 126)

1904–5   The Government and the Centre party clash over the question of colonial affairs. Centre opposition to his policies in West Africa causes Bülow to dissolve the Reichstag and allowed Bülow to manipulate a 'bloc' of Conservatives and National Liberals against the Centre, holding it together by proposing some mildly liberal measures and retaining ministers such as Posadowsky whom the liberals and socialists regard as too conservative. This 'bloc' is never particularly strong and collapses in summer 1909.

1907   Britain, France and Russia sign the Triple Entente.

1908 Oct.	'The *Daily Telegraph* Affair' – the Emperor's article in the *Daily Telegraph* published in Britain increases Anglo–German tension. The Bosnian Crisis (see p. 127).
1909 July 14	Defeat of Bülow's finance bill; in order to cover an increasing deficit Bülow intends to raise indirect taxation and extend the scope of death duties. Various parties in the Reichstag oppose Bülow and on the defeat of his finance bill he resigns. His successor Bethmann-Hollweg is appointed by William who accepts Bülow's resignation to be merely tactical.
1910	Amalgamation of the previously split radical groups into the *Fontschmitte Vereinigung* which supports the socialists entering into an electoral pact with them. Increasing demand for electoral reform in Prussia prompts Bethman-Hollweg to introduce a bill to the Landtag which is to increase the middle-class vote at the expense of the landowners and workers. Bitter Conservative and Centre party opposition leads to the withdrawal of this proposal.
1911 July	The Agadir incident (see p. 127).
1912 Jan.	Public dissatisfaction with the right results in 110 seats for the socialists in the Reichstag, making them the largest party. An Anglo–German conference on naval strength fails to halt the naval race. Passing of another Naval Bill and large increase in the army approved.
Oct.	War in the Balkans (see p. 127).
1913 Jan.	A new army bill further increases the peace-time strength of Germany's land forces.
Nov.	The Zabern 'Incident' shows continued ability of the army to operate with little formal constitutional restraint.
1914 Aug. 4	With the outbreak of war, the Emperor, in a speech to the Reichstag declares 'I know no parties any more, only Germans'; the party leaders respond with a political truce for the duration of hostilities, the 'Burgfriede'. Bethman-Hollweg speaks of Germany as the victim of unprovoked aggression, and war credits are passed unanimously before the Reichstag adjourns.
Aug. 8	Rathenau, director of the giant industrial combine AEG, persuades the War Minister Falkenhayn to establish the War Raw Materials Department.
Aug. 25–30	Hindenburg and Ludendorff smash one of two invading Russian armies at the battle of Tannenberg.
Sept. 5–14	The battle of the Marne; the German advance into France is halted; Moltke breaks down and is replaced by Falkenhayn. The conflict now develops into static trench warfare.

1915 Feb.	The waters around the British Isles are declared a war zone; enemy warships become liable to be sunk without warning. The Russians are defeated decisively at the battle of the Masurian Lakes.
May	The sinking of the liner *Lusitania* with great loss of life outrages allied public opinion and that of the United States.
Sept.	Unrestricted submarine warfare ceases in British waters.
Oct.	Austro–German forces defeat Serbia.
Dec.	Spahn of the Centre Party on behalf of all non-socialist parties presents a declaration in which are demanded territorial acquisitions to safeguard Germany's military, economic and political interests.
1916 Jan.	In a bid to retain socialist support Bethman-Hollweg persuades the Emperor to promise reform of the Prussian Constitution.
Feb.–June	Battle of Verdun; Germany and France both suffer massive losses as Falkenhayn attempts to 'bleed France white'.
Feb.	German submarines ordered to sink any merchant ships in the war-zone without warning.
Apr.	The sinking of the liner *The Sussex* causes the United States to threaten to break off diplomatic relations; to avert this Bethmann-Hollweg, to the annoyance of the Conservatives, places restrictions on submarine warfare.
July–Oct.	Battle of the Somme; Germany and Britain suffer huge losses. The Conservatives demand the replacement of Falkenhayn by Hindenburg. Bethmann-Hollweg joins the campaign to replace Falkenhayn; he holds the misguided view that a strong, popular figure like Hindenburg can achieve a negotiated peace without alienating the right.
Aug. 29	Falkenhayn replaced as Chief of General Staff by Hindenburg. Ludendorff appointed Chief Quarter-Master-General. Auxiliary Service Act passed by the Reichstag; Ludendorff has demanded the immediate mobilisation of the whole population, including compulsory labour for women and restrictions on the workers' freedom to change jobs. The aim is to establish an equality of sacrifice between soldiers and civilians. However the Act itself is less far reaching; it introduces direction of labour for all males between 17 and 60, but safeguards the right of the working population to change jobs. Though women and children are excluded, an intensive campaign is launched to mobilise them for the war effort. The Majority Socialists and the Labour Fellowship vote against the budget.
Oct. 1916– Mar. 1917	The 'turnip winter'. Severe cold destroys the potato crop causing widespread hardship; the hardship is

increased by a lack of transport, Bethmann-Hollweg realises constitutional changes will be necessary to avoid serious disturbances.

Dec.	Hindenburg and Ludendorff demand unrestricted submarine warfare.
1917 Jan. 9	Bethmann-Hollweg agrees to unrestricted submarine warfare.
Jan. 31	America informed of German decision to renew unrestricted submarine warfare on 1 February.
Feb. 1	Unrestricted submarine warfare begins.
Feb. 25	Three Americans killed when Germans sink *Laconia*.
Mar. 1	Telegram from German Foreign Minister, Zimmermann, to German Minister in Mexico, calling for German–Mexican alliance and Mexican invasion of USA in the event of an American declaration of war, published in the American press after interception by British naval intelligence.
Mar. 17	Bethmann-Hollweg hints at the need for change during a speech to the Prussian Landtag; however news of the Russian revolution stirs the Reichstag into life, the Radicals demand universal suffrage in all states, the Independent Socialists demand parliamentary government and peace without annexations. The Majority Socialists supported by the National Liberals manage to establish a committee to consider constitutional reform.
Apr. 6	USA enters the war.
Apr.	The Chancellor persuades William to issue an Easter message promising reform of the Prussian upper chamber after the war and the introduction of the secret ballot and direct election for the lower house. The Emperor's message arouses little enthusiasm and produces consternation among the conservatives.
July 6	Matthias Erberger, a rising figure on the left of the Centre Party, declares unrestricted submarine warfare a failure and urges Germany to commit itself to a policy of peace and reconciliation.
July 12	Bethmann-Hollweg falls from power.
July 14	Michaelis is appointed Chancellor.
July 19	In the Reichstag a peace resolution is carried by 212 votes to 126. Ludendorff and Hindenburg threaten to resign if it is accepted.
Sept. 11	Michaelis demands that Germany give up its claim to Belgium.
Nov. 1	Count Hertling replaces Michaelis as Chancellor and promises to base his foreign policy on the peace resolution and to reform the Prussian franchise.
Dec. 5	German and Russian delegates sign armistice at Brest-Litovsk.
1918 Jan. 8	President Wilson outlines his 'Fourteen Points'.
Mar. 3	Treaty of Brest-Litovsk with Russia. Only Independent Socialists in the Reichstag vote against it.

Mar. 21	Ludendorff begins 'St Michael' offensive on the Western Front.
Mar. 26	After initial success the first German offensive comes to a halt within 75 miles of Paris.
Apr. 9	Renewed German offensive in Flanders.
May 27	Germans reach the Marne.
July 18	Allied counter-attack begins.
Aug. 8	'The Black Day of the German Army' (Ludendorff) as German forces break under fresh allied offensive.
Sept. 11	Allies break through the Hindenburg line.
Sept. 28	Ludendorff concedes that military victory is impossible.
Sept. 30	Hertling resigns in the face of proposals to transform Germany into a democracy.
Oct. 1	Ludendorff asks parliament to make peace.
Oct. 3	Prince Max of Baden appointed Chancellor and asks the USA for an armistice on the basis of the 'Fourteen Points'.
Oct 12	Germany and Austria–Hungary agree to Wilson's terms that they withdraw from occupied territory, but hesitate over demands for a democratic, civilian government.
Oct. 20	Germany suspends submarine warfare.
Oct. 21	German sailors at Wilhelmshaven mutiny.
Oct. 23	Wilson refuses to make peace with an autocratic regime in Germany.
Oct. 26	Ludendorff is forced to resign. The Reichstag makes the Chancellor dependent on parliament and military appointments to be countersigned by the Minister of War.
Oct. 29	The Emperor leaves Berlin for army headquarters at Spa.
Nov. 2	Scheidemann, one of the Majority Socialist leaders, writes to Prince Max requesting William's abdication.
Nov. 3	German Grand Fleet mutinies at Kiel. Sailors set up their own workers' and sailors' councils, mainly for redress of grievances.
Nov. 7	Bavaria is proclaimed a republic and a Socialist government is set up in Munich. In Berlin the majority Socialist Party executive threaten to withdraw support from the Government unless the Emperor abdicates.
Nov. 9	General Strike in Berlin. The Emperor flees to Holland. Prince Max resigns and hands over office to Ebert. Scheidemann proclaims a Republic from the Reichstag building and Ebert forms a Socialist-dominated government. Ebert makes pact with Groener with the army assuring army support in return for suppression of Bolshevism.
Nov. 11	German representatives sign armistice with allies at Compiègne.
Nov. 22	Agreement reached for transitional government until National Constituent Assembly meets.

Dec. 20	Workers' and soldiers' delegates in Berlin demand nationalisation of major industries.
Dec. 30	German Communist Party (KPD) founded by Spartacists and other groups. They decide to boycott the elections for the National Constituent Assembly and stage a rising in Berlin.
1919 Jan. 5–11	Spartacist revolt in Berlin put down by Ebert-Noske government using 'Free Corps (*Freikorps*) of ex-soldiers.
Jan. 15	Rosa Luxemburg and Karl Liebknecht, leaders of the Spartacists, are arrested and murdered by Free Corps.
Jan. 19	National Constituent Assembly elected on basis of proportional representation but fails to give any party an outright majority.
Feb. 8	National Constituent Assembly meets at Weimar.
Feb. 11	Ebert becomes President of Weimar Republic, following formation of coalition of Majority Socialists and the Centre and Democratic Parties under Scheidemann.
Feb. 13	Scheidemann forms a Cabinet.
Feb. 21	Assassination of the Premier of the Bavarian Republic, Kurt Eisner, by right wingers.
Apr.	Socialist Bavarian Republic overthrown by Federal German forces.
June 29	Treaty of Versailles signed (see pp. 194–5).
1920 Mar. 13–17	Kapp Putsch; Freikorps officers attempt to make Wolfgang Kapp Chancellor of the Reich in pro-monarchist coup d'état in Berlin. Although troops refuse to fire on the Freikorps, and the Government is forced to flee Berlin, a general strike frustrates the putsch.
Apr.	Hitler's German Workers' Party changes its name to the National Socialist German Workers' Party (Nazis).
1921 Aug. 29	Assassination of Matthias Erzberger, leader of Centre Party, by right-wing officers.
1922 Apr. 16	Treaty of Rapallo provides for economic and military cooperation between Germany and Russia.
June 24	Assassination of Walter Rathenau, foreign secretary, by right-wing nationalists.
1923 Jan. 11	Non-payment of reparations leads to French and Belgian troops occupying the Ruhr. Germany adopts passive resistance to the occupation.
Aug. 12	Stresemann becomes Chancellor.
Sept.–Nov.	Massive inflation in Germany. Interest rates raised to 90 per cent (15 Sept.) but by October German mark trading at rate of 10,000 million to the £.
Sept. 26	Passive resistance in Ruhr ends. A state of military emergency is declared.
Oct. 22	Bavarian troops take an oath of allegiance to right-wing regime in Bavaria. Communist revolt in Hamburg

	is put down and left-wing governments are deposed in Saxony and Thuringia.
Nov. 8–9	Unsuccessful 'Beer Hall' putsch in Munich led by Hitler and Ludendorff. Hitler captured.
Nov. 20	German currency stabilised by establishment of the *Rentenmark*, valued at one billion old marks.
Nov. 23	Stresemann becomes foreign minister.
1924 Apr. 1	Hitler sentenced to five years' imprisonment for part in Munich putsch (but released in December).
Apr. 9	Dawes Plan provides a modified settlement of the reparations issue.
May 4	In Reichstag elections, Nationalists and Communists gain many seats from the moderate parties.
Dec. 7	In further elections, Nationalists and Communists lose seats to Socialists.
Dec. 15	Beginning of Cabinet crisis in Germany.
1925 Jan. 15	Hans Luther, an independent, succeeds Wilhelm Marx of the Centre as Chancellor with Stresemann as foreign minister
Feb. 28	Death of President Ebert.
Apr. 26	Hindenburg elected President.
July 7	French troops begin to leave Rhineland.
Oct. 16	Locarno Pact guarantees Franco–German and Belgian–German frontiers and the demilitarisation of the Rhineland. (Signed, 1st Dec.).
1926 May 17	Marx takes over from Luther as Chancellor.
Sept. 8	Germany admitted to the League of Nations.
1927 Jan. 29	Marx takes over from Luther as Chancellor.
May 13	'Black Friday' with collapse of economic system.
Sept. 16	Hindenburg while dedicating the Tannenburg memorial repudiates Article 231 of the Versailles Treaty, the 'War Guilt' clause.
1928 May 20	Social Democrats win victory at elections, mainly at the expense of the Nationalists.
June 28	Hermann Müller, a Socialist, is appointed Chancellor, following resignation of Marx's ministry on the 13th.
1929 Feb. 6	Germany accepts Kellogg-Briand Pact, outlawing war and providing for the pacific settlements of disputes.
June 7	Young Committee provides for a rescheduling of German reparation payments in the form of annuities, on the security of the German railways, for the next sixty years.
Aug. 6–13	At Reparations Conference in The Hague, Germany accepts the Young Plan and the Allies agree to evacuate the Rhineland by June 1930.
Oct. 3	Stresemann dies.
Oct. 29	Wall Street Crash leads to the cessation of American loans to Europe.
Dec. 22	German referendum upholds the Young Plan.

France 1851–1945

1851 Dec. 2   Coup d'état of Louis Napoleon: leaders of Orléanists and Republicans seized and imprisoned, national assembly dissolved, and constitution annulled.

Dec. 3–4   Protests in Paris against the coup are crushed.

Dec. 14   Plebiscite ratifies Louis Napoleon as President for ten years and empowers him to frame a constitution by 7,430,000 votes to 640,000.

1852 Jan. 9   Opponents of regime banished by decree of the President.

Jan. 14   Louis Napoleon establishes a constitution with a Senate, Council of State and Legislative Assembly.

Jan. 22   Orléans family banished from France by decree of the President.

Feb. 17   Press censorship introduced.

Nov. 7   Senate proposes creation of Empire.

Nov. 21   Plebiscite ratifies revival of French Empire by 7,824,189 votes to 253,145.

Dec. 2   Second Empire proclaimed and Louis Napoleon takes title of Emperor Napoleon III.

1853 Jan. 29   Marriage of Napoleon III to Eugénie de Montijo.

June 14   French squadron joins British fleet at the Dardanelles.

1854 Mar. 12   Britain and France conclude alliance with Turkey against Russia.

Mar. 27   France declares war on Russia and enters Crimean War.

May 26   Franco–British forces occupy Piraeus in Greece to enforce Greek neutrality.

June   French forces land at Varna on the Black Sea.

Sept. 14   French, British and Turkish troops land in the Crimea.

Sept. 20   Franco–British forces defeat Russians at Alma.

Oct. 17   Siege of Sebastopol begins.

Nov. 5   Franco–British forces defeat Russians at Inkerman.

1855 Sept. 11   French and British occupy Sebastopol.

1856 Feb. 25   Peace Conference at Paris ends Crimean War.

Mar. 16   Birth of the Prince Imperial.

Dec. 2   Franco–Spanish frontier defined.

1857 June 14   Commercial Treaty between Russia and France.

Dec.   Occupation of Canton by French and British forces.

1858 Jan. 14   Orsini plot to assassinate Napoleon III fails.

Feb. 19   *Loi de sûreté generale* permits the government to arrest and exile without trial in certain cases.

July 20   Napoleon and Cavour begin meetings at Plombières to plan unification of Italy.

1859 Jan. 19	Treaty of alliance between France and Sardinia.
Apr. 17	Louis Napoleon grants an amnesty for political prisoners.
May 3	France declares war on Austria, following Austrian invasion of Sardinian territory.
June 4	French defeat the Austrians at Magenta.
June 14	French and Sardinians defeat the Austrians at Solferino.
July 8	Franco–Austrian armistice.
July 11	Peace of Villafranca. Austria cedes Parma and Lombardy to France for subsequent transfer to Sardinia.
1860 Jan. 23	Free trade treaty (Cobden–Chevalier treaty) signed between Britain and France.
Mar. 24	Sardinia cedes Nice and Savoy to France.
Nov. 24	Decree extends power of the French legislature by allowing an address to the throne. Senate and assembly allowed to discuss policy once a year and Ministers 'without Portfolio' appointed to the assembly to explain government policy. Full publication of debates permitted in *Journal Officiel*.
1861 Oct. 31	France, Britain and Spain sign London Convention to protect their interests after Mexico suspends repayment of debts by sending a joint expedition to enforce payment.
Nov. 11	Financial powers of French legislature extended.
1862 Feb. 19	Joint expedition to Mexico forces treaty of La Soledad on Juarez, who promises to pay an indemnity and arrears of debt. England and Spain withdraw from the expedition but Napoleon III decides to maintain forces there with a view to setting up a new monarchy.
Mar. 28	French acquire six provinces of Cochin China.
May	After repulse of French troops from Puebla, 25,000 French troops are sent as reinforcements to Mexico.
Aug. 2	Prusso–French commercial treaty.
1863 May 1	French elections show increase in opposition from five to thirty-five, supported by two million voters. Paris elects nine opposition deputies, including Thiers.
Nov. 23	Thiers forms opposition Third Party.
1864 Apr. 10	Archduke Maximilian of Austria becomes Emperor of Mexico with the support of French troops.
1865 Oct. 4–11	Biarritz meetings between Napoleon III and Bismarck. Napoleon sanctions Prussian supremacy in Germany.
1866 June 12	Secret treaty between Austria and France. Napoleon III promises French neutrality in return for Venezia which France will hand over to Italy.
July 4	Napoleon III announces Austria's cession of Venezia.
1867 Mar. 12	French troops withdrawn from Mexico. Maximilian refuses to leave.

May 11	London Conference guaranteeing the neutrality of Luxembourg forestalls Napoleon III's attempt to purchase it.
June 19	Execution of Maximilian in Mexico.
Oct. 28	French troops sent to assist the Pope whose territories have come under attack from Italian volunteers. Napoleon III declares former treaty with Italians broken.
Nov. 3	Italian forces defeated by French and Papal forces at Mentana and Garibaldi captured. Rome receives a French garrison.
1868 June 11	Freedom of press and limited right of public meeting granted in France.
1869 May	Although the Government receives a large majority at the elections there is the first evidence under the Empire of active participation by opposition parties. Radicals win victories in Paris and Lyons.
July 12	Parliamentary system adopted by Napoleon III.
1870 Jan. 2	Ollivier becomes French Premier. Repeal of the *loi de sûreté* and dismissal of the prefect of the Seine, Hausmann.
Apr. 20	A new liberal constitution introduced by a decree of the Senate, making the Senate an upper house sharing legislative powers with the Assembly.
Apr. 23	Imperial decree calls on French nation to accept or reject by plebiscite the 'liberal empire' and the alteration of the constitution.
Apr. 24	Imperial proclamation circulated in support of the plebiscite.
May 8	Plebiscite gives positive vote of 7,336,000 against 1,560,000 no's.
July 2	News of acceptance of Spanish throne by Leopold, Prince of Hohenzollern reaches France.
July 12	Leopold's candidature withdrawn.
July 13	French ambassador seeks assurances from the King of Prussia at Ems that the Spanish candidature will not be renewed. The King's report of the conversation to Bismarck is doctored by him and released to the press (the 'Ems Telegram') to inflame Franco–Prussian relations. As anticipated, the result is 'war fever' in France.
July 19	France declares war on Prussia.
Aug. 4	French under MacMahon defeated at Weissenberg.
Aug. 6	French defeats at Worth and Spicheren.
Aug. 10	Fall of Ollivier Ministry and formation of new ministry under Montauban-Palikao, the Bonapartist Minister of War.
Aug. 14	French defeated at Colombey-Nouilly.
Aug. 16	French worsted at Vionville.
Aug. 18	French defeated at Gravelotte and St Privat.
Aug. 19	French army in Metz besieged.

Sept. 1	French defeated at Sedan.
Sept. 2	Napoleon III capitulates with his army at Sedan and is taken to Wilhelmshohe.
Sept. 4	Republic proclaimed in Paris. Formation of Government of National Defence. Flight of Empress Eugénie to England.
Sept. 19	Siege of Paris begun by Prussians following failure of negotiations.
Oct. 27	Capitulation of French troops at Metz.

1871 Jan. 8   Prussians begin bombardment of Paris.

Jan. 19	Last sortie from Paris repulsed.
Jan. 28	Capitulation of Paris by the convention of Versailles and three weeks' truce.
Feb. 8	Elections held for a National Assembly.
Feb. 12	National Assembly meets at Bordeaux.
Feb. 23	Thiers Ministry formed.
Feb. 26	Preliminary Peace of Versailles between France and Germany:

    (i) France cedes Alsace (except for Belfort and its surrounding territory) and Lorraine, including Metz, a total of 4,700 square miles and 1½ million inhabitants;

    (ii) France agrees to pay 5,000,000 francs indemnity in three years.

Mar. 1	German troops enter Paris. The National Assembly ratifies the peace treaty.
Mar. 18	Rising of the Paris Commune. Hotel de Ville taken over by Central Committee of National Guard. Thiers leaves Paris for Versailles.
Mar. 19	National Guard announces elections in Paris for a Commune.
Mar. 22	Commune proclaimed at Lyons, but shortly collapses.
Mar. 23	Marseilles Commune declared.
Mar. 28	Proclamation of the Paris Commune and first decrees issued the next day.
Apr. 4	Communard forces retreat from Versailles. Collapse of Marseilles Commune.
Apr. 6	Paris communards besieged by troops of the National Assembly.
Apr. 19	Commune's 'Declaration to the French People'.
May 1	Communards set up a Committee of Public Safety. Versailles troops begin bombardment of Paris.
May 10	Definitive Treaty of Frankfurt signed by France and Germany.
May 21–28	Versailles troops enter Paris and begin a week of fighting to subdue the Commune's strongholds. Hostages taken by the communards, including the archbishop of Paris, are shot. Widespread summary executions of communard prisoners.
May 28	Last communard barricades captured.
Aug. 31	Thiers elected President of France.

1872 Jan. 25	Henry, Count of Chambord, legitimist claimant to the throne of France makes Antwerp Declaration, calling for a 'Revolutionary Monarchy' in France.
July 28	France adopts conscription.
Nov. 5	Anglo–French commercial treaty signed.
Nov. 22	Count of Paris, head of Orléanist line, accepts compensation for confiscation of his French estates. Execution of leading communards
1873 Jan. 9	Death of Napoleon III at Chislehurst, England.
May 24	Thiers forced to resign by coalition of Monarchist parties. Marshal MacMahon elected president of the national assembly.
Oct. 27	Count of Chambord, after reconciliation with the Count of Paris, virtually ends hope of monarchical restoration by refusing to accept the tricolour.
Nov. 20	French monarchists confer MacMahon with presidential powers for seven years.
1875 Jan. 30	Republican Constitution in France passed by one vote. Legislative power exercised by two chambers: the Chamber of Deputies, elected by direct elections and manhood suffrage for four years; and the Senate, partly elected by the Senate itself, and the majority by electoral colleges composed of deputies, councils of departments and districts, and delegates from the communes. Executive power is entrusted to a president who after the expiry of MacMahon's term (after 1878) is to be elected by the Senate and Chamber of Deputies united as a national assembly, for a period of seven years. The president may be impeached by the Chamber.
July 16	French constitution finalised.
Dec.	Adoption of new electoral law, *scrutin d'arrondissement* (see p. 325), and separation of the national assembly into its two components, the Chamber and Senate.
1876 Jan.–Feb.	New elections result in a Senate balanced between republicans and monarchical parties, with republicans in a majority in the Chamber.
1877 May 16	'Seize Mai' crisis. Ministry headed by Simon is replaced by act of the President. De Broglie forms a pro-monarchist government. 363 members of the Chamber vote against the action of the President.
Sept. 4	Death of Thiers.
Oct.	Republican majority returned at the elections.
Nov. 19– Dec. 13	De Broglie resigns, but MacMahon forms a royalist ministry under Rochebouet (23 Nov.). Continuing refusal of the Chamber to work with the ministry results in formation of republican ministry under Dufaure.

(see p. 325)

1879	Jan. 16	Pardon of 2,000 communards.
	Jan. 30	MacMahon resigns and is succeeded by Grévy.
	June 25	Anti-Jesuit legislation passed.
	July 1	Death of Prince Louis Napoleon in South Africa.
	Aug. 4	Alsace-Lorraine declared integral part of the German Reich.
	Nov. 27	French Chamber moves from Versailles to Paris.
1880	Mar. 30	Proclamation dispersing the Jesuits. Non-authorised religious associations have to regularise their positions or leave.
	June 30	Jesuits forcibly removed from religious houses.
	July 11	General amnesty for communards.
	Sept. 19	Ferry ministry.
	Oct. 16	Unauthorised congregations expelled from their religious houses.
1881	Apr. 30	French troops invade Tunis from Algeria.
	May 12	Tunisia becomes a French protectorate.
	Nov. 14	Ferry resigns after attacks on his Tunisian policy and Gambetta forms ministry.
1882	Jan. 27	Gambetta falls on a motion to adopt *scrutin de liste* (see p. 325). Freycinet forms ministry.
	Mar. 29	Free, compulsory primary education introduced. Religious teaching in schools abolished.
	Nov. 9	Franco–British dual control of Egypt established.
1883	June 1	French war with Madagascar.
	Aug. 24	Death of Count of Chambord without an heir effectively ends legitimist line.
	Aug. 25	French establish protectorate in Indo-China.
1884	Mar. 21	Legislation on trade unions.
	Aug. 5	The 75 life senatorships set up in 1875 are abolished. Members of former dynasties are excluded from the Presidency.
1885	Sept. 19	Grévy re-elected President.
1886	Jan. 7	General Boulanger becomes Minister of War in Freycinet Ministry.
	June 23	Orléanist and Bonaparte families banned from France.
1887	Apr. 20	Schnaebele incident. A French officer and spy is illegally arrested by the Germans. Grévy is criticised for taking the issue too lightly and Boulanger makes himself the spokesman for nationalist feeling over the incident.
	May 18	Boulanger excluded from the Rouvier Ministry.
	Oct. 1	Boulanger attempts coup d'état amidst the growing scandals associated with Grévy's Presidency.
	Dec. 2	Grévy resigns as President as a result of scandal surrounding the sale of honours. Carnot becomes President.

1888 Mar. 27	Boulanger retires from the French army making him eligible for election.
Mar. 15	Boulanger elected to the Chamber, standing for several constituencies. He advocates a revision of the Constitution through 'a specially elected constituent assembly'.
Oct. 30	France makes a large loan to Russia.
1889 Jan. 10	French establish protectorate over the Ivory Coast.
Jan. 27	Boulanger's attempt to provoke a 'crisis' in Paris fails.
Apr. 8	Flight of Boulanger fearing arrest. Republicans remain entrenched as the major party in the elections, securing over 54 per cent of the vote.
July 17	French law forbids multiple candidature in elections.
1890 Aug. 5	Anglo–French agreement on spheres of influence in Africa.
1891 July 23	Visit of French squadron to Kronstadt and further French loan to Russia.
Aug. 27	Franco–Russian entente.
Sept. 30	Boulanger commits suicide in Brussels.
1892 Aug. 17	Franco–Russian military convention.
Aug. 18	Leo XIII orders French catholics to accept the Republic.
Nov. 10	'Panama Canal Scandal'. De Lesseps and others committed for trial for alleged corruption.
1893 Jan. 17	Russo–French alliance.
Mar. 8–21	Panama Trial in Paris; De Lesseps fined.
June 10	Franco–Russian Commercial Treaty.
July 15–31	Franco–British crisis over Siam. Agreement reached that it should be kept as a buffer state.
Oct. 13–29	Russian squadron visits Toulon.
Nov. 17	France makes Dahomey a protectorate.
Dec. 27	Franco–Russian military convention comes into force.
1894 Mar. 15	Franco–German agreement over African spheres of influence.
June 24	President Carnot assassinated in Lyons; succeeded by Casimir-Périer.
Oct. 15	Dreyfus arrested on charge of spying for Germany.
Nov. 10	French begin invasion of Madagascar.
Dec. 22	Dreyfus convicted by court martial and sentenced to imprisonment on Devil's Island.
1895 Jan. 12	French trade unions declare in favour of General Strike.
Jan. 13	President Casimir-Périer resigns; succeeded by Faure (17th).
Apr. 23	France, Germany and Russia intervene against Japan's invasion of China.
1896 Jan. 5	Anglo–French agreement over Siam.
Aug. 18	France annexes Madagascar.
Sept. 30	Franco–Italian convention over Tunisia.

1897 Sept. 18	Anglo–French agreement about Tunisia.
Nov. 15	Discovery that the document on which Dreyfus had been convicted was produced by Major Esterhazy. Government enquiry into Dreyfus case.
1898 Jan. 11	Acquittal of Esterhazy for forgery in the Dreyfus case prompts Zola's *J'accuse* letter to the President.
Feb. 23	Zola imprisoned for *J'accuse* letter.
June 14	Anglo–French agreement over Nigeria and Gold Coast.
July 10	French occupy Fashoda in Sudan, confronting British forces under Kitchener.
Aug. 30	Forgery admitted by Colonel Henry in the Dreyfus case.
Nov. 4	After period of tension the 'Fashoda incident' is settled by Marchand marching away from Fashoda.
Nov. 26	Franco–Italian commercial agreement ends tariff war.
1899 Jan. 19	Anglo–French convention on the Sudan.
Feb. 18	Loubet becomes President of France.
Mar. 21	Anglo–French convention on North Africa ends period of tension between the two countries.
June 3	Dreyfus trial verdict annulled and retrial ordered.
Aug. 9	French foreign minister Delcassé visits St Petersburg and strengthens Franco–Russian alliance.
Sept. 9	Dreyfus retried and condemned but 'with extenuating circumstances'.
Sept. 19	Dreyfus pardoned by Presidential decree.
1900 Apr. 30	Republicans form bloc to defend Republic against anti-Dreyfusards.
Dec. 14	Secret Franco–Italian agreement to support each other's interests in Morocco and Tunisia respectively.
1901 July 1	Association Law promulgated for compulsory regulation of all religious congregations and associations and the dissolution of those not authorised by the state.
1902 June 2	Waldeck-Rousseau ministry resigns and succeeded by the more vigorously anti-clerical Combes ministry.
Nov. 1	Franco–Italian Entente. Italy agrees to remain neutral in the event of war between France and Germany.
1903 Mar. 18	Dissolution of religious orders in France.
Apr.	Britain and France oppose construction of Baghdad Railway.
May 1	Edward VII's visit to Paris marks beginning of improved Anglo–French relations.
July 6	Diplomatic conversations begin in London on the *Entente Cordiale*.
1904 Apr. 8	*Entente Cordiale* settles Anglo–French colonial disputes in North Africa.
May 17	French ambassador withdrawn from the Vatican.
Oct. 3	Franco–Spanish treaty on Morocco.
Nov. 18	Combes introduces legislation to separate Church and State in France.

1905 Apr. 30	Anglo–French military conversations following the first Moroccan crisis.
July 8	France agrees to a conference on Morocco.
Dec. 6	Church and State separated in France.
1906 Jan. 10	Further Anglo–French military and naval conversations.
Jan. 16	Opening of Algeçiras conference on Morocco.
Apr. 8	Algeciras Act signed, giving France and Spain major control in Morocco.
July 12	Dreyfus completely exonerated by French government.
1907 Apr. 8	Anglo–French convention confirms independence of Siam.
June 10	Franco–Japanese agreement on 'open-door' policy in China.
Aug. 4	French fleet bombards Casablanca.
1909 Feb. 9	France's dominant position in Morocco recognised by Germany in return for economic concessions.
1910 Jan. 15	Reorganisation of French Congo as French Equatorial Africa.
Oct. 10	Troops called out during railway strike and General Strike averted.
1911 Jan. 17	Assassination attempt on French Premier Briand in Chamber of Deputies.
Feb. 23	French Chamber votes for building two battleships.
Apr. 11	Jean Jaurès produces scheme for socialist organisation of France.
July 1	'Agadir incident' increases tension between France and Germany.
July 10	Russia confirms her support for France as a result of the Moroccan crisis.
Aug. 31	Franco–Russian military conversations.
Nov. 4	France and Germany sign convention giving France a free hand in Morocco in return for concessions of territory in the Congo.
1912 Feb. 6	French Senate ratifies Moroccan agreement.
Mar. 30	Morocco becomes a French protectorate.
Sept.	Anglo–French naval convention apportions responsibilities in the event of war.
Nov. 22–30	Grey–Cambon correspondence strengthens Entente.
1913 Jan. 17	Poincaré elected President of France.
Aug. 7	French army bill imposes three years' military service.
Nov. 20	Zabern incident, in which a German officer insults recruits in Alsace-Lorraine, inflames Franco–German relations
1914 Jan. 8	*Le Figaro* makes charges against Caillaux, French finance minister.
Feb. 15	Franco–German agreement on Baghdad Railway.
Mar. 16	Editor of *Le Figaro*, Calmette, assassinated by Mme

	Caillaux for publishing private letters.
July 20	President Poincaré visits Russia.
July 30	Jean Jaurès murdered in Paris.
Aug. 1	Germany declares war on Russia; France mobilises.
Aug. 3	Germany declares war on France.
Aug. 4	Britain declares war on Germany.
Aug. 8	First British troops land in France. Britain and France occupy German Togoland.
Aug. 12	France declares war on Austria.
Aug. 14	Beginning of 'Battle of the Frontiers'; French receive crushing defeats in Lorraine, the Ardennes, and on the Somme. (For full military chronology, see pp. 129–33.)
Aug. 24	Allies retreat in northern France in face of German advance.
Aug. 26	Germans cross the Meuse and occupy Lille. French cabinet reconstructed.
Aug. 30	Germans take Amiens.
Sept. 3	French government moves to Bordeaux. Germans cross the Marne and occupy Rheims.
Sept. 4	France, Russia and Britain agree by Pact of London not to make a separate peace.
Sept. 5–9	Battle of the Marne. Paris saved from capture; and Germans retreat.
Sept. 15–18	Battle of the Aisne in which German forces withstand allied attacks establishes trench line on Western Front.
Nov. 5	France and Britain declare war on Turkey.
Dec. 10	French government returns to Paris.
1915 Apr. 22	Anglo–French forces land at Gallipoli.
Sept. 29	US loan to France and Britain.
Oct. 29	Briand forms a new ministry in France.
Dec. 3	Joffre becomes French Commander-in-Chief.
1916 Jan. 29	First air attack on Paris by zeppelin.
Feb. 21	Battle of Verdun opens.
June 1	French and British troops join Somme offensive.
Oct. 24	French move onto the offensive east of Verdun.
Dec. 3	Nivelle succeeds Joffre as French Commander-in-Chief.
Dec. 12	French War Ministry formed.
Dec. 16	Germans end Verdun offensive.
1917 Feb. 23	Germany begins withdrawal to Hindenburg Line.
Mar. 19	Ribot cabinet formed in France.
Apr. 16	French offensive on the Aisne begins; halted (20th) with heavy loss. Further offensive in Champagne costs 200,000 men.
Apr. 29	Pétain becomes chief of French staff.
May 3	Mutinies in several French corps.
May 15	Pétain succeeds Nivelle as French Commander-in-Chief with Foch as chief of staff.
May 20	Mutinies begin in French army in Champagne.
June 26	First US troops arrive in France.

Sept. 3	Painlevé forms cabinet in France.
Nov. 16	Clemenceau forms cabinet on Painlevé's fall.
1918 Jan. 14	Cailloux, former Premier, arrested for treason.
Mar. 21	German offensive brings them within 75 miles of Paris. Paris bombarded by long-range guns.
Mar. 26	Foch assumes united command of armies on Western Front.
Apr. 27	Renewed German offensive captures Rheims.
July 15–Aug.4	Second battle of the Marne halts German offensive.
July 22	Allies cross the Marne.
Sept. 4	Germans retreat to Siegfried Line.
Oct. 30	Allies sign armistice with Turkey.
Nov. 1	Anglo–French forces occupy Constantinople.
Nov. 3	Allies sign armistice with Austria–Hungary.
Nov. 11	Allies sign armistice with Germany at Compiègne.
1919 June 28	Versailles Treaty signed.
Nov.	Victory of right-wing 'Bloc National' in elections to the Assembly.
1920 Jan. 17	Deschanel elected President of France. Resignation of Clemenceau; Millerand forms ministry.
May 16	Joan of Arc canonised.
Sept. 7	Franco–Belgian military convention.
Dec. 23	Millerand becomes French president.
Dec. 29	French socialists at Tours agree to join Moscow International; formation of French Communist Party.
1921 Jan. 16	Briand becomes prime minister.
Jan. 24–29	Paris conference agrees reparations for France.
Feb. 19	Franco–Polish alliance.
1922 Jan. 15	Poincaré becomes prime minister and foreign minister.
Dec. 9–11	International conference in London considers Germany's request for a reparations moratorium.
1923 Jan. 11	Franco–Belgian occupation of the Ruhr in retaliation for non-payment of reparations; passive resistance by German workers.
1924 Apr. 9	Germany accepts Dawes Plan on reparations and agreement reached that France should withdraw from the Ruhr.
May	Cartel des Gauches wins victory at the elections.
June 10	Millerand resigns as President. Doumergue elected President (13th); Herriot becomes prime minister (15th).
1925 Apr. 10	Painlevé becomes French prime minister.
July 27	French begin evacuation of Ruhr.
Dec. 1	Locarno Treaties guaranteeing Franco–German and Belgo–German frontiers signed.

1926 Jan. 31	First part of the Rhineland evacuated.
May 26	Rebel Abd-El-Krim submits to France.
July 15	Briand resigns over financial crisis; Poincaré becomes premier of French National Union Ministry. Measures taken to stabilise the franc.

| 1927 Nov. 11 | Treaty of friendship between France and Yugoslavia. |

1928 Apr. 22–29	Left parties win victory at elections.
June 24	Devaluation of the franc. Decision to build Maginot Line; Military Service cut to one year.
Aug. 27	France and 64 other states sign the Kellogg–Briand Pact, outlawing war and providing for peaceful settlement of international disputes.

| 1929 July 27 | Poincaré resigns as prime minister and is succeeded by Briand. |
| Sept. 5 | Briand proposes a European federal union. |

| 1930 May 17 | Young Plan of reduced German reparations comes into force. Briand produces memorandum on united states of Europe. |
| June 30 | Last portion of Rhineland evacuated. |

1931 Jan. 27	Laval becomes French premier.
May 13	Doumer elected French president.
June 20	Hoover Plan of moratorium of one year on reparations and war debts in view of world economic crisis.

1932 Feb. 21	Tardieu ministry formed.
May 1	Cartel des Gauches successful in elections.
May 6	President Doumer assassinated; succeeded by Lebrun (10th).
June 4	Herriot ministry formed.
Dec. 18	Paul-Boncour ministry formed.

| 1933 Jan. 31 | Daladier ministry formed. |
| Dec. | Flight of Stavisky brings about scandal of financial corruption amongst politicians. |

1934 Jan. 30	Daladier ministry formed.
Feb. 6–7	Rioting in Paris. Police kill 14 right-wing demonstrators.
Feb. 7	Daladier resigns and Doumergue forms National Union ministry of centre and moderate parties (8th).
Feb. 12	French CGT calls General Strike. Demonstrations in defence of the Republic.
Mar. 16	French complete suppression of rebel Berber tribes in Morocco.
Oct. 9	Barthou, Foreign Minister, and King Alexander of Yugoslavia assassinated at Marseilles.

1935 Mar. 7	Saar district restored to Germany following plebiscite (13 Jan.).
Apr. 11–14	Stresa Conference of Britain, France and Italy.
May 2	Franco–Russian treaty of mutual assistance.
July 14	Mass demonstrations throughout France demanding

	democracy and the dissolution of right-wing Leagues.
July 27	French government granted emergency financial powers.
Nov. 3	Socialist groups merge as Socialist and Republican Union under Léon Blum; later forming with Radical Socialists and Communists a Popular Front.
1936 Jan.	Popular Front agrees common programme.
May 3	Popular Front wins major success in elections with 387 seats to 231.
June 4	Blum forms Popular Front government.
June 7	40-hour week decreed, collective labour agreements, and paid holidays.
Sept.	Widespread strikes in French industry.
Oct. 2	Franc devalued.
Nov. 18	In spite of protests from the Left, Blum proposes non-intervention in the Spanish Civil War.
1937 Jan.	Blum slows down social reform programme.
Feb. 27	French Chamber passes defence plan; Schneider-Creusot factory nationalised and Maginot Line extended.
June 21	Chamber rejects Blum's programme of financial reforms. Blum resigns and replaced by the radical Chautemps.
1938 Mar. 13	Blum forms second Popular Front government, but Senate rejects financial reforms.
Apr. 10	Blum resigns and replaced by Daladier.
Sept. 29	France signs Munich Agreement.
Nov. 9	France recognises Italian conquest of Abyssinia.
1939 Feb. 27	France recognises Franco's government in Spain; Pétain sent as first ambassador.
Mar. 17	Daladier granted powers to speed rearmament.
Mar. 31	France and Britain guarantee support for Poland.
Apr. 13	France and Britain guarantee independence of Romania and Greece.
Aug. 26–31	Negotiations by Daladier and Chamberlain with Hitler fail.
Sept. 3	Britain and France declare war on Germany.
Sept. 4	Franco–Polish agreement.
Sept. 26	Daladier dissolves French Communist Party.
Sept. 30	British Expeditionary Force sent to France.
Nov. 3	Roosevelt allows France to purchase US arms on 'cash and carry' basis, amending Neutrality Act of May 1937.
1940 Mar. 21	Reynaud succeeds Daladier as Premier.
May 10	German attack on Holland, Belgium and Luxembourg.
May 12	German panzer forces cross into France.
May 14	German forces cross the Meuse.
May 19	General Weygand takes command of the French army from General Gamelin.
May 20	German forces reach Channel cutting off allied armies in the north.

May 29	British begin evacuation from Dunkirk.
June 10	Italy declares war on France.
June 14	Germans enter Paris.
June 16	Reynaud resigns and replaced by Pétain.
June 18	De Gaulle, from London, calls for continued resistance.
June 22	French sign armistice with Germany at Compiègne.
June 23	British government supports London-based French National Committee, 'Free French', headed by de Gaulle and breaks off relations with Pétain government.
June 24	Armistice signed with Italy.
July 1	French government moves to Vichy.
July 3	British attack on French fleet at Mers-el-Kebir.
July 5	Vichy regime breaks off relations with Britain.
July 10	National Assembly votes full powers to Pétain as 'Head of the French State', ending Third Republic.
Oct. 22–24	Laval, followed by Pétain, holds discussions with Hitler at Montoire.
Dec. 13	Laval dismissed. Replaced by Darlan.
1941 Apr. 18	Vichy government withdraws from League of Nations.
May	Darlan offers French air bases in Syria to the Germans.
June 8	Allied invasion of Syria.
June 30	Vichy government breaks off relations with Russia.
1942 Apr. 18	Laval returns to head government.
Nov. 11	German troops occupy Vichy France.
Nov. 27	French fleet scuttled at Toulon.
1944 June 6	Allied landings in Normandy.
Aug. 25	Paris is liberated.
Oct. 23	De Gaulle's provisional government recognised by allies.

The Eastern Question

1768–74 Turkey at war with Russia.

1774 Treaty of Kutchuk-Kainardji: Russia receives mouth of Dneiper and Crimea, and gains right to intervene on behalf of Christians in Moldavia and Wallachia.

1775 Austria annexes Bukovina from Turkey.

1787–92 Turkey at war with Russia and Austria.

1789 Austrians take Belgrade.

1791 Turkey cedes Orsova to Austria by Peace of Sistova.

1792 By Peace of Jassy between Russia and Turkey, Russia obtains Black Sea coast.

1798 French expedition to Egypt; Turkey declares war on France.

1800 Turks and Mamelukes defeated by Kleber at Heliopolis.

1801 France returns Egypt to Turkey.

1804 Revolt of Serbs.

1806–12 Turkey at war with Russia.

1807 British ships force a passage up the Dardanelles.

1811 Russians take Belgrade.

1812 Under Treaty of Bucharest, Russia receives Bessarabia from Turkey.

1815 Revolt of Serbs.

1817 Turkey grants autonomy to Serbs.

1821–30 Greek War of Independence.

1826 Convention of Ackermann between Russia and Turkey.

1827 Battle of Navarino: Turkish fleet destroyed by British and French.

1828 Russia intervenes on behalf of Greeks and takes Varna.

1829 Under Treaty of Adrianople, Russia obtains territory south of Caucasus; Russia occupies Moldavia and Wallachia.

1830 Greece is declared independent under protection of Britain, Russia and France.

1832 Turkey declares war on Egypt.

1833 Treaty of Unkiar Skelessi: Dardanelles are closed to all but Russian ships.
Turkey recognises independence of Egypt.

1839 War between Turkey and Egypt.

1840   Britain, Russia, Austria and Prussia establish Quadruple Alliance for protection of Turkey.

1841   Straits Convention: Dardanelles are closed to all foreign warships while Turkey was at peace.
Egypt loses Syria to Turkey.

1848   Russia suppresses nationalist revolt in Wallachia.

1849   Convention of Balta Liman provides for joint Russo–Turkish supervision of Danubian Principalities.

1853   Russia reoccupies Danubian Principalities and claims protectorate over Christians in Turkey.

1854   Outbreak of Crimean War: Britain and France declare war on Russia in support of Turkey.

1856   Treaty of Paris: Black Sea is declared neutral and Turkey's integrity is guaranteed.

1858   Separate administrations are established in Danubian Principalities; war between Turkey and Montenegro.

1860   Massacre of Christians in Syria.

1862   Danubian Principalities become autonomous principality of 'Romania'.

1871   London Conference abrogates Black Sea neutrality clauses of 1856.

1875   Bulgarian revolt; revolt in Bosnia–Herzegovina.

1876   Bulgarian massacres by Turks.

1877   London Protocol: Great Powers demand that Turkey undertakes internal reforms.   First Turkish parliament meets.

1877–78   Russo-Turkish war.

1878   Treaty of San Stefano creates Bulgaria.   Romanian independence confirmed.   Congress of Berlin.   Austria occupies Bosnia–Herzegovina, though Turkey retains sovereignty.

1885   Turkey refuses Britain passage up the Straits.

1886   Bulgaria is recognised as an autonomous united principality.

1894–97   Christian risings in Crete against Turkey.

1895   Turkey refuses Britain passage up the Straits. Lord Salisbury suggests the partition of Turkey.

1897   Greece declares war on Turkey.

1898   William II visits Constantinople.

1908   'Young Turks' rising.   Bulgarian independence is formally recognised.   Austrian annexation of Bosnia–Herzegovina leads to 'Bosnian Crisis'.

1909   Russia accepts Austrian annexation of Bosnia–Herzegovina; Young Turks depose Sultan Abdul Hamid; succeeded by Mohammed V.

1912   First Balkan War: Turkey attacked by Bulgaria, Serbia, Greece and Montenegro.

1913   Turkey cedes most of her European territory.   Second and Third Balkan wars.   Treaty of Bucharest.   German–Turkish military convention.

1914   Turkey becomes Germany's ally and declares war on Britain, France and Russia.

1915   Secret Constantinople Agreements on fate of Ottoman territory after War.

1918   Turkey surrenders unconditionally.

International background to the First World War, 1882–1914

1882 May   Germany, Austria–Hungary, and Italy form the Triple Alliance.

1890 June   Germany allows Reinsurance Treaty with Russia to lapse.

1894 Jan.   France and Russia sign defensive alliance.

1896 Jan.   'Kruger Telegram' incident. William II sends a telegram of congratulation to President Kruger of the Boer Republic on the failure of the Jameson raid on the Transvaal. Widely interpreted in Britain as an antagonistic act.

1898 Mar.–Apr.   Anglo–German negotiations for agreement to resist Russian expansion in the Far East break down.

     Sept.   British forces under Kitchener and French expeditionary force under Marchand confront each other at Fashoda in the Sudan. After a period of great tension between the two countries a compromise is reached allowing the French to withdraw.

1899 Mar.   Anglo–French agreement over the spheres of influence in Africa. France is excluded from the Nile valley but is allowed to consolidate its position in northern-west and Saharan Africa.
First German Naval Law passed.

     May–July   The Hague Peace Conference fails to achieve agreement on disarmament.

     Oct.   Outbreak of Boer War increases British diplomatic isolation.

1900 June   Second German Naval Law.

1901 Mar.–May   Franco–German negotiations for an alliance break down.

1902 Jan.   Great Britain and Japan sign defensive alliance.

1904 Apr.   *Entente Cordiale*. Great Britain and France sign agreement on colonial disputes.

1905 Feb.–July   First Morocco crisis. William II intervenes in Moroccan affairs, a French area of influence. Germany fails to obtain international support but France agrees to an international conference.

1906 Jan.–Apr.   Algeçiras conference provides peaceful settlement of the Moroccan crisis, but increases German isolation. During the crisis France and Britain hold military talks including a British expeditionary force to be sent to the continent.

Feb.	Great Britain launches the *Dreadnought*, the first all big-gun battleship, rendering existing naval vessels obsolete and intensifying the naval race with Germany.
1907 June–Oct.	Germany rejects any scheme for disarmament at the second Hague Peace Conference.
July	Triple Alliance renewed for six years.
Aug.	Britain and Russia sign a convention; Britain, France and Russia are known as the Triple Entente.
1908 Oct.	Austria–Hungary annexes Bosnia–Herzegovina: Russia backs down from intervention. William II's comments in an interview in the *Daily Telegraph* increase Anglo–German antagonism.
1909 Jan.	Agreement made for international exploitation of Moroccan mines.
Feb.	France and Germany sign an agreement recognizing France's political rights in Morocco in return for economic equality.
1911 July 1	Second Morocco crisis. German gunboat, the *Panther*, arrives in Agadir.
July 4	Germany warned of Great Britain's concern for Moroccan question.
July–Nov.	Talks between France and Germany result in end of crisis. Germany recognizes the French protectorate in Morocco (11 Oct.) while France signs agreement to pay compensation to Germany (4 Nov.).
Sept. 28	Italy sends ultimatum to Turkey not to resist troops sent to Tripoli in Libya.
Sept. 29	Italy declares war on Turkey; Italian forces bombard Tripoli and make landings.
Nov. 5	Italian Prime Minister declares Tripoli annexed.
1912 Feb.	Haldane mission to Germany fails to end naval race.
Mar.	Germany publishes third Naval Law.
Apr. 18	Italian fleet bombards Turkish forts in the Dardanelles.
Sept.	Serbia, Montenegro, Greece and Bulgaria form Balkan League against Turkey.
Oct. 6	Major powers back French proposals to avert Balkan War.
Oct. 8	Montenegro declares war on Turkey.
Oct. 12	Turkey refuses to undertake reforms in its Balkan territories proposed by great powers.
Oct. 17	Turkey declares war on Bulgaria and Serbia.
Oct. 18	Italy and Turkey sign peace treaty at Lausanne leaving Tripoli and Cyrenaica under Italian suzerainty.
Oct. 24	Turks suffer defeats by Bulgarians at Kirk-Kilisse and by the Serbs at Kumanovo.
Nov. 9	Greeks take Salonica.
Dec. 3	Armistice between Turkey, Bulgaria, Serbia and Montenegro. Russia and Austria-Hungary mobilise.

1913	Jan. 6	Peace conference between Turkey and Balkan states suspended.
	Mar.	Greeks take Janina; Adrianople surrenders to Bulgarians.
	Apr. 15	Turks and Bulgarians cease fighting.
	Apr. 22	Austria–Hungary moves forces to near Montenegrin border.
	May 30	Preliminaries of peace signed between Balkan states and Turkey.
	May 31	Serbs and Greeks sign secret military convention against Bulgaria.
	June	Germany makes fiscal provisions to double the strength of her army.
	June 30	Fighting breaks out between Bulgaria and her former allies.
	Aug. 10	Balkan states sign Treaty of Bucharest.
	Sept. 30	Treaty of Constantinople between Turkey and Bulgaria ends second Balkan War.
1914	June 15	Anglo–German agreement on Baghdad Railway and Mesopotamia.
	June 28	Archduke Francis Ferdinand assassinated by Slav extremists at Sarajevo.
	July 23	Austria–Hungary sends Serbian government a ten-point ultimatum demanding firm steps to suppress anti-Austrian activities by Slav extremists and (clause 6) participation of Austrian delegates in official inquiry into the assassination.
	July 24	Russian government declares it will defend Serbia against Austro–Hungarian attack.
	July 25	Serbia makes conciliatory reply to Austrian ultimatum, but will not accept clause 6 as contrary to the constitution. Austria–Hungary finds the reply unsatisfactory and mobilises against Serbia.
	July 26	Grey's proposal of an international conference to settle the Austro–Serbian dispute is rejected by Austria–Hungary and Germany. Austrian forces mobilise on Russian frontier.
	July 28	Austria–Hungary declares war on Serbia.
	July 30	Russia begins general mobilisation.
	July 31	Germany demands that Russia cease mobilisation.
	Aug. 1	Germany declares war on Russia; France mobilises. Italy declares her neutrality. German–Turkish treaty signed.
	Aug. 2	Germany occupies Luxembourg and sends ultimatum to Belgium demanding passage for her troops. Russians invade East Prussia.
	Aug. 3	Germany declares war on France and begins invasion of Belgium. British ultimatum to Germany.
	Aug. 4	Germany declares war on Belgium; Great Britain declares war on Germany.
	Aug. 5	Austria–Hungary declares war on Russia.
	Aug. 10	France declares war on Austria–Hungary.
	Aug. 12	Britain declares war on Austria–Hungary.

The First World War

1914 June 28   Francis Ferdinand assassinated in Sarajevo.
July 28   Austria–Hungary declares war on Serbia.
Aug. 1   Germany declares war on Russia.
Aug. 2   Germany invades Luxembourg; British fleet mobilised.
Aug. 3   Germany declares war on France.
Aug. 4   Germany invades Belgium; Britain and Belgium declare war on Germany.
Aug. 5   Turkey closes Dardanelles.
Aug. 5–12   Germans seize Liège.
Aug. 6   Austria declares war on Russia.
Aug. 7   British troops arrive in France.
Aug. 10   Austrians invade Russian Poland.
Aug. 10–20   Austrian advance on Serbia halted at Battle of the Jadar.
Aug. 12   Britain and France declare war on Austria.
Aug. 14–24   French suffer defeats in Lorraine, the Ardennes and on the Sambre; British retreat from Mons.
Aug. 17–20   Russians invade East Prussia and Galicia.
Aug. 20   Germans occupy Brussels.
Aug. 22   Hindenburg becomes German Commander in East Prussia.
Aug. 26–28   Germans cross the Meuse.
Aug. 26–29   Russians defeated at Tannenberg.
Sept. 5–9   Battle of the Marne.
Sept. 5–11   Austrians defeated in the Battle of Rawa Ruska.
Sept. 8–16   Serbs halt second Austrian invasion.
Sept. 10–14   Russians forced to retreat from East Prussia following Battle of the Masurian Lakes.
Sept. 14   Falkenhayn replaces Moltke as German Commander-in-Chief.
Sept. 14–18   Allied offensive fails at first Battle of the Aisne.
Sept. 27   Russians invade Hungary.
Sept. 28–
Nov. 1   Austro–German offensive in east checked, leading to withdrawal from Poland.

Sept.–Oct.   'Race for the Sea': series of outflanking manoeuvres towards the Channel fails.
Oct. 9   Germans take Antwerp.
Oct. 12–
Nov. 11   First Battle of Ypres: Germans fail to reach Channel ports; Allied counter-attack fails.
Oct. 16   'Race for the Sea' concluded by Battle of the Yser.
Nov. 1   Hindenburg becomes German Commander-in-Chief on Eastern front.
Nov. 2   Russians renew advance on East Prussia.
Britain declares North Sea a war-zone and begins blockade of Germany.
Nov. 5–Dec. 15   Serbs repel third Austrian invasion.
Nov. 11–Nov. 24   Russians retreat after Battle of Łódz.

Nov. 14	Turkey proclaims Holy War.
Dec. 2	Austrians take Belgrade.

1915 Jan 8–15   French attack halted by Germans at Battle of Soissons.

Jan. 23   German and Austrian armies launch offensive in Carpathians.

Feb. 7–21   Germans encircle Russian Tenth Army at Battle of Masuria; Austrian attack in Carpathians collapses.

Feb. 11   British air raid on Ostend and Zeebrugge.

Feb. 18   Germany commences submarine warfare against merchant vessels.

Feb. 19–Mar. 18   British Navy fails to force the Dardanelles Straits.

Mar. 10–13   British advance checked at Battle of Neuve-Chapelle.

Mar. 14–15   Battle of Saint-Eloi.

Mar. 19–20   Germans mount raid on Yarmouth and King's Lynn.

Mar. 31   Zeppelin raids on southern English counties begin.

Apr. 22–May 25   Second Battle of Ypres: Germans employ poison gas for the first time.

Apr. 25   Allied forces land on Gallipoli Peninsula.

May 2–4   Russian line between Gorlice and Tarnow broken by German–Austrian offensive, forcing Russians to retreat.

May 4   Italy leaves the Triple Alliance.

May 7   *Lusitania* sunk.

May 9–June 18   Second Battle of Artois.

May 15–25   Battle of Festubert.

May 23   Italy enters war on Allied side and declares war on Germany and Austria.

June 1   German air raid on London.

June 20–July 14   German offensive in the Argonne fails.

July 16–18   Russians defeated in Battle of Krasnotav.

Aug. 4–5   Germans enter Warsaw.

Aug. 6–21   Allied attacks in Dardanelles fail.

Sept. 18   Germany limits submarine attacks.

Sept. 25–Nov. 6   Allied offensives at Loos and in Champagne.

Sept. 28   British enter Kut el Amara after defeating Turks.

Oct. 5   Allied forces land in Salonika.

Oct. 7   Serbian army collapses in face of joint German–Austrian–Bulgarian offensive, and is evacuated to Corfu.

Dec. 3   Joffre becomes French Commander-in-Chief.

Dec. 7   Turkish forces lay siege to British at Kut el Amara.

Dec. 19   Haig replaces French as British Commander-in-Chief.

Dec. 20   Allied forces evacuated from Anzac and Suvla Bay in Dardanelles (completed 9 Jan. 1916).

1916 Feb. 21–Dec. 18   Battle of Verdun results in 550,000 French and 450,000 German casualties.

Mar. 15   Admiral von Tirpitz resigns.

Apr. 29   British surrender at Kut el Amara.

May 15–June 17   Austrians defeat Italians at Asiago but withdraw to strengthen Eastern front.

May 24   Britain introduces conscription.

May 31–June 1   Battle of Jutland.

June 4–Sept. 20   Massive Russian offensive south of Pripet Marshes results in heavy casualties on both sides.

June 5   Arab revolt against Turkish rule begins.

June 6   *HMS Hampshire* sunk: Lord Kitchener drowns.

June 10   Russians cross Dniester.

June 21   Turks begin offensive against Persia.

July 1–Nov. 18   Allied offensive at Battle of the Somme fails to achieve major breakthrough.

Aug. 26   Italy declares war on Germany.

Aug. 27   Romania enters war and commences invasion of Transylvania.

Aug. 29   Hindenburg becomes German Chief of General Staff.

Sept. 10–Nov. 19   Allied forces launch offensive in Salonika.

Sept. 15   British use tanks for first time during Battle of the Somme.

Oct. 24–Dec. 18   French launch successful counter-attacks at Verdun.

Dec. 3   Nivelle succeeds Joffre as French Commander-in-Chief.

Dec. 6   Bucharest captured; Russians and Romanians forced to retreat.

Dec. 7   Lloyd George forms Coalition government in Britain.

Dec. 12   Central Powers make peace offer.

Dec. 13   British begin offensive in Mesopotamia.

Dec. 30   Allies reject peace offer made by Central Powers.

1917 Jan 31   Germans announce resumption of unrestricted submarine warfare.

Feb. 23–Apr. 5   Expecting an Allied offensive, Germans withdraw to Hindenburg Line.

Feb. 25   British recapture Kut el Amara.

Mar. 11   British enter Baghdad.

Mar. 12   Revolution in Russia leads to abdication of Tsar Nicholas II.

Mar. 16–19   Germans take stand along Siegfried Line.

Mar. 26–27   British fail to capture Gaza.

Apr. 4   British launch offensive in Artois.

Apr. 6   USA declares war on Germany.

Apr. 9   French begin offensive in Champagne.

Apr. 9–May 3   Canadians take Vimy Ridge during Battle of Arras.

Apr. 16–May 9   French offensive fails at second Battle of the Aisne.

Apr. 17–19   British attack fails in second Battle of Gaza.

May 15   Pétain becomes French Commander-in-Chief.

May 3–20   Outbreak of mutinies in French Army.

June 7–8   British capture Messines Ridge.

June 25   US troops land in France.

July 31–Nov. 6   Third Battle of Ypres results in capture of Passchendaele.

Sept. 20   British resume offensive near Ypres.

Oct. 24–Nov. 12   Italians forced to retreat after Battle of Caporetto.

Oct. 31–Nov. 7   Turks forced to withdraw following third Battle of Gaza.

Nov. 2   Germans retreat behind Aisne–Oise and Ailette Canals.

Nov. 4	British forces reach Italian front.
Nov. 6	British take Passchendaele.
Nov. 7	Bolshevik Revolution in Russia.
Nov. 17	Clemenceau becomes French Premier.
Nov. 20–Dec. 3	First mass use of tanks at Battle of Cambrai leads to temporary breach of Hindenburg Line.
Dec. 2	Fighting ceases on Russian front.
Dec. 3	Austro–German campaign in Italy suspended.
Dec. 7	USA declares war on Austria–Hungary.
Dec. 9	Romania signs armistice.
	Allenby enters Jerusalem.
1918 Jan. 8	President Wilson issues Fourteen Points.
Feb. 18	Fighting resumes between Russia and Germany.
Mar. 3	Bolsheviks accept German peace terms at Brest-Litovsk.
Mar. 21–Apr. 4	Germans launch offensive on the Somme.
Apr. 9–29	Germans launch offensive on the Lys.
Apr. 14	Foch becomes supreme commander of Allied forces in France.
Apr. 22–23	British raid on Zeebrugge.
May 7	Romania concludes Treaty of Bucharest with Central Powers.
May 27–June 6	Germans launch offensive on the Aisne.
June 9–13	Germans launch Noyon-Montidier offensive.
June 15–24	Italians repulse Austrian attack across the Piave.
July 13	Final Turkish offensive in Palestine.
July 15–17	Germans launch final (Champagne–Marne) offensive.
July 18–Aug. 6	Allied forces launch Aisne–Marne offensive, leading to reduction of Marne salient.
Aug. 8–Sept. 3	Amiens salient is reduced.
Sept. 3	German armies commence retreat to Hindenburg Line.
Sept. 14	Allied armies begin offensive against Bulgarians.
Sept. 19	Turkish army defeated in Battle of Megiddo.
Sept. 25	Bulgaria requests armistice.
Sept. 26	Foch launches final offensive, breaching Hindenburg Line on 27 Sept.
Sept. 29	Bulgaria concludes armistice.
Oct. 1	French forces take St Quentin. British forces enter Damascus.
Oct. 3	Prince Max of Baden becomes German Chancellor.
Oct. 9–10	British take Cambrai and Le Cateau.
Oct. 14	USA demands cessation of submarine warfare.
Oct. 17	British reach Ostend.
Oct. 20	Submarine warfare abandoned by Germany.
Oct. 24–Nov 4	Italians defeat Austrians at Vittorio Veneto.
Oct. 31	Armistice with Turkey comes into force.
Nov. 3	Austria agrees to Allied peace terms.
	Mutiny in German High Seas fleet.
Nov. 4	Armistice concluded on Italian front.
	Germans withdraw to Antwerp–Meuse line.
Nov. 9	Revolution in Berlin leads to proclamation of Republic.

Nov. 10	William II flees to Holland; Emperor Charles of Austria abdicates.
Nov. 11	Armistice concluded on Western Front.
Nov. 21	German High Seas fleet surrenders to British.

Manpower and casualties of major European powers, 1914–1918

	Standing armies and trained reserves	Total mobilised	Killed or died of wounds	Total military casualties
Austria–Hungary	3,000,000	7,800,000	1,200,000	7,020,000
British Empire	975,000	8,904,000	908,000	3,190,235
France	4,017,000	8,410,000	1,363,000	6,160,800
Germany	4,500,000	11,000,000	1,774,000	7,142,558
Italy	1,251,000	5,615,000	460,000	2,197,000
Russia	5,971,000	12,000,000	1,700,000	9,150,000
Turkey	210,000	2,850,000	325,000	975,000

Naval strength of major European powers in 1914

	Britain	Germany	France	Italy	Russia	Austria–Hungary	Turkey
Dreadnoughts	24	13	14	1	4	3	1
Pre-Dreadnoughts	38	30	9	17	7	12	3
Battle cruisers	10	6	0	0	1	0	0
Cruisers	47	14	19	5	8	3	0
Light cruisers	61	35	6	6	5	4	2
Destroyers	228	152	81	33	106	18	8
Submarines	76	30	67	20	36	14	0

Naval losses of major European powers, 1914–1918

	Britain	Germany	France	Italy	Russia	Austria–Hungary	Turkey
Dreadnoughts	2	0 (18)*	0	1	2	2	0
Pre-Dreadnoughts	11	1 (0)	4	3	2	1	1
Battle cruisers	3	1 (6)	0	0	0	0	0
Cruisers	13	6 (0)	5	1	2	0	0
Light cruisers	12	17 (23)	0	2	0	3	1
Destroyers	67	66 (92)	12	8	20	6	3
Submarines	54	199 (all)	14	8	20	14	0

* Figures in brackets indicate vessels surrendered

Chronology of Italian Fascism

1919	Mar. 23	Foundation of the first *Fascio di Combattimento* by Mussolini in Milan.
	Aug. 25	Italian forces evacuate Fiume.
	Sept. 2	Universal suffrage and proportional representation introduced.
	Sept. 12	D'Annunzio seizes Fiume.
	Nov. 11	The Pope lifts the prohibition against Catholics participating in political life.
	Nov. 16	Socialists and Catholics receive strong support in the elections; fascists gain only a fraction of the vote.
1920	June 9	Giolitti takes over as prime minister from Nitti.
	Aug. 31–Sept.	Widespread strikes and lockouts in engineering, metal and steel industries.
	Nov. 12	Treaty of Rapallo settles disputes between Italy and Yugoslavia. Fiume to be an independent state.
	Nov. 21	Fascists fire on crowd in Bologna during inauguration of Mayor.
	Dec. 1	D'Annunzio declares war on Italy.
	Dec. 24–25	Clashes between Italian troops and Fiuman troops. *Andrea Doria* shells the royal palace.
	Dec. 31	D' Annunzio makes peace with Italy.
1921	Jan. 5	D'Annunzio leaves Fiume.
	Feb. 27	Communists and Fascists clash in Florence.
	May 15	Liberals and Democrats successful at the elections.
	June 26	Giolitti cabinet falls, replaced by Bonomi.
1922	Feb. 9	Bonomi government resigns.
	Feb. 25	Facta heads new government.
	May	Fascist takeover in Bologna.
	Aug. 3–4	Fascist takeover in Milan.
	Oct. 24	Mussolini calls on Facta to resign and for the formation of a Fascist cabinet. Facta refuses.
	Oct. 28	Fascist 'March on Rome'.
	Oct. 30	Mussolini arrives in Rome and organises victory march.
	Oct. 31	Mussolini forms cabinet.
	Nov. 25	Mussolini is granted temporary dictatorial powers to institute reforms.
1923	Jan. 14	King Victor Emmanuel authorises voluntary Fascist Militia.
	July 21	Electoral law passed, guaranteeing two-thirds of the seats in the Chamber to the majority party.
1924	Jan. 27	Treaty with Yugoslavia recognises Fiume as Italian, but cedes surrounding area to Yugoslavia.

Apr. 6	Fascists obtain almost two-thirds of votes in election amidst widespread use of violence and intimidation.
May 30	Matteotti launches attack on the Fascist government.
June 10	Matteotti is abducted and murdered. Non-fascists resign from Chambers and condemn violence.
July	Press censorship introduced.

1925 Oct. 2   Palazzo Vidoni pact between 'industrialists' association (Confindustria) and the fascist syndicates.

Dec. 24   Mussolini's dictatorial powers increased. Press censorship tightened, secret non-fascist organisations banned, and widespread arrests.

1926 Jan. 31   Government decrees given the power of law.

Apr. 3   Right to strike abolished: collective contracts reserved to the fascist syndicate.

Apr. 7   Mussolini wounded in assassination attempt.

Nov. 25   Law for defence of the state; creation of a special tribunal for political crimes; death penalty introduced for plotting against royal family or head of state.

1927 Dec. 21   Exchange rate fixed at 'quota 90' (92.45 Lira to £1).

1929 Feb. 11   Lateran Treaties with Papacy creating the Vatican City as a sovereign independent state (see p. 260).

1932 Oct. 30   *Decennale* celebrations – fascists celebrate tenth year of power in Italy.

1934 Mar. 17   Mussolini signs the Rome Protocols with Austria and Hungary.

June 14   Meeting of Hitler and Mussolini at Venice.

July   Mussolini sends troops to the Austrian frontier following Hitler's attempted coup.

Nov. 10   Council of Corporations inaugurated at Rome.

1935 Oct. 3   Italy begins invasion of Abyssinia (Ethiopia).

1936 May 5   Italian forces occupy Addis Ababa.

Oct. 24   Rome–Berlin Axis formed.

1938 July 14   Publication of *Manifesto della Razza* – first anti-semitic measures.

1939 Jan. 19   Creation of the *Camera del Fascie delle Corporazioni*, replacing parliament.

Apr. 7   Italy invades Albania.

May 22   Pact of Steel signed between Hitler and Mussolini.

1940 June 10   Mussolini declares war and invades France. First air attacks on Malta.

Aug. 3   Italy invades British Somaliland.

Sept. 13   Italian forces invade Egypt.

Oct. 28   Italy invades Greece.

Nov. 11–12   Destruction of large part of Italian fleet at Taranto by British aircraft.

Dec. 9   British offensive in North Africa routs the army of Graziani.

1941	Mar. 24	Italians defeated in British Somaliland.
	Mar. 27–28	Italian fleet defeated at Cape Matapan.
	Apr. 6	British enter Addis Ababa.
	May 16	Capitulation of Italian forces under the Duke of Aosta.
	Dec. 11	Italy declares war on United States.
1942	June	Allied convoys resupply Malta.
	Nov. 4	British break through Axis line at El Alamein.
1943	May	Surrender of Axis forces in North Africa.
	July 10	Allied invasion of Sicily.
	July 25	Grand Council of Fascism votes Mussolini out of power. Badoglio takes over the Italian government.
	Aug. 17	Sicily finally conquered by the Allies.
	Sept. 8	Italian surrender announced. Nazis take over power in Italy.
	Sept. 9	Salerno landing by US 5th Army.
	Sept. 12	Skorzeny rescues Mussolini.
	Sept. 23	Mussolini announces creation of fascist social republic of Salo.
1944	Jan. 22	Anzio landing by US 5th Army; German counterattack stalls advance.
	Mar. 15	Allies bomb Monte Cassino.
	Mar. 17	Monte Cassino falls.
	June 4	Rome falls.
1945	Apr. 28	Mussolini executed by partisans at Dongo.

Germany, 1929–1945

1929 Feb.–June	Nazis combine with Hugenberg and German Nationalists to oppose the Young Plan.
June 7	Publication of Young Plan for rescheduling German reparation payments in the form of annuities over 59 years, amounting to a quarter of the sum demanded in 1921.
July 9	Nationalists and Nazis form a National Committee to fight the Young Plan with Hugenberg as chairman and Hitler a leading member.
Oct. 3	Death of Stresemann.
Oct. 29	Wall Street Crash and cessation of American loans to Europe.
Dec. 29	National referendum accepts Young Plan, frustrating Nationalist hopes.
1930 Mar.	Young Plan approved by Reichstag and signed by Hindenburg.
Mar. 17	Müller's Socialist cabinet resigns in Germany.
Mar. 30	Heinrich Brüning, of the Centre, forms a minority coalition of the Right.
May 17	Young Plan reparations come into force.
June 30	Last allied troops leave Rhineland.
July 16	Hindenburg authorises German budget by decree on failure of Reichstag to pass it.
Sept. 14	In Reichstag elections, Hitler and the Nazi Party emerge as a major party with 107 seats, second only to the Socialists with 143 seats.
Oct.	Röhm becomes leader of SA or 'Brownshirts'.
1931 July	Worsening economic crisis in Germany. Unemployment reaches over $4\frac{1}{4}$ million. Bankruptcy of German Danatbank (13 July) leads to closure of all banks until 5 August.
Oct. 11	Hitler forms an alliance with the Nationalists led by Hugenberg at Hartzburg – the Hartzburg Front.
1932 Jan. 7	Brüning declares that Germany cannot and will not resume reparations' payments.
Mar. 13	In presidential elections Hindenburg receives 18 million votes against Hitler's 11 million, and the communists' 5 million. With failure to achieve an overall majority, a new election is called for 10 April.
Apr. 10	Hindenburg re-elected President with an absolute majority of 19 million against Hitler's 13 million and the communists' 3 million.
Apr. 14	Brüning attempts to disband the SA and SS.
Apr. 24	Nazis achieve successes in local elections.
May 30	At Hindenburg's withdrawal of support for disbanding the SA and SS, Brüning resigns.

June 1	Franz von Papen forms a ministry with von Schleicher as minister of defence and von Neurath as foreign minister.
June 16	Ban on SA and SS in operation since April is lifted.
July 31	In Reichstag elections Nazis win 230 seats and become largest party, producing a stalemate since neither they nor the Socialists (133 seats) will enter a coalition.
Aug. 13	Hitler refuses Hindenburg's request to serve as vice-chancellor under von Papen.
Sept. 12	Von Papen dissolves the Reichstag.
Sept. 14	Germany leaves disarmament conference.
Nov. 6	New elections fail to resolve the stalemate, with the Communists only gaining a few seats from the Nazis.
Nov. 17	Von Papen forced to resign by Schleicher; Hitler rejects Chancellorship.
Dec. 2–4	Schleicher becomes Chancellor and forms a ministry, attempting to conciliate the Centre and Left.
1933 Jan. 28	Schleicher's ministry is unable to secure a majority in the Reichstag and resigns.
Jan. 30	Hindenburg accepts a Cabinet with Hitler as Chancellor, von Papen as Vice-Chancellor and nationalists in other posts.
Feb. 27	Reichstag fire blamed on Communists and made pretext for suspension of civil liberties and freedom of press.
Mar. 5	In elections the Nazis make gains, winning 288 seats, but fail to secure overall majority.
Mar. 13	Goebbels becomes minister of propaganda and 'enlightenment'. Pius XI praises Hitler's anti-communism.
Mar. 17	Schacht becomes President of the Reichsbank.
Mar. 23	Hitler obtains Enabling Law with the support of the Centre Party, granting him dictatorial powers for four years.
Mar. 30	German bishops withdraw opposition to Nazis.
Apr. 1	National boycott of all Jewish businesses and professions.
Apr. 7	Civil Service law permits removal of Jews and other opponents.
July 5	Centre Party disbands.
July 8	Concordat signed between Nazi Germany and Holy See.
July 14	All parties, other than the Nazis, suppressed. The Nazi Party is formally declared the only political party in Germany.
July 20	Concordat ratified.
Sept.	Ludwig Müller, leader of minority 'German Christians', becomes 'Bishop of the Reich'.
1934 Mar. 21	'Battle for Work' begins.
May	German Protestants at Barman synod express disapproval of Müller and 'German Christians', close complicity with Nazis.

June 14	Hitler visits Mussolini in Italy.
June 20	Hindenburg demands dissolution of SA.
June 30	'Night of the Long Knives'. Nazis liquidate thousands of opponents within and without the Party. Over seventy leading Nazis lose their lives including Röhm, leader of the SA, and Gregor Strasser, leader of Berlin Nazis. General von Schleicher also a victim.
Aug. 2	Death of President Hindenburg. Hitler assumes Presidency, but retains title Der Führer. Army swears oath of allegiance. Schacht becomes minister of economics.
Oct. 24	German Labour Front founded, Nazi organisation to replace trade unions.
1935 Jan. 13	Saar plebiscite favours reabsorption into Germany.
Mar. 16	Germany repudiates disarmament clauses in Treaty of Versailles, restores conscription and announces expansion of the peace time army to over half a million men.
June 18	By Anglo–German Naval Agreement Germany agrees that her naval tonnage shall not exceed a third of that of the Royal Navy.
Sept. 15	Nuremberg laws prohibit marriage and sexual intercourse between Jews and German nationals.
1936 Mar. 7	German troops reoccupy the demilitarised Rhineland in violation of the Treaty of Versailles.
Aug.	Olympic Games in Berlin turned into an advertisement for Nazi Germany.
Aug. 24	Germany adopts two-year compulsory military service.
Oct. 19	Hitler announces four-year plan under Goering as economics minister.
Nov. 1	Rome–Berlin Axis proclaimed.
Nov. 18	Germany and Italy recognise the Franco Government.
1937 Dec.	Schacht resigns as minister of economics.
Dec.	Leading members of the Protestant opposition arrested, including Pastor Niemoller.
1938 Feb. 4	Hitler appoints Joachim von Ribbentrop foreign minister. Fritsch is relieved of his duties as Commander-in-Chief of the army. Hitler takes over personal control of the armed forces. The War Ministry is abolished and OKW (High Command of the Armed Forces) is set up.
Mar. 11	German troops enter Austria which is declared part of the Reich (13th).
Apr. 23	Sudeten Germans demand autonomy.
Aug. 18	Beck resigns as Chief of the Army General Staff.
Aug. 12	Germany mobilises over Czech crisis.
Sept. 30	Munich Agreement gives Sudetenland to Germany.
Nov. 9–10	Anti-Jewish pogrom, the *Kristallnacht*.
1939 Jan. 21	Schacht dismissed as president of Reichsbank.
Mar. 15	German troops occupy remaining part of Czechoslovakia.

Aug. 23	Nazi–Soviet Pact signed.
Sept. 1	Germany invades Poland.
Sept. 3	Great Britain and France declare war on Germany.
Sept. 21	Polish Jews ordered into ghettos.
Sept. 27	Warsaw surrenders, end of Polish campaign.
Oct. 7	Himmler appointed Reich Commissioner.
Oct. 8	Western Poland incorporated in Reich.
Oct. 12	Austrian Jews deported to east.
Nov. 23	Polish Jews ordered to wear the Yellow Star of David.

1940 Apr. 7   Germany invades Norway and Denmark.
May 10   Germany invades Holland, France and Belgium.
May 14   Dutch army surrenders.
May 28   Belgium capitulates.
May 29–June 3   British and allied forces evacuate from Dunkirk.
June 14   Germans enter Paris.
June 22   France concludes armistice with Germany.
July–Sept.   Battle of Britain fails to destroy the RAF.
Aug. 23   Beginning of 'Blitz' on Britain by Luftwäffe.
Postponement of 'Operation Sealion', the invasion of Britain.
Dec. 18   Hitler issues secret plan for invasion of Russia – Operation Barbarossa.

1941 Feb. 9   German troops under Rommel sent to assist Italians in North Africa.
Apr. 6   German ultimatum to Greece and Yugoslavia.
Apr. 18   Yugoslav opposition collapses.
May 10   Rudolf Hess lands in Scotland on mysterious mission and is captured.
May 13   Bormann succeeds Hess as Party chancellor.
June 22   German forces launch invasion of Russia.
July 16   Germans take Smolensk.
July 31   Goering gives Heydrich a written order to achieve a 'general solution to the Jewish problem in areas of Jewish influence in Europe'.
Sept. 3   Germans lay siege to Leningrad.
Oct. 25   German offensive against Moscow fails, followed by Russian counter-offensive (5 Dec.).
Dec. 11   Hitler declares war on America.

1942 Jan. 20   Heydrich puts forward 'final solution' to the 'Jewish Problem'.
Feb.   Speer becomes Reich minister of armaments and production.
Mar.   Sauckel made plenipoteniary general for allocation of labour.
May 30   First '1,000 bomber' raid against Cologne by RAF.
June 28   German offensive begins in Southern Russia.
July   Beginning of liquidation of Jewish ghetto in Warsaw.
Aug.–Sept.   German advance in North Africa halted at El Alamein.
Oct. 23–   British forces defeat and pursue Axis forces at El
Nov. 4   Alamein.
Nov. 8   Anglo–American landings in North Africa – Operation Torch.

1943	Jan. 27	USAAF makes first raid on Germany.
	Feb. 2	German army at Stalingrad surrenders.
	Feb. 18	Goebbels declares mobilisation for total war at mass demonstration in Berlin Sportspalast. Under direction of Speer, arms production rises threefold.
	Mar. 13	Attempt to kill Hitler on a flight between Smolensk and Rastenburg fails.
	July 5–12	Mass air-raids on Hamburg kill many thousands and destroy large parts of the city.
	Sept. 3	Italy forced out of the war.
	Oct.	American air-raids on Schweinfurt ball-bearing factories cause extensive damage but at insupportable cost to attackers.
	Nov.	Series of mass air-raids on German capital known as the 'Battle of Berlin'.
1944	May	Americans begin air attacks on German synthetic oil production.
	June 6	D-Day. Opening of second front with Anglo–American landings in Normandy.
	June 23	Russian offensive begins on central front.
	July 20	'July Plot'. Hitler wounded in bomb attack at headquarters in East Prussia. Attempted coup d'état is put down by loyal troops and leading conspirators and thousands of suspects are arrested and executed.
	July 26	Russians reach the Vistula.
	July 31	Allied break-out in Normandy.
	Aug. 17	Russians reach East Prussian border.
	Dec. 16	Germans begin counter-offensive in the Ardennes.
1945	Jan. 12	Red Army begins final campaign against Germany.
	Feb. 1	American forces reach Siegfried Line.
	Feb. 13	Allied bombing of Dresden.
	Mar. 22	Allies cross Rhine.
	Apr. 11	Western allies halt on the Elbe.
	Apr. 16	Russian offensive against Berlin begins.
	Apr. 21	Russians reach outskirts of Berlin.
	Apr. 30	Hitler commits suicide with his wife Eva Braun in the Berlin bunker, along with Goebbels and his family. Admiral Dönitz is named Hitler's successor.
	May 2	Fall of Berlin to Russian forces.
	May 7	General Jodl makes final capitulation of Germany to General Eisenhower.
	May 8	Von Keitel surrenders to Zhukov near Berlin. Official end of the war in Europe.
	June 5	Admiral Dönitz surrenders his powers to the allied occupation forces.

The Russian Revolution 1914–1924

1914	Aug. 1	Germany declares war on Russia.
	Aug. 26	Russia defeated at battle of Tannenberg.
	Sept. 3–12	Russians force Austrians from Galicia.
	Sept. 5	Russia suffers severe losses at battle of the Masurian Lakes.
1915	May	Austro–German offensive in Galicia defeats Russians.
	July	Further Austro–German offensive leads by the autumn to over a million Russian casualties.
	Aug. 1	Duma meets to consider the way the war is being conducted.
	Aug. 22	Six parties in the Duma form the Progressive Bloc and demand a responsible ministry.
	Sept. 6	Tsar assumes supreme command of the armed forces.
	Sept. 8	Reform programme put before Council of Ministers by Progressive Bloc.
	Sept. 15	Tsar rejects offer of resignation by his ministers to make way for a more popular administration.
	Sept. 16	Tsar prorogues Duma.
1916	Feb. 15	Duma meets. Goremykin replaced as prime minister by Sturmer.
	June–Oct.	Brusilov offensive gains territory but fails to achieve decisive victory and costs over a million casualties.
	Sept.–Oct.	Wave of strikes in Russia; sporadic mutinies of soldiers at the front.
	Oct.	Survey of manpower resources reveals that after February 1917 the Russian army will begin to decline in numbers.
1917	Feb. 27	Duma meets.
	Mar. 7	Tsar leaves Petrograd for army GHQ; beginnings of large-scale demonstrations in the capital.
	Mar. 8	Queues at bakers' shops and crowds continue to demonstrate against the regime.
	Mar. 9	Police fire on crowds.
	Mar. 10	Strikes break out and soldiers join with the people; the Tsar orders suppression of the trouble.
	Mar. 11	Police fire at demonstrators, but more soldiers join the protesters. Tsar prorogues Duma.
	Mar. 12	Formation of Committee of State Duma to replace Tsarist government. Formation of Petrograd Soviet of Workers' and Soldiers' Deputies.
	Mar. 13	Soviet news sheet *Izvestia* calls on people to take affairs into their own hands.
	Mar. 14	Appointment of Ministers of the Provisional Government. 'Army Order No. 1' issued by Petrograd Soviet puts armed forces under its authority and urges rank and file to elect representatives to the Soviet.

Mar. 15	Tsar abdicates in favour of his brother, Grand Duke Michael, at the same time confirming the new ministry and asking the country to support it. Grand Duke Michael chooses not to accept the throne unless he is bid to do so by the Assembly. The Provisional Government forbids the use of force against rioting peasants.
Mar. 16	Constituent assembly meets; abdication of Grand Duke Michael.
Apr. 11	All-Russian Conference of Soviets overwhelmingly votes to continue war in spite of Bolshevik opposition.
Apr. 16	Lenin arrives back in Petrograd.
May 3–5	Bolshevik-organised demonstrations by garrison in Petrograd against the Ministers Guchkov and Milyukov. Kornilov resigns command of forces in Petrograd, and Milyukov and Guchkov resign from the government.
May 18	Kerensky helps to reorganise provisional government.
June 18	Start of renewed offensive on southern front.
June 26	Soldiers at front refuse to obey orders. Kornilov insists on offensive being called off and is appointed commander-in-chief.
July 2	Start of northern offensive backed by Kerensky, Minister of War. Germans and Austrians drive Russians back after early successes.
July 12	Provisional government restores capital punishment and courts martial.
July 16–18	Bolsheviks organise demonstrations by sailors and Red Guards but the unrest is put down by loyal troops.
July 18	Fearing arrest, Lenin flees to Finland.
July 20	Lvov and Kadet ministers resign.
July 21	Formation of new government with Kerensky as Prime Minister.
Aug. 1	Kornilov appointed Commander-in-Chief.
Aug. 3	Kerensky resigns. Party leaders give him a free hand to form new government.
Aug. 25–28	Kerensky holds Moscow State Conference to settle differences with Kornilov, but fails to reach agreement.
Sept. 3	Riga falls to Germans.
Sept. 8	Troops begin to move against Petrograd, and Kerensky denounces Kornilov 'plot' against the government. Collapse of movement followed by arrest of Kornilov and fellow generals.
Sept. 19	Bolshevik majority in Moscow Soviet.
Oct. 6	Trotsky becomes Chairman of Petrograd Soviet.
Oct. 23	Decision by Bolshevik Central Committee to organise an armed rising.
Oct. 25	Formation of Military Revolutionary Committee by Bolsheviks.
Nov. 1	Provisional government tries to remove units from the Petrograd garrison, but Bolsheviks prevent this.
Nov. 2	Parliament refuses to give Kerensky powers to suppress the Bolsheviks.

Nov. 6	Bolsheviks organise headquarters in Peter and Paul fortress and move on strategic points. Lenin takes command.
Nov. 7	Bolsheviks seize power in Petrograd, taking key installations and services. The Winter Palace cut off and ministers of provisional government arrested. Kerensky flees. Lenin announces the transfer of power to the Military Revolutionary Committee and the victory of the socialist revolution.
Nov. 8	Lenin makes the Decree on Peace, an appeal for a just peace without annexations and indemnities, and the Decree on Land, affirming that all land is the property of the people. A Bolshevik government is formed.
Nov. 13	Counter-offensive by Kerensky against Petrograd fails.
Nov. 15	Bolsheviks establish power in Moscow.
Dec. 1	Left-wing social revolutionaries enter government after agreement with Bolsheviks.
Dec. 2	Escape of Kornilov and fellow generals from prison in Bykhov.
Dec. 3	Bolsheviks occupy Supreme Headquarters at Mogilev.
Dec. 17	Russia and Germany agree a ceasefire and start negotiations for a peace treaty in Brest-Litovsk (22nd).
Dec. 20	Establishment of the *Cheka*.
1918 Jan. 18	Opening of Constituent Assembly.
Jan. 19	Constituent Assembly dispersed.
Feb. 1–14	Introduction of the Gregorian calendar.
Feb. 9	Central Council of the Ukraine concludes separate peace with Central Powers having declared its independence.
Feb. 10	Brest-Litovsk negotations broken off after German ultimatum.
Feb. 18	Germany resumes hostilities in the Ukraine.
Feb. 24	Soviet government decides to accept German peace ultimatum.
Mar. 2	Germans occupy Kiev.
Mar. 3	Russians sign Treaty of Brest-Litovsk, giving up large areas of pre-Revolutionary Russia (see p. 194). German troops continue to advance into central Russia and the Crimea.
Mar. 12	Soviet government moves from Petrograd to Moscow.
Mar. 13	Trotsky appointed Peoples Commissar of War.
Apr. 5	Allied ships and troops arrive in Murmansk.
Apr. 13	Kornilov killed fighting with anti-Bolshevik 'Volunteer army'. Bolsheviks mount drive against anarchists and other deviant elements. Germans take Odessa.
Apr. 14	Germans and Finns occupy Helsinki.
Apr. 29	Germans set up puppet Ukrainian government.
May	Georgia, Armenia, and Azerbaidjan declare independence.
May 8	Germans occupy Rostov.
May 14	Czech Legion (ex-prisoners recruited into service

against the Central Powers) clash with Soviets at Chelyabinsk on their way to Vladivostock.

May 25	Revolt of Czech Legion who seize eastern part of Trans-Siberian Railway.
May 29	Partial conscription introduced for Red Army.
June 23	Allied reinforcements arrive in Murmansk.
July 16	Execution of Imperial family at Ekaterinburg.
Aug. 2	Establishment of anti-Bolshevik government at Archangel, followed by landing of more troops.
Aug. 6	White forces take Kazan.
Aug. 14	Allied forces land at Baku. British, Japanese and American forces land at Vladivostock.
Sept. 10	Bolsheviks take Kazan.
Sept. 13	Allied forces leave Baku.
Sept. 23	'White' forces set up Directorate as All Russian provisional government.
Oct. 9	Directorate fixes capital at Omsk.
Nov. 13	Following armistice between allies and Germany, the Soviet government denounces the Brest-Litovsk Treaty.
Nov. 18	Directorate suppressed at Omsk. Kolchak assumes supreme power.
Dec. 14	Collapse of Skoropadsky regime in the Ukraine.
Dec. 17	French land in Odessa.
1919 Jan. 3	Red Army takes Riga and Kharkov.
Feb. 6	Red Army occupies Kiev.
Feb. 15	Denikin assumes supreme command of white forces in south-east Russia.
Mar. 2–7	First Congress of Communist International in Moscow. Creation of Politburo and Communist International.
Mar. 13	Spring offensive by Kolchak.
Mar. 21	Allies decide to withdraw forces from Russia.
Apr. 5	British and Indian troops leaves Transcaspia.
Apr. 8	French evacuate Odessa.
Apr. 10	Soviet troops enter Crimea.
May 19	Denikin begins offensive against Bolsheviks.
June 4	Kolchak defeated in centre and south, but Denikin continues advance, capturing Kharkov by end of month.
July 15	Red Army takes Chelyabinsk.
Aug. 23	Denikin takes Odessa.
Aug. 31	Denikin occupies Kiev.
Sept. 19	Allies evacuate Archangel.
Sept. 28	Yudenich reaches suburbs of Petrograd.
Oct. 14–20	Denikin takes Orel, but is forced to retreat; general retreat of White armies.
Nov. 14	Defeat of Yudenich by Red Army and occupation of Omsk.
Dec. 12	Red Army occupies Kharkov.
Dec. 16	Red Army occupies Kiev.
1920 Jan. 4	Abdication of Kolchak as Supreme Ruler.
Jan. 8	Red Army takes Rostov.

Jan. 15	Czechs hand Kolchak over to revolutionaries in control of Irkutsk.
Feb. 7	Execution of Kolchak.
Feb. 19	Northern government at Archangel collapses.
Apr. 4	Denikin succeeded by Wrangel.
Apr. 24	Outbreak of Russo–Polish War. Poles invade the Ukraine.
May 6	Polish forces take Kiev.
June 12	Red Army retakes Kiev.
July 11	Russian counter-attack takes Minsk and Vilna (14th).
July 20	Second Congress of Communist International.
Aug. 17	Russian forces almost reach Warsaw; beaten back by Polish counter-offensive.
Sept. 21	Start of Russo–Polish peace negotiations.
Oct. 12	Russo–Polish provisional peace treaty.
Oct. 25	Red Army offensive against Wrangel.
Nov. 2	Wrangel forced to retreat to the Crimea.
Nov. 11–14	Defeat and evacuation of Wrangel's forces in the Crimea.
1921 Feb.	Strikes in Petrograd. Red Army invades Georgia.
Mar. 1	Beginnings of revolt of Kronstadt sailors.
Mar. 5	Trotsky delivers ultimatum to sailors.
Mar. 16–17	Bombardment and assault of Kronstadt.
Mar. 18	Kronstadt Rising crushed. Treaty of Riga defines Russo-Polish frontier. 10th Party Congress; Lenin introduces New Economic Policy (NEP), allowing peasants to keep their surplus grain for disposal on the open market.
Apr.	Beginnings of famine in the Volga regions.
Aug.	Famine relief agreements signed with America and the Red Cross.
1922 Mar.–Apr.	11th Party Congress. Stalin becomes General Secretary. Lenin forced to convalesce after operation to remove two bullets, the result of Kaplan's attempted assassination in 1918.
Apr. 16	Treaty of Rapallo with Germany establishes close economic and military co-operation.
May 26	Lenin has stroke.
Oct. 2	Lenin returns to Moscow.
Dec.	Lenin's second stroke.
Dec. 23–26	Lenin dictates the *Letter to the Congress*.
Dec. 30	Formation of Union of Soviet Socialist Republics, federating Russia, the Ukraine, White Russia and Transcaucasia.
1923 Jan. 4	Lenin adds codicil to the *Letter*, warning of Stalin's ambitions.
Mar.	Lenin's third stroke.
Apr.	12th Party Congress.
July	Constitution of USSR published.
1924 Jan. 21	Death of Lenin.

Russia, 1924–1953

1924	Jan. 21	Death of Lenin.
	Feb. 1	Great Britain recognises Soviet Union.
	Feb. 3	Rykov elected prime minister.
	May 23	13th Party Conference opens. Zinoviev demands Trotsky's recantation of belief in 'Permanent Revolution'.
1925	Jan. 16	Trotsky dismissed as War Commissar.
	Jan. 21	Japan recognises Soviet Union.
	Apr.	14th Party Conference adopts 'socialism in one country'.
1926	Oct. 19	Trotsky and Kamenev expelled from Politburo.
1927	May 26	Britain temporarily severs relations with Soviet Union because of continued Bolshevik propaganda.
	Nov.	Trotskyists organise political demonstrations and Trotsky expelled from Party.
	Dec.	15th Party Conference condemns all deviations from party line and resolves upon the collectivisation of agriculture. Stalin emerges as dominant voice.
1928	Jan.	Trotsky banished to provinces.
	Spring	Serious grain procurement crisis.
	Sept.	Bukharin publishes opposition articles in *Pravda* in support of peasants.
	Oct. 1	Beginning of First Five Year Plan aiming to develop heavy industries.
	Nov.	Bukharin and Tomsky exiled to Turkey.
1929	Jan.	Trotsky exiled to Turkey.
	Autumn	Start of forced collectivisation and dekulakisation.
	Nov. 17	Bukharin and other 'rightists' expelled from Party.
1930	Jan.	Quickening of tempo of collectivisation; resistance harshly dealt with by force and deportation. Widespread disorder and destruction in rural areas.
	Mar.	Stalin publishes *Dizzy with Success* calling for slowing down of collectivisation.
	Nov.–Dec.	Trial of so-called 'Industrial Party' for alleged conspiracy within the State Planning Commission Gosplan.
1931	Mar.–July	Trial of Mensheviks. Harvest failure as a result of chaos of collectivisation.
1932	Apr.	Central Committee resolves reform of literary artistic organisations. Beginnings of famine in Ukraine and other parts of Russia.
	Dec.	Introduction of internal passport.

1933 Nov.	Second Five-Year Plan inaugurated. USA recognises the Soviet government.
1934 Jan.	17th Party Conference.
July	GPU (former *Cheka*) reorganised as NKVD.
Sept.	USSR joins League of Nations.
Dec.	Assassination of Kirov by Nikolayev leads Central Executive Committee to issue a directive ordering summary trial and execution of 'terrorists' without appeal.
Dec. 28–29	Nikolayev and 13 'accomplices' tried in secret and executed.
1935 Jan.	Zinoviev, Kamenev and 17 others tried in secret for 'moral responsibility' for Kirov's assassination and sentenced to imprisonment. Widespread arrests of 'oppositionists'.
Feb.	Statute regulating collective farms promulgated. Commission appointed to draw up a new constitution.
June	Draft constitution presented to Central Committee for approval.
Aug.	'Stakhanovite' programme launched to encourage industrial production.
Sept.	Reintroduction of ranks in Red Army.
Dec.	Central Committee declares that the purge is complete.
1936 Jan.	Renewed purge of party members.
Aug. 19–24	Trial and execution of Zinoviev, Kamenev and other members of the 'Trotskyite – Zinovievite Counter-Revolutionary Bloc' for alleged plotting against the leadership. Tomsky commits suicide following accusations made at their trial.
Sept. 25	Yagoda dismissed as head of NKVD and replaced by Yezhov.
Dec. 5	Eighth Congress of Soviets approves the new Constitution.
1937 Jan.	Trial of Radek, Pyatakov and 15 others for alleged conspiracy with Trotsky and foreign powers to overthrow the Soviet system. Four are imprisoned, the rest shot.
Mar.	Bukharin, Rykov and Yagoda expelled from the Party.
June	Tukachevsky, Chief of the General Staff, and other senior officers tried in secret for plotting with Germany and executed. Widespread purge of the armed forces begins, removing over 400 senior officers.
1938 Mar. 2–13	Third Five-Year Plan inaugurated. Trial of Bukharin, Rykov, Krestinsky, Rakovsky, Yagoda, and other leading party and NKVD members for terrorism, sabotage, treason and espionage.
Mar. 28	Stalin offers support to Czechoslovakia if attacked.
Mar. 9	Russia offers to assist Czechoslovakia if Romania and

	Poland will allow the passage of Russian troops across their territory; both refuse.
Dec.	Beria succeeds Yezhov as head of NKVD.
1939 Mar.	18th Party Congress.
Apr. 18	USSR proposes defence alliance with Great Britain and France. Offer not taken up by the western allies.
May 3	Molotov replaces Litvinov as commisar of foreign affairs in the USSR.
Aug. 12	Anglo–French mission to USSR begins talks in Moscow.
Aug. 18	Germany makes commercial agreement with USSR.
Aug. 22	Ribbentrop, German Foreign Minister, arrives in Moscow.
Aug. 23	Nazi-Soviet Pact signed. A non-aggression pact, it also contains secret clauses on the partition of Poland and allocation of Finland, Latvia, Estonia and Bessarabia to Soviet sphere of influence.
Aug. 31	Supreme Soviet ratifies German non-aggression pact.
Sept. 17	Red Army invades eastern Poland.
Sept. 22	Red Army occupies Lvow.
Sept. 28	Secret accord with Germany transfers Lithuania to Soviet sphere of influence.
Sept. 29–Oct. 10	Estonia, Latvia, and Lithuania conclude treaties with USSR allowing Soviet military bases in their territory.
Oct. 12	Talks in Moscow between Finland and USSR. Stalin presents his territorial demands.
Nov. 9	Finns reject Soviet demands.
Nov. 29	USSR breaks off diplomatic relations with Finland.
Nov. 30	Russians bomb Helsinki and Red Army crosses Finnish frontier.
Dec.	Finnish forces inflict heavy defeats on Russia in the south and east.
1940 Feb. 1–12	Major Russian offensive on Karelian isthmus.
Mar. 12	Treaty of Moscow concludes war. Finns cede 10 per cent of their territory including the Karelian Isthmus and territory in the north-east.
June 15–17	Soviet troops occupy Lithuania, Latvia, and Estonia.
June 28	Soviet troops occupy Bessarabia and north-eastern Bukovina.
July 21	Lithuania, Latvia, and Estonia 'request' incorporation into USSR.
Nov. 17	USSR demands control of Bulgaria and withdrawal of German troops from Finland before joining Tripartite Pact of Germany, Italy and Japan.
Dec. 18	Hitler issues directive for Operation Barbarossa, the invasion of Russia.
1941 Apr. 13	Non-aggression Pact signed with Japan.
June 22	Germany invades USSR.
June 29	State Defence Committee formed.
July 3	Stalin broadcasts to the people.

July 12	Anglo–Soviet mutual assistance agreement signed.
July 15	Fall of Smolensk.
Aug. 7	Stalin becomes Supreme Commander of the Soviet Armed Forces.
Sept. 8	Kiev captured.
Oct. 2	German offensive against Moscow opens.
Oct. 19	Declaration of state of siege in Moscow. Stalin remains in city, though thousands are evacuated or flee in panic.
Nov. 27	German forces come within 20 miles of Moscow.
Dec. 5	Russian counter-offensive in Moscow sector. Hitler abandons Moscow offensive for winter.

1942 Mar.	Soviet winter offensive ends.
June 28	German offensive in the south.
Aug. 9	German Army Group A reach Caucasus.
Sept.	Army Group B reaches Stalingrad.
Nov. 23	Army Group B surrounded by Russian offensive.

1943 Feb. 2	Last German forces surrender at Stalingrad.
May	Comintern dissolved as a gesture of reassurance towards western allies.
July 5	Beginning of Operation Citadel, the German attack on the Kursk Salient. Counter-attack by Red Army (from 12 July) begins fresh Soviet advance.
Aug. 23	Kharkov captured by the Red Army. End of the battle of Kursk.
Sept.	Re-establishment of Patriarchate and Church administration in Russia. Seminaries and many churches reopened.
Sept. 25	Smolensk recaptured.
Nov. 6	Red Army recaptures Kiev.
Nov. 28–Dec. 1	Roosevelt, Churchill and Stalin meet at Tehran.

1944 Jan. 27	Siege of Leningrad lifted.
Mar.	Red Army enters Poland.
Mar. 26	Red Army enters Romania.
Aug. 1	Home army rises in Warsaw but receives no support from Russian forces. Rising quelled by October.
Aug. 24	Romania accepts Armistice terms.
Sept. 8	Russians enter Bulgaria.
Sept. 26	Estonia occupied by the Russians.
Oct. 6	Russians enter Hungary and Czechoslovakia.
Oct. 15	Russo–Bulgarian armistice.

1945 Jan. 12	Final Red Army offensive begins.
Feb. 4–11	'Big three', Churchill, Roosevelt, and Stalin meet at Yalta.
Apr. 13	Russian forces reach Vienna.
Apr. 16	Russians begin final drive on Berlin.
May 9	Surrender of Germany. Victory day in the Soviet Union.
July 17–Aug. 1	Potsdam meeting of Stalin, Truman, and Churchill (Attlee after 27 July).

1946		Fourth Five-Year Plan inaugurated.
	Aug.	Central Committee establish party high schools.
	Sept.	Decree that all land being privately cultivated to be returned to the collectives.
1947 Sept.		Cominform established.
	Dec.	Currency reform.
1948 Jan.		Solomon Milhoels, Chairman of the Jewish State Theatre in Moscow murdered.
	June	Yugoslavia expelled from Cominform.
	Autumn	Purge of Leningrad party following death of Zhdonov.
	Nov.	Dissolution of Jewish Anti-Fascist Committee.
1948		Beginnings of collectivisation in Baltic provinces.
1949		Closure of Jewish State Theatre in Moscow and arrest of leading Yiddish cultural figures.
1951		Fifth Five-Year Plan inaugurated.
1953 Jan.		'Doctors' Plot' announced, alleged to have planned 'to wipe out the leading cadres of the USSR' by medical means.
	Mar. 5	Death of Stalin: Malenkov becomes prime minister.
	July	Arrest and execution of Beria.
	Sept.	Khrushchev confirmed as First Secretary.

Spain, 1909-1939

1909 July 26	*Semana Tragica*. Committee of anarchists and socialists call a general strike in Barcelona. The strike is accompanied by the burning of ecclesiastical property, especially convents.
July 31	Strike suppressed with over 100 deaths.
1912 Dec. 12	Canalejas, Spanish Premier, murdered by anarchists in Madrid.
1917 Aug. 13	General strike in Spain, calling for Catalan independence.
1921 Mar. 8	Dato, Spanish Premier, murdered by anarchists in reprisal for police actions against anarcho-syndicalists in Catalonia, following widespread campaign of terror and assassination.
1923 Dec. 14	Primo de Rivera assumes Spanish dictatorship, supported by military and middle classes and with acquiescence of King Alfonso XIII.
1930 Dec. 28	The King accepts the resignation of Primo de Rivera, following Spain's deteriorating economic condition and failure to achieve progress towards constitutional government.
1931 Apr. 14	King Alfonso XIII abdicates. Spain becomes a constitutional republic.
May 10	Left-wing Republican, Azana, becomes Premier.
Oct. 20	'Protection of the Republic' Law passed in Spain.
Dec. 9	Spanish Republican Constitution introduced; Zamora elected President.
1933 Jan. 2–12	Rising of anarchists and syndicalists in Barcelona.
Nov. 19	Spanish Right wins elections to the Cortes. Foundation of *Falango Española* by José Antonio Primo de Rivera (son of the dictator, Primo de Rivera).
1934 Jan. 14	Catalan elections won by the Left.
Oct. 4	Right forms a Ministry; followed by Socialist rising in Asturias and Catalan separatist revolt in Barcelona. Moroccan troops used to suppress risings with great ferocity.
1936 Feb. 16	Popular Front wins elections: Azana elected President and re-establishes 1931 constitution. Amnesty granted to rebels of 1934; growing clashes between left and right with assassinations and attacks on church property.
Apr. 20	Cortes dismiss President Zamora.
May 10	Azana elected Spanish President, although large

	numbers of voters boycott the elections.
July 17–18	Outbreak of Spanish Civil War with rising of the army in Morocco under General Franco; revolt spreads to mainland led by General Mola.
July 19	Rebels reject offer of a cease-fire and the formation of an all-party national government. Republican Giral government formed and orders arming of revolutionary organisations.
July 20–31	Republican forces seize the Montana barracks in Madrid and secure Catalonia, the Basque country and much of the south. The rebels, or Nationalists, overrun Morocco, parts of southern Spain and much of the north.
July 26	Léon Blum declares that France cannot intervene on behalf of the Republic. Communist Comintern decides to raise international force of volunteers – the International Brigades – for service in Spain. Hitler offers aircraft and supplies to the Nationalists, as does Mussolini.
Aug. 6	France and Britain submit draft 'non-intervention' agreement to the European powers.
Aug. 19	Britain imposes embargo on arms to Spain.
Aug. 21	Italy accepts non-intervention, but makes exceptions for 'volunteers' and financial support.
Aug. 23	Germany accepts non-intervention, as does the Soviet Union, although both continue to supply advisers and other support.
Sept. 4	Formation of Largo Caballero government in Madrid, composed of Republicans, Socialists and Communists.
Sept. 27	Nationalists capture Toledo.
Oct. 1	Nationalists appoint Franco Generalissimo and head of state.
Oct. 22	Most of Spanish gold reserves shipped to the Soviet Union. Russian advisers supervise reorganisation of Republican army and appoint political commisars.
Nov.	Nationalist forces advance on Madrid. Air raids on Madrid and Republican forces by German Condor Legion. First International Brigades go into action and assist in repelling Nationalist advance. Republican government moves to Valencia.
Nov. 18	Germany and Italy recognise Franco government.
Dec. 16	Protocol signed in London by major powers agreeing non-intervention in Spain.
1937 Feb. 8	Malaga falls to Nationalists.
Mar. 3–12	Republican government orders disarming of workers' and anarchist militias in Catalonia following clashes between them and the communists.
Mar. 20–23	Battle of Guadalajara. Republicans defeat Italian forces advancing on Madrid.
Apr. 19	Franco orders unification of the Nationalist movement, fusing the Falange and other political bodies into a single political body, and para-military groups into a militia responsible to the army.

Apr. 26	German Condor Legion destroys town of Guernica in Basque country.
Apr. 30– May 6	Street fighting in Barcelona between workers' militias and Republican-Communists.
May 15	Largo Caballero resigns in opposition to communist call for greater control and suppression of rival groups.
May 17	Negrin government formed with backing of Comintern to pursue victory by means of Communist control of the Republican forces.
June 18	Anarchist militia (POUM) dissolved and leaders arrested; anti-Stalinist leader, Nin, executed.
June 19	Nationalists capture Basque capital of Bilbao.
July 5–28	Failure of Republican offensive at Brunete to restore position in north.
Sept. 10–14	Following attacks on shipping by Italian submarines and aircraft. Nyon Conference of nine European powers agree to patrol the Mediterranean and sink submarines attacking non-Spanish ships. Italy and Germany do not attend, but sinkings cease.
Oct. 17	Largo Caballero denounces repressive policies of Negrin government.
Oct. 20–22	Franco's forces complete reduction of north-west with capture of Gijon and Oviedo.
Oct. 31	Republican government moves to Barcelona.
Dec. 15–26	Republican forces go over to the offensive at Teruel to avert threat to Madrid.
1938 Feb. 5–22	Nationalists launch counter-offensive at Teruel; recaptured (23rd). Nationalist offensive in Aragon.
Mar.	Nationalists begin advance from Aragon to the Mediterranean with aim of cutting Republican territory in half and achieve rapid early success.
Apr. 15	Nationalist forces reach Mediterranean at Vinaroz, cutting off Catalonia from the rest of Republican Spain.
Apr.–May	Opening of French frontier permits some resupply of Republican forces. 200,000 new conscripts called up and organised on flanks of the Nationalist corridor.
July–Aug.	Last Republican offensive on the Ebro forces Franco to suspend attack on Valencia.
Aug.	Basque and Catalan separatist ministers resign from Negrin ministry.
Nov. 15	Last Republican forces driven out of Ebro bridgehead.
Dec.	Nationalists begin offensive against Catalonia.
1939 Jan. 26	Fall of Barcelona to Nationalist forces.
Feb. 7	President Azana goes into exile in France (resigns on 24th).
Feb. 9	End of resistance in Catalonia by Republican forces; over 200,000 cross French frontier and are disarmed. Negrin makes last attempts to obtain a negotiated peace without reprisals.
Feb. 26	Negrin tries to organise last stand of Republic at Cartagena naval base.

Mar. 4	Negrin appoints communist military leaders to key defence positions.
Mar. 5–12	Military commander in Madrid, Casado, leads rebellion against Negrin government on account of its communist domination and sets up a National Defence Council. On Comintern instructions, communists attempt to defeat the rebellion, but are themselves defeated by non-communist elements. Negrin flees to France.
Mar. 23	Casado sends emissaries to Nationalist capital in Burgos to negotiate peace terms. Franco demands surrender of Republican Air Force by 25 March and rest of armed forces by 27 March.
Mar. 25	Franco breaks off negotiations because his terms not met.
Mar. 27	Last meeting of National Defence Council.
Mar. 28	Nationalist forces enter Madrid.
Apr. 1	General Franco announces end to the Civil War.

International background to the Second World War

1933 Jan. 30   Hitler becomes Chancellor of Germany
Mar. 16   Britain's plan for disarmament fails as Germany insists on exclusion of the SA.
Mar. 19   Mussolini proposes pact between Britain, France, Italy and Germany, signed as the Rome Pact.
July 15   Rome Pact binds Britain, France, Germany and Italy to the League Covenant, the Locarno Treaties, and the Kellogg–Briand Pact.
Oct. 14   Germany leaves disarmament conference and League of Nations.

1934 June 14–15   Hitler meets Mussolini for the first time in Venice.
July 25   Austrian Chancellor Dollfuss murdered in Nazi coup.
July 30   Dr Kurt Schuschnigg becomes new Austrian Chancellor.
Dec. 5   Italian and Ethiopian troops clash at Walwal inside Ethiopia.

1935 Feb. 1   Anglo–German conference on German rearmament; Italy sends troops to East Africa.
Mar. 15   Hitler repudiates the military restrictions on Germany imposed by the Treaty of Versailles, restores conscription and announces that the peacetime army strength is to be raised to half a million men. Germany announces the existence of the Luftwäffe.
Apr. 11–14   Britain, France and Italy confer at Stresa to establish a common front against Germany.
May 2   France and the Soviet Union sign a treaty of mutual assistance for five years.
May 16   Czechoslovakia and Soviet Union sign mutual assistance pact.
May 19   Pro-Nazi Sudeten Party makes gains in Czechoslovak elections.
June 18   Anglo–German Naval Agreement. Germany undertakes that her navy shall not exceed a third of the tonnage of the Royal Navy.
June 27   League of Nations Union 'Peace Ballot' in Britain shows strong support for the League.
Sept. 3   League of Nations attempts to defuse the Walwal Oasis incident by stating that neither country was to blame as possession was unclear.
Oct. 2   Italian forces invade Ethiopia.
Oct. 7   League of Nations declares Italy the aggressor in Ethiopia and votes sanctions (11th)
Oct. 19   League of Nations sanctions on Italy come into force.
Dec. 9   Hoare–Laval Pact, lenient to Italy, is met by hostile public reaction in Britain and France.

Dec. 13	Beneš succeeds Masaryk as President of Czechoslovakia.
1936 Feb. 16	Popular Front wins a majority in the Spanish elections.
Mar. 3	Britain increases defence expenditure, principally on the air force.
Mar. 8	German troops reoccupy the demilitarised Rhineland in violation of the Treaty of Versailles.
May 5	Italians take Addis Ababa; Emperor Haile Selassie flees. Italy annexes Ethiopia (9th).
July 11	Austro–German convention acknowledges Austrian independence.
July 18	Army revolt under Emilio Mola and Francisco Franco begins Spanish Civil War.
Aug. 24	Germany introduces compulsory conscription.
Sept. 9	Conference held in London on non-intervention in Spanish Civil War.
Oct. 1	Franco appointed 'Chief of the Spanish State' by the Nationalist rebels.
Oct. 14	Belgium renounces its military pact with France in order to ensure its liberty of action in the face of German reoccupation of the Rhineland.
Oct. 19	Germany begins four-year economic plan to develop its economic base for war.
Nov. 1	Mussolini proclaims Rome–Berlin Axis.
Nov. 18	Germany and Italy recognise Franco's government.
Nov. 24	Germany and Japan sign Anti-Comintern Pact.
Dec. 16	Protocol signed in London for non-intervention in Spain.
1937 Jan. 2	Mussolini signs agreement with Britain ensuring the safety of shipping in the Mediterranean.
Jan. 15	Amnnesty granted for Austrian Nazis.
Feb. 27	France extends Maginot Line.
Mar. 18	Defeat of Italian push on Madrid.
Apr. 27	Basque town of Guernica destroyed by German Condor Legion.
June 18	Spanish Nationalist forces take Bilbao.
June 23	Germany and Italy withdraw from non-intervention committee.
July 17	Naval agreements between Britain and Germany and Britain and Soviet Union.
Sept. 10–14	At Nyon Conference, nine nations adopt system of patrol in Mediterranean to protect shipping.
Oct. 13	Germany guarantees inviolability of Belgium.
Oct. 17	Riots in Sudeten area of Czechoslovakia.
Oct. 21	Franco's forces complete conquest of Basque country.
Nov. 5	Hitler informs his generals in the Hossbach memorandum that Austria and Czechoslovakia will be annexed as the first stage in Lebensraum for Germany.
Nov. 6	Italy joins Anti-Comintern Pact.
Nov. 17–21	Lord Halifax (Lord President of the Council) accepts unofficial invitation to visit Germany where he has

	inconclusive discussions with Hitler on a European settlement.
Nov. 29	Sudeten Germans secede from Czech Parliament following a ban on their meetings.
Dec. 11	Italy leaves the League of Nations.
1938 Feb. 4	Von Ribbentrop becomes German foreign minister.
Feb. 12	At Berchtesgaden Hitler forces the Austrian Chancellor Schusnigg to accept a Protocol promising the release of Nazis in Austria, accepting a pro-Nazi (Seyss-Inquart) as Minister of the Interior and virtually attaching the Austrian army to that of Germany, subject to the consent of Austrian President Miklas.
Feb. 16	Amnesty for Nazis proclaimed in Austria; Seyss-Inquart becomes Minister of the Interior.
Feb. 20	In a speech to the Reichstag Hitler proclaims the need to protect the ten million Germans on the frontiers of the Reich.
Mar. 6	President Miklas of Austria accepts Schusnigg's proposal of a plebiscite on the future independence of Austria. Announced on 9 March, voting was to take place on the 13th.
Mar. 10	Hitler mobilises for immediate invasion of Austria.
Mar. 11	Schusnigg accepts Hitler's ultimatum demanding that the plebiscite not be held.
Mar. 12	German army marches into Austria.
Mar. 13	Austria is declared part of Hitler's Reich.
Mar. 28	Hitler encourages German minority in Czechoslovakia to make such demands as will break up the state.
Apr. 16	In Anglo–Italian pact Britain recognises Italian sovereignty in Ethiopia in return for withdrawal of Italian troops from Spain.
Apr. 24	Germans in Sudetenland demand full autonomy.
Apr. 29	Britain reluctantly joins France in diplomatic action on behalf of the Czech government.
May 9	Russia promises to assist Czechoslovakia in the event of a German attack if Poland and Romania will permit the passage of Russian troops. Both, however, refuse.
May 18–21	German troop movements reported on Czech border; Czech government calls up reservists (20th); and partial mobilisation (21st).
May 22	Britain warns Germany of dangers of military action, but makes it clear to France that she is not in favour of military action herself.
Aug. 3	Walter Runciman visits Prague on mediation mission between Czechs and Sudeten Germans.
Aug. 11	Under British and French pressure, the Czech Prime Minister Beneš opens negotiations with the Sudeten Germans.
Aug. 12	Germany begins to mobilise.
Sept. 4	Henlein, leader of the Sudeten Germans, rejects Beneš's offer of full autonomy and breaks off relations with the Czech government (7th).

Sept. 7	France calls up reservists.
Sept. 11	Poland and Romania again refuse to allow the passage of Russian troops to assist Czechoslovakia.
Sept. 12	Hitler demands that Czechs accept German claims.
Sept. 13	Unrest in Sudetenland put down by Czech troops.
Sept. 15	Chamberlain visits Hitler at Berchtesgaden. Hitler states his determination to annex the Sudetenland on the principle of self-determination.
Sept. 18	Britain and France decide to persuade the Czechs to hand over territory in areas where over half of the population is German.
Sept. 20–21	Germany completes invasion plans. The Czech government initially rejects the Anglo–French proposals, but accepts them on the 21st.
Sept. 22	Chamberlain meets Hitler at Godesberg. Hitler demands immediate occupation of the Sudetenland and announces 28 September for the invasion. The Czech cabinet resigns.
Sept. 23	Czechoslovakia mobilises; Russia promises to support France in the event of her aiding the Czechs.
Sept. 25	France and Britain threaten Hitler with force unless he negotiates.
Sept. 26	Partial mobilisation in France.
Sept. 27	The Royal Navy is mobilised.
Sept. 28	Hitler delays invasion for 24 hours pending a four-power conference at Munich.
Sept. 29	At the Munich conference Chamberlain, Daladier, Hitler and Mussolini agree to transfer the Sudetenland to Germany, while guaranteeing the remaining Czech frontiers.
Sept. 30	Hitler and Chamberlain sign 'peace in our time' communiqué.
Oct. 1	Czechs cede Teschen to Poland. Germany begins occupation of the Sudetenland.
Oct. 5	Beneš resigns.
Oct. 6–8	Slovakia and Ruthenia are granted autonomy.
Oct. 25	Libya is declared to be part of Italy.
Dec. 1	British prepare for conscription.
Dec. 6	Franco–German pact on inviolability of existing frontiers.
Dec. 17	Italy denounces 1935 agreement with France.
Dec. 23	Franco begins final offensive against last Republican stronghold in Catalonia.
1939 Jan. 10	Chamberlain and Halifax visit Rome for discussions with Mussolini.
Jan. 26	Franco's forces take Barcelona.
Feb. 27	Britain and France recognise Franco's government.
Mar. 14	Under Hitler's prompting, the Slovak leader Tiso proclaims a breakaway 'Slovak Free State'.
Mar. 15	German troops march into Prague and occupy Bohemia and Moravia.
Mar. 28	Hitler denounces 1934 non-aggression pact with

	Poland. Spanish Civil War ends with surrender of Madrid.
Mar. 31	Britain and France promise aid to Poland in the event of a threat to Polish independence.
Apr. 7	Italy invades Albania. Spain joins the anti-Comintern Pact.
Apr. 13	Britain and France guarantee the independence of Greece and Romania.
Apr. 15	The United States requests assurances from Hitler and Mussolini that they will not attack 31 named states.
Apr. 16–18	The Soviet Union proposes a defensive alliance with Britain and France, but the offer is not accepted.
Apr. 27	Britain introduces conscription. Hitler denounces the 1935 Anglo–German naval agreement.
Apr. 28	Hitler rejects Roosevelt's peace proposals and denounces the German–Polish non-aggression pact.
May 22	Hitler and Mussolini sign a ten-year political and military alliance – the 'Pact of Steel'.
Aug. 11	Anglo–French mission to the Soviet Union begins talks in Moscow.
Aug. 18	Germany and the Soviet Union sign a commercial agreement.
Aug. 23	Germany and the Soviet Union sign non-aggression pact, with secret clauses on the partition of Poland. Chamberlain warns Hitler that Britain will stand by Poland, but accepts the need for a settlement of the Danzig question. Hitler states that Germany's interest in Danzig and the Corridor must be satisfied. The Poles refuse to enter negotiations with the Germans. Hitler brings forward his preparations to invade Poland to the 26th (from 1 Sept.).
Aug. 25	Anglo–Polish mutual assistance pact signed in London. Hitler makes a 'last offer' on Poland and postpones his attack until 1 September.
Aug. 28–31	Britain and France urge direct negotiations between Germans and Poles, but the Poles refuse.
Aug. 31	Hitler orders attack on Poland.
Sept. 1	German forces invade Poland and annex Danzig. Britain and France demand withdrawal of German troops.
Sept. 2	Britain decides on ultimatum to Germany.
Sept. 3	Britain and France declare war on Germany.

The Second World War

1939 Sept. 1   Germany invades Poland and annexes Danzig.

Sept. 2   Great Britain introduces National Service Bill calling up men aged between 18 and 41.

Sept. 3   Britain and France declare war on Germany.

Sept. 7   Germans overrun western Poland.

Sept. 17   Soviet Union invades eastern Poland.

Sept. 19   Polish government leaves Warsaw.

Sept. 28   Fall of Warsaw.

Sept. 30   Germany and Soviet Union settle partition of Poland. Last of British Expeditionary Force (BEF) arrives in France.

Oct. 6   Peace moves by Hitler rejected by Britain and France.

Oct. 8   Western Poland incorporated into the Reich.

Nov. 3   United States allows Britain and France to purchase arms in US on a 'cash and carry' basis.

Nov. 30   Soviet Union invades Finland.

Dec. 13   German battleship *Graf Spee* forced to scuttle itself off Montevideo after battle of the River Plate.

1940 Mar. 12   Finland signs peace treaty with Soviet Union ceding territory on the Karelian Isthmus and in north-eastern Finland.

Apr. 9   Germany invades Norway and Denmark.

Apr. 14   British forces land in Norway.

May 2   Evacuation of British forces from Norway.

May 10   Resignation of Chamberlain as British premier, replaced by Winston Churchill.

May 14   Dutch army surrenders after bombing of Rotterdam.

May 28   Belgium capitulates.

May 29–   Over 300,000 British and allied troops evacuated from
June 3   Dunkirk.

June–Sept.   Battle of Britain.

June 10   Italy declares war on Britain and France.

June 14   Germans enter Paris. French government moves to Bordeaux.

June 16   France declines offer of union with Britain. Marshal Pétain replaces Paul Reynaud as head of French administration.

June 17–23   Russians occupy Baltic states.

June 22   France concludes armistice with Germany.

June 24   France signs armistice with Italy.

June 27   Russia invades Romania.

July 3   Britain sinks French fleet at Oran.

Aug. 5   Britain signs agreement with Polish government in exile in London and (7th) with Free French under de Gaulle.

Aug. 23   Beginning of 'Blitz' on Britain.

Oct. 7	Germany seizes Romanian oilfields.
Oct. 12	Hitler cancels Operation Sealion for the invasion of Britain.
Oct. 28	Italy invades Greece. Britain offers help.
Nov. 11	Major elements of Italian fleet sunk at Taranto, Sicily.
Dec. 9–15	Italian forces defeated at Sidi Barrani in North Africa.
1941 Jan. 6	F. D. Roosevelt sends Lend-Lease Bill to Congress.
Jan.–Feb.	Further Italian reverses in North Africa.
Feb. 6	German troops under Rommel sent to assist Italians in North Africa.
Apr. 6	German ultimatum to Greece and Yugoslavia. Britain diverts troops from North Africa to Greece.
Apr. 7	Rommel takes offensive in North Africa.
Apr. 11	Blitz on Coventry.
Apr. 13	Stalin signs neutrality pact with Japan.
Apr. 17	Yugoslavia signs capitulation after Italian and German attack.
Apr. 22–28	British forces evacuated from Greece.
May 10	Rudolf Hess flies to Scotland and is imprisoned.
May 27	*Bismarck* sunk by Royal Navy.
May 20–31	German capture of Crete.
June 22	Germans launch invasion of Russia, Operation Barbarossa. Finnish forces attack on Karelian Isthmus.
July 6	Russians abandon eastern Poland and Baltic States.
July 12	Britain and Russia sign agreement for mutual assistance in Moscow.
July 16	Germans take Smolensk.
Aug. 11	Churchill and Roosevelt sign the Atlantic Charter.
Sept. 8	Germans lay siege to Leningrad.
Sept. 19	Germans take Kiev.
Sept. 30–Oct. 2	Germans begin drive on Moscow.
Oct. 16	Russian government leaves Moscow but Stalin stays.
Oct. 30	German attacks reach within 60 miles of Moscow.
Nov. 15	Renewed German offensive takes advance elements within 20 miles of Moscow.
Nov. 20–28	German forces take, but retreat from, Rostov.
Dec. 5	Germans go on to defensive on Moscow front as Russians launch counter-offensive.
Dec. 7	Japanese bomb Pearl Harbor, Hawaii and British Malaya.
Dec. 8	Britain and the USA declare war on Japan.
Dec. 11	Germany and Italy declare war on USA.
1942 Jan. 2	Britain, United States, Soviet Union and 23 other nations sign Washington Pact not to make separate peace treaties with their enemies.
Feb. 1	Pro-Nazi Quisling becomes premier of Norway.
Feb. 6	Roosevelt and Churchill appoint Combined Chiefs of Staff.
Feb. 11	German battleships make Channel 'dash' from Brest to Germany.
Feb. 15	Surrender of Singapore to Japanese.

Mar. 10   Rangoon falls to Japanese.
Mar. 28   RAF destroys much of Lubeck, first major
            demonstration of area bombing.
May 12–17   Russian offensive on Kharkov front defeated.
May 26   Anglo–Soviet treaty signed for closer cooperation.
May 29   Soviet Union and United States extend lend-lease
            agreement.
May 30   First 1,000 bomber raid on Cologne.
June 6   Germans wipe out village of Lidice in Czechoslovakia in
            retaliation for assassination of Gestapo leader Heydrich.
June 10   German offensive in the Ukraine.
June 21   Fall of Tobruk after Rommel's advance in North Africa.
            Eighth Army retreats to El Alamein.
June 25   Dwight Eisenhower appointed Commander-in-Chief of
            US forces in Europe.
July 2   Fall of Sevastopol.
July 28   Germans take Rostov and northern Caucasus in drive
            to take Baku oilfields. Zhukov takes over command of
            southern armies.
Aug. 14   Raid on Dieppe ends in failure.
Oct. 23–Nov. 4   Defeat and pursuit of Axis forces at El Alamein.
Nov. 11–12 Vichy France occupied.
Nov. 19–20 Russians began counterattack at Stalingrad, cutting off
            von Paulus's troops.
Nov. 27   French Navy scuttled in Toulon.
Dec. 29   Final failure of effort by German forces to relieve von
            Paulus.

1943 Jan. 2 German withdrawal from Caucasus begins.
Jan. 14–24 Churchill and Roosevelt meet at Casablanca
            Conference and declare 'Unconditional Surrender'
            required of Germany.
Jan. 31   Paulus surrenders at Stalingrad.
Feb. 2   Last German forces surrender at Stalingrad.
Feb. 8   Russian offensive takes Kursk.
Feb. 14   Russians capture Rostov.
Feb. 16   Russians take Kharkov.
Mar. 15   Russians forced out of Kharkov.
Apr. 20   Massacre of Jews in Warsaw ghetto.
Apr. 26   Discovery of the Katyn massacre and demand by
            Polish government in London for investigation by the
            Red Cross. Stalin breaks off diplomatic relations with
            London Poles.
May 12   Axis armies in Tunisia surrender.
May 17   RAF bombs Ruhr dams causing widespread
            destruction.
June 4   French Committee of National Liberation formed
            under General Charles de Gaulle.
July 4   General Sikorski killed in an air crash.
July 5   Germans launch an offensive on Kursk Salient,
            Operation Citadel.
July 10   Allied landings in Sicily.
July 12   Russian counter-offensive against Orel Salient causes
            Germans to halt Kursk offensive.

July 26	Mussolini forced to resign. King Victor Emmanuel asks Marshal Badoglio to form a government. Secret armistice signed with allies.
Aug. 4	Russians take Orel.
Aug. 23	Russians take Kharkov.
Sept. 3	Allied landings in Italy; Italy surrenders unconditionally.
Sept. 25	Russians take Smolensk.
Nov. 2	Moscow Declaration of Allied foreign ministers on international security.
Nov. 6	Russians take Kiev.
Nov. 28–Dec. 1	Churchill, Roosevelt and Stalin meet at Tehran.
Dec. 20	Britain and USA agree to support Tito's partisans.
Dec. 26	*Scharnhorst* sunk in Barents Sea by British ships.
1944 Jan. 22	Allied landing at Anzio in attempt to by-pass German forces blocking the road to Rome.
Jan. 27	Relief of Leningrad.
Feb. 15	Bombing of Monte Cassino by Allies fails to dislodge German defenders.
Mar. 18	Fall of Monte Cassino to Allied forces.
Apr. 2	Russians enter Romania.
June 4	Fall of Rome to Americans.
June 6	'D-Day' landings in Normandy.
June 13	V-I, 'Flying Bomb', campaign opened on Britain.
July 1	Monetary and financial conference at Bretton Woods, New Hampshire lays foundation for postwar economic settlement.
July 9	Fall of Caen to Allied troops.
July 20	Failure of 'July Plot' to assassinate Hitler.
July 26	Soviet Union recogizes the Lublin Committee of Polish Liberation in Moscow as the legitimate authority for liberated Poland.
Aug. 1	Rising of Home Army in Warsaw. American armies begin breakout from Normandy bridgehead at Avranches.
Aug. 11	Allied landings in Southern France.
Aug. 13–20	German forces destroyed in Falaise Pocket in France.
Aug. 25	De Gaulle and allied troops enter Paris.
Aug. 30	Russians enter Bucharest.
Sept. 4	Ceasefire between Soviet Union and Finland. Armistice signed on 19th.
Sept. 5	Brussels liberated by allied troops.
Sept. 8	V-2 rockets begin landing in Britain.
Sept. 17	Arnhem airborne landings in allied attempt to seize vital river crossings for advance into northern Germany.
Oct. 3	Final suppression of Warsaw rising by German forces.
Oct. 14	British troops liberate Athens.
Oct. 20	Belgrade liberated by Russians and Yugoslav partisans.
Oct. 23	De Gaulle's administration recognised by the allies as provisional government of France.

Dec. 3	Rioting in Athens and British police action sparks off Communist insurrection.
Dec. 16	Germans begin Ardennes offensive, the 'Battle of the Bulge'.
Dec. 31	Regency installed in Greece by British.
1945 Jan. 3	Allied counterattack begins in Ardennes.
Jan. 11	Truce declared in Greek Civil War.
Jan. 17	Russians take Warsaw.
Feb. 4–11	Yalta Conference. Churchill, Roosevelt and Stalin plan for Germany's unconditional surrender, the settlement of Poland, and the United Nations Conference at San Francisco.
Feb. 12	Amnesty granted to Greek Communists.
Feb. 13	Fall of Budapest to Russians.
Mar. 23	American armies cross Rhine at Remagen.
Mar. 28	End of V-Rocket offensive against Britain.
Apr. 3	Beneš appoints a National Front government in Czechoslovakia.
Apr. 20	Russians reach Berlin.
Apr. 25	Renner becomes chancellor of provisional Austrian government.
Apr. 26	Russian and American forces link up at Torgau.
Apr. 28	Mussolini killed by partisans.
Apr. 30	Hitler commits suicide in Berlin. Doenitz is appointed successor.
May 1	German army in Italy surrenders.
May 2	Berlin surrenders to Russians.
May 7	General Jodl makes unconditional surrender of all German forces to Eisenhower.
May 8	Victory in Europe, 'VE' day. Von Keitel surrenders to Zhukov near Berlin.
May 9	Russians take Prague.
May 14	Democratic Republic of Austria established.
June 5	Allied Control Commission assumes control in Germany which is divided into four occupation zones.

Manpower and casualties of major European Powers 1939–1945

	Total mobilised	Killed or died of wounds	Civilians killed
Belgium	625,000	8,000	101,000
Britain	5,896,000	265,000*	91,000[†]
Bulgaria	450,000	10,000	N.A.
Czechoslovakia	150,000	10,000	490,000
Denmark	25,000	4,000	N.A.
Finland	500,000	79,000	N.A.

	Total mobilised	*Killed or died of wounds*	*Civilians killed*
France	5,000,000	202,000	108,000
Germany	10,200,000	3,250,000	500,000
Greece	414,000	73,000	400,000
Hungary	350,000	147,000	N.A.
Italy	3,100,000	149,000	783,000
Netherlands	410,000	7,000	242,000
Norway	75,000	2,000	2,000
Poland	1,000,000	64,000	2,000,000
Romania	1,136,000	520,000	N.A.
Soviet Union‡	22,000,000	7,500,000	6–8,000,000
Yugoslavia	3,741,000	410,000	1,275,000

* Includes overseas troops serving in British forces
† Includes 30,000 merchant seamen
‡ Approximate figures
N.A. Not available

The Cold War and Eastern Europe, 1942–1985

1942 May 26   Twenty year Anglo–Soviet treaty signed but without any territorial agreement for postwar Europe.

June–Aug.   Stalin steps up demands for opening of 'second front' to relieve pressure on Russia.

July   British suspension of convoys to Russia because of losses causes Stalin to accuse allies of lack of genuine support.

1943 Jan. 14–24   Churchill and Roosevelt agree to insist on the 'unconditional surrender' of Germany. The decision to mount an invasion of Italy, agreed by the allied commanders, leads to bitter recriminations from Stalin who sees it as bad faith on the part of the Western powers.

Aug.   Stalin objects to not being consulted about the surrender of Italy and demands a say in the Italian settlement.

Oct.   Three-power foreign ministers' conference in Moscow agrees upon an advisory council for Italy and makes broad plans for a world security organisation.

Nov. 28–
Dec. 1   Meeting of Big Three (Churchill, Roosevelt, and Stalin) at Tehran, the first conference attended by Stalin. As well as discussing arrangements for the allied landings in Europe and a renewed Soviet offensive against Germany, the main lines of a territorial settlement in Eastern Europe are agreed, including the Polish frontiers. No agreement is reached about the future of Germany, although there is discussion of the dismemberment of Germany.

1944 Aug. 21–
Oct. 9   Dumbarton Oaks Conference draws up broad framework of the United Nations.

Sept. 11–17   Churchill and Roosevelt meet at Quebec and move towards acceptance of Morgenthau Plan for the destruction of German industry and the conversion of Germany into a pastoralised state.

Oct. 9–10   Churchill and Stalin meet in Moscow and decide on 'spheres of influence'. Romania and Bulgaria are ceded predominantly to Russian influence, Greece to Britain, and Yugoslavia and Hungary equally between Russia and Great Britain.

Dec. 3   Attempted Communist insurrection in Athens.

1945 Jan. 11   Communists in Greece seek truce.

Feb. 4–11   Meeting at Yalta between Churchill, Roosevelt and Stalin decides upon four occupation zones in Germany, the prosecution of war criminals, and prepares Allied Control Council to run Germany on the basis of 'complete disarmament, demilitarisation and dismemberment'. Removals of national wealth from Germany are to be permitted within two years of the end of the war and reparations are tentatively agreed. Agreement reached that the Provisional government already functioning in Poland, i.e. the Communist Lublin-based group, with the addition of other groups including the London Poles, act as the government. A three-power commission based in Moscow would supervise the setting up of the new regime. The provisional government was pledged to hold free and unfettered elections as soon as possible. Declaration on Liberated Europe signed by three powers to allow European states to 'create democratic conditions of their own choice'.

Feb. 12	Greek Communists granted amnesty and lay down arms.
Apr.	Members of non-communist delegation to the three-power commission in Moscow arrested. Russians conclude a treaty of alliance with the Lublin administration of Poland.
July 5	Great Britain and United States recognise Provisional government of National Unity in Poland.
July 17– Aug. 1	Stalin, Truman, Churchill (after 25 July Attlee) meet at Potsdam and finalise four-power agreement on administration of Germany and the territorial adjustments in Eastern Europe. The Oder–Neisse line is to mark the new boundary between Germany and Poland. Although Germany is to be divided into zones, it is to be treated as a single economic unit. Germans living in Poland, Hungary and Czechoslovakia are to be sent to Germany.
Oct. 28	Provisional Czech National Assembly meets, representing Communist and non-Communist parties.
Nov.	Tito elected President of Yugoslavia.
1946 Mar. 6	Churchill makes 'Iron Curtain' speech at Fulton, Missouri: 'From Stettin in the Baltic to Trieste in the Adriatic, an Iron Curtain has descended upon the Continent.'
May 26	At Czech elections Communists win 38 per cent of the vote and set up a single party 'National Front' government.
May	Fighting breaks out in Northern Greece, marking renewal of civil war between monarchist forces assisted by Britain and communist guerrillas, backed by Albania, Bulgaria and Yugoslavia.
1947 Feb. 21	The British inform the Americans that they cannot afford to keep troops in Greece because of their domestic economic difficulties and intend to withdraw them by the end of March.
Feb. 27	Dean Acheson privately expounds the 'Truman

Doctrine' of economic and military aid to nations in danger of Communist take-over.

Mar. 12   In message to Congress President Truman outlines the Truman Doctrine 'to support free peoples who are resisting attempted subjugation by armed minorities or by outside pressures', effectively committing the United States to intervene against Communist or Communist-backed movements in Europe and elsewhere.

Apr. 22   Truman Doctrine passed by Congress.

Apr. 24   Council of Foreign Ministers in Moscow ends without formal peace treaties for Germany and Austria.

May 22   Congress passes Bill for $250 million of aid for Greece and Turkey.

June 5   George Marshall, American Secretary of State, calls for a European recovery programme supported by American aid.

June 12–15   Non-communist nations of Europe set up Committee of European Economic Co-operation to draft European Recovery Programme.

Aug.   First American aid arrives in Greece, followed by military, 'advisors' to assist in the Civil War against the communists.

1948 Feb. 25   Czech President Beneš accepts a Communist-dominated government.

Mar. 10   Czech Foreign Minister, Jan Masaryk, found dead in suspicious circumstances.

Mar. 14–31   Congress passes the Foreign Assistance Act, the Marshall Plan. $5,300 million of 'Marshall Aid' is initially allocated for European recovery.

Mar. 17   Belgium, France, Luxembourg, The Netherlands and Great Britain sign a treaty setting up the Brussels Treaty Organisation for mutual military assistance.

Mar. 20   Russian representative walks out of Allied Control Council.

Mar. 30   Russians impose restrictions on traffic between Western zones and Berlin.

Apr.   Paris Treaty sets up Organisation for European Economic Co-operation to receive Marshall Aid.

May 30   At Czech elections no opposition parties are allowed to stand and electors called on to vote for a single list of National Front candidates.

June 7   Beneš resigns as President of Czechoslovakia; succeeded by Gottwald.

June 24   Russians impose a complete blockade of traffic into Berlin. Berlin airlift begins (25th).

June   Yugoslavia expelled from Comintern, effectively putting it outside direct Soviet control.

Sept. 5   Head of Polish Communist Party, Gomulka forced to resign.

Nov. 30   Russians set up separate municipal government for East Berlin.

1949 Jan.	Comecon, Communist economic co-operation organisation, set up.
Apr. 4	Creation of NATO. North Atlantic Treaty signed by members of Brussels Treaty Organisation, with Canada, Denmark, Iceland, Italy, Norway, Portugal and the United States. It pledges mutual military assistance.
May 4	Representatives of four occupation powers in Germany come to an agreement for ending of Berlin blockade.
May 12	Berlin blockade lifted.
May 15	Communists take power in Hungary on the basis of a single-list election for the 'Peoples Front', replacing the communist-dominated coalition which had been elected in 1947.
May	Federal Republic of Germany (West Germany) comes into existence.
June	Purge of Albanian Communist Party.
Sept. 30	End of Berlin airlift.
Oct. 16	Greek Communists cease fighting.
Oct.	German Democratic Republic (East Germany) comes into existence.
Nov.	Russian Marshal takes command of Polish army.
Dec. 1949– Jan. 1950	Purge of Bulgarian Communist Party; 92,000 expelled.
1950 May 28	Pro-Stalinist Hoxha confirmed in power in single-list elections in Albania.
May–June	Last non-communists expelled from Hungarian government.
July	Romanian Communist Party admits to expulsion of almost 200,000 members in past two years.
Sept.	United States proposes German rearmament.
1951 Sept.	First Soviet atomic bomb exploded.
1952 Feb. 18	Greece and Turkey join NATO.
May 27	Belgium, France, Italy, Luxembourg, the Netherlands, and West Germany sign mutual defence treaty for proposed creation of a European Defence Community.
1953 Mar. 5	Death of Stalin. Khrushchev confirmed as First Secretary of the Communist Party (September).
June	Risings in East Germany suppressed.
1954 May 5	Italy and West Germany enter Brussels Treaty Organisation.
1954–6	Khrushchev launches 'virgin land' campaign to increase grain output in marginal land.
1955 May 9	West Germany admitted to NATO.
May	Warsaw Pact formed.
1956 Feb.	At Russian Twentieth Party Congress Khrushchev attacks abuses of Stalin era.

June	Workers' riots in Poznan, Poland suppressed; Gomulka becomes First Secretary of Polish United Workers' Party (October).
Oct.–Nov.	General strike and street demonstrations in Budapest. Russians intervene and depose Nagy and crush the rising. Kadar becomes the First Secretary of the Hungarian Communist Party and Premier. Thousands of Hungarian refugees flee to the West.
1958 Feb.	Khrushchev replaces Bulganin as Prime Minister.
1961 Apr.	First manned Soviet space flight. Arrests of dissident writers.
July	Anti-clerical legislation in Russia, restricting role of the clergy in parish councils.
Aug.	Berlin Wall constructed to prevent flight from East to West Berlin.
Oct.	Twenty-second Party Congress; new Party programme and further 'de-Stalinisation', including the removal of Stalin's body from Red Square mausoleum.
1962 Oct.	Cuban missile crisis after Soviet Union attempts to set up ballistic missile bases in Cuba. Imposition of naval 'quarantine' by the United States forces the Soviet Union to back down in the face of the threat of nuclear war.
Nov.	Publication of Solzhenitsyn's *A Day in the Life of Ivan Denisovitch* marks first public recognition of the conditions in Soviet labour camps.
1963 Mar.	Khrushchev warns Writers' Union of 'bourgeois influences'.
Aug. 5	Partial Test Ban Treaty signed in Moscow, banning nuclear weapon tests in the atmosphere, outer space, and under water (in force from October).
1964 Oct.	Brezhnev replaces Khrushchev as First Secretary.
1965 Mar.	Central Committee of the Soviet Union makes a number of agricultural reforms.
Sept.	Central Committee approves further set of economic reforms.
1966 Feb.	Trial of leading 'dissidents', Sinyavsky and Daniel who are given periods of imprisonment.
1967 June	Arab–Israeli 'Six-Day' War leads to acute tension between United States and Soviet Union.
1968 Jan.	Dissidents Ginsburg and Galanskov tried and imprisoned. Dubcek becomes First Secretary of Czechoslovak Communist Party and process of liberalisation begins – 'Socialism with a human face', including decentralisation of economic planning and more open contacts with the West.
July 1	Non-proliferation treaty signed in London, Moscow and Washington.

Aug.	The Soviet Union and the other Warsaw Pact forces invade Czechoslovakia and end the 'Prague Spring'. The Czech leaders are forced to agree in Moscow to the reimposition of censorship, return to centralised planning, and abandon closer links with the West. Husak takes over Party Secretaryship from Dubcek.
1969 Mar.	Dubcek demoted and sent as ambassador to Turkey; he is eventually expelled from the Party and given menial work.
Oct.	Czechoslovakia repudiates its condemnation of the Warsaw Pact invasion and consents to the stationing of Russian troops.
1970 Dec.	Widespread rioting in Poland over food prices and economic conditions; Gierek replaces Gomulka as First Secretary of Polish United Workers' Party.
1971 Feb.	Mass Jewish demonstration at Supreme Soviet building. Jewish emigration to Israel grows.
1972 Jan.	Seizure of documents and leading intellectuals in the Ukraine.
May 26	Visit of President Nixon to Moscow. Strategic Arms Limitation Treaty (SALT 1) signed between United States and Soviet Union on limitation of anti-ballistic missile systems (in force from October) and interim agreement on limitation of strategic offensive arms.
May	Disturbances in Lithuania.
1973 Apr.	Andropov and Gromyko join Politburo.
1974 Feb.	Solzhenitsyn deported from Soviet Union.
1975 Aug.	Helsinki agreement on European Security and Co-operation provides for 'Human Rights'.
Oct.	Soviet physicist and dissident Andre Sakharov awarded Nobel peace prize.
1976 June	Strikes and sabotage in Poland in opposition to attempted price rises which were temporarily withdrawn, although unrest is severely put down.
1977 Jan.	Dissident civil rights group 'Charter 77' formed in Prague.
June	Brezhnev replaces Podgorny as President of the Soviet Union.
1978 July	Trial of Jewish dissident and civil rights activist Shcharansky.
1979 June	Visit of Pope John Paul II to Poland helps to arouse strong national feeling.
Dec.	Soviet invasion of Afghanistan. The United States imposes a grain embargo on Russia. Large commemorative services held in Poland for those killed in the disturbances of 1970.
1980 Jan.	Sakharov sentenced to internal exile in Gorky.

Mar.–Apr.	Dissident groups in Poland advocate boycott of official Parliamentary elections on 23 March and mass commemorative service for Polish officers killed at Katyn in April 1940 leads to arrests.
July	Olympic Games in Moscow boycotted by the United States.
July–Sept.	Widespread strikes amongst Polish workers at Gdansk (Danzig) and elsewhere as a result of rise in meat prices. In August, Gdansk workers publish demands calling for free trade unions. Soviet Union begins jamming of Western broadcasts. Resignation of Babinch as prime minister (24 Aug.) and of Gierek as First Secretary of the Polish United Workers Party (6 Sept.); replaced by Pinkowski and Kania. Gierek's departure followed by the signing of the 'Gdansk agreement' with Lech Walesa, the leader of the Gdansk 'inter-factory committee'. This recognises the new Solidarity unions, grants a wage agreement and promises a 40-hour week, permits the broadcast of church services on Sunday, relaxes the censorship laws, promises to re-examine the new meat scales and review the cases of imprisoned dissidents. National Confederation of Independent Trade Unions, 'Solidarity', formed under leadership of Lech Walesa (8 Sept.) attracts an estimated 10 million members. 'Rural Solidarity' claims an estimated ½ million farmers.
Dec.	Death of Russian Prime Minister Kosygin.
1981 Jan.	Walesa visits Pope in Rome.
Feb.	General Jaruzelski replaces Pinkowski as prime minister.
Dec.	After visiting Moscow General Jaruzelski declares martial law in Poland. The leading members of Solidarity are arrested and the organisation banned.
1982 Nov.	Death of Brezhnev. Andropov becomes First Secretary of the Communist Party of the Soviet Union.
1984 Feb.	Death of Andropov. Chernenko becomes First Secretary of the Communist Party of the Soviet Union.
1985	Death of Chernenko. Gorbachev becomes First Secretary of the Communist Party of the Soviet Union.

The Movement for European Unity

1948   Organisation for European Economic Co-operation (OEEC) set up to receive Marshall Aid from the United States, consisting of Austria, the Benelux (Belgium, Netherlands, and Luxembourg), Denmark, France, West Germany, Greece, Iceland, Ireland, Italy, Norway, Portugal, Spain, Sweden, Switzerland, Turkey and the United Kingdom.

1949   Council of Europe set up for 'political co-operation', consisting of the OEEC states except for Spain and Portugal. A Consultative Assembly is set up with Strasbourg as headquarters.

1950   At Strasbourg, Churchill advocates a single European army, but Macmillan rejects the idea of joining a coal and steel organisation.

1951   Paris Treaty between the Benelux countries, France, Italy and West Germany. 'The Six' sets up a 'common market' in coal and steel. A European Commission is set up as the supreme authority, a Council of Ministers, Court of Justice and an appointed Parliament – the prototype for the European Community.

1953   European Court of Human Rights set up in Strasbourg.

1954   Western European Union proposed by the British as a substitute for a single European army.

1955   Messina Conference of 'the Six' discusses a full customs union. Britain expresses preference for a larger free trade area of the OEEC countries.

1957   The Rome Treaties between 'the Six' set up the European Economic Community (EEC) and Euratom.

1959   European Free Trade Association (EFTA) set up as a counterweight to the EEC, comprising Austria, Denmark, Norway, Portugal, Sweden, Switzerland and the United Kingdom.

1961   Britain, Ireland and Denmark decide to apply for membership of the EEC; Norway in 1962.

1962   Common Agricultural Policy (CAP) agreed between EEC members to come into operation in 1964; a system of high guaranteed prices for European farmers paid for out of a common agricultural fund with protective tariffs against imports.

1963   De Gaulle announces veto on British application for membership. Irish, Danish and Norwegian applications suspended.

1967   Britain, Ireland, Denmark and Norway re-apply to the EEC, but still opposed by de Gaulle.

1970   Plans to enlarge the EEC and give it its own resources are agreed.

1973   Britain, Denmark and Ireland join the EEC but Norway declines to join after a referendum.

1975   Britain confirms membership of the EEC by referendum. Greece applies for membership as do Spain and Portugal.

1979   European Monetary System introduced with a common European Currency Unit (ECU) linking the exchange rates of individual countries. First direct elections held to the European Parliament.

1981   Greece becomes a member of the EEC, phased over five years.

1985   Spain and Portugal sign accession treaty to join the EEC from 1 January 1986.

War, diplomacy and imperialism

Principal European wars and campaigns

First Russo-Turkish War 1768-1774

Turkey declared war on 6 October 1768 after Russian troops burnt the Turkish town of Balta. By 1771 the Russians had occupied Moldavia, Wallachia and the Crimea, but the Pugachev Revolt at home forced them to end the war by the Treaty of Kutchuk Kainardji in 1774, before Turkey was completely defeated.

War of American Independence 1775-1783

Beginning as a struggle between Britain and the American rebels, the conflict increasingly involved European powers after Britain's unexpected defeat at Saratoga (1777). In 1778 France declared war on Britain, and Spain entered the war in 1779. Britain was further isolated by the Armed Neutrality of the North, formed by Russia, Sweden and Denmark in 1780, and by war with Holland, the same year. Military operations took place in India and the West Indies, and Spain besieged Gibraltar, but the decisive battle came in America in 1781, when the French and Americans beat the British at Yorktown. This forced Britain to admit defeat in the Treaty of Versailles of 1783.

The 'Potato War' 1778-1779

Also known as the War of the Bavarian Succession, the war began after Frederick the Great of Prussia invaded Bohemia in order to forestall Austrian claims to Bavaria. The struggle was called the 'Potato War' because no battles occured and the main military efforts were devoted to finding food supplies. In 1779 peace was made at Teschen, by which Austria made only small gains in Bavaria.

The Second Turkish War 1787-1792

Turkey declared war on Russia in August 1787 but Austria joined the Russians in February 1788 and Turkey soon faced major setbacks. In 1788 Austria overran Moldavia and Russia defeated Turkey at sea and in 1789 the scale of the Austro-Russian advance seemed to point to the collapse of Turkey. The Russians, however, were diverted by war with Sweden, and Austria faced diplomatic pressure from Prussia and Britain to make peace. In 1791 Austria agreed to the Treaty of Sistova with Turkey and Russia made peace at Jassy in 1792.

The Russo–Swedish War 1788–1790

In June 1788 Gustavus III of Sweden took advantage of the Turkish War to declare war on Russia, but a mutiny in his army and a Danish invasion prevented the advances he had planned for 1788. Gustavus defeated the Danes and internal opposition, and in 1790 routed the Russian fleet at Svenskund, but he agreed to make peace with Russia soon afterwards on the basis of the pre-war situation.

The French Revolutionary Wars 1792–1799

Austria and Prussia went to war with the French revolutionaries in 1792, but, after initial advances into France, the Prussians were checked at Valmy on 20 September and the Austrians were defeated at Jemappes on 6 November. The French themselves made advances in the Low Countries, Germany and Italy and this, together with the execution of Louis XVI, led to the formation of the First Coalition, between Austria, Prussia, Britain, Spain and Holland in 1793. The coalition had some successes, notably the Austrian victory of Neerwinden in March and the British seizure of Toulon in August, but the French soon retrieved their losses, and the coalition proved disunited. The French war minister Carnot reformed the army, which defeated the Austrians at Wattignies (16 Oct. 1793), overran Holland and invaded Spain and Piedmont. In 1795 Prussia, Spain, Holland and other minor states made peace with France. In 1796–7 the defeat of Austria was completed, mainly thanks to a series of victories by Napoleon Bonaparte in northern Italy, and the Franco–Austrian treaty of Campo Formio was made. Only Britain remained to challenge the French. British landings on the continent, at Toulon and in the Low Countries, had been defeated, but at sea the British were supreme.

The Egyptian Expedition 1798–1801

The expedition was planned as an attempt to defeat Britain by threatening her possessions in the East, and was placed under Bonaparte's control. But, though Bonaparte defeated the Mameluke rulers of Egypt in 1799 in the Battle of the Pyramids (21 July), the British fleet under Nelson destroyed the French fleet in the Battle of the Nile (2 Aug.) and cut Bonaparte's force off from France. An expedition to Syria in 1799 was halted at Acre and Bonaparte decided to return to France. The troops he left behind were forced to surrender to the British in August 1801.

The Napoleonic Wars 1799–1815

The War of the Second Coalition 1799–1802

By early 1799 British diplomacy had brought together the second coalition against France with Russia, Austria, Portugal and Naples.

A series of Allied victories in 1799 in Italy and Germany were soon reversed, however and on 14 June 1800 Bonaparte, now First Consul of France, won a great victory over the Austrians at Marengo. Russia left the coalition in 1800, Austria made peace at Lunéville in 1801, and even the British decided to come to terms with France in 1802 at Amiens.

The War of the Third Coalition 1803–7

In 1803 war again broke out between Britain and France and in 1804 a new anti-French coalition was formed by Britain, Russia, Austria and Sweden. But whilst the British fleet was triumphant at Trafalgar (21 Oct. 1805), the Austrians and Russians were defeated by Bonaparte, who had crowned himself Emperor of France, at Austerlitz (2 Dec. 1805). Austria was forced to make peace, and when Prussia joined the coalition in 1806 she in turn was defeated at Jena-Auerstadt (14 Oct.). Napoleon proved unable to defeat the Russians at Eylau, on 8 February 1807 but had greater success at Friedland on 14 June, after which Russia and Prussia made the peace of Tilsit.

The Peninsular War 1808–1814

In 1808 Napoleon, who had conquered Portugal in 1807, tried to make his brother, Joseph, King of Spain, but the Spaniards resisted and were aided by the British. A British army landed in Lisbon in August and drove the French from Portugal. Although Sir John Moore's expedition into Spain was defeated by Napoleon, Wellington was able to resume the British advance in 1809. His victories at Talavera (1809), Salamanca (1812) and Vittoria (1813) eventually allowed the war to be carried into southern France in 1814. Throughout, the guerrilla war of the Spaniards sapped French morale and assisted Wellington's efforts.

The Austrian War 1809

Austria was encouraged by the Peninsular War to open hostilities against France in April, 1809 but in May Napoleon captured Vienna. The Austrians were able to defeat the French at Aspern (22 May) but Napoleon had his revenge at Wagram (6 July), after which peace was made.

The Russian Campaign 1812

In June, 1812 the peace between France and Russia, which had been established at Tilsit finally broke down and Napoleon invaded Russia. He had early successes, capturing Smolensk (18 Aug.) and worsting the Russians at Borodino (7 Sept.) before taking Moscow (14 Sept.). But the army had already suffered heavy losses and the Russians refused to come to terms. In October Napoleon was forced to abandon Moscow, in the face of winter, and carry out a long retreat through the snow, constantly harassed by the Russians. In all over 500,000 men had taken part in the invasion, but by the time they left Russia in December only several thousand remained in the army.

The Wars of Liberation 1813–14

In March Prussia joined Russia in the war against France, and Sweden soon followed. In May Napoleon won two victories at Lutzen and Bautzen but in August Austria joined the Allies and, despite another French victory at Dresden, Napoleon was finally decisively defeated at Leipzig (16–19 Oct.). The war was carried into France, and despite gallant resistance by Napoleon Paris was taken on 31 March 1814. Napoleon was exiled to Elba.

The Hundred Days 1815

In March, 1815 Napoleon returned from Elba to Paris, regained power, and moved quickly to attack the British, Dutch and Prussian armies in Belgium. He defeated the Prussians at Ligny (16 June) but, on 18 June, was unable to overcome Wellington's Anglo–Dutch army at Waterloo. The Prussians joined the battle late in the day, and helped Wellington rout the French. Napoleon abdicated soon after.

The Third Russo–Turkish War 1806–1812

Turkey declared war due to Russian claims on her territory, but again the Russians proved the dominant power. The imminent danger of war with France induced Russia to sign the Treaty of Bucharest in 1812 in which Turkey lost Bessarabia.

The Spanish Uprising 1820–1823

In early 1820 Spanish troops broke into revolt in order to secure a liberal constitution and forced King Ferdinand VII to agree to their aims. By 1822 Spain was in a state of virtual civil war however and in 1823 a French army invaded and helped restore Ferdinand to full control.

The Greek Revolt 1821–1829

In April 1821 the Greeks rose against Turkish rule and a bitter struggle began in which the Christian powers of Europe were sympathetic to Greek aims. In 1827 Britain, France and Russia agreed to use force against the Turks and on 20 October destroyed their fleet at Navarino. In April 1828 Russia went to war with Turkey and in 1829 the Treaty of Adrianople made Greece an autonomous state.

The Belgian Revolt 1830–1833

The Belgians rose against Dutch rule in August 1830, encouraged by the

July Revolution in France. Britain, France and Prussia, who held a
conference at London in November, favoured ending the Dutch-Belgian
union of 1815 but the Dutch resisted this, and finally had to be coerced
by the great powers to accept Belgian independence in 1833.

The Polish Revolt 1830–1832

In November 1830, encouraged by the revolution in France, Polish
nationalists seized Warsaw. But the Russians would not negotiate Polish
independence and in September 1831 retook Warsaw. In 1832 Poland
became a mere province of Russia and many Poles were sent to Siberia.

The Carlist Wars 1834–1839 and 1872–1876

The First Carlist War broke out in 1834 when regional (largely Basque)
and Catholic groups supported the claims of Don Carlos to the throne of
Spain, instead of his niece, Isabella. Isabella was supported by the army,
liberals and foreign powers (France and Britain) however, and the
Carlists came to heel in 1839. They rose again in 1872, after a Republican
government was established in Madrid, but they again had only local
support. In 1874, with the monarchy restored, the Carlists were confined
to the Basque territories and in 1876 Don Carlos fled into exile.

The Egyptian–Turkish War 1839–1841

In April 1839 war broke out between Mehemet Ali, ruler of Egypt, and the
Turks, to whom he was nominally subject. France showed sympathy for
Ali but Britain, Russia, Austria and Prussia all acted to restore order in
the area. In 1841 peace was made between the two sides and all the
powers joined together in the 'Straits Convention' to settle their
differences over Turkey.

The Hungarian Rising 1848–1849

The Hungarians rose against Austrian control in March, 1848,
encouraged by revolution in France. The Austrians were able to recapture
Budapest in January, 1849 but Hungarian resistance continued, and it
was only with Russian military assistance that the Austrians finally
defeated the rebels in the Battle of Vilagos on 13 August.

The Austro–Sardinian War 1848–1849

Encouraged by revolts elsewhere in Italy and Europe the Sardinians declared war on Austria on 24 March 1848 but were defeated at Custozza in July and agreed to an armistice. In March 1849 Sardinia ended the armistice but was almost immediately defeated at Novara and forced to make peace.

The First Schleswig War 1848–1850

In late March 1848 the provinces of Schleswig and Holstein rose against Danish rule. The Prussians went to the aid of their fellow Germans, and forced the Danes to accept a truce in August. War was revived for a short time in 1849 but peace was finally made the following year.

The Crimean War 1853–1856

In October 1853 Turkey declared war on Russia, and the Turkish fleet was destroyed the following month at Sinope. Britain and France, fearing Russian success, joined Turkey in March 1854 and launched an invasion at the Crimea in September. Bloody battles were fought at Alma, Balaclava and Inkerman before the Russian port of Sevastopol was taken in September 1855. Russia agreed to make peace at Paris in 1856.

The Franco–Austrian War and Italian risings 1859–1861

In 1858 Napoleon III of France agreed to help Sardinia make war on Austria. War was declared in April 1859 and the French proved victorious at Magenta and Solferino in June. But Napoleon, shocked by the bloodshed at these battles, agreed to make peace before Austria was completely defeated. Nonetheless the Sardinians were able to unite most of Italy into a new state by March, 1861 aided by popular risings and the efforts of Garibaldi.

The Polish Rising 1863–1864

The Poles again rose against Russian rule in early 1863 but were unable to gain support from other powers, and by late 1864 the rising had been crushed.

The Second Schleswig War 1864

In February 1864 Austria and Prussia went to war with Denmark over the future of Schleswig–Holstein, and by July had overrun strong Danish defensive fortifications and captured much of the Danish army. The Danes, who had rejected terms offered at a meeting in London in May–June, were now forced to accept peace at Vienna.

The Austro–Prussian War (Six Weeks War) 1866

In June 1866 Prussia declared war on Austria over the future of Schleswig–Holstein, and completely defeated their opponents at Sadowa-Königgrätz on 3 July. Austria managed to defeat Prussia's Italian allies at Custozza (24 June) but had to accept the end of their former domination of Italy and Germany in the Treaty of Prague in August.

The Franco–Prussian War 1870–1871

On 19 July 1870 Napoleon III declared war on Prussia after a disagreement over the Spanish succession. As in the war against Austria, the Prussians completely outmanoeuvred their opponents, capturing most of the French army at Sedan (2 Sept.) and Metz (27 Oct), and bringing the downfall of Napoleon. Paris itself fell in January 1871 and at Frankfurt, in May, the French accepted complete defeat.

The Russo–Turkish War 1877–1878

In 1875–6 revolts had broken out against Ottoman rule in Bosnia and Bulgaria, and the Turks responded ruthlessly. On 24 April 1877 the Russians declared war on Turkey but their invasion stalled with the siege of Plevna, which did not fall until December. By the time the Turks made peace at San Stefano, in March 1878, the great powers were ready to oppose large-scale Russian gains and forced a new settlement in the Balkans at the Congress of Berlin in July.

The Serbo–Bulgarian War 1885–1886

In November 1885 Serbia declared war on Bulgaria but was soon defeated at Slivnitsa and peace was restored, under Austrian influence, on the basis of the pre-war situation.

The Cretan Rising 1896–1898

In May 1896 the Cretans rose against Turkish rule, and gained support from Greece, which declared war on Turkey in April 1897. Within a month the Greeks were defeated but the great powers intervened to ensure that Crete received autonomy in 1898.

The Italo–Turkish War 1911–1912

On 29 September 1911 Italy declared war on Turkey, with the aim of
seizing Cyrenaica and Tripoli (modern Libya) to which they had long
advanced claims. By November they had defeated the Turks in North
Africa and in May 1912 occupied the Dodecanese islands in the Aegean.
Italian finances suffered severely in the war, but Turkey recognised their
gains by the Treaty of Ouchy in October.

The Balkan Wars 1912–1913

Encouraged by Italy's success the Balkan states of Serbia, Bulgaria,
Greece and Montenegro went to war with Turkey in October 1912 and
soon overran most of Turkey-in-Europe. Turkey acknowledged her losses
at London in May 1913 but in June war broke out between Bulgaria, who
felt cheated by the peace, and her Serb and Greek allies, supported by
Turkey and Romania. The Bulgarians were defeated and forced to
surrender territory.

The First World War 1914–1918

On 28 July 1914 Austria–Hungary declared war on Serbia whom she
blamed for the assassination of the Austrian heir to the throne a month
earlier. Austria was supported by her ally Germany, but they were faced
by the 'Entente' powers, Russia, France and Britain. In late 1914
the Germans failed to capture Paris despite the boldness of their invasion
plan (the Schlieffen Plan), and the war settled into the deadlock of trench
warfare. In 1915 the Entente tried to break the deadlock by expeditions to
the Dardanelles and Salonika in south-east Europe, and by inducing Italy
to attack Austria, but to no avail. In 1916 both sides launched grand
offensives on the Western Front, the Germans against Verdun and the
Allies on the Somme, but despite enormous casualties the deadlock
continued. At sea the British and Germans fought the drawn battle of
Jutland. In 1917 both sides were given hope, the Germans by the
Russian Revolution (which eventually removed Russia from the war) and
the Allies by the United States' entry into the war. The next year proved
decisive. The Germans launched a last great offensive in Spring 1918 but
this was halted and American support tipped the scales the Allied way.
Germany agreed to an armistice in November. Her allies, Austria and
Turkey, had already given up the fight, the Austrians defeated at Vittorio
Veneto in Italy and the Turks defeated by the British in Palestine and
Mesopotamia.

The Russian Civil War 1917–1920

In November 1917 the Communists seized power in Russia but were
opposed by the Tsarists and others. In 1918 the victorious Allied powers

intervened to help the Tsarists, but the divisions between the 'White' generals, and the strong central position of the Bolsheviks, ensured that the intervention ended in failure. The Poles, who invaded Russia in April 1919 were able to make gains, following their unexpected victory over the Russians in 1920, and Estonia, Latvia and Lithuania gained their independence, but the Communist government survived.

The Hungarian–Romanian War 1919

In 1919 a Communist government under Bela Kun took power in Hungary. Resentful of the armistice terms proposed by the Allies after the war, the Hungarians invaded Slovakia and the Romanians, fearing that they too would be attacked, attacked Hungary to forestall any further Communist advances. In August the Romanians captured Budapest and Bela Kun fled. The Romanians left in November. In 1920 Hungary's territorial losses were confirmed by the treaty at Trianon.

The Greek–Turkish War 1920–1923

By the treaty of Sèvres, 1920, the Allies handed territory in Asia Minor to Greek control, but the Turks refused to accept this change, and General Mustapha Kemal resisted the Greek occupation. In 1922 he drove the Greeks from their last stronghold at Smyrna, secured control of the area around Constantinople, and overthrew the Ottoman Sultan. In 1923 the Allies renegotiated the peace treaty with Turkey at Lausanne.

The Italo–Abyssinian War 1935–1936

In October 1935 Mussolini invaded Abyssinia (Ethiopia) and caused an international outcry. An Anglo–French plan to partition Abyssinia between its ruler, Haile Selassie, and Italy failed, as did economic sanctions against Italy to force her to end her aggression. In May 1936 the Italian conquest was complete.

The Spanish Civil War 1936–1939

In July 1936 Spanish generals, led by Franco, rose against the Republican government and plunged Spain into civil war. Despite international declarations against foreign involvement, Italy, Germany and Portugal aided the generals and Russia and France helped the Republicans. In addition International Brigades were formed by volunteers from many states to fight for the Republicans, and helped to defeat the Nationalists in the battle of Guadalajara, 1937. But by early 1939 the Nationalists held most of Spain. They finally captured Madrid on 28 March.

The Second World War 1939–1945

Britain and France declared war on Germany on 3 September 1939 following Hitler's invasion of Poland. Poland soon fell and in 1940 Germany overran Denmark. Norway, the Low Countries and, finally, France. Italy joined the Germans, and for a year Britain and her Empire stood alone against the 'Axis' powers. In 1941 however the war was vastly extended, Japan joining the Axis and Russia, China and America joining Britain. The Japanese rapidly overran many of the European colonies in East Asia, but Hitler's invasion of Russia (June 1941) eventually proved a decisive mistake. In 1942 the Germans were defeated in North Africa and Russia, in 1943 the Allies invaded Italy, and in 1944 Britain and America opened the 'Second Front' in France. The Third Reich finally collapsed on 8 May 1945 and in August the Japanese were defeated by the use of atomic bombs.

The Russo–Finnish War (The Winter War) 1939–1940

War broke out on 30 November 1939 over Russian border claims, but Finnish resistance along the Mannerheim Line ensured that Russia's victory was hard-fought. The war ended in March and peace was made at Moscow. In June 1941 the Finns joined the German invasion of Russia but were again defeated.

The Greek Civil War, 1944–9

The Greek Civil War developed out of the rivalry between communist and monarchist partisans for control of Greece as the Axis forces retreated at the end of the Second World War. British troops were sent to aid the pro-monarchist forces in 1944, while the Soviet Union took the side of the communist insurgents. After 1945 American aid enabled British troops to remain in Greece and assist the return of the monarchy. Communist resistance was seriously weakened by the break between Yugoslavia and Russia in 1948 resulting in the closure of much of Greece's northern border to infiltration and aid. The Greek communists announced an end to open conflict in October 1949.

East European Risings since 1945

In 1944–8 Russia established domination of most of Eastern Europe through local Communist parties. There have been risings against Russian control, in East Germany (June 1953), Hungary (October 1956) and Czechoslovakia (1968) but all were put down by Russian troops aided, in the case of Czechoslovakia, by other East European forces.

Wars of Decolonisation since 1945

There have been numerous struggles linked to the process of decolonisation since 1945. Two of the worst defeats were suffered by the French in the Indochina War, 1946–54, and Algeria, 1956–62. The Dutch were forced to recognise Indonesian independence in 1949, the British were forced to abandon Palestine in 1948, and in 1956 the British and French were forced to give up an attempt to reassert control of the Suez Canal. (See also pp. 210–13).

The Partition of Cyprus 1974

In July 1974 a coup in Cyprus brought to power a government favouring 'enosis' (union) with Greece, but Turkey quickly responded by invading the islands to safeguard the Turkish half of the population. An armistice was agreed on 16 August, which left Turkish rule over one third of the island.

Key European treaties and alliances

1763   Treaty of Paris, 10 February, between Britain, France and Spain. France ceded Canada, Grenada and Senegal to Britain. Spain ceded Florida to Britain. Treaty of Hubertusburg, 15 February, between Prussia, Austria and Saxony restored all conquests by the signatories.

1764   Treaty of alliance, 11 April, between Prussia and Russia agreed to make Stanislaus Poniatowski King of Poland.

1772   First Partition of Poland, 5 August, between Russia, Prussia and Austria. Each obtained parts of Poland.

1774   Treaty of Kutchuk-Kainardji, 21 July, ended war between Russia and Turkey. Russia gained territory and rights of navigation in Turkish waters.

1778   Alliance between France and the United States, 6 February.

1779   Treaty of Teschen, 13 May, between Austria and Prussia regarding the future of Bavaria.

1780   Armed Neutrality of the North, August, formed by Russia. Sweden and Denmark, to safeguard shipping from British searches.

1783   Treaty of Versailles, 3 September, between Britain. United States, France and Spain, established American independence. France received Senegal, St Lucia and trading posts in India.

1784   Convention of Constantinople, 6 January, Turkey recognised Russian acquisition of the Crimea. Peace between Britain and Holland, 20 March.

1785   Treaty of Fontainebleau, 10 November, between Austria and Holland, regarding Dutch fortresses.

1788   Treaty of Uddevalla, 6 November. The Danes agreed to evacuate Sweden, which they had invaded.

1790   Convention of Reichenbach, 27 July, between Prussia and Austria regarding Turkey and The Netherlands. Treaty of Varala, 15 August, ended war between Russia and Sweden.

1791   Treaty of Sistova, 4 August, ended war between Austria and Turkey. Declaration of Pillnitz, 27 August, by Austria and Prussia promised intervention against the French revolutionaries if other powers agreed.

1792   Treaty of Jassy, 9 January, between Russia and Turkey established the river Dneister as their mutual border.   Treaty of Berlin, 7 February, between Austria and Prussia promised mutual support in war with France.

1793   Second Partition of Poland, 23 January, by Russia and Prussia.

First Coalition against France formed by Britain, Austria, Prussia, Holland, Spain and Sardinia.

1795   Treaties of Basle between France and Prussia, 5 April, France and Holland, 16 May, and France and Spain, 22 July, effectively marked the defeat of the First Coalition.   Third Partition of Poland, 24 October, by Russia, Prussia and Austria ended Polish independence.

1796   Armistice of Cherasco, 28 April, between France and Sardinia, made Sardinia neutral in the war against France.

1797   Treaty of Campo Formio, 17 October, established peace between France and Austria. Austria recognised French conquests.

1798   Formation of the Second Coalition against France by Britain, Russia, Austria, Portugal and Naples.

1800   Revival of the Armed Neutrality of the North, 15 December, by Russia, Sweden and Denmark.

1801   Treaty of Lunéville, 9 February, established peace between France and Austria.

1802   Treaty of Amiens, 25 March, established peace between Britain and France; Britain obtained Ceylon and Trinidad.

1804   Third Coalition against France by Britain, Russia, Austria and Sweden.

1805   Treaty of Schönbrunn, 15 December, between France and Prussia. Prussia obtained Hanover in return for territorial losses.   Treaty of Pressburg, 26 December, established peace between Austria and France. Austria lost territory to French client states and agreed to pay a war indemnity of 40,000 francs.

1807   Treaty of Bartenstein, 26 April, between Russia and Prussia promised to maintain the war against France.   Treaty of Tilsit, 7 July, established peace between France and Russia, whilst (9th) Prussia ceded all lands west of the Elbe to new Kingdom of Westphalia. Treaty of Fontaineblau, 27 October, between France and Spain, agreed to partition Portugal.

1808   Convention of Cintra, 30 August, allowed French troops to evacuate Portugal without harassment by the British. Conference of Erfurt, 12 October, reaffirmed co-operation between France and Russia.

1809   Sweden ceded Finland to Russia by the Treaty of Fredericksham, 17 September. Treaty of Vienna or Schönbrunn, 14 October, established peace between France and Austria. Austria ceded territory to France and her clients.

1812   Treaty of Abo, 9 April, established an alliance between Russia and Sweden. Treaty of Bucharest, 28 May, ended war between Russia and Turkey, Russia annexing Bessarabia.

1813   Treaty of Kalisch, 27 February, established an alliance between Prussia and Russia against France.   Treaty of Teplitz, 9

September, between Russia, Prussia and Austria agreed on their aims in war against France.

1814   Treaty of Kiel, 14 January, between Sweden and Denmark, exchanged Norway for Swedish Pomerania.   Treaty of Chaumont, 1 March, between Britain, Russia, Prussia and Austria promised not to make a separate peace with Napoleon.   Treaty of Fontainebleau, 6 April, gave Napoleon rule over Elba, and a pension, following his abdication.   Treaty of Paris, 3 May, between France and the Allies reduced France to her 1792 borders and gave territorial concessions to the Allies. A comprehensive peace would be discussed in Vienna.

1815   Britain, Russia, Prussia and Austria formed a new alliance to defeat Napoleon. Act of the Congress of Vienna, 9 June, between Britain, Russia, Prussia, Austria, France, Sweden and Portugal, established a comprehensive peace in Europe, including a complete reorganisation of Germany.   The Holy Alliance, 26 September, between Russia, Austria and Prussia declared the faith of their monarchs in Christian brotherhood.   Second Treaty of Paris, 20 November, reduced France to her 1789 borders, forced her to pay an indemnity and provided for a five year occupation. On the same day Britain, Russia, Austria and Prussia agreed to hold regular meetings in future to discuss pressing problems.

1818   The Quadruple Alliance between Britain, Russia, Austria and Prussia was renewed on 15 November in secret, to safeguard against another possible revolution in France, and these powers declared their intention to maintain their close union.

1820   Troppau Protocol, 19 November, between Austria, Russia and Prussia promised united action if revolutionary changes threatened international order.

1826   Protocol of St Petersburg, 4 April, between Britain and Russia agreed that Greece should become an autonomous state.

1827   Treaty of London, 6 July, between Britain, Russia and France threatened to use force if Turkey did not agree to the Protocol of St Petersburg.

1829   Treaty of Adrianople, 14 September, between Russia and Turkey gave Russia navigation rights in the Straits and confirmed Greek independence. Russia occupied Moldavia and Wallachia.

1833   Treaty of Unkiar Skelessi, 8 July, formed a defensive alliance between Russia and Turkey, but was practically meaningless. Treaty of Berlin, 15 October, between Austria, Russia and Prussia reaffirmed the Troppau Protocol of 1820.

1834   Quadruple Alliance, 22 April, between Britain, France, Spain and Portugal, to re-establish stability in the Iberian peninsula through liberal constitutions.

1839   Treaty of London, 19 May. The great powers guaranteed Belgian neutrality and independence.

1840 Quadruple Alliance, 15 July, between Britain, Russia, Austria and Prussia agreed to protect the Turkish Sultan from being overthrown.

1841 The Straits Act, 13 July, between Turkey, Britain, Russia, Austria, Prussia and France closed the Dardanelles to all but Turkish warships.

1849 Treaty of Milan, 6 August, established peace between Austria and Sardinia.

1850 Treaty of Berlin, 2 July, established peace between Prussia and Denmark.   Convention of Olmutz, 29 November, between Austria and Prussia regarding Schleswig–Holstein and Hesse–Cassel.

1852 Treaty of London, 8 May, between Britain, France, Russia, Austria, Prussia and Sweden guaranteed Danish integrity and decided the Danish succession.

1854 Treaty of alliance, 12 March, between Britain, France and Turkey, made at Constantinople.   Treaty of alliance, 2 December, between Britain, France and Austria, made at Vienna.

1855 Turin military convention, 26 January, between Britain, France and Sardinia, against Russia.

1856 Treaty of Paris, 30 March, between Britain, France, Russia, Turkey, Sardinia, Austria and Prussia ended the Crimean War and neutralised the Black Sea. On 15 April Britain, France and Austria guaranteed Turkish integrity.

1858 Secret alliance between France and Sardinia made at Plombières, 20 July. Paris agreement, 19 August, between Britain, France, Russia, Turkey, Sardinia, Austria and Prussia, united the provinces of Moldavia and Wallachia which later became Romania.

1859 Peace of Villafranca, 11 June, ended war between Austria and France. Sardinia to obtain Lombardy.   Treaty of Zurich, 10 November, between Austria, France and Sardinia, confirmed the peace of Villafranca.

1860 Treaty of Turin, 24 March, between France and Sardinia. French annexation of Nice and Savoy.

1864 Treaty of Vienna, 27 October, between Prussia, Austria and Denmark, ended war between them. The Danish King renounced claims to Schleswig and Holstein.

1865 Convention of Gastein, 14 August, between Prussia and Austria regarding the future of Schleswig and Holstein.

1866 Treaty of Prague, 23 August, established peace between Prussia and Austria. Prussia obtained territory and the leadership of the North German Confederation.   Austria ceded Venetia to Italy.

1870 London agreements between Britain and Prussia, 9 August, and Britain and France, 11 August, confirmed Belgian neutrality.

1871 London agreement, 13 March, between Britain, Russia, Germany, France, Austria–Hungary, Turkey and Italy ended the neutralisation of the Black Sea. Treaty of Frankfurt, 10 May, ended the Franco–Prussian War. France ceded Alsace–Lorraine to Germany, paid on indemnity and was subjected to occupation.

1872   The Emperors of Germany, Austria–Hungary and Russia meeting in Berlin, September, formed the Three Emperors' League (Dreikaisersbund), an informal alliance.

1877   Treaty of Reichstadt, 15 January, between Austria–Hungary and Russia, promised Austrian neutrality in war between Russia and Turkey.

1878   Treaty of San Stefano, 3 March, ended war between Russia and Turkey and created a large, new Bulgarian state. But this was superceded by the terms of the Congress of Berlin, 13 June, between Britain, Russia, Austria–Hungary, Germany, France, Italy and Turkey which created a small, autonomous Bulgaria and semi-independent Eastern Roumelia. Britain obtained Cyprus; Austria–Hungary to administer Bosnia–Herzegovina.

1879   The Dual Alliance, 7 October, between Germany and Austria–Hungary signed in Vienna. Mutual aid in the event of war with Russia; neutrality in the event of war with other powers.

1881   Formal agreements were made under the League of the Three Emperors, 18 June, between Germany, Austria–Hungary and Russia, including a commitment to consultation in the event of problems in the Balkans.   Alliance between Austria–Hungary and Serbia, 28 June, made in Belgrade.

1882   Triple Alliance, 20 May, between Germany, Austria–Hungary and Italy formed in Vienna, extended the Dual Alliance of 1879. Renewed in 1887, 1891, 1902 and 1912. Alliance between Austria–Hungary and Romania, 30 October. Later extended to Germany and Italy. Renewed 1892, 1896, 1902 and 1913.

1884   The League of the Three Emperors was renewed in Berlin, 27 March.

1885   Act of the Conference of Berlin, 26 February, between Austria–Hungary, Belgium, Britain, Denmark, France, Germany, Holland, Italy, Portugal, Russia, Spain, Sweden and Turkey settled claims with regard to colonisation in Africa.

1886   Treaty of Bucharest, 3 March, ended war between Serbia and Bulgaria.

1887   Mediterranean Agreements, 24 March and 16 December, between Britain, Austria–Hungary and Italy, to preserve stability in the Balkans and Mediterranean, made in London. Lapsed in 1896. The Reinsurance Treaty, 18 June, between Germany and Russia, made in Berlin, following the end of the League of the Three Emperors. Neutrality in war with another power. Lapsed in 1890.

1890   Berlin agreement, 1 July, between Britain and Germany on colonies.

1893   'Dual Entente', 27 December, formed between France and Russia in St Petersburg. Mutual aid in the event of war with Germany. Ratified in 1894.

1897   Vienna agreement,17 May, between Austria–Hungary and Russia on policy in the Balkans.   Treaty of Constantinople, 4 December, established peace between Turkey and Greece.

1900   Exchange of letters, 20 March, between Britain, France, Germany, Italy, Russia, the United States and Japan, accepted an open door for trade with China.

1902   Secret treaty between France and Italy, November. Italy to be neutral in any war France was involved in.

1904   Treaty of Sofia, 31 March, established an alliance between Serbia and Bulgaria. The 'Entente Cordiale', 8 April, between Britain and France settled colonial disputes and promised friendship.

1906   Act of the Conference of Algeciras, 7 April, between Austria–Hungary, Belgium, Britain, France, Germany, Holland, Italy, Morocco, Portugal, Russia, Spain, Sweden and the United States regarding the future of Morocco.

1907   'Triple Entente' of Britain, France and Russia came into being with an agreement between Britain and Russia, 31 August, in St Petersburg on areas of influence in Asia.

1911   Berlin Convention, 4 November, between France and Germany gave France predominance in Morocco in return for German gains elsewhere in Africa.

1912   The 'Balkan League' of Bulgaria, Serbia, Greece and Montenegro was formed against Turkey by a series of agreements, February–September. Treaty of Ouchy, 15 October, between Italy and Turkey. Turkey ceded Tripoli and Cyrenaica to Italy.

1913   Treaty of London, 13 May, established peace between Turkey and the Balkan League. Turkey-in-Europe reduced to the area around Constantinople; Albania established. Treaty of Bucharest, 10 August, established peace between Bulgaria, Serbia, Greece, Romania and Montenegro. Bulgaria reduced in size.

1914   London agreement, 15 June, between Britain and Germany concerning the Baghdad railway.   London Declaration, 5 September, by Britain, France and Russia not to make a separate peace with the Central Powers.

1915   Treaty of London, 25 April, between Britain, France and Italy promised Italy territorial gains in return for entering the First World War.

1918   Treaty of Brest-Litovsk, 3 March, between Russia and the Central Powers. Russia ceded territory, and made Finland and the Ukraine independent. Later invalidated.

1919   Treaty of Versailles, 28 June, between Germany and the Allies. Germany ceded territory and all her colonies to the Allies, returned Alsace–Lorraine to France, promised to pay large reparations and had her armed forces restricted. The Rhineland was demilitarised and occupied, and the League of Nations was created. Germany admitted 'war guilt'.   Treaty of St Germain, 10 September, between Austria and the Allies, reduced Austria to a rump state following concessions to Czechoslovakia, Poland, Yugoslavia, Hungary, Italy and Romania, from the old Austria–Hungary. Treaty of Neuilly, 27 November, between Bulgaria and the Allies reduced Bulgaria and provided for reparations payments.

1920   Treaty of Trianon, 4 June, between Hungary and the Allies, reduced Hungary to a rump state and provided for reparations payments.   Treaty of Sèvres, 10 August, between Turkey and the Allies, reduced Turkey in size but was not accepted by the Turks.

1921   Alliance between France and Poland, 19 February. Treaty of Riga, 18 March, between Russia and Poland, ended war between them and defined their mutual border.

1922   Washington Naval Agreement, 6 February, between Britain, France, the United States, Japan, Italy and others restricted the size of navies.   Treaty of Rapallo, 16 April, formed an alliance between Russia and Germany. The 'Little Entente', 31 August, formed between Czechoslovakia, Yugoslavia and Romania under French auspices.

1923   Treaty of Lausanne, 24 July, between Turkey and the Allies replaced the treaty of Sèvres. Confined Turkey to Asia Minor and the area around Constantinople.

1925   Locarno Pact between Britain, France, Germany, Italy and Belgium guaranteed the current West European borders.

1928   Briand–Kellogg Pact, 27 August, between Britain, France, the United States, Germany, Italy and Japan, renounced war as a means to settle disputes. Later adhered to by other states.

1930   London Naval Agreement, 22 April, between Britain, France, the United States, Japan and Italy, expanded the 1922 Washington agreements.

1934   Non-aggression pact, between Germany and Poland, 26 January.

1935   Franco–Italian agreement, 6 January, concerning colonies and Austria. Alliance between France and Russia, 2 May, providing for mutual aid against aggression.   Anglo–German naval agreement, 18 June.

1936   Non-intervention agreement, 7 August, between Britain, France, Germany, Italy, Russia and others, regarding the Anti-Comintern Pact, 25 November, between Germany and Japan.

1937   Italy joined the Anti-Comintern Pact, 6 November.

1938   Munich Agreement, 29 September, between Britain, France, Germany and Italy forced Czechoslovakia to cede territory to Germany, Hungary and Poland.

1939   France and Britain guaranteed Polish integrity, 31 March. 'Pact of Steel', 22 May, between Germany and Italy formalised the Rome–Berlin 'Axis'.   German–Soviet Pact, 23 August, promised Russian neutrality in war involving Germany.

1940 Treaty of Moscow, 12 March, established peace between Russia
      and Finland. Tripartite Pact, 27 September, between Germany,
      Italy and Japan.

1942 Alliance between Britain and Russia, 26 May, promised mutual aid
      against German aggression. Twenty-year term, but abrogated by
      Russia in 1955.

1944 Alliance between France and Russia, 10 December, promised
      mutual aid against German aggression. Twenty-year term but
      abrogated by Russia in 1955.

1945 Yalta Agreement, 11 February, between Britain, Russia and the
      United States on the future of Germany, Europe and world
      security.   United Nations Charter, 26 June, established new
      world security system, with Britain, Russia, France, the United
      States and China as leading powers. Potsdam Agreement, 2
      August, between Britain, Russia and the United States expanded
      on the Yalta Agreement.

1947 Peace Treaties, 10 February, with Italy, Finland, Hungary, Bulgaria
      and Romania.   Treaty of Dunkirk, 4 March, between Britain and
      France promised mutual aid against German aggression. Benelux
      customs union created, 14 March, between Belgium, Holland and
      Luxembourg.

1948 Brussels Treaty, 17 March, between Britain, France, Belgium,
      Holland and Luxembourg providing for mutual aid against
      aggression, economic and social co-operation.   Organisation
      for European Economic Co-operation (OEEC) formed by sixteen
      West European nations, 16 April.

1949 North Atlantic Treaty, 4 April, between the United States, Canada,
      Britain, France, Belgium, Holland, Luxembourg, Norway,
      Denmark, Portugal and Iceland. Later joined by Greece, Turkey
      and West Germany. Mutual aid against aggression. Statute of the
      Council of Europe signed in London, 5 May, by ten West
      European states.

1952 Treaty signed in Paris between France, West Germany, Italy,
      Belgium, Holland and Luxembourg, 27 May, to create a European
      Defence Community and common army. Later rejected by France
      and common army failed to develop.

1954 London agreement, 3 October, to extend the Brussels Pact to
      West Germany and Italy, forming the West European Union.

1955 London and Paris agreements, 5 May, gave West Germany full
      sovereignty and brought her into the North Atlantic Treaty
      Organisation. Warsaw Pact, 13 May, between Russia, East
      Germany, Poland, Czechoslovakia, Hungary, Bulgaria, Romania
      and Albania. Mutual assistance in the event of war.   Austrian
      State Treaty, 15 May, between Britain, the United States, Russia
      and France established a neutral but sovereign Austria.

1957 Treaty of Rome, 22 March, between France, West Germany, Italy,
      Belgium, Holland and Luxembourg established the European

Economic Community. Extended to Britain, Denmark and Eire, 1973.

1960   Stockholm Convention, 3 May, between Britain, Denmark, Norway, Portugal, Austria, Sweden and Switzerland established the European Free Trade Association. Later joined by Finland and Iceland. Britain and Denmark left, 1972, to join the EEC.

1961   Organisation for Economic Co-operation and Development (OECD), 30 September, replaced the OEEC, and included the United States and Canada.

1963   Treaty of co-operation between France and West Germany, 22 January. Nuclear test-ban treaty, 5 August, between Britain, the United States and Russia limited nuclear tests.

1966   France withdraws from military commitments to NATO.

1970   Treaty between West Germany and Russia, 12 August, renounced use of war. Treaty between West Germany and Poland, 18 November, renounced use of war and confirmed their present mutual border.

1975   Act of the Helsinki Conference, 1 August, between thirty-five nations regarding European security, including a reaffirmation of human rights and proposals for economic collaboration between Eastern and Western 'blocs'.

Europe and the wider world

1760 Jan.	Battle of Windewash ends French power in India.
Sept.	Montreal taken by British forces. Under secret agreement with East India Co., Mir Kasim becomes Nawab of Bengal.
1761 Jan.	Shah Alam defeated by British at Patna. Pondicherry taken by Coote. Britain conquers Cuba and Antilles.
1762	Under secret treaty, France cedes Louisiana to Spain.
1763 Feb.	Treaty of Paris: all French possessions in North America east of Mississippi, Grenada, St Vincent, Tobago, Windward Islands, Dominica and Senegal ceded to Britain. Britain returns Guadeloupe to France. Spain cedes Florida to Britain.
1764 Oct.	British defeat Nawab of Oudh at Buxar.
1765 Mar.	Britain passes Stamp Act affecting Thirteen Colonies. Clive appointed Governor of Bengal. Privileges of the East India Co. are confirmed and increased by the Mogul.
1766 Mar.	Britain passes Declaratory Act, affirming right to tax American colonies. First Mysore War breaks out. British occupy Turks and Caicos Islands and Falkland Islands.
Nov.	Under treaty, Nizam Ali cedes Northern Circars to Britain.
1770	French East India Co. dissolved. Britain claims New South Wales.
Mar.	Boston Massacre. Spanish expedition from Buenos Aires expels British from Falkland Isles.
1771 Jan.	Spain surrenders Falkland Islands to Britain after threat of war.
1772 Feb.	Boston Assembly threatens secession unless rights of American colonies are upheld.
Apr.	Hastings becomes Governor of Bengal. Parliamentary enquiry into Clive's administration begins.
1773	Lord North's Regulating Act: British to rule in India in name of Crown.
Dec.	Boston Tea Party.
1774 July	By Treaty of Kutchuk-Kainardji, Russia acquires mouth of Dneiper and Crimea from Turkey.
Sept.	Quebec Act makes Canada a Crown colony and confirms rights of French Canadians. First Congress of Thirteen Colonies (except Georgia) meets at Philadelphia.
1775 Apr.	Battles of Lexington and Concord (in Massachusetts).
May	Second Congress meets.

June	Washington is appointed American commander-in-chief. Austria acquires Delagoa Bay (Mozambique).
1776 July	American colonies declare independence. Viceroyalty of River Plate formed (Argentina, Bolivia, Paraguay and Uruguay).
1777	Equatorial Guinea ceded by Portugal to Spain. France enters American War of Independence against Britain.
Oct.	General Burgoyne surrenders at Saratoga.
Nov.	Confederation Articles issued as first constitution of USA.
1778	Britain takes St Lucia.
Feb.	France and America establish alliance.
Sept.	Dominica seized by France. Annabon and Fernando Pó become Spanish possessions.
1779	First Maratha War begins. French cede Senegal and Gorée to Britain.
1780	Second Mysore War begins.
1781	Portugal acquires Delagoa Bay from Austria.
Oct.	Cornwallis surrenders at Yorktown.
1782 Feb.	Britain cedes Minorca.
1783 Sept.	Treaty of Versailles: Britain recognises American independence, recovers possessions in West Indies, and retains Gibraltar; France recovers stations in India, Senegal, St Lucia, Tobago and possessions in East Indies; Florida is restored to Spain. Russia annexes Georgia from Turkey.
1784 Aug.	Under India Act, political and commercial responsibilities of East India Co. are separated.
1785 June	Rajah of Kedah (in Malaya) cedes Penang to Britain.
1786	Cornwallis is appointed Governor-General of India.
1787	France intervenes in Annam (Indo-China). Freetown, Sierra Leone, is founded as settlement for freed slaves.
1788 Jan.	Convict settlement established at Port Jackson, Sydney.
Feb.	Trial of Warren Hastings opens.
1789 Dec.	Third Mysore War begins.
1790 June	Maratha princes form alliance with Britain.
July	Nizam of Hyderabad forms alliance with Britain.
Oct.	Spain cedes British Columbia to Britain.
1791 May	Under Canada Act, Canada becomes two provinces (Upper and Lower Canada) each having its own government subject to a joint Governor-General.
1792 Jan.	Peace of Jassy between Russia and Turkey: Russia acquires coast of Black Sea and Ochakov fortress; Turkey recognises Russia's annexation of Crimea.

	Feb.	Tipu Sahib, Sultan of Mysore, defeated at Seringapatam and cedes half his territory to British. Sierra Leone Co. receives its Charter.
1793		British occupy French settlements in India.
1794		Slavery abolished in French colonies.
	Feb.	British capture Seychelles, Martinique and St Lucia.
1795	Feb.	Dutch cede Ceylon to Britain.
	Apr.	Warren Hastings acquitted of accusation of financial misconduct.
	June	French retake St Lucia.
	Sept.	British occupy Cape of Good Hope. Spain cedes half of San Domingo to France.
1796		British take Demerara, Essequibo and Berbice (in Guiana).
1797	Feb.	British seize Trinidad from Spain, and St Lucia.
1798	Sept.	British take Honduras from Spain. Nizam accepts Treaty of Hyderabad with British.
	Nov.	British seize Minorca from Spain.
1798–1801		Egyptian expedition. See p. 179.
1800	Sept.	British capture Malta from the French.
	Oct.	France buys Louisiana from Spain.
1801	Mar.	British capture Danish and Swedish islands in West Indies.
	June	Portugal cedes part of Guiana to Spain.
	Sept.	Russia annexes Georgia.
	Oct.	France restores Egypt to Turkey.
1802	Dec.	East India Co. assumes control of Peshawar.
1803	Apr.	France sells Louisiana to USA.
	June	British take Tobago.
	Aug.	Second Maratha War begins.
	Sept.	British seize Dutch Guiana.
1806	Jan.	British occupy Cape of Good Hope.
1807		Britain abolishes slave trade. Heligoland seized by Britain from Denmark. Sierra Leone and The Gambia become Crown colonies.
1809		British take Martinique and Guadeloupe from France.
	Apr.	Treaty concluded between British and Sikhs.
	Sept.	Russia acquires Finland.
1810		Sukhumi (in Georgia) annexed by Russia from Turkey.
	July	British occupy Mauritius.
1811	Aug.	British occupy Java.
	Oct.	Paraguay renounces links with Spain and Argentina.
1812	May	Treaty of Bucharest: Russia receives Bessarabia.
1813		Colombia declares itself independent of Spain.
	July	East India Co. loses its monopoly of Indian trade. Under

terms of Peace of Gulistan, Russia receives Caucasus region from Persia.

1814	Following defeat of Napoleon, Britain acquires St Lucia, Malta, Mauritius, British Guiana, Seychelles, Windward Islands and Cape of Good Hope as recognised colonies. Uruguay declares itself independent of Spain.
1815	Britain establishes protectorate over Ionian Islands.
Oct.	British occupy Ascension Island.
Dec.	Brazil becomes an empire under John, Prince Regent of Portugal.
1816	Chile declares itself independent of Spain.
Dec.	Java is restored to Dutch.
1817 Dec.	Third Maratha War destroys Maratha power. Possessions in Guiana and Senegal restored to France.
1818	Rajputana States come under British protection (Jan).
1819 Feb.	East India Co. founds Singapore.
Dec.	Republic of Colombia established.
1820 Oct.	Spain cedes Floridas to USA.
1821	Amalgamation of North West Co. and Hudson's Bay Co. Royal African Co. dissolved and its possessions taken over by British Crown.
July	Peru declares itself independent of Spain.
Nov.	Panama declares itself independent of Spain and unites with Colombia.
1822	California becomes part of Republic of Mexico.
Sept.	Brazil proclaims its independence of Portugal.
Oct.	Dom Pedro proclaimed Emperor of Brazil.
1823	New South Wales becomes a Crown colony.
Dec.	Promulgation of 'Monroe Doctrine'.
1824 Feb.	First Burmese War breaks out.
1825 Aug.	Portugal recognises independence of Brazil. Bolivia and Uruguay declare themselves independent of Spain.
1826	Penang, Malacca and Singapore are joined to form Straits Settlements.
1827	Russia seizes Erivan from Persia. Spain leases Equatorial Guinea to Britain.
Jan.	Peru withdraws from union with Colombia.
1828 Feb.	By Peace of Turkmentchai, Russia acquires part of Armenia from Turkey and Azerbaijan from Persia.
1829 Sept.	Under Treaty of Adrianople, Russia receives land south of Caucasus from Turkey.
1830	Edward Gibbon Wakefield founds the Colonisation Society.
June	French invade Algiers. East India Co. annexes Mysore and Cachar (in Assam).

1832 Apr.	Britain proclaims sovereignty over Falkland Islands.
1833	East India Co. ceases trading. Slavery abolished in British Empire.
1834	Britain authorises colonisation of South Australia.
1835	Boers begin Great Trek from Cape Colony.
1837 Jan.	Boer settlers found Natalia. Rebellion of Papineau and Mackenzie in Canada.
1838	Earl of Durham becomes Governor-General of Canada.
Oct.	First Afghan War begins.
Dec.	Boers defeat Zulus on Blood River, Natal.
1839	Britain annexes Aden. First 'Opium War' between Britain and China. Natal Republic established. Durham Report published.
1840 Feb.	Treaty of Waitangi secures British sovereignty over New Zealand. Upper and Lower Canada re-united under a single administration. Transportation of convicts to New South Wales ends.
1841	British forces retreat from Kabul. Sultan of Brunei cedes Sarawak to Britain.
1842 Jan.	British forces in Afghanistan suffer major defeat.
Aug.	Treaty of Nanking ends war between Britain and China: Hong Kong is ceded to Britain and five treaty ports are opened to British trade. Ashburton Treaty defines Maine boundary between USA and Canada. British conquest of Assam and Burma begins. Tahiti becomes a French protectorate. New South Wales gains representative government.
1843	Maori Wars begin. British conquer Sind and annex Natal. France acquires Ivory Coast and Dahomey, and establishes protectorate over Mayotte (Comoro Islands).
1844	Spain re-acquires Fernando Pó.
1845	Anglo–French expedition against Madagascar.
Dec.	First Sikh War begins.
1846	Sultan of Brunei cedes Labuan to Britain.
June	Oregon Treaty defines boundary of Canada at 49th Parallel.
Dec.	British establish control over Punjab.
1847	Straits Settlements become a Crown colony. Governor of Cape Colony becomes High Commissioner for South Africa.
Aug.	Liberia becomes independent.
1848	Orange Free State becomes a Crown colony.
Mar.	Second Sikh War begins. Nova Scotia becomes first British colony to attain responsible government.
1849 Mar.	Britain annexes Punjab.
May	Britain repeals Navigation Acts. Portugal claims

sovereignty over Macao.   France founds Libreville (Gabon) as settlement for freed slaves.

1850 Aug.   Britain buys Denmark's Gold Coast possessions.

1851   Australian gold rush.   Victoria becomes a separate colony.
    Sept.   Cuban revolt suppressed by Spain.

1852   Second Burmese War: Burma becomes a province of India.
    Jan.   Sand River Convention establishes South African Republic. New Zealand gains responsible government.

1853   Cape Colony gains representative government.
    Dec.   Britain annexes Nagpur (India).   Russia annexes Khiva (in Central Asia).   France annexes New Caledonia (in Pacific).

1854 Feb.   Under Bloemfontein Convention, Orange Free State gains self-rule.

1855   New South Wales, Victoria and Newfoundland gain responsible government.

1856 Feb.   Britain annexes Oudh.
    Mar.   At Paris Peace Congress, Russia cedes Bessarabia.
    May   Natal becomes a separate colony.   South Australia and Tasmania gain responsible government.
    Oct.   War between Britain and China renewed.

1857   Port of Dakar founded in Senegal (French West Africa).
    Mar.   Indian Mutiny begins at Meerut.
    Dec.   British and French forces take Canton.
1858   Britain, France and China conclude Treaty of Tientsin, giving European traders access to Chinese ports.
    Nov.   British Crown assumes direct control of India, replacing rule of East India Co.
    Dec.   British Columbia becomes a Crown colony.   French begin to occupy Mekong Delta area, Cochin China.

1859   Construction of Suez Canal begins.   French occupy Saigon.   Timor divided between Portuguese and Dutch. Sir George Grey, Governor of Cape Colony, proposes South African federation.
    May   Queensland gains responsible government.

1860   Britain attains full free trade.
             Kowloon Peninsula ceded to Britain.
    Sept.   Anglo–French occupation of Peking.
    Apr.   Maori Wars resume.   French occupy Gabon.

1861 Mar.   Spain annexes San Domingo.
    Aug.   Britain annexes Lagos.
    Oct.   French expedition to Mexico.

1862 Apr.   France annexes Cochin–China and buys Obok (opposite Aden).

1863 Aug.   France establishes protectorate over Cambodia.
    Nov.   Britain cedes Ionian Islands to Greece.

1864 Apr.	Maximilian proclaimed Emperor of Mexico. Russia annexes Abkhazia (Central Asia).
1865	Morant rising in Jamaica suppressed.
Sept.	Second Maori War ends.
Oct.	Transportation of convicts to Australia abolished.
1866	French troops evacuate Mexico.
1867 Mar.	USA buys Alaska from Russia.
June	Emperor Maximilian executed in Mexico.
July	British North America Act creates Dominion of Canada as self-governing federation. Russia establishes Governor-Generalship of Turkestan. Straits Settlements become a Crown colony.
1868 Jan.	Britain expedition against Ethiopia.
Mar.	Britain claims Basutoland.
May	Russia occupies Samarkand.
1869 Mar.	Territorial rights of Hudson's Bay Co. transferred to Dominion of Canada. Rebellion of Louis Riel in Canada.
Nov.	Suez Canal opens.
1870	Manitoba enters Dominion of Canada. Western Australia gains representative government.
1871	British Columbia joins Dominion of Canada. Basutoland united with Cape Colony.
Oct.	Britain annexes diamond-producing area around Kimberley, Griqualand West.
1872 Feb.	Netherlands sells Gold Coast trading stations to Britain.
Oct.	Cape Colony gains responsible government.
1873 Apr.	Beginning of British expedition against Ashanti on Gold Coast.
June	Sultan of Zanzibar abolishes slave trade under British pressure.
Aug.	Russia claims suzerainty over Khiva and Bokhara.
1874 Mar.	Treaty of Fomena ends Ashanti War and promises Britain freedom of trade on Gold Coast. France declares Annam a protectorate and secures trading rights in southern China.
Oct.	Britain annexes Fiji Islands.
1875	Lord Carnarvon reveals proposals for South African Confederation.
Nov.	Britain buys majority holding in Suez Canal Co.
1876	Victoria created Empress of India.
Apr.	Khedive of Egypt suspends payment on treasury bills.
Sept.	Brussels Conference leads to formation of *Association Internationale Africaine* by Leopold II of the Belgians.
1877 Apr.	Britain annexes Transvaal.
1878 Mar.	Britain occupies Walvis Bay (South-West Africa).
July	Britain occupies Cyprus following Treaty of Berlin. Russia acquires Bessarabia. Anglo–French Dual Control established in Egypt.

Sept.	Second Afghan War begins.
Nov.	Leopold II founds *Comité d'Etudes du Haut Congo* in order to finance occupation of Congo.

1879 Jan.   Anglo–Zulu War begins.   Treaty between Germany and Samoa initiates international rivalry in Pacific.

Sept.   British resident in Kabul murdered.

Oct.   Britain invades Afghanistan.

Dec.   Transvaal Republic proclaimed.   Algeria enters semi-colonial relationship with France.   Portuguese Guinea becomes a separate colony.

1880 June   France annexes Tahiti.

Sept.   Britain recognises independence of Afghanistan.

Oct.   Transvaal declares its independence.   First Boer War begins.

1881 Feb.   Boers defeat British at Majuba Hill.

May   Tunisia becomes a French protectorate.

Aug.   By Pretoria Convention, Britain recognises independence of Transvaal.

Sept.   Egyptian nationalist rising under Col. Arabi.   Mahdist rising in the Sudan.   Sino–French war over future of Annam.

Dec.   Stanley founds Leopoldville, Congo.

1882   Bahrain becomes a British protectorate.

Apr.   French occupy Hanoi.

July   British naval bombardment of Alexandria.

Sept.   British defeat Egyptians at Tel-el-Kebir.   Britain occupies Egypt and Sudan.

Dec.   Italy occupies Assab, Eritrea.

1883 May   Kruger becomes President of South African Republic.

June   French commence invasion of Madagascar.

Aug.   Treaty of Hué secures French control of Annam and Tonkin.

Nov.   After military defeat, Britain decides to evacuate Sudan.

1884 Jan.   Russia occupies Merv in Central Asia.

Feb.   Under terms of London Convention, Britain recognises Transvaal as South African Republic.

Apr.–   Germany occupies South-West Africa, Togoland and
Aug.   Cameroons.

July   Anglo–French treaty concerning Mekong Basin. Basutoland, Somali Coast, Nigeria and remainder of New Guinea become British protectorates.

Oct.   Fall of Omdurman.

Nov.   Britain annexes Walvis Bay.

1885 Jan.   Death of Gen. Gordon at Khartoum.

Feb.   Congo Free State established under Leopold II.   Italy occupies Massawa, Eritrea.   Germany declares protectorates over Tanganyika and Zanzibar.

Mar.   Russia occupies Penjdeh, on Afghan–Turkestan border. Northern Bechuanaland becomes a British protectorate.

May   Germany annexes northern New Guinea and Bismarck Archipelago.

| June | Lower Niger area becomes a British protectorate.   France establishes protectorate over Madagascar. |
| Dec. | Indian National Congress founded. |

1886 Jan.	Britain annexes Upper Burma.
June	France establishes colonies of Gabon and Congo.
July	Royal Niger Co. receives charter.
July–Nov.	Britain and Germany define their African and Pacific interests.
Oct.	Socotra (Gulf of Aden) becomes a British protectorate. Gold discovered in Transvaal.

1887	British Somaliland declared a protectorate. Indo–Chinese Union established.
June	Britain annexes Zululand.
July	Anglo–Russian agreement over Afghanistan.
Oct.	India absorbs Baluchistan.
Nov.	Anglo–French condominium over New Hebrides agreed.

| 1888 May | North Borneo, Brunei and Sarawak become a British protectorate.   British East Africa Co. receives charter. |
| Oct. | Matabele Chief Lobengula grants Rudd Concession. Pacific island of Nauru becomes a German protectorate. |

1889 Jan.	Ivory Coast becomes a French protectorate.
May	Treaty of Ucciali between Italy and Ethiopia.
June	Samoa becomes a British, German and US condominium.
July	Brussels Act on slavery.
Oct.	Rhodes's British South Africa Co. receives charter.

1890	Germany occupies Ruanda–Urundi.
July	Britain cedes Heligoland to Germany in return for Zanzibar and Pemba. Rhodes becomes prime minister of Cape Colony.
Aug.	Anglo–French agreement over Nigeria. Anglo–Portuguese agreement over Zambesi and Congo.
Oct.	Western Australia attains responsible government.
Dec.	Britain occupies Sikkim, Uganda and Mashonaland.

1891 Mar.	Anglo–Italian agreement over Ethiopia.
Apr.	Anglo–Portuguese treaty recognises British protectorate in Nyasaland.
May	Work begins on Siberian Railway (completed 1904).

| 1892 | Gold discovered in Western Australia. |
| Oct. | Anglo–German agreement over Cameroons. |

1893 May	Natal gains responsible government.
July	Matabele War leads to British occupation of Bulawayo.
Oct.	Siam cedes left bank of Mekong to France.
Nov.	Britain and Germany agree on their respective frontiers in West Africa. Frontier between India and Afghanistan defined. Dahomey and Laos become French protectorates.
Dec.	Anglo–French agreement over Siam.

1894 Jan.   Britain occupies Matabeleland.
   Apr.   Uganda becomes a British protectorate.
   May   Anglo–Italian agreement over boundaries in West Africa.
   July   Italy begins expedition to occupy Ethiopia.   Togoland
            becomes a German protectorate.
   Nov.   France begins military conquest of Madagascar.

1895   British East African protectorate established.
   June   Joseph Chamberlain appointed British Colonial Secretary.
   Dec.   Jameson Raid into Transvaal fails.

1896 Jan.   Rhodes resigns premiership of Cape Colony.   William II
            sends 'Kruger Telegram'.   Britain and France agree on
            their mutual interests in Siam.   Second Ashanti War.
   Mar.   Italian forces defeated at Adowa, Ethiopia.
   June   Marchand begins mission from Gabon to Nile at Fashoda.
   Aug.   France annexes Madagascar.   Rising in Philippines
            against Spanish rule.
   Sept.   France and Italy reach agreement over Tunis.   Russia
            and China reach agreement over Manchuria.
   Oct.   By Treaty of Addis Ababa, Italy revokes protectorate over
            Ethiopia.

1897   Milner becomes High Commissioner of Cape Colony.
   Sept.   Britain and France agree over Tunis.
   Nov.   Germany occupies Kiao-Chow Bay (in Shantung Peninsula,
            China) as a naval base.
   Dec.   Russia occupies Port Arthur (China).

1898 Mar.   Chinese treaty ports (Kiao-Chow, Port Arthur, Kwangchow,
            Wei-Hai-Wei) leased to Germany, Russia, France and Britain
            respectively.
   Apr.   USA declares war on Spain.
   June   Britain and France conclude Niger Convention.
   July   Marchand reaches Fashoda.
   Aug.   Anglo–German agreement over Portuguese African
            colonies.
   Sept.   Kitchener defeats Mahdist army at Omdurman and
            encounters Marchand at Fashoda, precipitating the Fashoda
            incident (see p. 311).
   Nov.   France evacuates Fashoda.   Sudan declared an
            Anglo–Egyptian condominium.
   Dec.   Treaty of Paris: Spain cedes Cuba, Puerto Rico, Philippines
            and Guam to USA.
1899 Mar.   Anglo–French agreement over Nile Valley.
   Aug.   Britain buys Niger Co.'s territories.
   Oct.   Second Boer War begins.

1900 May   Britain annexes Tonga Islands and Orange Free State.
            Boxer rising in China.
   Sept.   Britain annexes Transvaal.
   Oct.   Russia completes occupation of Manchuria.
   Dec.   France and Italy secretly agree over respective claims to
            Morocco and Tripolitania.

1901	Jan.	Commonwealth of Australia established. North West Frontier Province created in India as buffer with Afghanistan.
	June	Cook Islands annexed to New Zealand.
1902	May	Peace of Vereeniging ends Boer War.
	Nov.	Franco–Italian agreement over Northern Africa.
1903	July	Negotiations between Russia and Japan over Manchuria collapse.
1904	Jan.	Herrero rising in South-West Africa.
	Feb.	Outbreak of Russo–Japanese War.
	Apr.	Anglo–French *entente* resolves outstanding colonial disputes.
	Sept.	Hottentot rising in South West Africa.
	Oct.	Federation of French West Africa created. France and Spain reach agreement over Morocco.
1905		Partition of Bengal.
	Mar.	Moroccan Crisis.
	Sept.	Treaty of Portsmouth ends Russo–Japanese War: Russia cedes Port Arthur and Talienwan to Japan.
1906	Jan.	Algeciras Conference meets to discuss future of Morocco.
	July	Britain, France and Italy agree on independence of Ethiopia.
	Aug.	Anglo–Chinese Convention on Tibet.
	Dec.	All-India Muslim League formed. German Reichstag opposes funding colonial wars. Transvaal and Orange Free State given self-government.
1907		Australia and New Zealand achieve dominion status.
	Aug.	Anglo–Russian Convention on Persia, Afghanistan and Tibet.
1908	June	Gabon, Congo and other territories federated as French Equatorial Africa.
	Aug.	Leopold II transfers sovereignty over Congo Free State to Belgium.
1909	Feb.	Franco–German agreement over Morocco. 'Morley–Minto reforms' in India introduce participation of Indians in government.
1910	July	Union of South Africa established, with dominion status. Russia and Japan reach agreement over Manchuria and Korea.
1911	May	French occupation of Moroccan capital results in German gunboat *Panther* being sent to Agadir (July).
	Aug.	Italy declares war on Turkey and seizes Tripoli.
	Nov.	France and Germany reach agreement on interests of France and Spain in Morocco.
1912	Mar.	Under Treaty of Fez, Morocco becomes a French protectorate.
	Oct.	Italy receives Tripoli from Turkey under Treaty of Ouchy.

Nov.	Spain establishes a protectorate over her Moroccan territories.
1914 Jan.	North and South Nigeria united under a single Governor-General.
Aug.	Outbreak of First World War.
Aug.–Sept.	Allied troops begin to occupy German colonies.
Nov.	Britain annexes Cyprus.
Dec.	Egypt declared a British protectorate.
1916 Apr.	Easter Rising in Dublin.
1917 Aug.	Montagu Declaration states Britain's eventual goal in India is self-government.
Nov.	Balfour Declaration promises a national home in Palestine for the Jews.
1919 Apr.	'Massacre' of Indians at Amritsar by British troops under Brigadier-General Dyer.
June	Under Treaty of Versailles, Germany relinquishes all her colonial possessions. These are redistributed as mandates of the League of Nations among the Allies. Nationalist rising in Egypt.
1920 Apr.	Transjordan becomes a British mandated territory.
July	British East Africa is divided into colony of Kenya and protectorate of Uganda.
Aug.	Gandhi begins non-co-operation campaign in India.
1921 Jan.	New All-Indian parliament meets; India is given fiscal and tariff autonomy.
Mar.	Britain accepts League of Nations mandate over Iraq.
Dec.	Southern Ireland is granted dominion status as the Irish Free State. Washington agreement between USA, Britain, France and Japan over Pacific territories.
1922 Feb.	Britain withdraws protectorate over Egypt.
July	League of Nations Council confirms British and French mandates over Togo, Cameroons, Tanganyika and Palestine.
Aug.	Arab Congress rejects Britain's Palestine mandate.
1923 Aug.	Rwanda–Urundi becomes a Belgian mandated territory.
Oct.	Southern Rhodesia becomes a self-governing colony.
1924 Apr.	Protectorate of Northern Rhodesia established.
1925 May	Cyprus becomes a British Crown colony.
July	Insurrection against French rule begins in Syria.
1926 Nov.	Imperial Conference declares that Britain and her dominions are autonomous and equal though 'freely associated as members of the British Commonwealth of Nations'. Communist rising begins in Java against Dutch rule.
1927	Simon Commission sent to investigate the effect of the Montagu–Chelmsford reforms of 1919.

1928 Aug.	Italy and Ethiopia conclude treaty of friendship.
1930 Mar.	Gandhi initiates civil disobedience campaign in India. Nehru declares Indian independence.
Oct.	Britain evacuates base at Wei-Hai-Wei.
Nov.	Round Table Conference on Indian self-government meets.
1931 Mar.	'Gandhi-Irwin Pact' ends civil disobedience in India.
Dec.	Statute of Westminster defines status of dominions, and allows them to claim full sovereignty.
1932 July	Imperial Economic Conference meets at Ottawa and introduces limited preferential tariffs within the British Empire.
Oct.	Iraq becomes independent.
1934 Apr.	Gandhi once more calls off civil disobedience.
Dec.	Incident on border between Ethiopia and Italian Somaliland heightens tensions.
1935 Aug.	Government of India Act gives India new constitution with provincial self-government and separates Burma and Aden from India.
Oct.	Italy invades Ethiopia. League of Nations imposes sanctions against Italy.
1936 May	Italian forces occupy Addis Ababa.
July	League of Nations withdraws sanctions against Italy.
Aug.	Anglo–Egyptian treaty re-defines Britain's rights in Egypt.
Sept.	France agrees to grant Syria independence in 1939.
1937 Nov.	Rising in Tunisia against French rule.
1940 Aug.	Britain evacuates Somaliland following Italian invasion.
Sept.	Italians invade Egypt. Japan invades Indo-China.
1941 Jan.	British forces begin to occupy Italian East Africa.
June	British and Free French occupy Syria.
Dec.	Japan occupies Hong Kong and Siam.
1942 Jan.	Japanese forces begin occupation of British, French, US and Dutch possessions in South East Asia and Western Pacific.
Feb.	Singapore surrenders to Japanese.
Apr.	Indian nationalists reject offer of self-government made by Cripps.
1944 Jan.	Free French hold Brazzaville Conference to discuss future of French possessions in Africa. Ho Chi Minh proclaims Vietnamese independence from France.
1946 Mar.	Transjordan becomes independent (formerly a British mandate).
Apr.	Malayan Union established.
May	Sarawak is ceded to Britain.
July	North Borneo becomes a British colony.
1947 Mar.	Netherlands recognises independence of Indonesia.
June	Partition of India announced.

Aug.   India and Pakistan become independent.
Sept.   Britain announces withdrawal from Palestine.

1948 Jan.   Burma becomes independent and leaves the
            Commonwealth.
Feb.   Malayan Union becomes Federation of Malaya.   Ceylon
        becomes independent.
May   State of Israel established.   Conflict with communist
        guerrillas in Malaya begins.

1949 Apr.   Eire withdraws from Commonwealth.
July   Laos becomes independent of France.
Dec.   Netherlands grants formal independence to Indonesia.

1950 Jan.   Dutch colonies in Latin America are promised autonomy.

1951 Jan.   Gold Coast constitution becomes operative.
Dec.   Libya becomes independent.

1952   Beginning of Mau Mau conflict in Kenya.
Jan.   Nigerian constitution becomes operative.
Sept.   Eritrea is united with Ethiopia.

1953 Feb.   Anglo–Egyptian agreement on Sudan reached.
Aug.   Southern Rhodesia, Nyasaland and Northern Rhodesia are
        united in the Federation of Rhodesia and Nyasaland.
Nov.   Cambodia becomes independent of France.

1954 May   French forces surrender to Vietminh at Dien Bien Phu,
            Vietnam.
July   French Assembly approves Indo-China settlement.
Nov.   National Liberation Front begins revolt in Algeria.

1955 June   French agreement on Tunisian home rule.

1956 Jan.   Sudan becomes independent (formerly under
            Anglo–Egyptian rule).
Mar.   France recognises independence of Morocco and Tunisia.
Nov.   Suez Crisis: Britain and France intervene in war between
        Egypt and Israel.   Mau Mau insurgency in Kenya
        suppressed.

1957 Mar.   Gold Coast becomes independent as Ghana.
Aug.   Malay States become independent as Federation of Malaya.

1958 Jan.   Federation of West Indies is established.   French Guinea
        becomes independent.
May.   Revolt of French settlers and Army in Algeria.

1960 Jan.   Cameroun gains independence from France.
Feb.   Harold Macmillan makes 'Wind of change' speech.
Apr.   Togo becomes independent from France.
June   Mali and Madagascar win independence from France.
Aug.   Ivory Coast, Dahomey, Upper Volta, Niger, Chad, Gabon,
        (French) Congo, and Central African Republic gain
        independence from France.   Cyprus becomes
        independent.   British Somaliland gains independence,
        and unites with Italian Somaliland to form the Somali
        Republic (Somalia).

Oct.   Nigeria becomes independent.
Nov.   Mauritania and Senegal win independence from France.

1961 Mar.   South Africa leaves the Commonwealth.
Apr.   Army revolt in Algeria collapses.   Sierra Leone becomes independent.
June   Northern Cameroons (British) unites with Nigeria.
Oct.   Southern Cameroons (French) unites with Cameroun.
Dec.   Tanganyika becomes independent.

1962 Jan.   Western Samoa gains independence.
Mar.   French and Algerians agree to cease-fire.
July   Algeria becomes independent.   Rwanda and Burundi become independent (formerly under Belgian rule).
Aug.   Federation of West Indies dissolves when Jamaica and Trinidad and Tobago become independent.
Oct.   Uganda becomes independent.

1963 Sept.   Federation of Malaysia established.
Dec.   Zanzibar and Kenya become independent.   Federation of Rhodesia and Nyasaland is dissolved.

1964 July   Nyasaland becomes independent as Malawi.
Sept.   Malta becomes independent.
Oct.   Northern Rhodesia becomes independent as Zambia.

1965 Feb.   The Gambia becomes independent.
July.   The Maldive Islands gain independence.
Nov.   Southern Rhodesia unilaterally declares its independence.

1966 May   British Guiana becomes independent as Guyana.
Sept.   Bechuanaland becomes independent as Botswana.
Oct.   Basutoland becomes independent as Lesotho.
Nov.   Barbados becomes independent.
Dec.   Negotiations between Britain and Rhodesia aboard HMS *Tiger* collapse.

1967 Nov.   Aden gains independence.

1968 Jan.   Nauru becomes independent.
Mar.   Mauritius becomes independent.
Aug.   French military support given to Chad to combat rebels.
Sept.   Swaziland becomes independent.
Oct.   Spanish Equatorial Guinea becomes independent.   Talks between Britain and Rhodesia aboard HMS *Fearless* reach stalemate.

1969 Mar.   British police despatched to Anguilla.   French troops called into Chad.

1970 Mar.   Rhodesia declares itself a republic.
June   Tonga becomes independent.
Oct.   Fiji Islands become independent.

1971 Aug.   Bahrain becomes independent.
Sept.   Qatar becomes independent.
Nov.   Oman becomes independent.
Dec.   Britain leaves Gulf States.

1973 July   Bahamas become independent.

1974 Feb.   Grenada becomes independent.
Sept.   Portuguese Guinea gains independence as Guinea–Bissau.

1975 June   Mozambique gains independence from Portugal.
July   Cape Verde Islands, São Tomé e Principe gain independence
from Portugal.   Comoro Islands declare themselves
independent of France.
Sept.   Papua New Guinea becomes independent.
Nov.   Angola gains independence from Portugal.   Surinam is
granted independence by The Netherlands.

1976 Feb.   Spain relinquishes all rights over the Western Sahara.
June   Seychelles becomes independent.
July   Timor becomes a province of Indonesia.

1977 June   French territory of the Afars and Issas becomes independent
as Djibouti.
Sept.   Anglo–American peace plan for Rhodesia receives support
of 'front-line states' and provides for first elections on the
basis of universal suffrage in April 1979, though still
opposed by major guerrilla armies.

1978 July   Solomon Islands become independent.
Oct.   Ellice Islands gain independence as Tuvalu.
Nov.   Dominica becomes independent.

1979 Feb.   St Lucia gains independence.   French paratroops sent to
Chad (withdrawn in May).
July   Kiribati becomes independent (formerly the Gilbert Islands).
Oct.   St Vincent and the Grenadines gain independence.
Dec.   Lancaster House agreement on future of Rhodesia. Cease-
fire arranged and constitutional agreement reached.
Commonwealth troops to supervise elections.   Soviet
troops invade Afghanistan. Widespread guerrilla resistance
begins.

1980 Feb.   Elections in Rhodesia result in sweeping victory for
Mugabe's ZANU.
Apr.   Rhodesia becomes independent republic of Zimbabwe.
July   Vanuatu becomes independent (formerly known as New
Hebrides).

1981   Belize becomes independent republic.

1982 Apr.   Argentine troops invade Falkland Islands and South
Georgia. Britain organises task force to recapture islands.
June   Argentine forces in Falklands surrender.

1983 June   French troops sent to assist Chadian troops against rebel
and Libyan forces.

1984   Brunei becomes independent.
Sept.   Agreement with China, whereby Hong Kong reverts to
Chinese sovereignty after 1 July 1997.

Section IV
Social and economic

Comparative population of European countries, 1750–1981*

(millions, rounded up to the nearest 100,000)

	c. 1750	1800	1850	1900	1950	1981
Austria	–	14.0	17.5	26.2	6.9	7.6
Hungary	3.5	5.0	13.2	19.3	9.2	10.7
Belgium	–	3.1	4.3	6.7	8.5	9.9
Bulgaria	–	–	–	3.8	7.0	8.7
Czechoslovakia	–	–	–	–	12.3	15.1
Denmark	–	0.9	1.4	2.5	4.3	5.1
Finland	0.4	0.8	1.6	2.7	4.0	4.8
France	21.0	27.4	35.8	38.5	42.8	53.4
Germany	18.0	23.0	33.4	56.4	69.1	78.2
Great Britain	7.4	10.5	20.8	37.0	49.0	55.5
Greece	–	0.9	1.0	2.4	7.6	9.7
Ireland	3.2	5.2	6.6	4.5	3.0	3.0
Italy	14.7	17.2	24.4	32.5	46.7	56.0
Netherlands	1.6	2.1	3.1	5.1	9.6	13.9
Norway	0.6	0.9	1.4	2.2	3.3	4.1
Poland	–	9.0	–	25.1	25.0	35.0
Portugal	2.3	2.9	3.8	5.4	8.4	9.8
Romania	–	–	3.9	6.0	15.9	21.8
Russia	28.0	40.0	68.5	126.4	208.8	255.5
Spain	8.2	10.5	15.5	18.6	28.0	37.0
Sweden	1.8	2.4	3.5	5.1	7.0	8.3
Switzerland	–	–	2.4	2.3	4.7	6.3
Yugoslavia	–	–	–	–	15.7	22.1

* Figures are given for the nearest year where not otherwise available.

(*Sources*: B. R. Mitchell, *European Historical Statistics*, 1750–1975 (2nd edn) Macmillan 1980; C. M. Cipolla (ed.), *The Fontana Economic History of Europe*, vol. vi, Collins/Fontana, 1975; J. Paxton (ed.), *The Statesman's Year-Book*, *1985–86*, Macmillan, 1985.)

Population of individual European countries

(millions, figures rounded up to nearest 100,000)

Austria, Austria–Hungary, Hungary

	Austria	*Hungary*
1750	–	3.5
1800	14.0	5.0
1851	17.5	13.2

	Austria–Hungary*
1861	35.8
1880	37.8
1900	45.5
1910	51.4

	Austria	*Hungary*
1920	6.5	8.0
1940	6.7	9.3
1951	6.9	9.2 (1949)
1981	7.6	

* Figure for 1910 includes Bosnia–Herzegovina.

Belgium

1750	2.2	1880	5.5	1961	9.2
1800	3.1	1900	6.7	1983	9.9
1831	4.1	1920	7.4		
1856	4.5	1940	8.3		

Bulgaria

1881	2.0	1920	4.8	1965	8.2
1900	3.8	1946	7.0	1983	8.9

Czechoslovakia

1921	13.6	1947	12.2	1983	15.4
1930	14.7	1961	13.8		

Denmark*

1769	0.8	1850	1.4	1930	3.6
1801	0.9	1880	2.0	1950	4.3
1834	1.2	1901	2.5	1984	5.1

* Excludes Schleswig–Holstein up to 1930 after which figures include the part of Schleswig ceded to Denmark by Germany in 1919.

Finland

1750	0.4	1850	1.6	1940	3.7
1775	0.6	1880	2.1	1960	4.5
1800	0.8	1900	2.7	1983	4.9
1830	1.4	1920	3.2		

France*

1750	21.0	1881	37.4	1962	46.5
1801	27.4	1901	38.5	1984	54.5
1831	32.6	1921	39.2		
1851	35.8	1946	39.9		

* Figures for 1881 and 1901 exclude Alsace and Lorraine, incorporated into Germany in 1871, but returned to France in 1919.

Germany*

1750	18.0	1880	45.2
1800	23.0 (est.)	1910	64.9
1828	26.7	1925	62.4
1852	33.4	1939	69.5

	West Germany	East Germany
1950	47.7	17.3
1961	56.1	17.0 (1964)
1983	61.4	16.7

* Figures to 1852 relate to the lands comprising the German Empire in 1870. Figures for 1880 and 1910 include territories ceded by Austria, Denmark and France in 1864–71. Figures for 1925 exclude the Saarland and other territories removed at Versailles, principally the Saarland. Figure for 1939 includes the recovered Saarland but excludes acquisitions of Austria and the Sudetenland.

Great Britain*

1750	7.4	1851	20.8	1931	44.9
1801	10.5	1881	29.7	1951	49.0
1831	16.3	1901	37.0	1981	55.5

* Figure for 1750 is an estimate, including an estimate for Scotland in 1755. Figures for 1801–1901 exclude Ireland. Figures for 1931–1981 include Northern Ireland.

Greece*

1821	0.9	1907	2.6	1981	9.7
1853	1.0	1928	6.2		
1889	2.2	1951	7.6		

* Figures from 1889 include Thessaly, annexed in 1881. Figures after 1907 also include parts of Thrace and Macedonia acquired from Turkey and Bulgaria.

Ireland*

1754	3.2 (est.)	1851	6.6	1936	3.0
1791	4.8	1881	5.2	1956	2.9
1821	6.8	1911	4.4	1981	3.0

* Figures after 1911 exclude Northern Ireland.

Italy*

1770	14.7 (est.)	1852	24.4	1931	40.3
1800	17.2 (est.)	1881	28.5	1951	46.7
1833	21.2	1911	35.4	1983	56.9

* Figures for 1770 to 1852 are based upon estimates for the states comprising the Kingdom of Italy in 1870.

Netherlands*

1750	1.6	1849	3.1	1930	7.9
1800	2.1	1879	4.0	1947	9.6
1829	2.6	1909	5.9	1984	14.4

* Figure for 1829 excludes the Belgian provinces.

Norway

1750	0.6	1851	1.4	1930	2.8
1801	0.9	1875	1.8	1950	3.3
1831	1.1	1900	2.2	1984	4.1

Poland*

1800	9.0 (est.)	1921	27.2	1983	36.4
1870	16.9 (est.)	1946	23.9		
1900	25.1	1960	29.8		

* Figures for 1800, 1870 and 1900 are estimates for the territory comprising the Polish state in 1920. The boundaries of the Polish state were very substantially altered after the Second World War.

Portugal

1750	2.3	1854	3.8	1930	6.8
1801	2.9	1878	4.6	1950	8.4
1835	3.1	1911	6.0	1981	9.8

Romania*

| 1859 | 3.9 | 1912 | 7.2 | 1956 | 17.5 |
| 1899 | 6.0 | 1930 | 18.1 | 1984 | 22.6 |

* Figure for 1930 includes substantial territorial gains from the first Balkan War and the First World War. Figures for 1956 and 1981 reflect further boundary changes after the Second World War.

Russia*

1750	28.0 (est.)	1880	97.7	1959	208.8
1800	35.5/40.0 (est.)	1910	160.7	1970	241.7
1831	56.1	1926	147.0	1984	273.8
1851	68.5	1939	170.5		

* Figures for 1750 and 1800 are estimates for European Russia excluding Finland. Figures thereafter relate to present area of the Soviet Union excluding Polish lands and Finland.

Spain

1750	8.2	1887	17.6	1970	33.8
1797	10.5	1910	19.9	1983	38.2
1830	14.6	1930	23.6		
1857	15.5	1950	28.0		

Sweden

| 1750 | 1.8 | 1800 | 2.4 | 1850 | 3.5 |
| 1780 | 2.1 | 1830 | 2.9 | 1890 | 4.8 |

1910	5.5	1950	7.0
1930	6.1	1983	8.3

Switzerland

1837	2.2	1910	3.8	1983	6.4
1850	2.4	1930	4.0		
1880	2.9	1950	4.7		

Yugoslavia*

1921	12.0	1961	18.6
1948	15.7	1983	22.9

* Figures after 1948 include territory acquired from Italy in 1945.

Note It is important to recognise that virtually all population statistics relating to the late eighteenth and early nineteenth centuries are based on inadequate statistical records. Where these are particularly subject to discussion, this has been indicated by (est.).

(*Sources*: B. R. Mitchell, *European Historical Statistics, 1750–1975* (2nd edn), Macmillan 1980); C. M. Cipolla (ed.), *The Fontana Economic History of Europe*, vol. iv, Collins/Fontana 1975; J. Paxton (ed.), *Statesman's Year-Book 1985–86*, Macmillan 1985.)

Population of major European cities
(thousands)

	1800	1850	1900	1950	1981*
Amsterdam	201	224	511	804	965
Athens	12	31	111	565	886
Barcelona	115	175	533	1,280	1,754
Belgrade	30	–	69	368	1,400
Berlin	172	419	1,889	3,337	3,083[†]
Birmingham	71	233	523	1,113	1,050
Brussels	66	251	599	956	1,029
Budapest	54	178	732	1,571	2,093
Cologne	50	97	373	595	1,014
Copenhagen	101	127	401	1,168	1,214
Dresden	60	97	396	494	509
Edinburgh	83	194	394	467	464
Genoa	100	120	235	648	804
Glasgow	77	345	776	1,090	832
Hamburg	130	132	706	1,606	1,717
Leipzig	30	63	456	618	567
Lisbon	180	240	356	790	1,708
Liverpool	80	376	704	789	537
London	1,117	2,685	6,586	8,348	6,970[†]
Lyons	110	177	459	650	1,153[§]
Madrid	160	281	540	1,618	3,146
Manchester	75	303	645	703	491
Marseilles	111	195	491	661	1,005[§]
Milan	170	242	493	1,260	1,723
Moscow	250	365	989	5,046	7,734
Munich	40	110	500	832	1,315
Naples	350	449	564	1,011	1,221
Palermo	140	150	228	491	666
Paris	547	1,053	2,714	2,850	2,317
Prague	75	118	202	922	1,889

Rome	153	175	463	1,652	2,884
St Petersburg/Leningrad	220	485	1,267	3,321	4,372
Stockholm	76	93	301	744	1,375
Turin	78	135	336	711	1,199
Vienna	247	444	1,675	1,766	1,581
Warsaw	60	114	423	279	1,463

Note: As totals are based on varying definitions of the conurbations concerned, they are not exactly but only generally comparable between countries.

* Where no figure for 1981 is available, given to the nearest census.

† East and West Berlin totals combined.

‡ Based on a more restricted boundary of the area controlled by the Greater London Council after 1966.

§ Conurbation totals.

(*Sources*: B. R. Mitchell, *European Historical Statistics, 1750–1975* (2nd edn), Macmillan 1980; C. M. Cipolla (ed), *The Fontana Economic History of Europe*, vol iv, Collins/Fontana 1975; A. F. Weber, *The Growth of Cities in the Nineteenth Century*, Macmillan, New York 1899); J. Paxton (ed.), *The Statesman's Year-Book 1985–86*, Macmillan 1985.)

Emigration from Europe, 1851–1960: selected countries
(in thousands)

	1851–60	1861–70	1871–80	1881–90	1891–1900	1901–10	1911–20	1921–30	1931–40	1941–50	1951–60
Austria–Hungary*	31	40	46	248	440	1,111	418	61	11	–	53
Belgium	1	2	2	21	16	30	21	33	20	29	109
Denmark	–	8	39	82	51	73	52	64	100	38	68
Finland	–	–	–	16	59	159	67	73	3	7	32
France	27	36	66	119	51	53	32	4	5	–	155
Germany†	671	779	626	1,342	527	274	91	564	121	618	872
Italy	5	27	168	992	1,580	3,615	2,194	1,370	235	467	858
Netherlands	16	20	17	52	24	28	22	32	4‡	75‡	341‡
Norway	36	98	85	187	95	191	62	87	6	10	25
Poland	–	–	–	–	–	–	–	634	164	–	–
Portugal	45	79	131	185	266	324	402	995	108	69	346
Russia	58	288	481	911	420	–	–	–	–	–	–
Spain	3	7	13	572	791	1,091	1,306	560	132	166	543
Sweden	17	122	103	327	205	324	86	107	8	23	43
UK and Ireland§	1,313	1,572	1,849	3,259	2,149	3,150	2,587	2,151	262	755	1,454

* Austria only after 1921.

† West Germany only after 1941

‡ Excludes emigration to Dutch colonies.

§ Excludes direct emigration from Irish ports.

(Source: B. R. Mitchell, European Historical Statistics, 1750–1970, Macmillan 1975, p. 135.)

Output of grain crops, 1800–1914: selected countries
(Annual averages in million quintals)

	1800–13	1835–44	1855–64	1885–94	1905–14
Austria	–	49.4	60.0	66.2	85.9
Hungary	–	51.0	68.1	102.6	131.7
France	94.5*	131.4	158.5	160.1	171.9
Germany	–	–	153.7	304.6	457.9
Italy	–	–	57.2	63.1	88.8
Russia	268.6	310.1	381.2	515.4	543.1
Sweden	5.0	8.4	14.7	21.7	26.1
U.K.	43.0	64.0[†]	68.0	56.9	51.7
Ireland	–	23.4[†]	16.7	11.2	11.3

* Average of 1803–12 only.

[†] Figures for 1845–54.

(*Source*: C. M. Cipolla (ed.), *The Fontana Economic History of Europe*, vol. IV, Collins/Fontana 1975, p. 752)

Output of wheat, 1913–1983: selected countries
(thousands of metric tons)

	1913	1924	1938	1950	1962	1972	1983
Bulgaria	1,184	672	2,149	1,757	2,086	3,582	3,600
Czechoslovakia	–	877	1,764	1,430	1,644	4,017	5,820
France	8,690	7,650	9,800	7,700	14,050	17,850	24,781
Germany*	5,094	3,053	6,250	2,614	4,592	7,134	8,998
Greece	357†	210	980	850	1,722	1,768	2,026
Hungary	4,119	1,403	2,688	2,040	1,973	4,095	4,800
Italy	5,690	4,479	8,184	7,774	9,497	9,421	8,514
Poland	–	884	2,172	1,888	2,700	5,147	5,165
Romania	2,291	1,917	4,821	2,219	4,054	6,041	5,000
Spain	3,059	3,314	4,300	3,374	4,812	4,562	4,330
USSR	28,000¶	13,000	40,800	31,100	70,800	85,993	82,000
UK	1,566	1,435	1,990	2,646	3,968	4,780	10,880
Yugoslavia	417‖	1,662	3,030	1,833	3,514	4,844	5,519

* West Germany after 1938   † 1914   ¶ Includes Baltic States   ‖ Serbia only   § 1934   ‡ Estimated

(Source: B. R. Mitchell, *European Historical Statistics, 1750–1870*, Macmillan 1975, pp. 249–75; J. Paxton (ed.) *The Statesman's Year-Book, 1985–86*, Macmillan 1985, p. xiii.)

Output of coal and lignite, 1820–1939: selected countries

(Annual averages for quinquennia in million metric tons)

	Belgium	France	Germany	UK	Russia
1820–24	–	1	1	18	–
1825–29	–	2	2	22	–
1830–34	2	2	2	23	–
1835–39	3	3	3	28	–
1840–44	4	4	4	34	–
1845–49	5	4	6	47	–
1850–54	7	5	9	50	–
1855–59	9	8	15	68	–
1860–64	10	10	21	86	–
1865–69	11	13	31	105	1
1870–74	15	15	41	123	1
1875–79	15	17	50	136	2
1880–84	18	20	66	159	4
1885–89	18	22	78	168	5
1890–94	20	26	94	183	7
1895–99	22	31	120	205	11
1900–04	23	33	157	230	17
1905–09	25	36	201	260	24
1910–14	23	40	247	274	27
1915–19	15	24	244	247	28
1920–24	23	34	249	240	11
1925–29	26	52	316	227	31
1930–34	25	50	265	223	73
1935–39	29	47	351	233	133

(*Source*: C. M. Cipolla (ed.), *The Fontana Economic History of Europe*, vol. iv, 1975, p. 770.)

Output of coal and lignite, 1950–1984: selected countries
(Annual totals in million metric tons)

	1950	1955	1960	1965	1970	1975	1984
Austria	4	7	6	6	4	3	3*
Belgium	27	30	22	20	13	7	6
Bulgaria	6	9	16	25	29	24	34†
Czechoslovakia	45	61	85	101	107	107	123†
France	53	57	58	54	41	27	19‡
West Germany	188	223	240	239	220	214	207*
East Germany	140	203	228	253	256	245	278*
Hungary	13	22	26	31	27	26	25*
Italy	2	2	2	1	2	2	2§
Netherlands	12	12	12	11	5	–	–
Poland	83	101	114	141	166	211	227†
Romania	4	6	8	12	19	29	49*
Russia	261	390	509	577	624	701	716*
Spain	12	14	15	16	14	14	30§
UK	220	225	197	191	153	124	106
Yugoslavia	13	15	23	30	26	23	47*

* 1983   † 1982   ‡1979   § 1981

(*Sources*: B. R. Mitchell, *European Historical Statistics, 1750–1970*, Macmillan 1975, pp. 365–8; J. Paxton (ed.), *The Statesman's Year-Book, 1985–86*, Macmillan 1985.)

Raw cotton consumption, 1830–1970: selected countries
(thousands of metric tons)

	1830	1850	1880	1910	1930	1950	1970
Austria*	6	29	64	173	22	20	23
Hungary	–				15	30	67
Belgium	1	10	23	63	100	87	63
Czechoslovakia	–	–	–	–	113	60	108
Bulgaria	–	–	–	1	3	22	72†
Finland	–	–	3	7	7	11	16
France	34	59	89	158	361	252	244
Germany	8	26	137	383	346	189 (W) 43†(E)	255 89
UK	24	267	617	740	577	461	176
Greece	–					21	46
Italy	–	–	–	175	205	203	221
Netherlands	–		14	20	52	61	62
Poland	–				61	87	141
Portugal	–		3	16	18	36	85
Romania	–				3	17	80
Russia	2	20	94	362	257	953	1,713
Spain	–	16	45	73	99	59	108
Sweden	–	2	9	21	23	28	15
Switzerland	–	–	22	24	31	30	41
Yugoslavia	–	–	–	–	88	35	91

* Figures for Austro–Hungarian Empire to 1910; 1830 and 1850 also include Lombardy and Venetia in N. Italy

† 1951

(*Source*: B. R. Mitchell, *European Historical Statistics, 1750–1970*, Macmillan 1975, pp. 428–32.)

Output of pig-iron, 1820–1984: selected countries
(Annual production in million metric tons)

	UK	France	Belgium	Germany		Italy	Russia
1820	0.4	0.2	–	0.1		–	0.1
1850	2.3	0.4	0.1	0.2		–	0.2
1880	7.9	1.7	0.6	2.7		–	0.4
1910	10.2	4.0	1.9	14.8		0.3	3.0
1930	6.3	10.1	3.4	9.7		0.5	5.0
				W	E		
1950	9.8	7.8	3.7	9.5	0.3	0.5	19.2
1975	12.1	22.5	9.1	30.1	2.5	11.3	102.9
1984	9.6	19.4*	8.0†	26.6†	N.A.	N.A.	N.A.

* 1979   † 1983

(*Source*: B. R. Mitchell, *European Historical Statistics, 1750–1970*, Macmillan 1975, pp. 391–6.)

Output of steel, 1880–1984: selected countries
(Annual production in million metric tons)

	UK	France	Belgium	Germany		Italy	Russia
1880	1.3	0.4	0.1	0.7		–	0.3
1890	3.6	0.7	0.2	2.2		0.1	0.4
1900	5.0	1.6	0.7	6.6		0.1	2.2
1910	6.5	3.4	1.9	13.7		0.7	3.5
1930	7.4	9.4	3.4	11.5		0.5	5.8
1940	13.4	4.4	1.9	19.0		1.0	18.0
				W	E		
1950	16.6	8.7	3.8	12.1	1.0	2.4	27.3
1960	24.7	17.3	7.1	34.1	3.8	8.2	65.3
1975	20.2	27.0	11.6	40.4	6.5	21.8	141.3
1984	15.1	23.3*	10.2[†]	35.7[†]	N.A.	21.7[†]	154.0

* 1979   [†] 1983

(*Sources*: B. R. Mitchell, *European Historical Statistics, 1750–1970*, Macmillan 1975, pp. 399–402; J. Paxton (ed.), *The Statesman's Year-Book, 1985–86*, Macmillan 1985.)

Output of crude oil, 1900–1984: selected countries

(thousand metric tons)

	1900	1920	1930	1950	1960	1970	1984†
Austria	349	–	–	1,700	2,440	2,798	1,268
Germany*	50	35	174	1,119	5,560	7,536	4,100
Denmark	–	–	–	–	–	–	2,335
Netherlands	–	–	–	705	1,920	1,919	3,500
UK	–	–	–	40	90	84	125,000
France	–	55	76	128	2,260	2,308	2,000
Italy	2	5	8	8	1,990	1,408	2,400
Spain	–	–	–	–	–	156	2,500
Norway	–	–	–	–	–	–	34,500
Russia	10,684	3,851	18,451	37,878	147,859	352,667	615,500
Romania	247	1,109	5,792	5,047	11,500	14,637	12,000
Yugoslavia	–	–	–	110	1,040	2,854	4,000
Hungary	2	–	–	512	1,215	1,937	2,000
Poland	–	765	663	162	195	424	250

* West Germany from 1950   † Estimated output

(Sources: B. R. Mitchell, *European Historical Statistics, 1750–1970*, Macmillan 1975, p. 371; J. Paxton (ed.) *The Statesman's Year-Book, 1985–86*, Macmillan 1985, p. xxiii.)

Motor vehicles produced – major producers, 1910–1985

(in thousands, commercial and private)

	1910	1925	1930	1938	1950	1965	1975	1985
Czechoslovakia	–	–	17	13	31	94	168	176[†,‡]
France	38	177	142	227	357	1,616	1,694	3,148[‡]
Germany	10	49	96	338	301(W) 13(E)	3,063(W) 118[§](E)	3,172(W) N.A.	3,334[§](W) 118[§](E)
Italy	–	49	47	71	129	1,186	1,459	1,575[§]
Netherlands	–	–	–	–	–	36	N.A.	N.A.
Poland	–	–	–	–	1	71	229	275[‡]
Russia	–	–	4	231	259	814	763*	1,300
Spain	–	–	–	–	–	234	967	1,226[§]
Sweden	–	–	2	7	17	207	N.A.	N.A.
UK	34	198	136	445	784	2,180	1,647	N.A.

* Commercial vehicles only   [†] Cars only   [‡] 1982   [§] 1983

(*Source*: B. R. Mitchell, *European Historical Statistics, 1750–1970*, Macmillan 1975, pp. 467–9; J. Paxton (ed.), *The Statesman's Year-Book, 1985–86*, Macmillan 1985.)

Output of electricity, 1920–1984
(in million kWh)

	1920	1935	1955	1975	1984
Austria	1.8	2.6	10.6	35.2	42.6[†]
Belgium	1.2	4.3	10.9	39.0	49.9
Bulgaria	–	0.1	2.1	25.2	40.5[‡]
Czechoslovakia	1.4	2.6	15.0	56.0	74.8[‡]
Denmark	0.3	0.9	3.9	17.4	20.4[‡]
Finland	–	2.1	6.8	25.1	40.1[†]
France	5.8	17.5	49.6	180.0	262.8[‡]
Germany	15.0	35.7	78.9(W) 28.7(E)	301.8(W) 84.5(E)	366.9(W) 104.9(E)[†]
Greece	0.1	0.4	1.4	8.9*	21.7[§]
Hungary	–	0.9	5.4	20.5	25.8[†]
Ireland	–	0.2	1.6	N.A.	N.A.
Italy	4.0	12.6	25.6	140.8	182.9[†]
Netherlands	0.7	2.8	11.2	54.3	59.7[†]
Norway	5.3	7.8	22.6	76.7	93.2[‡]
Poland	–	2.8	17.8	97.2	118.03[‡]
Portugal	0.1	0.4	1.9	10.7	15.4[‡]
Romania	–	0.9	4.3	53.7	70.3[†]
Russia	0.5	26.2	170.2	1039.0	1418.0[†]
Spain	1.0	3.3	11.9	76.3	117.3[†]
Sweden	2.6	6.9	24.7	80.6	100.1[‡]
Switzerland	2.8	5.7	15.5	42.9	51.8[†]
UK	8.5	26.0	89.0	272.1	N.A.
Yugoslavia	–	0.6	4.3	40.0	64.6[†]

* 1970   † 1983   ‡ 1982   § 1981

(*Sources*: B. R. Mitchell, *European Historical Statistics, 1750–1970*, Macmillan 1975, pp. 479–82; J. Paxton (ed.), *The Statesman's Year-Book, 1985–86*, Macmillan 1985.)

Railway mileage open, 1840–1913: selected countries
(kilometres)

	1840	1860	1880	1900	1913
Austria–Hungary	144	4,543	18,507	36,330	44,748
Belgium	334	1,729	4,112	4,562	4,676
France	410	9,167	23,089[†]	38,109[†]	40,770[†]
Germany	469	11,089	33,838[‡]	51,678[‡]	63,378[‡]
UK	2,411	16,798	28,846	36,004	38,114
Italy	20	2,404	9,290	16,429	18,873
Russia	–	1,626	22,865	53,234	70,156
Sweden	–	527	5,876	11,303	14,377
Spain	–	1,649	7,290	13,214	15,088
Switzerland	–	1,053	2,571	3,867	4,832

* 1914 boundaries unless otherwise stated; countries with more than 4,000 km of track open in 1914   [†] Excludes Alsace-Lorraine   [‡] Includes Alsace-Lorraine

(*Source*: B. R. Mitchell, *European Historical Statistics, 1750–1970*, Macmillan 1975, pp. 581–4.)

Railway mileage open, 1920–1975
(kilometres)

	1920	1950	1975
Austria	6,639	6,734	5,858
Belgium	4,938	5,046	3,998
Bulgaria	2,205	3,967	4,045
Czechoslovakia	13,430	13,124	13,241
Denmark	4,328	4,815	2,493
Finland	3,988	4,726	5,963
France	38,200	41,300	34,787
Germany	57,545	36,924(W) 12,895(E)	32,072(W) 14,298(E)
Greece	2,396	2,553	2,572
Hungary	8,141	8,756	8,392
Ireland	5,542	2,440	1,361
Italy	20,385	21,550	20,176
Netherlands	3,606	3,204	2,825
Norway	3,286	4,469	4,241
Poland	13,763	26,312*	23,773
Portugal	3,268	3,597	3,618
Romania	4,968	10,853	10,403
Russia	71,600	116,900	138,300
Spain	15,886	18,098	13,497
Sweden	14,869	16,516	12,065
Switzerland	5,078	5,152	2,860
UK	32,707	31,353	17,093
Yugoslavia	9,321	11,541	10,068

* Figure reflects major boundary changes in 1945

(*Source*: B. R. Mitchell, *European Historical Statistics, 1750–1970*, Macmillan 1975, pp. 585–7.)

Merchant ships registered by country, 1840–1985
(thousand tons)

	1840	1880	1910	1938	1960	1985¶
Austria–Hungary*	199	262	414	–	–	–
Belgium	23	75	191	272	677	2,183
Denmark	69	250	522	1,233	2,389	5,075
Finland	–	272	411	644	801	2,360
France	663	920	1,452	1,664	4,809	10,580
Germany	352	1,104	2,890	2,482	4,724(W) 197(E)	7,060(W) 1,224(E)
Great Britain	2,768	6,575	11,556	10,702	11,988	23,200
Greece	111	361§	458	1,930	5,38	36,806
Ireland	–	–	–	115	76	198
Italy	N.A.	999	1,001	2,039	5,705	9,620
Netherlands	380†	328	534	2,242	4,661	4,796
Norway	205	1,520	1,526	2,782	11,402	18,000
Poland	–	–	–	102	578	3,005
Portugal	–	–	–	250	286	1,260
Russia		468	723	1,273	3,429	16,000
Spain	245‡	560	775	214	1,754	7,299
Sweden	159	543	670	1,105	3,851	3,060
Yugoslavia	–	–	–	401	718	2,500

* To 1919   † 1846   ‡ 1850   § 1884   ¶ or nearest figure

(*Sources*: B. R. Mitchell, *European Historical Statistics, 1750–1970*, Macmillan 1975, pp. 613–31; J. Paxton (ed.), *The Statesman's Year-Book 1985–86*, Macmillan 1985.)

Value of external trade, 1815–1913: selected countries

	Germany (million marks)	Austria–Hungary (million kronen)	France (million francs)	Russia (million roubles)	UK (million pounds)
1815	–	–	791	341	140
1830	–	297	942	470	100
1850	–	554	1,859	192[†]	186
1870	5,741*	1,663	5,669	696[†]	547
1900	10,380	3,638	8,807	1,342	877
1913	20,848	6,177	15,301	2,894	1,404

* 1880   † New roubles, c. 4 × old value

(*Source*: B. R. Mitchell, *European Historical Statistics, 1750–1970*, Macmillan 1975, pp. 487–97.)

Total value of external trade, 1913–1975: selected countries

	Germany (million marks)	France (million francs)	Russia (million roubles)	Italy (million lira)	(UK) (million pounds)
1913	20,848	15,301	2,894	6,143	1,404
1925	27,713	99,850	1,020*	44,370	2,248
1938	10,713	76,655	475	21,750	1,453
1955	50,089[†]	3,409,973	5,839	2,855[‡]	6,854
1965	142,099[†]	100,661[§]	14,610	9,111[‡]	10,652
1975	–[†]	458,854[§]	50,699	47,846[‡]	43,790

* New roubles   [†] West Germany   [‡] Thousand million lira   [§] New francs

(*Sources*: B. R. Mitchell, *European Historical Statistics, 1750–1970*, Macmillan 1975, pp. 494–500; J. Paxton (ed.), *The Statesman's Year-Book, 1977–78*, Macmillan 1977.)

Days lost in industrial disputes, 1888–1969: selected countries
(in thousands)

	France	Germany	Italy	Spain	UK	Sweden
1888	–	–	–	–	–	–
1889	–	–	–	–	–	–
1890	1,340	–	–	–	–	–
1891	1,717	–	–	–	6,809	–
1892	918	–	–	–	17,382	–
1893	3,175	–	–	–	30,468	–
1894	1,062	–	–	–	9,529	–
1895	617	–	–	–	5,725	–
1896	644	–	–	–	3,746	–
1897	781	–	–	–	10,346	–
1898	1,216	–	–	–	15,289	–
1899	3,551	3,381	–	–	2,516	–
1900	3,761	3,712	–	–	3,153	–
1901	1,862	2,427	–	–	4,142	–
1902	4,675	1,951	–	–	3,479	–
1903	2,442	4,158	–	–	2,339	642
1904	3,935	5,285	–	–	1,484	386
1905	2,747	18,984	–	–	2,470	2,390
1906	9,439	11,567	–	–	3,029	479
1907	3,562	9,017	–	–	2,162	514
1908	1,752	3,666	–	–	10,834	1,842
1909	3,560	4,152	–	–	2,774	11,800
1910	4,830	17,848	–	1,409	9,895	39
1911	4,096	11,466	–	364	10,320	570
1912	2,318	10,724	–	1,056	40,915	292
1913	2,224	11,761	–	2,258	11,631	303
1914	2,187	2,844	–	1,018	9,804	620
1915	55	46	–	383	9,878	83
1916	236	245	838	2,415	2,953	475
1917	1,482	1,862	849	1,785	2,446	1,109

	France	Germany	Italy	Spain	UK	Sweden
1918	980	1,453	912	1,819	5,875	1,436
1919	15,478	33,083	22,325	4,001	34,969	2,296
1920	23,112	16,755	30,569	7,262	26,568	8,943
1921	7,027	25,874	8,180	2,802	85,872	2,663
1922	3,935	27,734	6,917	2,673	19,850	2,675
1923	4,172	12,344	296	3,027	10,672	6,907
1924	3,863	36,198	–	605	8,424	1,205
1925	2,046	2,936	–	840	7,952	1,560
1926	4,072	1,222	–	247	162,233	1,711
1927	1,046	6,144	–	1,312	1,174	400
1928	6,377	20,339	–	771	1,388	4,835
1929	2,765	4,251	–	314	8,287	667
1930	7,209	4,029	–	3,745	4,399	1,021
1931	950	1,890	–	3,843	6,983	2,627
1932	1,244	1,130	–	3,590	6,488	3,095
1933	1,199	–	–	14,441	1,072	3,434
1934	2,393	–	–	11,103	959	760
1935	1,182	–	–	–	1,955	788
1936	–	–	–	–	1,829	438
1937	–	–	–	–	3,413	861
1938	–	–	–	–	1,334	1,284
1939	–	–	–	–	1,356	159
1940	–	–	–	–	940	78
1941	–	–	–	–	1,079	94
1942	–	–	–	–	1,527	53
1943	–	–	–	–	1,810	94
1944	–	–	–	–	3,710	228
1945	–	–	–	–	2,835	11,321
1946	386	–	–	–	2,158	27
1947	22,673	–	–	–	2,433	125
1948	13,133	–	–	–	1,944	151
1949	7,129	271*	16,578	–	1,807	21
1950	11,729	380	7,761	–	1,389	41
1951	3,495	1,593	4,515	–	1,694	531

	France	Germany	Italy	Spain	UK	Sweden
1952	1,733	443	3,531	–	1,792	79
1953	9,722	1,488	5,828	–	2,184	582
1954	1,440	1,587	5,377	–	2,457	24
1955	3,079	847	5,622	–	3,781	159
1956	1,423	1,580	4,137	–	2,083	4
1957	4,121	1,072	4,619	–	8,412	53
1958	1,138	782	4,172	–	3,462	15
1959	1,938	62	9,190	–	5,270	24
1960	1,070	38	5,786	–	3,024	18
1961	2,601	61	9,891	–	3,046	2
1962	1,901	451	22,717	–	5,798	5
1963	5,991	1,846	11,395	125	1,755	25
1964	2,497	17	13,089	141	2,277	34
1965	980	49	6,993	190	2,925	4
1966	2,523	27	14,474	185	2,398	352
1967	4,204	390	8,568	236	2,787	1
1968	N.A.	25	9,240	241	4,690	1
1969	2,224	249	37,825	560	6,846	112

* West Germany

(*Source*: B. R. Mitchell, *European Historical Statistics, 1750–1970*, Macmillan 1975, pp. 174–82.)

Number of children in school (primary and secondary), 1850–1985

(in thousands)

	1850	1880	1910	1938	1960	1985[12]
Austria	1,440	2,504	4,691	914[9,10]	825	1,296
Belgium	493	366[1]	965	1,141	1,010	1,596
Bulgaria	–	–	525	1,016	1,212	740[13]
Czechoslovakia	–	–	–	2,381[10]	2,465	2,418
Denmark	–	341[2]	432	476	689	834
Finland	–	37[1]	202	550	841	1,232
France	3,370	5,136	5,781	5,943	7,201	9,866
Germany	–	–	11,310	8,442	6,513(W) 2,005(E)	8,375(W) 2,019(E)
Greece	–	–	260	1,029[10]	1,143	1,562
Hungary	–	1,659	2,549	1,031[10]	1,633	1,670
Ireland	–	–	–	500	567	791
Italy	–	2,036	3,473	5,104	5,832	6,889
Netherlands	399	548	924	1,304	1,851	2,134
Norway	–	254	392	378	529	756
Poland	–	–	–	4,640[10]	5,088	6,402
Portugal	–	248[3]	236[7]	499	999	1,760
Romania	–	108	594	2,663	2,588	4,798
Spain	–	1,769	1,861[8]	2,627[10]	3,861	7,403
Sweden	–	677[5]	815	619	1,063	1,265
Switzerland	–	460[1]	647	510	646[11]	–
UK	282	3,274[6]	6,295	5,947[10]	7,839	–
USSR	–	–	–	–	–	54,300
Yugoslavia	–	39[4]	146[4]	1,443	2,844	3,845

[1] 1881   [2] 1893   [3] 1887   [4] Serbia   [5] 1886   [6] Primary only   [7] 1899
[8] 1914   [9] Reduced boundaries since 1919   [10] 1935 figure   [11] 1961   [12] or
nearest date   [13] to age 11 only

(*Sources*: B. R. Mitchell, *European Historical Statistics, 1750–1970*, J. Paxton (ed.), *The Statesman's Year-Book, 1985–86*, Macmillan 1985.)

Number of students in higher education, 1840–1985

(in thousands)

	1840	1880	1910	1935	1955	1985[9]
Austria	8.6[1]	13.3	39.4	17.8	21.1	51.7
Belgium	1.5	4.6	7.9	10.7	24.5	96.8
Bulgaria	–	–	2.4[3]	7.9	37.1	83.6
Czechoslovakia	–	–		29.3	49.5	154.4[10]
Denmark	–	–	0.8	6.7	8.3	50.0
Finland	0.4	0.7	3.2	8.1	12.7	127.7[10]
France	–	–	41.2	73.8	157.5	980.8[10]
Germany	–	21.4	70.2	76.3	144.9(W) 74.7(E)	981.8 108.1
Greece	–	–	–	8.3	16.3[7]	87.4
Hungary	–	4.4	13.0	10.8	45.4	62.9
Ireland	–	–	–	5.0	8.1	N.A.
Italy	–	11.9	26.9	64.9	139.0	985.6
Netherlands	1.4	1.5	4.1	12.6	29.6	159.0
Norway	0.6	0.8	1.5	3.9	3.7	41.0
Poland	–	–	–	47.0	157.5	423.5
Portugal	0.9	0.8	1.2[3]	5.9	18.5	73.0[10]
Romania	–	–	3.8	38.2	77.6	174.0[10]
Spain	–	–	20.5[4]	29.2	57.0	669.9
Sweden	–	–	7.6	11.7	23.1	168.0[10]
Switzerland	–	–	6.8	8.7	11.9	51.5
UK	–	–	41.0	63.6	101.5	605.71[10]
USSR	–	–	39.9[3]	–	1,527.0[8]	5,300.0[10]
Yugoslavia	–	0.1[2]	0.8[5]	15.1	51.6	386.4[10]

[1] 1842 [2] Serbia [3] 1911 [4] 1914 [5] 1907 [6] 1937 [7] 1959
[8] 'Higher education institutes' [9] or nearest available year [10] all full-time students in higher education

(*Sources*: B. R. Mitchell, *European Historical Statistics, 1750–1970*, Macmillan 1975, pp. 771–6; J. Paxton (ed.), *The Statesman's Year-Book, 1985–86*, Macmillan 1985.)

Major events in European religious history

1760	England	Wesley Methodist lay-preachers take out licenses as dissenting teachers and administer the sacrament.
1762	France	Louis XV forbids Jesuits to teach and recruit new members, and orders the sale of their property.
1764	France	The Jesuit Order is suppressed in France. Pope Clement XIII issues a Bull defending the Order.
	Bohemia	The Moravian Church is reformed by Spangenberg.
	Portugal	Communication between Portugal and the Papacy is broken off as a result of the execution of Malagrida as a heretic. Beginning of Pombal's work to suppress the Jesuits.
1765	Papacy	Cult of the Sacred Heart sanctioned by the Pope.
1766	Spain	Secular education, supervision of monasteries and tax on church lands introduced by D'Aranda.
	Russia	Religious toleration declared in Russia.
1767	Spain	Jesuits expelled from Spain, the Sicilies and Parma.
1769	Germany	List of anti-papal grievances the 'Coblenz Articles' presented by the Archbishops of Mainz, Cologne, and Trier to Maria Theresa.
	Other	Spain, France and Naples demand the abolition of the Jesuit Order.
1773	Papacy	Jesuits Order suppressed.
1774	Poland	Jesuits expelled from Poland.
1776	Bavaria	Illuminati founded in Bavaria.
1778	Great Britain	Catholic Relief granted in Ireland and mainland Britain. Agitation in Scotland begun by Lord George Gordon and Protestant Association for repeal.
1780	England	Gordon riots in London with widespread attacks on Catholic (and other) property.
1781	Austria	Joseph II grants religious toleration to Protestants and members of the Greek Church. 700 monasteries dissolved; Papal Bulls restricted; funds for Rome stopped, and six new bishoprics created without papal approval.
1782	Austria	Pope visits Vienna to protest at Joseph's actions but to no effect.
1783	Germany	Eichhorn's *Introduction to the Old Testament* investigates its sources and contents and attributes parts to several different authors.

	Austria	Joseph II makes marriage a civil contract and allows divorce. He proposes appointment of bishops without papal approval, suppresses diocesan seminaries and forms own schools for the education of clergy.
1784	Great Britain	Wesley ordains two Wesleyan 'superintendents' in America, effectively producing a major breach with the Anglican Church.
1787	Italy	Leopold II of Tuscany dismisses national synod in Florence for failing to agree with his church reforms and sets about them himself. King of the Two Sicilies refuses to pay annual tribute to the Pope.
	England	Evangelical revival focuses around Beilby Porteus, appointed Bishop of London, the Countess of Huntingdon, William Wilberforce, Charles Simeon, and Hannah More.
	France	Edict of Versailles grants religious freedom and legal civil status to Protestants.
1789	France	Mirabeau carries a motion that the property of the Church belongs to the nation.
1790	France	Church property confiscated and monasteries abolished. The Civil Constitution of the Clergy reduces the number of Bishops to one for each department; Bishops to be chosen by the Parliamentary electors and instituted by the Metropolitan; the clergy chosen by the electors to communal offices. Papal confirmation dispensed with. All clergy to take the oath to the Civil Constitution. Protestants become eligible for office and receive back property confiscated by Louis XIV. Jews also received civil rights.
1791	General	Volney's *Ruins of Empires* compares the chief religions of the world to the disadvantage of Christianity.
1792	France	Clergy who refuse to take the oath to the Civil Constitution of the Clergy are given 14 days to leave after 10 August. The religious orders are dissolved and civil marriage and divorce are introduced.
	Germany	Fichte's *Critique of all Revelation* rejects doctrinal Christianity.
1793	France	Convention abolishes Catholic faith and threatens recalcitrant clergy with death. Feast of Reason celebrated on 10 November in Church of St Eustache.
1794	General	Paine's *Age of Reason* adopts Deistic position, attacking Christianity and the Old Testament.
	France	Convention formally recognizes the existence of a Supreme Being and immortality (May). Robespierre presides over the Feast of the Supreme Being (June).
1795	Ireland	British government founds College of Maynooth in Ireland to train Catholic priests.

1797   *England*   Methodist New Connexion leaves the Wesleyans.

1801   *France*   Concordat with the Papacy. Catholicism is recognised as the religion of the nation; the State guarantees salaries and chooses bishops, subject to Papal confirmation. The clergy are chosen by the bishops but confirmed by the State. Some bishops refuse to recognise the Concordat and form La Petite Eglise.

1802   *France*   Concordat promulgated, but with Organic Articles which have not been discussed by the Pope. Papal bulls and representatives not allowed into France without government permission, nor synods held. Chateaubriand's *Genius of Christianity* published. It asserts the irrational and aesthetic values of Christianity in opposition to the criticism of the philosophes.

1804   *France*   Napoleon tightens control over Church, restoring laws against perpetual vows.

1805   *France*   Napoleon brings Jews under state control.

1806   *Papacy*   Following a series of disputes with Napoleon, principally over the extension of the *Code Napoleon* to Italy and Napoleon's seizure of Papal territory, the Pope refuses to expel French enemies from his territory, observe the continental system and appoint to the Venetian bishoprics under Napoleon's control.
       England   Leaders of Evangelical movement form 'Clapham sect', named after John Venn, Rector of Clapham.

1808   *Papacy*   Rome occupied by French troops.
       Spain   Napoleon abolishes the Inquisition and suppresses most of the monasteries.
       Italy   Napoleon abolishes Italian Inquisition.

1809   *Papacy*   Rome formally added to French Empire (17 May); Pius VII excommunicates Napoleon (11 June); Pius arrested and imprisoned in Savona (6 July). The Pope refuses to institute French bishops. Napoleon calls an Ecclesiastical Commission for France to seek a solution to the deadlock, but it fails to offer a solution acceptable to Napoleon and is suppressed (January 1810).

1810   *France*   Senate decrees that all future Popes and all the clergy of the Empire must accept the Gallican articles of 1682.
       Switzer-land   Zinzendorf circle in Geneva form a Society of Friends and begin a Protestant revival.

1811   *France*   Napoleon calls a Council in Paris to sanction a scheme for the institution of Bishops. Although securing Papal approval, Napoleon dissolves the Council because of the restrictions he requests.

1813   *France*   Napoleon brings Pope to France and forces a new Concordat giving Napoleon the nomination of bishops in France and Italy and the Metropolitan the power to institute if the Pope had not done so within six months. The Pope, however, later repudiates the agreement.

1814	Spain and Italy	Spanish and Italian Inquisitions refounded. Index renewed.
	Papacy	Jesuit Order and Index restored by the Pope.
1815	Germany	Wessenberg, Vicar-General of the diocese of Constance urges the Vienna Congress to found a German national Church under a German primate.
1817	Germany	Lutheran and Reformed Churches of Prussia unite in the Evangelical Union. The Union spreads to other German states.
	France	Lamennais's *Essay on Indifference* attacks individualism and scepticism.
1818	Germany	Representatives of several German states meet at Frankfurt to revive the idea of a German national Church but frustrated by Niebuhr, the Prussian envoy at Rome.
1820	England	Plymouth Brethren founded by Darby, an Anglican ex-clergyman, on the basis of strict Calvinism. The headquarters of the Brethren eventually moves to Switzerland.
1821	Germany	Concordat concluded between Prussia and the Papacy.
1824	France	Lamennais visits Rome and on his return advocates the political supremacy of the Pope.
1828	Great Britain	Repeal of Test and Corporation Acts removes last civil disabilities on Protestant Dissenters.
1829	Great Britain	Catholic Emancipation Act makes Catholics eligible for almost all offices of state. No oath of supremacy required to sit in either House of Parliament.
1832	Papacy	Gregory XVI issues an Encyclical condemning freedom of conscience and of the press in reaction to the new Belgian Constitution.
1833	England	Keble's Assize Sermon on National Apostasy, denouncing the suppression of Irish bishoprics, seen as the beginning of the high church Oxford Movement to revive Anglicanism.
1834	Portugal	Suppression of monasteries.
1835	Germany	Tubingen school of theology founded by Professor Baur, dealing with theology from an historical and philosophical point of view.
1837	Germany	Dispute with the king of Prussia over mixed marriages leads to the imprisonment of the Archbishop of Cologne and several other bishops.
1838	France	Dominican Order revived in France.

1839	Russia	Catechism approved by the Russian Holy Synod and distributed to schools and churches.
	Greece	Two million Uniate Christians incorporated within the Greek Church.
1841	England	Newman's Tract 90, draws hostile criticism from Anglicans for its Catholic tendency.
	Italy	Don Bosco founds the Oratory of St Francis de Sales for work amongst boys.
1843	Scotland	'Disruption' in Presbyterian Church. 474 clergy leave the established church over the issue of lay patronage.
1844	Germany	Short-lived German Catholic Church founded. The Pope condemns the rationalistic teaching of Hermes.
1845	England	Newman joins the Roman Church, with other leaders of the High Church movement.
	Norway	Dissenter law permits freedom of religious expression. All except civil servants can leave the national church and parents can exempt children from religious education in schools.
1846	England	Evangelical Alliance formed in England to oppose Romanism, Puseyism, and rationalism. It attracts support in America and on the Continent and holds conferences abroad.
	Papacy	Election of Pius IX. Begins reform of Papal States, including an amnesty for 1,000 prisoners and reform of courts.
1847	Germany	Edict of Toleration in Prussia. Prussian government recognises right of secession from state church.
	Papacy	Pope grants limited freedom of the press in Papal States and becomes focus of anti-Austrian feeling after protest to Austria over violation of the Papal States.
	Scotland	United Presbyterian Church formed.
1848	Germany	Separation of Church and State decreed by Frankfurt Parliament (March). Meeting of German Bishops at Wurzburg resolves to work for the full independence from secular control of ecclesiastical legislation, administration, and control of education. These are incorporated in Concordats with several of the southern German States. Five hundred clergy meet at Wittenberg to celebrate success against Revolution.
	France	Falloux, Minister of Education, introduces a bill permitting Catholics to be educated at Catholic primary and secondary schools, but only obtain degrees at secular universities. The numbers receiving clerical education greatly increase.
	Italy	Roman crowds demand lay ministers in Papal States. Papal armies cross into Austrian Italy. Pius IX states his unwillingness to declare war on Austrians and denies instigation of revolution. Effectively ended hopes of the Pope as champion of war against

Austrian domination. Pope flees to Gaeta after demonstrations in Rome.   Jesuits expelled from Kingdom of Sardinia and influence of clergy on education restricted.

Holland   Dutch Reformed Church disestablished.

1849   *Papacy*   Rome recaptured for the Pope. The Pope issues an encyclical to the Italian Bishops condemning socialism and communism. He also issues an encyclical inviting views on the immaculate conception.

Denmark   By the constitution the Evangelical Lutheran Church is supported by the state, parliament acting as legislative and money-voting authority, but full religious toleration also established.

1850   *Germany*   Prussian constitution provides that all religious associations should administer their affairs independently and remain in possession of their property and funds for religious, educational, and charity purposes. Communication with superiors and publication of ordinances largely unfettered. But nomination, election, and confirmation of ecclesiastical posts governed by the state.

Belgium   Pius IX protested against law making secondary education subject to state control. Bishops insist on there only being Catholic chaplains in state establishments.

England   Restoration of Catholic sees. Manning (later Cardinal) joins the Roman Church with other Anglicans.

Italy   Siccardi Laws suppress ecclesiastical immunities in Kingdom of Sardinia. Archbishops of Turin and Sardinia imprisoned.

1851   *Germany*   Prussian Evangelical Churches placed under control of a Church Council instead of the King.

Italy   Church's jurisdiction over heresy and sacrilege taken by civil power in Kingdom of Sardinia.

Spain   Concordat signed with the Papacy by which Catholicism is declared sole religion of the state. Church to supervise education and have sole jurisdiction over marriage disputes. Papacy guarantees the right of the Crown to appoint bishops and recognises loss of church lands already secularised.

1852   *Germany*   The Eisenach biennial conference is instituted, made up of representatives of the Protestants of each state. Under its direction a revision of Luther's Bible is instituted.

Italy   Church property secularised and civil marriage introduced in Kingdom of Sardinia.

1853   *Holland*   Catholic hierarchy re-established in spite of protests.

Russia   Dispute over Holy Places. Tsar Nicholas I intervenes to 'protect' Christians in Turkey and to confirm Russian rights over the Holy Places. Russia fails to obtain a

treaty with Turkey giving her protectorate over
Christians in the Ottoman Empire through opposition
of Great Britain.

1854	*Germany*	The New Lutherans attack pietism and individualism. Jewish seminary established at Breslau.
	Papacy	The Immaculate Conception of the Virgin is declared an article of faith for Roman Catholics. The Curia is reformed and the Sacred College. Greater centralisation of Papal power.
	Denmark	Kirkegaard–Martensen controversy on Christianity.
1855	*Austria*	Concordat with the Papacy. Austrian Catholic Bishops empowered to issue ordinances without the approval of the civil power, set penalties and supervise education, marriage and the press. State control of the Church abolished.
	Italy	A Monastic Law abolishes all religious orders in the Kingdom of Sardinia except those employed in preaching, education and the care of the sick.
	Sweden	Obligatory communion for public office holders ended.
	General	Spiritualist movement spreads from the United States to England and later to Europe.
1856	*Sweden*	Evangelical National Institute founded for lay work at home. Foreign missions and seamen's missions founded in 1861.
1858	*France*	First apparitions of the Virgin reported at Lourdes.
	Russia	Metropolitan Philaret and other bishops oppose emancipation of serfs.
1859	*Papacy*	Pope refuses to renounce temporal power.
	Great Britain	Darwin's *Origins of Species* provokes intense controversy about the literal accuracy of the Bible.
	Sweden	Members of non-Lutheran faiths allowed to practise freely.
1860	*Papacy*	Encyclical *Nullis Certe* threatens to excommunicate all who attack papal domains. Papal army defeated by Austrians and Rome only saved by French troops.
1861	*Italy*	Prota-Giurleo, a Dominican, attempts to found a National Church, with radical changes in organisation and liturgy. Monastic orders partially suppressed in Kingdom of Two Sicilies.
1863	*France*	Renan's *Vie de Jesus* (life of Jesus), a strictly historical account of Christ's life, is published and arouses controversy.
	Germany	Protestant Union founded, seeking federation into a National Church, greater power for the laity, and greater latitude in doctrinal matters.
	Romania	Monasteries secularised and transferred to the state.
	Russia	Concordat between Russia and Holy See repudiated by Tsar following the Russian repression of Polish rising.

1864	*Poland*	Catholic monasteries dissolved and control of Catholic affairs given to a Minister of Worship.
	Papacy	Pope issues encyclical, a syllabus *Quanta Cura*, with 80 errors, including Liberalism. Religious toleration, freedom of conscience and press, free discussion, and secularist legislation are challenged.
	Romania	Romanian Church proclaimed national and independent of the patriarchate of Constantinople.
	Russia	Diplomatic relations between Russia and Holy See broken off.
1865	*England*	General Booth begins evangelical and rescue work in East London, leading to the formation of the Salvation Army.
1866	*Papacy*	Pope condemns attempts at Anglican–Catholic reunion.
	Italy	Monasteries and congregations suppressed by law. Land held in mortmain sold by the state. Cathedral chapters and bishops forced to surrender their capital to the state. Seminarists made liable for military service and civil marriage made obligatory.
1867	*Papacy*	The Pope announces his intention to hold an Ecumenical Council. The doctrine of Papal Infallibility is widely canvassed.
1868	*Ireland*	Anglican Church in Ireland disestablished.
	Austria	Civil marriage is restored and the schools are freed from clerical control. The Church can only open new ones. Jews granted full civil liberty and Jewish immigration increases substantially from neighbouring states. Pope condemns the new laws.
	France	White Fathers founded by Lavigerie for missionary and educational work.
	Spain	Following Liberal Revolution the Cortes proclaims freedom of worship and teaching and introduces civil marriage. Religious houses suppressed and clergy deprived of salaries.
1869	*Papacy*	Vatican Council meets and begins discussion of papal infallibility
	Germany	Prince Hohenlohe, Minister President of Bavaria, invites powers to confer on the prospect of decree of papal infallibility. German Bishops at Fulda produce a pastoral to allay fears of a new dogma.
1870	*Papacy*	Vatican Council declares Papal *ex cathedra* definitions of faith and morals infallible by 533 votes to 2 (July). Rome falls to Piedmontese troops of Victor Emmanuel. Romans decide by plebiscite to become part of Italy. Decree of 9 October declares Rome and Roman provinces part of Kingdom of Italy. The Popes loses all temporal power.
	Austria	Austrian government forbids promulgation of Council's decree and cancels Concordat with Papacy.

	Germany	After first producing a memorial against the new dogma (Jan.), the German bishops accept the dogma of infallibility. Archbishop of Cologne orders theological professors of Bonn to accept the dogma on pain of being forbidden to lecture to Roman Catholic students or exercise their priestly function. Bavaria refuses to accept Papal Bill on infallibility. Clergy and Bishops accept and attempt to coerce opponents. Some German Catholics, now known as Old Catholics, prefer to secede from Rome rather than accept the decree. Several states give active support to the Old Catholic movement and its leaders Dr Dollinger and Dr Reinkens.
	France	Communards enact separation of Church and State, the abolition of a budget for religious affairs, and execute 24 clergy including the Archbishop of Paris.
	Switzer-land	Swiss Federal government breaks off relations with Papacy after disputes over mixed marriages, education, freedom of the press, and the doctrine of infallibility.
	Denmark	Sunday Schools introduced by Home Mission Movement (Indre Misjon).
1871	Germany	Catholic Centre Party founded to defend Catholic interests and wins 63 seats in Diet. Congress of Old Catholics held at Munich. Catholic members of the Prussian Landtag petition the Emperor to restore the temporal power of the Pope. He refuses to assist. When some Catholic bishops attempt to excommunicate those not accepting infallibility the Government declares them still Catholics with full civil rights. Political pronouncements from pulpit made a criminal offence and Roman Catholic Department of Spiritual Affairs abolished.
	Italy	The Law of Guarantees declares the Pope's person inviolable, accords the honours of a sovereign prince, allows the possession of the Vatican and other palaces, and grants an annuity (rejected by the Pope). Church and state separated and Church property secularised, though religious orders once again allowed to own property. Restrictions on Church lifted.
	Belgium	Prime Minister Frère-Orban obtains law creating free 'neutral' schools in which the Catholic faith may only be taught outside class hours. Catholic bishops protest and diplomatic relations with the Papacy ended. Private Catholic schools organised. Congrès des Oeuvres Sociales founded by Bishop of Liège.
1872	Germany	The Prussian government reduces 'clerical influence' in school. The Bishops protest and the Pope excommunicates the authors of the law. Bismarck banishes the Jesuits and forces clergy to swear allegiance before appointment.

1873   *Germany*   May Laws in Prussia give state control in the education of the clergy, jurisdiction over Church cases, excommunication, and the appointment and dismissal of ministers. Catholic bishops vote to oppose the laws and three are imprisoned and over 400 clergy dismissed.

        Italy   1866 law extended to Rome. Proceeds of property of religious corporations divided between Holy See and charitable activities.

        Sweden   By decree of toleration Swedes allowed to leave Lutheran Church to join another Christian community.

1874   *Great Britain*   Gladstone declares acceptance of the Papal decrees of 1870 inconsistent with civil allegiance.

        Germany   Civil marriage made compulsory in Prussia and priests who refuse to accept the May Laws are threatened with banishment. Catholic Centre Party grows in strength at the General Election.   German Old Catholics permit use of vernacular, allow marriage of priests, and abolish compulsory confession.

        Austria   The May Laws replace Concordat of 1855. Powers of Church restricted. Bishops say will only obey the laws in so far as in agreement with old Concordat.

        Italy   Church declares it 'inexpedient' to vote in General Election, though many Catholics disobey.

        Switzerland   Civil marriage made obligatory. No new monasteries to be founded, but religious freedom ensured.

1875   *Germany*   Pope declares recent anti-Catholic legislation in Germany invalid. The Prussian Government refuses payment to clergy who will not obey; two-thirds of Prussian bishoprics and 1,400 curacies become vacant. Civil marriage made obligatory throughout the Empire. All religious orders suppressed in Prussia except those engaged in nursing.

        Russia   Last Apostolic See of Roman Catholic Church suppressed.

        Papacy   Pope institutes the cult of the Sacred Heart.

1876   *Bulgaria*   Massacre of thousands of Bulgarian Christians by the Turks provokes intense outrage in many parts of Europe.

        Spain   Alfonso XII takes throne. Church property restored, Catholic schools reopened, diplomatic relations with Papacy restored. Catholicism once again official religion though recognised the existence of 'non-Catholic cults'. The state took responsibility for maintaining the Church. Civil marriage abolished and Protestant chapels closed.

1877   *Germany*   Eight Roman Catholic Archbishops and bishops removed in Prussia, leaving only four.

        Russia   Holy War against Turkey to 'liberate Balkan Christians' and re-establish Constantinople as a great Christian centre.

1878	*Germany*	Roman Catholic seminaries closed.
	Scotland	Catholic hierarchy restored in Scotland.
1879	*Germany*	Bismarck lessens persecution of Catholic Church after accession of Leo XIII.
	France	Jules Ferry's education bill forbids members of unauthorised communities to teach.
	General	Max Muller edits a translation of the sacred Books of the East.
1880	*France*	The Jesuit Order is dissolved, military chaplains are abolished, and candidates for the ministry are compelled to serve in the army for a year. State primary education made free and compulsory and religious teaching abolished.
	Belgium	Diplomatic relations between the Papacy and Belgian government broken off over the School Law of 1879.
	Germany	Bismarck relaxes application of the May Laws and reinstates clergy.
	Russia	Constantine Petrovich Pobedonostsev becomes Procurator of the Holy Synod. An active promoter of Russian Orthodoxy, he sanctions the persecution or conversion of other religious groups.
1881	*France*	Ferry expels the unauthorised congregations.
	Russia	Pobedonostsev begins a widespread persecution of the Jews following the assassination of Alexander II. Many Jews leave Russia for other parts of Europe and America. Pobedonostsev calls on Tsar Alexander III to reassert autocratic rule and opposes talks to improve the position of Catholics in Russia.
1882	*Russia*	Diplomatic relations between Russia and Holy See resumed. May Laws restrict Jews to the south-west of Russia; forbid Jews from becoming lawyers, owning land, holding administrative posts, appeal against court sentence or marry Christians without conversion. Jewish schools closed and Hebrew books banned.
1883	*Russia*	Pobedonostsev launches drive to establish parish schools throughout European Russia. Publishes Moscow Collection which sees religion as the foundation of a civilised life and threatened by modernism and democracy. He supports Leo Tolstoy's official removal from the Russian Orthodox Church for his support of student disorders. Act allows schismatics to hold religious services at home, to work, and hold internal passports, but not allowed to worship publicly, build new places of worship, nor proselytise.
	Britain	Salvation Army founded.
1884	*France*	The Pope calls on the French Bishops not to show hostility to the Republic.

	Belgium	Catholic government elected. New education law makes many public schools Catholic and restores relations with Papacy. First worker priests amongst miners.
1884	Russia	Lord Radstock and other Plymouth Brethren expelled from Russia. More parish schools established under direction of Holy Synod.
1885	Russia	Holy Synod forbids mixed marriages in largely Lutheran Baltic Provinces (Estonia and Latvia) unless children raised in Orthodox faith. Widespread protest.
1886	Portugal	Concordat with Vatican. Bishops to be nominated by the government, appointed by the Pope, and paid by the state. Parish clergy appointed by the state.
	France	Teachers belonging to religious orders removed from state schools.
	Germany	State examination and control of seminaries given up.
1887	Germany	Bismarck ends the *Kulturkampf*.
1888	Papacy	Papal encyclical *De libertate humana*, on human liberty.
1889	Italy	Penalties increased for clergy who use pulpit for political purposes.
1890	France	Pope Leo XIII's 'Ralliement' policy encourages Catholics to accept the Republic through encyclical, *Sapientiae christianae*. Right-wing and anti-Jewish Assumptionist Order dissolved.
	Italy	Compulsory tithes abolished and Church charities taken over by state.
1891	France	Five French cardinals indict the Government for its past anti-clerical legislation.
	Papacy	Encyclical *Rerum novarum* condemned condition of workers, advocates just wage, right of association and right of peasants to land; missions encouraged and Vatican archives opened; but modernism and rationalism also condemned.
1892	France	Further papal encyclical declares that 'acceptance of the new regime is not only permitted but demanded'.
	Germany	Revision of Luther's Bible completed.
	Russia	Salaries of clergy increased and training streamlined. Anti-Jewish pogrom in Moscow forces thousands to flee.
1893	Romania	Priests become government officials and maintenance of church and clergy becomes a charge on the general budget.
1894	France	Many Catholics support the prosecution of Dreyfus, intensifying anti-clerical feeling on the left.
	Poland	Papal encyclical states that Polish Catholic clergy will no longer oppose Russia.
	Russia	Pobedonostsev prevents appointment of papal nuncio

to St Petersburg and frustrates Church of England efforts to establish relations with the Orthodox Church. Protestant sects are persecuted.

Austria   Civil marriage made obligatory and declared sufficient without religious ceremony. Freedom of worship proclaimed.

Papacy   Discussion of reunion of Roman and Armenian churches.

Belgium   Religious instruction made obligatory in all state schools.

1897   *Jewry*   First Zionist Congress held at Basle to promote resettlement of Palestine.

Austria   *Los von Rom* (freedom from Rome) movement grows in Austria.

1898   *Italy*   Violence in Milan leads to suppression of 3,000 Catholic organisations.

1901   *France*   Law allows associations to be formed, but congregations have to be licensed.

1903   *Denmark*   Congregational councils of clergy and laity set up in each parish to manage church fabric and funds and elect clergy and bishops.

1904   *France*   Law suppressing teaching orders. Quarrel over choice of bishops between French government and Papacy.

1905   *France*   Separation of Church and State. Napoleon's concordat and organic articles repealed. Churches remained property of state but at the disposal of the ministers and orders.

Russia   Fr. Gapon leads ill-fated 'Bloody Sunday' procession. Group of 32 formed by St Petersburg priests and petition for church reform. Their leader Fr. Petrov elected to the second Duma, but sentenced by the Synod to 3 months confinement and unfrocked. Group of 32 produce a declaration, approved by Metropolitan Antoni, calling for freedon from state control, the restoration of the patriarchate abolished in 1700, and local religious councils.   Religious tolerance law passed. Now legal to leave state church. Evangelical sects form league of freedom whose platform includes schooling, equal rights for denominations, constitutional monarchy and equal suffrage.   Nonetheless persecution of evangelicals, Old Believers, Jews, and Roman Catholics (especially in Poland) continued.   Pobedonostsev replaced by Lukyanov.

Italy   Bishops allowed to decide if Catholics of diocese can participate in political life.

1906   *Papacy*   Pius X refuses to recognise the separation of church and state in France.

Netherlands   Catholic Social Weeks started.

	Russia	Fr. Gapon assassinated.
1907	*Russia*	Holy Synod declares it incompatible with priestly office to belong to parties opposed to the State and the Tsar.
	Britain	Three Methodist churches unite as United Methodist Church.
1908	*Portugal*	New Portuguese republic expels religious congregations, parish administration is taken over by lay committees, and financed solely from contributions. Religious teaching in schools abolished and religious oaths for university and other courses.
	Russia	Holy Synod tells bishops to encourage the participation of the Orthodox clergy in the right-wing League of the Russian People and other conservative societies. Russian Evangelical League founded, calling for moral regeneration to replace class struggle.
1909	*Papacy*	Pope condemns modernism in encyclical *Pascendi gregis*.
	Spain	During '*Semana Tragica*' in Barcelona over 50 religious buildings destroyed by the populace during socialist uprising.
1910	*General*	World Missionary Conference in Edinburgh sees beginning of modern ecumenical movement.
	Portugal	Prelates publish a pastoral censuring government. Minister of Justice orders its suspension. When defied, the Bishop of Oporto is deposed.
	Russia	Protestant conferences to be vetted by Minister of Interior. They are not allowed to educate their children in their Faith.
1911	*Portugal*	Law of separation. Church disestablished. Clergy forbidden to criticise the government or laws of the republic. Boards of laymen to take charge of Catholic worship. Ministers permitted to marry.
	Russia	Rasputin, whose influence at court is very great, causes increasing embarrassment to ecclesiastical and political authorities and is forced to make pilgrimage to Holy Land, but returns and causes fresh scandals.
1912	*Russia*	40 conservative clergy elected to the fourth Duma.
1914	*France*	Clemenceau condemns Pope Benedict XV as 'the Bosche Pope'.
1916	*Russia*	Duma condemns Rasputin.
1917	*Russia*	Synod refuses to condemn February revolution. Provisional government puts church schools under Ministry of Education. All Russian Council of the Church convened and rejects separation of Church and State. Patriarch Tikhon (elected November) and council oppose Soviet revolution. Liberal clergy support it.

1918	*Russia*	Separation of church and state (Jan.). Abolition of religious teaching and publications, censorship of sermons, and ban on church youth groups. Clergy deprived of vote, have to pay higher taxes, and children debarred from higher education. Churches may be used for secular purposes.
	Portugal	Conservative regime of Sidonia Pais revokes anti-clerical measures and reopens diplomatic relations with the Papacy. Cult of Our Lady of Fatima becomes increasingly popular after three children claim to have seen the Virgin on a hillside in Estremadura.
1919	*Italy*	Catholic Partito Popolare formed (Jan.). Pope lifts ban on Catholic participation in political life and in following elections (Nov.) Catholics strongly represented.
	Sweden	Religious instruction in schools made non-denominational.
	Germany	United Evangelical Protestant National Church reorganised.
1920	*France*	Moves towards reconciliation with Papacy. Canonisation of Joan of Arc.
	Germany	Cardinal Pacelli, later Pius XII, becomes papal nuncio in Berlin.
1921	*Russia*	Anti-Soviet clergy call a Sobor (Church council) at Karlovtsy in Yugoslavia, endorsing anti-Bolshevik cause and calling for return of the monarchy.
1922	*Russia*	Trial and execution of Metropolitan Veniamin for resistance to seizure of church treasure decreed by state for famine relief in Volga region. Patriarch Tikhon put under house arrest.
1923	*Russia*	Reformist clergy of so-called 'Living Church' hold Sobor, strip Patriarch Tikhon of titles and clerical status, pass resolutions in favour of socialist reconstruction of society; also give more influence to clergy in church administration and make married priests eligible to become bishops. Produces split amongst faithful and eventually amongst the 'Living Church'. Patriarch Tikhon offers muted support for Soviet state and is released from house arrest.
1927	*Russia*	After period of uneasy compromise Metropolitan Sergei proclaims full support for Soviet state. Beginnings of widespread persecution of Islam and Islamic customs; Mosques closed, mullahs displaced, veils banned, and Islamic courts and schools closed. Polygamy, bride-money and Ramadan stopped or discouraged.
	General	World Conference on Faith and Order at Lausanne.
1928	*General*	Ecumenical Missionary Conference in Jerusalem stresses partnership of churches.

1929	*Russia*	Legislation on 'religious associations'. Religious activity only permitted to registered congregations each of which has to consist of at least 20 people over eighteen, who can hire church buildings and engage a priest. All outside religious activity prohibited. Evangelism banned.
	Italy	Lateran treaties with Papacy recognising the Vatican as a state and the Pontiff as its head. The church assumes privileged status in Italy and formal reconciliation between the Papacy and Kingdom of Italy takes place.
	Scotland	Presbyterian Churches of Scotland unite in the Church of Scotland.
	General	World Conference of Lutherans at Copenhagen.
1931	*Spain*	Constitution of Republic separates Church and State; reduces clerical salaries; forbids Orders to teach and suppresses the Jesuits.
	Papacy	Pius XI publishes encyclical *Quadragesimo Anno* on his ideas of the corporate state.
1932	*Spain*	Widespread attacks on church property in Madrid, Barcelona and southern Spain. Over 55 churches or convents destroyed.
	Germany	Protestant group found pro-Nazi 'German Christians'.
1933	*Papacy*	Pope protests in encyclical *Dilectissima nobis* about anti-clerical measures in Spain.
	Germany	Pope Pius XI publicly praises Hitler for his stand against Communism and German bishops withdraw their opposition. Hitler and chairman of German Catholic Centre Party hold discussions and Centre Party supports Enabling Act (Mar.). Centre Party dissolves itself (July). Concordat signed between Nazi Germany and Holy See (July); ratified in September. Ludwig Muller of German Christians becomes Bishop of the Reich. Protestant Churches amalgamate as German Evangelical Church.
1934	*Spain*	Priests and religious in Oviedo murdered during Asturias rising.
	Germany	The Protestant Barman Synod accuses German Christians of departing from the Gospels and abandoning the legal basis of the Protestant churches.
1935	*Germany*	Nuremberg Laws deprive Jews of citizen rights and forbid sexual relations and inter-marriage. Hitler sets up ministry of Church affairs.
	Russia	Soviet Muslims prohibited from visiting Mecca.
	Spain	Widespread attacks on church property in the areas where anarchism and communism strong.
1936	*Russia*	Widespread purge of clergy and bishops. Of 163 bishops active in 1930 only 12 still at liberty in 1939.
	Spain	Attacks on church property following election of

Popular Front; 160 churches or convents destroyed and 269 clergy killed. Renewed attacks and atrocities following the outbreak of war. Twelve bishops and over 7,000 religious and clergy killed. Pius XI denounces 'the satanic enterprise' and blesses Franco's cause. Franco declares 'Spain shall be an empire turned towards God'.

1937 *Germany* Protestant Church deprived of control of its finances. Protestant opposition forbidden. Pastor Niemuller and other protestant pastors arrested and sent to concentration camps.

Papacy Papal encyclical on atheistic communism.

1938 *Spain* Diplomatic relations renewed between Papacy and Nationalists. The Pope calls for the re-establishment of a Catholic Spain.

Germany Anti-Jewish pogrom on 9–10 November, the *Kristallnacht*, arouses protests from some Church groups.

1939 *Papacy* Cardinal Pacelli becomes Pius XII.

1940 *Great Britain* In letter to *The Times* leading churchmen urge creation of a more egalitarian and just society as a postwar objective.

1941 *Jewry* Germans begin extermination of Jews in occupied territories of Poland and Russia. By 1942 an estimated 1,400,000 Jews massacred by *Einsatzgruppen* murder squads. Beginning of construction of camps primarily for the systematic murder of Jews. Mass deportations of Jews from Germany to camps in the east begin.

Russia Russian Orthodox Church pledges support for war with Germany.

Germany Cardinal Galen of Munster condemns Nazi euthanasia programme.

1942 *Jewry* Heydrich chairs 'Wannsee Conference' of Nazi officials in Berlin which adopts the 'final solution' of deportation and extermination of European Jewry. Extermination camps opened at Sobidor, Treblinka, Birkenau and elsewhere. Widespread deportations of French, Dutch, Polish, and Slovak Jews to the camps for forced labour and gassing. Continued massacres of Russian, Baltic and Yugoslav Jews.

Great Britain Archbishop William Temple's *Christianity and the Social Order* outlines advances in social welfare as necessary to a Christian society.

Papacy Hitler closes diplomatic channels with the Vatican.

Holland Dutch bishops issue a public protest against the deportation of Jews to Germany.

1943 *Russia* Patriarchate and ecclesiastical administration re-established. Seminaries and theological academies opened, and churches permitted to reopen.

		Government appoints special Council for Church Affairs to supervise.
	France	Archbishop Suchard of Paris founds worker-priest movement.
	Jewry	Continuation of mass extermination programme by the Nazis. Belsen concentration camp opened. Destruction of Jewish Ghetto in Warsaw.
1945	*Jewry*	Mass extermination of European Jews continues until the last days of the war. Between 5 and 6 million Jews estimated to have been murdered or died of ill-treatment out of a European total of over 8½ million in 1941.
1946	*Russia*	'Living Church' abolished.
	General	Committee of World Council of Churches drafts plan for a reconstructed World International Assembly. International Christian Conference at Cambridge aims at closer relations between Protestant and Orthodox Churches.
1948	*General*	Representatives of 147 churches from 44 countries meet in Amsterdam to inaugurate World Council of Churches.
	Jewry	End of British mandate in Palestine. Jews proclaim new state of Israel.
1950	*Papacy*	Papal decree, *Humani Generis*, against Existentialism and erroneous scientific theories. Pius XII pronounces dogma on bodily Assumption of the Virgin Mary.
1959	*Papacy*	Pope John XXIII announces the calling of the first Vatican Council since 1870. Vatican orders French worker-priest movement to discontinue.
1960	*Great Britain*	Archbishop of Canterbury visits Rome and meets the Pope. First to do so since the Reformation.
1961	*Russia*	Synod of bishops removes priests' function as legal administrator of parish and explicitly confines them to spiritual function. In next three years over half of existing parishes are disbanded, 10,000 churches and most monasteries closed. Closure of Jewish synagogues in Moscow.
	Papacy	Papal encyclicals on Catholic social doctrine and for Christian reconciliation under Rome's Primacy.
	General	Meeting of World Council of Churches at Delhi is joined by members of the Russian Orthodox Church and by Roman Catholic observers. The International Missionary Council is integrated with the World Council of Churches.
1962	*Papacy*	John XXIII insists on retention of Latin as the language of the Roman Catholic Church. Vatican Council opens with observer delegates from other Christian Churches.

1963   *Great Britain*   Anglican–Methodist 'Conversations' about unification.

        Papacy   Vatican Council approves use of vernacular liturgies. Encyclical *Pacem in Terris* deals with peaceful settlement of disputes and with relations with non-Catholics and Communists.

1964   *Papacy*   Paul VI makes pilgrimage to Holy Land.

1965   *Papacy*   Vatican Council promulgates documents exonerating the Jews from the death of Christ. The Catholic Church and the Eastern Orthodox Church agree to retract the excommunications put on each other in 1054. Worker Priests allowed to resume work.

1968   *Papacy*   Papal encyclical *Humanae Vitae* reaffirms Catholic doctrine of opposition to artificial birth control.

1970   *Papacy*   Pope reaffirms celibacy of clergy as a law of the Church.

1972   *Great Britain*   Presbyterian and Congregationalist Churches merge to form the United Reform Church.

1973   *Papacy*   Sacred Congregation for the Doctrine of the Faith reaffirms papal infallibility and the Church's unique claim to being the authentic Church of Christ.

1978   *Papacy*   Cardinal Karol Wojtyla of Cracow becomes first non-Italian Pope for 450 years as Pope John Paul II

1986   *Papacy*   First ever visit by a Pope to a Jewish synagogue.

Section V
Biographies

Adenauer, Konrad (1876–1967): German statesman. Mayor of Cologne, 1917–33. Removed by Nazis. Prominent member of Catholic Centre Party in Weimar Republic. President of Prussian State Council, 1920–33. Twice imprisoned by Nazis. Founded Christian Democratic Union, 1945. Elected first chancellor of Federal Republic, 1949; re-elected 1953, 1957. Also foreign minister, 1951–5. Negotiated German entry into NATO, EEC. Established diplomatic relations with USSR, 1955. Resigned 1963.

Alexander I (1777–1825): Tsar of Russia, 1801–25. Son of murdered Paul I. Entered War of Third Coalition against France, 1805. Obliged to conclude treaty of Tilsit with Napoleon, 1807. Active in Fourth Coalition against France. Leading figure at Congress of Vienna, 1814–15. Secured creation of Polish Kingdom. Established 'Holy Alliance' with Prussia and Austria. Early promise of liberal rule gave way to reactionary policy, under influence of Metternich.

Alexander II (1818–1881): Tsar of Russia, 1855–81. 'The Liberator'. Son of Nicholas I. Succeeded to throne during Crimean War. Embarked on wide-ranging modernisation of government. Most important reform was liberation of serfs, 1861. Innovations in legal code, 1862, and local government, education and army administration. Encouraged railway construction and banking. In foreign policy, concerned chiefly with expansion into Balkans, encouraging Pan-Slav movement. In Central Asia, Bokhara and Samarkand acquired, 1868. Russian troops reached Constantinople, 1878. Later in reign, more conservative in response to discontent in Poland, growth of revolutionary societies (e.g. Nihilists) and assassination attempts. Killed by bomb, 1881, before able to implement new constitution.

Alexander III (1845–1894): Tsar of Russia, 1881–94. Autocratic ruler, applying stern political repression. Pursued policy of 'Russification' of non-Russian nationalities within Empire, affected Jewish population in particular. Political opposition forced underground. First Marxist group formed in St Petersburg, 1883. In foreign policy, *Dreikaiserbund* lapsed following Bulgarian Crisis: 1885–6. Secret alliance with France concluded 1894. In last years of reign, promoted development of Far Eastern territories, e.g. authorised building of Trans-Siberian Railway.

Andrássy, Count Gyula (1823–1890): Hungarian statesman. Radical nationalist and supporter of Kossuth, 1848–9, during struggle for Hungarian independence. Exiled until 1858. On return, supported moves towards *Ausgleich*. First prime minister of Hungary, 1867–71. Foreign minister of Austria–Hungary, 1871–9. Headed Austro–Hungarian delegation at Congress of Berlin, 1878, at which Austria–Hungary acquired control of Bosnia and Herzegovina. Sought to balance threat of Russian encroachment by allying with Germany.

Azaña, Manuel (1881–1940): Spanish president. Founded Republican Party, 1924. Subsequently imprisoned. War minister, 1931. First prime minister of Second Republic, 1931–3, again 1936. Imprisoned for advocacy of Catalan self-rule, 1934. President, 1936–9. Fled to France, February 1939.

Babeuf, François (1760–1797): French journalist and early socialist. Emerged during Revolution as 'Gracchus Babeuf', publishing own newspaper, *Tribun du peuple*, advocating an egalitarian, communistic society. Formed 'Society of Equals', in Paris. Plotted armed rising to overthrow Directory, 1796. Arrested and executed. Influential on later French left-wing revolutionary thought.

Bakunin, Mikhail (1814–1876): Russian anarchist. Resigned military commission over Russian treatment of Poles. Active in German revolutionary movement, 1848–9, also in Paris and Prague. Sentenced to death, transferred to Russian custody and exiled to Siberia, escaping 1861. Remaining years spent in Western Europe, funded by Herzen, encouraging anarchist revolution. Involved in risings in Lyons, 1870, and Spain, 1873. Opposed Marx and Engels in First International, 1869–72. Expelled at Hague Congress, 1872. Especially influential on Spanish and Italian anarcho-syndicalist thought.

Beneš, Eduard (1884–1948): Czech statesman. Worked with Masaryk in Paris during First World War, seeking Czech independence. Principal Czech representative at Paris Peace Conference. Prime minister, 1921–2. Foreign minister, 1918–35. Active diplomat, chief proponent of Little Entente (Czechoslovakia, Romania and Yugoslavia, with French support). President of League of Nations Assembly, 1935. Succeeded Masaryk as president, 1935. Resigned, 1938, following Munich Agreement. President of Czech government-in-exile in London, 1941–5. Re-elected president, 1946. Resigned shortly after Communist coup, 1948.

Bernadotte, Jean-Baptiste (1763–1844): Marshal of France, King of Sweden. Distinguished soldier, fought at Austerlitz and Wagram. Minister of war, 1799. Created Marshal, 1804. Created Duke of Ponte Corvo, 1806. Married into Bonaparte family. Governor of Hanseatic cities, 1807–9. Elected heir to Swedish throne, 1810. Ascended throne as Charles XIV, 1818. Encouraged pact with Britain and Russia against France. Received Norway in peace settlement. Liberal monarch, accepted principle of ministerial accountability to parliament, which also controlled finance.

Bismarck, Otto von (1815–1898): Prussian–German statesman, architect of German unification. Ultra-Royalist member of Prussian parliament, 1847. Hostile to liberal–national Revolution, 1848. Prussian member of German Diet at Frankfurt, 1851–9. Ambassador to St Petersburg, 1859. Ambassador to Paris, 1862. Recalled, 1862, to become Prussian chief minister. Dissolved parliament, undertook reorganisation of army. Sought German unification under Prussian leadership, with exclusion of Austria. Engineered wars over Schleswig-Holstein, 1864, Seven Weeks' War with Austria, 1866, and Franco–Prussian War, 1870. Created Count, 1866. Chancellor of North German Confederation, 1867–71. Prince and Imperial Chancellor, 1871. Internal political struggles with Catholic Church, 1870s (*Kulturkampf*), and Socialists, 1880s. Introduced anti-Socialist legislation, universal suffrage, social insurance and protective tariffs. Foreign policy was geared to securing newly unified Germany. Devised system of alliances (*Dreikaiserbund*, Triple Alliance, Reinsurance

Treaty), designed to preserve balance of power and isolate France. Presided at Congress of Berlin, 1878. After disagreements over policy with William II, resigned 1890.

Blanc, Louis (1811–1882): French Socialist politician and writer. Chief work was *Organisation du Travail*, 1839, idealistic, stressing need for equality of wages. Critical of July Monarchy. Member of provisional government, 1848. Headed Luxembourg Commission on employment problems. Attacked for failure of 'National Workshops'. Accused of involvement in disorders, summer 1848. Elected to National Assembly, 1871. Elected to Chamber of Deputies, 1876, supporting left wing. Unpopular with French Marxists. Continued to advocate nationalisation of property and establishment of worker co-operatives.

Blum, Léon (1872–1950): French Socialist statesman. Elected to Chamber of Deputies, 1919. By 1925, established as a leader of Socialist Party. First Socialist prime minister, 1936, leading 'Popular Front'. Introduced important social reforms, including 40-hour working week. Formed second Popular Front, 1938. Imprisoned by Vichy régime, 1940. Accused of being responsible for French military weakness and tried, 1942. Interned in Germany during Second World War. Briefly prime minister of caretaker government, 1946.

Boulanger, General Georges (1837–1891): French soldier. Active in defence of Paris during Franco–Prussian War. As minister of war, 1886–7, replaced Royalist army officers with Republicans. Dismissed, 1888. Politically ambitious. Elected deputy, 1888, advocating nationalistic, expansionist policies. Sought limitations on Constitution, won backing of militarists and royalists, and 'League of Patriots'. Suspected of planning coup, fled from France. Condemned in absence as a traitor. 'Boulangism' subsequently disintegrated. Death by suicide.

Brandt, Willy (1913–   ): West German Social Democratic statesman. Active in opposition to Hitler. Member of *Bundestag*, 1949–57. President of *Bundesrat*, 1955–7. Mayor of West Berlin, 1957–66. Chairman of Social Democratic Party, 1964–   . Joined coalition with Christian Democrats under Chancellor Kiesinger, 1966. Chancellor in SPD – Free Democrat coalition, 1969. Awarded Nobel Peace Prize, 1971. Resigned following spy scandal, 1974, remaining Chairman of SPD. Consistent advocate of improved relations with Eastern Europe ('*Ostpolitik*').

Brezhnev, Leonid Ilyich (1906–1982): Soviet politician. Communist Party official in Ukraine and Moldavia. Held military posts, 1933–4. Member of Praesidium of Supreme Soviet, 1952–7. President of Praesidium, 1960–4, succeeding Marshal Voroshilov. Succeeded Khrushchev as First Secretary of Central Committee, 1964. General Secretary of Central Committee, 1966.

Briand, Aristide (1862–1932): French statesman. Allied with Socialists, 1894–1906. Elected deputy, 1902. Expelled by Socialists for accepting office as minister of public instruction and worship in Radical coalition, 1906–9. Drafted and implemented separation of Church and State. Prime minister 11 times between 1909 and 1929. Used force to end railway strike, 1910. Foreign minister, 1925–32. Major diplomatic role, worked for European unity. Sought rapprochement between France and Germany. Successes include Locarno Treaty, 1925, and Kellogg–Briand Pact, 1928. Awarded Nobel Peace Prize with Stresemann, 1926. Defeated in Presidential elections, 1931.

Caballero, Francisco Largo (1869–1964): Spanish Socialist politician. Elected to parliament, 1918. Became leader of UGT, 1925. Minister of labour in several governments, 1931–3. Proponent of genuinely Socialist policy, helping to provoke military reaction against government, 1936. Prime minister, 1936–7. During Civil War, failed to achieve cohesion among parties of the left. Went into exile in France, 1939. Interned by Germans, 1942–5. Minister of interior of Republican government-in-exile, 1946.

Calonne, Charles Alexandre de (1734–1802): French statesman and financier. Appointed controller-general of finance, 1783. Policy of heavy borrowing aggravated financial problems. Advised Louis XVI to summon Assembly of Notables, 1786, in order to achieve fairer distribution of taxes. Aroused aristocratic opposition by threatening privileged with taxation. Banished when Assembly requested explanation of national budgetary deficit. Served as finance minister in émigré government in London during Revolution.

Carnot, Lazare (1753–1823): French politician. Known as the 'organiser of victory' during French Revolutionary Wars. Entered Legislative Assembly, 1791. Endorsed execution of Louis XVI. Won victory at Wattignies. Member of Committee of Public Safety, 1793–4. Responsible for raising 14 Revolutionary armies. Sought to limit Robespierre's powers. Member of Directory. Imprisoned for opposition to Barras, 1797. Returned to power following Napoleon's coup of Brumaire. Minister of war, 1800–1. Partly responsible for French military success in Rhineland and Italy. Resigned in protest at Napoleon's Imperial ambitions. Returned, 1814, to defend Antwerp. Minister of interior during 'Hundred Days'. Exiled by restored Louis XVIII.

Castlereagh, Viscount, Robert Stewart, 2nd Marquess of Londonderry (1769–1822): British statesman. Secretary for Ireland, 1798–1801. Secretary for war and colonies, 1805–6, 1807–9. Secured appointment of Wellington as commander in Portugal. Foreign secretary, 1812–22. Favoured union of Britain and Ireland. Resigned when George III vetoed Catholic Emancipation. Influential figure at Congress of Vienna, 1814–15. Advocate of balance of power in Europe. Disappointed with operation of 'Congress System'. Death by suicide.

Catherine II, the Great (1729–96): German-born Empress of Russia, 1762–96. Married Peter, heir to Russian throne, 1745. Peter dethroned and murdered, Catherine made Empress. 'Enlightened Despot', favouring French philosophers, e.g. Voltaire. Few reforms actually introduced; abolished capital punishment (except for political crimes). During reign, number of serfs in Russia rose, as did economic burdens on peasantry. Turned to repression after Pugachev Revolt, 1773–5. Main development in reign was rapid territorial expansion: three Partitions of Poland, 1772, 1793 and 1795. Wars with Turkey, 1774 and 1792. War with Sweden, 1790. Annexed Crimea and Ukraine.

Cavour, Count Camillo Benso di (1810–1861): Italian statesman. Architect of Italian unification. In newspaper, *Il Risorgimento*, called for republican system. Piedmontese minister of agriculture, marine and commerce, 1850. Succeeded D'Azeglio as prime minister of Piedmont, 1852. Strengthened constitutional government, reduced influence of Church and encouraged economic development. Brought Italian question before Congress of Paris, 1856. Made pact with Napoleon III to expel Austrians from Italy (Plombières Agreement), 1858. Resigned when Napoleon failed to honour agreement. Returned, 1860; negotiated union of Parma, Modena, Tuscany and the Romagna with Piedmont–Sardinia. Encouraged Garibaldi's sweep through Sicily while occupying Papal States. First prime minister of unified Italian kingdom, 1861.

Chamberlain, Neville (1869–1940): British Conservative politician. Son of Joseph Chamberlain. Lord Mayor of Birmingham, 1915–16. Director General of National Service, 1916–17. Member of parliament, 1918–40. Postmaster General, 1922–3. Paymaster General, 1923. Minister of health, 1923, 1924–9. Chancellor of the exchequer, 1923–4, 1931–7. Prime minister, 1937–40. Resigned, 1940, becoming Lord President of the Council in wartime coalition, following rebellion by Conservative MPs in favour of Churchill. Much criticised for attempts to appease Germany and Italy, especially in Munich Agreement, 1938. Retired from politics, 1940.

Charles X (1757–1836): King of France, 1824–30. Brother of Louis XVIII. Lived in Britain during French Revolution. Returned to France to lead revolt in Vendée, 1795. Appointed Lieutenant-General of France, 1814. After 1815, led reactionary 'Ultras' in struggle with Constitutionalists. Ascended throne, 1824. At first, promised loyalty to Constitution of 1814. Provoked opposition through his support of clerical party, favourable treatment of former émigrés and reactionary religious legislation. Appointed Prince de Polignac as head of government, 1829. Dissolved parliament, 1830. 'Five Ordinances', July 1830, limiting political and civil rights, led to revolution. Abdicated in favour of Comte de Chambord, but succeeded by his cousin, Louis Philippe.

Churchill, Sir Winston (1874–1965): British statesman. Conservative MP, 1900–4. Became a Liberal in protest at Tariff Reform policies. Liberal MP, 1906–8, 1908–22. Constitutionalist, later Conservative MP, 1924–45. Conservative MP for Woodford, 1945–64. Under-secretary at Colonial Office, 1906–8. President of the Board of Trade, 1908–10. Home secretary, 1910–11. First Lord of the Admiralty, 1911–15. Chancellor of the Duchy of Lancaster, 1915. Minister of munitions, 1917–19. Secretary for war and air, 1919–21. Secretary for air and colonies, 1921. Colonial secretary, 1921–2. Chancellor of the exchequer, 1924–9. First Lord of the Admiralty, 1939–40. Prime minister and minister of defence, 1940–5. Leader of the Opposition, 1945–51. Prime minister, 1951–5. Minister of defence, 1951–2. Knighted, 1953. Resigned, 1955. Chequered career; during First World War involved in disputes over Admiralty policy and

Gallipoli campaign. Opposed Conservative policies over India and rearmament during 1930s. Advocated prevention of German expansion. Wartime leadership earned him legendary status, though not returned to power in 1945. Negotiated wartime alliance with USA and USSR. After Second World War, favoured alliance with USA against USSR.

Ciano, Count Galeazzo (1903–1944): Italian politician. Son-in-law of Mussolini. Prominent Fascist Minister of propaganda, 1935. Minister of foreign affairs, 1936–43. Negotiated 'Axis' agreements with Germany. Supported expansionist policy, e.g. annexation of Albania, 1939 and entry into Balkans, 1940–1. Began to oppose policy when its failure became clear after 1943, with defeats in North Africa. Appointed Ambassador to Vatican. Voted against Mussolini in Grand Council. Tried and executed by Fascists.

Clausewitz, Karl von (1780–1831): German military strategist. His theory of war outlined in *Vom Kriege*, dominated Prussian military thinking.

Clemenceau, Georges (1841–1929): French Radical statesman. Mayor of Montmartre, 1870–1. Entered National Assembly, 1871. Elected deputy, 1876, becoming leader of extreme left, 1876–93. Founded radical newspaper, *La Justice*, 1880. Critical of government. Contributed to downfall of several ministries. Instrumental in securing resignation of President Grévy after honours scandal, 1887. Lost seat in Chamber, 1893. Returned after supporting Dreyfus. Senator, 1902–20. Minister of interior, 1906. Prime minister, 1906–9. Completed Church–State separation. Strike-breaking measures aroused Socialist opposition. Attacked military mismanagement during First World War. Appointed prime minister and minister of war, 1917–20. Semi-dictatorial rule. Secured appointment of Foch as Chief of Allied forces, March 1918. Presided at Paris Peace Conference, 1919, pressing for harsh penalties on Germany. Lost presidential election, 1920.

Danton, George (1759–94): French Revolutionary politician. Became an administrator of Paris, 1791. Founded Cordeliers Club with Marat and Desmoulins. Minister of justice, 1792. Voted for execution of Louis XVI, 1793. Original member of Committee of Public Safety. President of Jacobin Club, 1793. Achieved suppression of Girondins. Later sought conciliation, moving to right wing of Jacobins. Sought to moderate Revolutionary Tribunal. Opposed by Robespierre and the 'Mountain'. Arrested, 1794 and guillotined.

De Gaulle, Charles (1890–1970): French soldier and statesman. Member of French military mission to Poland: 1919–20. Lectured at Staff College. Sought to modernise Army. Published *The Army of the Future*, 1932–4. Ideas subsequently employed by German Army. Briefly a member of Reynaud's government, 1940. Fled to Britain after fall of France. Became head of Committee of National Liberation ('Free French'), 1943. Claimed status of head of government. Led unsuccessful attempt to recapture Dakar. Entered Paris, August 1944. President of provisional government, 1945. Suspected of authoritarian ambitions. Resigned, 1946. Founded political party (Rally of the French People), retiring from its leadership, 1953. During Algerian Crisis, 1958, invited by President Coty to form temporary government with wide executive powers. Won overwhelming victory in referendum on new Constitution. Elected first president of Fifth Republic, 1959. Granted independence to former French colonies in Africa, 1959–60. Granted Algeria independence, 1962. Developed independent nuclear deterrent. Encouraged closer ties with West Germany. Twice vetoed British entry to EEC, 1962–3, 1967. Re-elected on second ballot, 1965. Re-elected after May 1968 'Events', but resigned, 1969, following opposition to his plans to reform Constitution.

Delcassé, Théophile (1852–1923). French politician. Elected Deputy, 1889. Minister of colonies, 1893–5, favouring territorial expansion. Foreign minister, 1898–1905, 1914–15. Encouraged *Entente Cordiale* with Britain, 1904. Active in Moroccan Crisis, 1905. Forced to resign. Naval minister, 1911–13. Ambassador to St Petersburg. Involved in negotiations for treaty of London, 1915.

De Valera, Eamon (1882–1975): Irish statesman. Led group of Irish Volunteers in Easter Rising, 1916. Imprisoned, released 1917. Elected MP, 1917. Leader of Sinn Fein, 1917–26. Elected president of Dáil Eireann. Opposed 1921 treaty with Britain. Led extreme nationalists during Civil War, 1922–3. Leader of Fianna Fail, winning 1932 elections. Between 1932–8, reduced links with Britain. After 1937, prime minister under revised Constitution. Maintained Irish neutrality during Second World War. Lost power, 1948. Re-elected, 1951–4, 1957–9. President, 1959–73.

Disraeli, Benjamin, 1st Earl of Beaconsfield (1805–1881): British Conservative politician. Member of parliament, 1837–76. Opposed repeal of Corn Laws, 1846, heading Protectionist group until 1852. Leader of the Commons and chancellor of the exchequer, 1852, 1858–9, 1866–8. Prime minister, 1868, 1874–80. Lord Privy Seal, 1876–8. Created Earl of Beaconsfield, 1876. Leader of Conservative Party until shortly before death. Introduced franchise reform, 1867, almost doubling electorate. Stressed Tory concern over social and imperial issues. Bought almost half share in Suez Canal Co., 1875. Created Queen Victoria Empress of India, 1876. Aimed to restrict Russian penetration of Eastern Europe. Attended Congress of Berlin, 1878, winning recognition of Britain's right to occupy Cyprus. Retired after election defeat, 1880.

Dollfuss, Engelbert (1892–1934): Austrian politician. Leader of Christian Socialist party. Chancellor, 1932–4. Opposed by Nazis and Socialists. Used political violence as pretext for dictatorial government. Suspended parliamentary rule, 1933. Provoked and suppressed Socialist revolt. Granted authority by parliament to implement new fascist-style constitution. Murdered during attempted Nazi coup.

Dreyfus, Alfred (1859–1935): French soldier. Artillery captain appointed to General Staff. Wrongly accused of espionage and imprisoned. Case revealed depth of anti-Semitism within French establishment (Dreyfus was himself Jewish), and provoked bitter division between 'Dreyfusards' (the Left, intellectuals, anti-clericals) and 'anti-Dreyfusards' (especially Army and Church). Retried and pardoned. Verdict finally overturned, 1906.

Engels, Friedrich (1820–1895): German political philosopher. Associate and colleague of Karl Marx. After 1842, lived mostly in Britain. Wrote *The Condition of the Working Classes in England*, 1844. Involved in revolutionary movement in Baden, 1848. With Marx, wrote *The Communist Manifesto*, 1848. Helped Marx financially. Final years engaged in preparing Marx's writings for publication, completing *Capital* in 1894.

Ferry, Jules (1832–1893): French politician. Critic of Second Empire. Elected to *Corps Législatif*, 1869. Opposed war with Prussia, 1870. Mayor of Paris, 1870–1. Prominent on Republican left. Minister of public instruction, 1879. Organised reformed, non-sectarian education system. Prime minister, 1880–1, 1883–5. Main interests were education and colonies. Responsible for colonial growth in North Africa and Indo-China. Assassinated by religious fanatic.

Foch, Ferdinand (1851–1929): French soldier, Marshal of France. Served as military instructor, 1894–9. Director of École de Guerre, 1907–11. Wrote *Principles and Conduct of War*, 1899. Appointed chief of staff, 1917. Created Generalissimo of Allied forces from March 1918. Field marshal, 1919. Supervised implementation of military provisions of Treaty of Versailles.

Fouché, Joseph, Duke of Otranto (?1759–1820): French minister of police. Elected to National Convention, 1792. During Revolution, crushed rebellions in Vendée and Lyons. Endorsed execution of Louis XVI. Initially lent support to Robespierre, but came to oppose him over question of 'Cult of the Supreme Being'. Minister of police under Directory, 1799, and Napoleon, 1802, 1804–10. Maintained internal order by repressive means. Returned as minister of police, 1815. Under Louis XVIII held office briefly as ambassador to Dresden. Exiled as a regicide.

Francis Ferdinand (1863–1914): Archduke of Austria. Nephew of Emperor Francis Joseph. Became heir to throne, 1896. Hoped to give autonomy to subject Slav peoples. Assassinated by Bosnian Serb at Sarajevo, 28 June 1914, immediate cause of First World War.

Francis Joseph (1830–1916): Emperor of Austria, 1848–1916. Succeeded during Revolution. King of Hungary from 1867. Quickly restored order after 1848 in Hungary and Lombardy. Abolished Constitution, 1851. Ruled personally until 1867. Favoured government by strong central bureaucracy. Hostile to party politics. Allied monarchy with Catholic Church. Accepted *Ausgleich*, 1867. Sought to maintain balance of power in Europe, but by annexing Bosnia–Herzegovina, 1908, provoked ill-feeling. Precipitated First World War by attacking Serbia, 1914.

Franco, Francisco (1892–1975): Spanish soldier and military dictator. Held command of Foreign Legion in Morocco. Chief of staff, 1935. Governor of Canaries, 1936. On outbreak of Civil War, integrated Foreign Legion and Moorish troops into rebel army. Became leader of Nationalist forces, 1936. Defeated Republican government, 1939. Established corporatist, authoritarian state, acting as *'Caudillo'* ('Leader'), and permitting only one political party, the Falange. Maintained Spanish neutrality during Second World War. Presided over Spain's rapid postwar economic development. Faced growing problem of regional separatism in last years. Ensured his own succession by King Juan Carlos I.

Frederick II, the Great (1712–1786): King of Prussia, 1740–86. Son of Frederick William I. Laid claim to Silesia. Encouraged War of Austrian Succession, 1740–8. Made alliances with France and Bavaria. Won military victories at Mollwitz, 1741, and Chotusitz, 1742. Invaded Bohemia, 1744. Acquired Silesia by Peace of Dresden, 1745. Entered Seven Years' War, 1756–63, in alliance with England against Austria, France, Russia, Sweden and Saxony. Position of Prussia greatly strengthened after Peace of Hubertusburg, 1763. Took part in First Partition of Poland with Russia, 1772. Entered War of Bavarian Succession, 1778. Established *Fürstenbund*, 1785, in order to safeguard Imperial Constitution against Austria. Despite some reversals, a great military commander. Encouraged economic development. Began codification of Prussian law. Some liberalisation, e.g. on laws of torture, religion and censorship. Chief interest was modernisation of army.

Gambetta, Léon Michel (1838–1882): French politician. As a lawyer defended critics of Second Empire. Elected deputy, 1869. One of group who declared the Republic, September 1870. Minister of the interior in government of National Defence. During siege of Paris, escaped to Tours, becoming nominal dictator for five months. Continued war against Germany even after fall of Paris. Re-elected, 1871. Not involved in crushing of Paris Commune. Emerged as leader of more radical Republicans, playing important part in downfall of President Macmahon, 1877. Became President of Chamber of Deputies, 1879. Formed government, 1881. Resigned when accused of having dictatorial ambitions, 1882.

Garibaldi, Giuseppe (1807–1882): Italian patriot. Involved in 'Young Italy' movement, 1834. Escaped to South America after sentenced to death for role in attempted seizure of Genoa. Fought against Austrians in Italy, 1848. Joined revolutionary government in Rome, 1849. Voted for a republic, repulsed French troops but forced to retreat by Austrians. Summoned by King Victor Emmanuel, 1859, and helped to liberate north Italy. Swept through Naples and Sicily, 1860, handing conquests over to Piedmont–Sardinia. Active in campaign against Austria in which Italy acquired Venice. Tried to seize Rome, 1867, but thwarted by French. Eventually secured Rome for Italy during Franco–Prussian War. Supported French Republican government after fall of Napoleon III.

Gioberti, Vincenzo (1801–1852): Italian philosopher and politician. Ordained a priest, 1825. Held nationalist views. Saw Papacy as most appropriate vehicle for Italian independence and unity, as he argued in *Del primato morale e civile degli Italiani*, 1843, which influenced supporters of Pius IX. Briefly prime minister of Piedmont, 1848.

Giolitti, Giovanni (1842–1928): Italian statesman. Entered parliament as a liberal, 1882. Became minister of finance, 1889. Prime minister five times between 1892 and 1921. First ministry, 1892–3, was ended by 'Tanlongo Scandal', involving irregularities at Bank of Rome. Prime minister again, 1903–5, 1906–9. Sought reconciliation with Church. Fourth ministry, 1911–14, saw annexation of Tripoli, war with Turkey, acquisition of Libya, Rhodes and Dodecanese. Ministry fell after general strike in protest at heavy taxation. Fifth ministry, 1920, saw Italy convulsed by civil strife and disputes over Fiume. Resigned 1921. Had introduced universal suffrage, attempted to maintain Italian neutrality during First World War. Introduced wide-ranging social reforms after war. Critical of Mussolini after 1924.

Gladstone, William Ewart (1809–1898): British Liberal politician. Entered parliament, 1832. Held several junior offices under Peel. President of the Board of Trade, 1843. Colonial secretary, 1845. Out of office following split over repeal of Corn Laws, 1846–52. Chancellor of the exchequer, 1852–5, 1858–66. Cut government expenditure and advocated free trade. Became leader of Liberal Party, 1866. Prime minister, 1868–74. Introduced national education system. Disestablished Church of Ireland, 1869. Introduced secret ballot in elections, army reforms under Cardwell. Second ministry, 1880–5, formed after success of 'Midlothian' election campaign. Widened franchise, 1884. Main preoccupation (as in last two administrations, 1885–6, 1892–4) was Home Rule for Ireland. Issue caused decisive breach in Liberal Party. Both Home Rule Bills, 1886 and 1893, were defeated. Drawn into several colonial wars in Africa. Retired, 1894.

Goebbels, Joseph (1897–1945): German Nazi propagandist. Early recruit to Nazi Party. Party chief in Berlin, 1926–30. Became Party's propaganda chief, 1929. Elected to Reichstag, 1930. Minister of propaganda, 1933–45. Held powerful position in Nazi leadership. Made skilful use of oratory, parades, demonstrations and radio. Attracted to 'radical' aspect of Nazi ideology. Death by suicide.

Goering, Hermann (1893–1946): German Nazi military and political leader. First World War ace pilot. Joined Nazi Party, 1922. Given command of Storm Troopers, 1923. Elected to Reichstag, 1928. President of Reichstag, 1932–3. Entered government, 1933, as Reich Commissioner for Air, Minister President of Prussia and Prussian Minister of the Interior (hence controlled Prussian police). Created Gestapo, 1933. Head of Luftwäffe. Responsible for preparing Germany's war economy. Created general, 1933, field marshal, 1938 and reich marshal, 1940. Became Hitler's deputy during Second World War. Influence declined after Battle of Britain, 1940. Disgraced after plotting to oust Hitler, 1945. Condemned to death at Nuremberg Trials. Death by suicide.

Gorbachev, Mikhail (1931–   ): Soviet statesman who succeeded Chernenko as general secretary of the Communist Party in 1985. His advent to power, after a succession of ailing old guard leaders, marked a major departure in the Soviet leadership.

Gorchakov, Prince Alexander Michaelevich (1798–1883): Russian statesman. Ambassador to Vienna, 1854–6. Foreign minister, 1856–82. Chancellor, 1863. Secured Austrian neutrality during Franco–Prussian

War, 1870. Co-operated with Prussia, winning release of Russia from provisions of treaty of Paris in 1870. Most powerful minister in Europe until advent of Bismarck.

Grey, 1st Viscount, Sir Edward Grey (1862–1933): Liberal MP Berwick-on-Tweed, 1885–1916; foreign secretary, 1905–16. His support of Britain's obligation to help Belgium in 1914 took Britain into the First World War; believed in international arbitration, used successfully in Balkan Wars: later a champion of the League of Nations.

Gromyko, Andrei Andreevich (1909–   ): Soviet statesman. Attached to Soviet embassy in Washington, 1939. Ambassador in Washington, 1943. Attended Teheran, Yalta and Potsdam Conferences. Elected deputy of Supreme Soviet, 1946. Became deputy foreign minister, and permanent delegate to United Nations Security Council, using veto frequently. Ambassador to Britain, 1952–3. Foreign minister, 1957–85. Signed partial nuclear test ban agreement, 1963. President of the USSR, 1985.

Guizot, François (1787–1874): French statesman. Professor of modern history at Sorbonne, 1812–22. Deprived of his posts because of his liberalism. Prevented from lecturing, 1825. Elected to Chamber of Deputies, 1830. Minister of the interior, minister of public instruction. Introduced system of primary education. Imposed restrictions on press freedom. Ambassador to London, 1840. Foreign minister, 1840–7. Prime minister, 1847–8. Resorted to repressive measures, contributing to fall of July Monarchy by refusal to make political concessions. Returned to Paris after 1848 Revolution, seeking to rally monarchists. Abortive coup attempt, 1851, led to his retirement from politics.

Heath, Edward (1916–   ): British Conservative politician. Entered Parliament, 1950. Party whip, 1951–5. Chief whip, 1955–9. Minister of labour, 1959–60. Lord privy seal, 1960–3. Secretary for trade and industry, 1963–4. First leader of Conservative Party to be elected by ballot, 1965. Prime minister, 1970–4. Proponent of European integration. Achieved British entry into EEC, January 1973. Failed to tackle problems of inflation and industrial relations. Improved British relations with China. Following electoral defeats of 1974, replaced as leader of Party by Margaret Thatcher, 1975.

Hegel, George (1770–1831): German philosopher. Became professor of philosophy at Berlin, 1818. Described process of 'dialectic', i.e. interaction of two conflicting half-truths (thesis and antithesis), to produce synthesis. At first welcomed French Revolution and Napoleon. Later supported idea of an authoritarian state and became hostile to liberalism. Ideas on dialectic, in modified form, used by Marx. Writings include *The Philosophy of Right*, 1821, *The Science of Logic*, 1812–16.

Herzen, Alexander (1812–70): Russian political thinker. Civil servant, 1835–42; aroused suspicion of authorities because of his westernising ideas. Went to Paris, 1847. Much influenced by experience of Revolution, 1848. Went to London, 1851. Stressed need for realism in revolutionary planning. Gave financial help to Bakunin and others.

Herzl, Theodor (1860–1904): Zionist leader, born in Hungary. Influenced by the anti-Semitism of the Dreyfus Affair. In pamphlet, *Judenstaat*, 1896, proposed creation of a Jewish State. Called first Zionist Congress at Basel, 1897. First President of World Zionist Organisation. Later years spent in unsuccessful negotiations with Kaiser, Sultan, Russian prime minister etc. with aim of securing land for new state.

Himmler, Heinrich (1900–45): German Nazi leader and Chief of Police. Early member of Nazi party. Involved in Munich Putsch, 1923. Head of *Schutzstaffel* (SS), 1929. Head of Gestapo, 1934, subsequently of all police forces, 1936. Head of Reich administration, 1939. Minister of the interior, 1943. Commander-in-chief of Home Forces, 1944. Used elaborate system of terror, espionage, detention and murder to reinforce totalitarian state. Bore major responsibility for racial extermination policies. Made attempts to negotiate unconditional surrender before end of war. Tried at Nuremberg. Death by suicide.

Hindenburg, Paul von (1847–1934): German soldier and President. Fought at Königgratz, 1866, and in Franco–Prussian War, 1870–71. Became general, 1903. Retired, 1911. Recalled to duty on outbreak of First World War. Victories won with Ludendorff at Tannenberg, 1914, and Masurian Lakes, 1915 made him a national hero. Became chief of general staff, 1916. Organised withdrawal from Western Front, 1918 (giving rise to myth of undefeated German Army). Advised Kaiser to abdicate and arranged Armistice. Retired, 1919. Elected president of Weimar Republic, 1925–34. Defeated Hitler in presidential election, 1932, but appointed him chancellor, January 1933.

Hitler, Adolf (1889–1945): Dictator of Germany. Born in Austria. Served in Bavarian Army during First World War, becoming lance corporal, twice decorated with Iron Cross. Joined German Workers' Party in Munich, 1919, transforming it into National Socialist German Workers' Party (NSDAP/Nazi Party), based on extreme nationalism and anti-Semitism. Attempted putsch in Munich, 1923, which proved abortive, though making him a national figure. While in prison, wrote political testament, *Mein Kampf*. Began to reorganise Nazi Party, 1925. Established unrivalled position as leader of party. Created efficient propaganda machine and organised elite guard, *Schutzstaffel* (SS). Helped to power by Great Depression. Nazi Party won 107 seats in 1930 *Reichstag* elections, becoming second largest party. In elections, July 1932, won 230 seats (highest they ever achieved). Appointed chancellor by Hindenburg, January 1933, though Nazis still a minority in *Reichstag*. Following *Reichstag* fire and Enabling Act, assumed dictatorial powers. Other political parties dissolved. Nazi Party purged of rivals by 1934. On death of Hindenburg, 1934, became President, uniting position with that of chancellor as *Führer* ('Leader'). Internal opposition ruthlessly suppressed. Rearmament programme expanded, 1935, aiding economic recovery. Occupied Rhineland, 1936. Rome–Berlin 'Axis' negotiated, 1936. Annexed Austria, 1938 (*Anschluss*). Gained Sudetenland after Munich Agreement, 1938. Seized remainder of Czechoslovakia, 1939. After Non-Aggression Pact with USSR (Molotov–Ribbentrop Pact, August 1939), invaded Poland, 1 September 1939, precipitating Second World War. Achieved swift military successes through *'Blitzkrieg'* campaigns, but fatal error was in attacking Russia, June 1941. Faced combined opposition of USSR, USA and Britain. Survived assassination attempt, July 1944. Committed suicide during closing stage of war.

Horthy de Nagybánya, Miklós (1886–1957): Hungarian admiral and Regent. Commander-in-Chief of Austro–Hungarian Navy, 1917. Minister of war in 'White' government, 1919. With Romanian help, crushed Communist regime of Béla Kun, 1920. Chosen to be Regent, acting as head of state, on behalf of absent King Charles. Refused to give up office in favour of King Charles, 1921. Ruled virtually as a dictator. Formed alliance with Germany, 1941, but withdrew 1944. Imprisoned by Germans but freed by Allies. Retired to Portugal.

Izvolski, Alexander (1856–1919): Russian statesman. Entered diplomatic service, 1875. Held important post in Tokyo, 1899. Transferred to Copenhagen, 1903. Unexpectedly appointed Foreign Minister, 1905, holding post for five years. Worked for better relations with Britain and Japan. Successes marred by Bosnian Crisis, 1908–9. Aggrieved by Austria's seizure of Bosnia–Herzegovina before Russia had secured 'compensation' through fresh solution to Straits Question. As ambassador in Paris, 1910–16, strengthened military alliance between Russia and France.

Jaruzelski, General Wojciech (1923–   ): Polish soldier and politician. Long and distinguished army career. Became chief of general staff, 1965, minister of defence, 1968, and member of Politburo, 1971. Became prime minister after resignation of Pinkowski, 1981. Declared martial law in effort to tackle economic crisis and to counter growth of Solidarity movement. Solidarity banned and its leaders detained and tried. Lifted martial law, July 1983.

Jaurès, Jean (1859–1914): French Socialist leader and writer. Elected deputy, 1885, again 1889, 1893. Founded Socialist newspaper, *L'Humanité*, 1904, giving support to Dreyfus. By 1905 had become leader of united Socialist party. Never held office, in accordance with decision of Congress of Socialist International, 1905. Not a Marxist, but in French Revolutionary tradition. Hoped to mobilise French and German workers to prevent outbreak of war. Assassinated by French nationalist fanatic.

Joseph II (1741–1790): Holy Roman Emperor, 1765–90; Archduke of Austria, 1780–90. Succeeded his father, Francis I. Ruled Habsburg possessions jointly with his mother, Maria Theresa. Ruled alone after her death, 1780, as an enlightened monarch. Limited clerical influence, granted religious toleration, 1781. Abolished serfdom, extended education, reformed taxation. Established strong, centralised government. Aroused hostility, expressed in several revolts, 1788. Also in 1788, waged unsuccessful war with Turkey.

Kapp, Wolfgang (1868–1922): German civil servant. Collaborated with group of ex-soldiers in attempt to overthrow Weimar Republic, 1920. Thwarted by general strike. Fled to Sweden. Returned to Germany, 1922. Died awaiting trial.

Károlyi, Count Mihály (1875–1955): Hungarian statesman. Entered parliament, 1905 . Politically liberal, became increasingly radical. Led Independent Party during First World War. Became prime minister, 1918 and sought Armistice. Provisional president of Hungarian Republic, aimed to introduce reforms. Overthrown by Communist coup,1919, and went into exile. Returned, 1946, after downfall of Horthy. Served as a diplomat, 1946–9, before resuming exile.

Kautsky, Karl (1854–1938): German Socialist of Czech descent. Colleague of Marx. Collaborated with Engels in London, 1881–2. Founded Socialist newspaper, *Die Neue Zeit*, 1883. Criticised 'revisionism' of German Social Democrats. Disagreed with Lenin over interpretation of Marxism. Condemned Russian Revolution and refused to join German Communist Party. Remained a pacifist during First World War. Joined Austrian Social Democrats after war. Fled to Holland after *Anschluss*.

Kemal Atatürk (Mustafa Kemal) (1881–1938): Creator of modern Turkish nation. Joined Young Turk reform movement. Entered army, winning quick promotion. Fought Italians in Tripoli, 1911, and in Balkan Wars. Involved in Gallipoli campaign during First World War. Led national resistance after Greek invasion following Turkey's defeat. Renounced loyalty to Sultan and formed provisional government in Ankara, 1920. Led Turks in War of Independence until 1922, expelling Greeks, deposing Sultan and establishing Republic. Became first president of Republic, 1923–38. Architect of modern, secularised state. Emancipated women. Sought to build strong nation from homelands of Anatolia and residue of European Turkey. Did not attempt to regain former Arab possessions. Territorial settlement with Greece achieved at Treaty of Lausanne, 1923.

Kerensky, Alexander (1881–1970): Russian politician. Entered *Duma*, 1912, as critic of Tsarist government. Led Social Revolutionary Party. Leading role in Revolution, March 1917. Became minister of justice, then minister of war. Prime minister of Provisional government, July 1917. Continued war with Germany and attempted major offensive which reduced his popularity. Defeated Kornilov's military rising, September 1917. Overthrown by Bolsheviks in November Revolution, 1917. Spent rest of life in exile in France, Australia and USA.

Keynes, John Maynard, 1st Baron Keynes (1883–1946): British economist. Worked at Treasury during First World War. Chief representative at negotiations prior to treaty of Versailles. Criticised reparations plans in *The Economic Consequences of the Peace*, 1919. Made radical proposals for dealing with unemployment by provision of public works. Ideas influenced Liberal Party's election manifesto, 1929. Full proposals on economic controls in interests of maintaining full employment appeared in *The General Theory of Employment, Interest and Money*, 1936. Inspired 'Keynesian Revolution' during and after Second World War. Rejected classical belief in self-regulating economy. Argued need for government expenditure to be adjusted to control level of public demand. Advised chancellor of the exchequer during Second World War. Chief British delegate at Bretton Woods Conference, 1944. Involved in discussions leading to creation of International Monetary Fund and World Bank.

Khrushchev, Nikita Sergeyevich (1894–1971). Soviet politician. Joined Communist Party, 1918. Fought in Civil War. Member of Central Committee of Party, 1934. Full member of Politburo and of Praesidium of Supreme Soviet, 1939. Organised guerrilla warfare against Germans during Second World War. Premier of Ukraine, 1944–7. Undertook major restructuring of agriculture, 1949. Became First Secretary of All Union Party on death of Stalin, 1953. Denounced Stalinism, 1956. Relegated Molotov, Kaganovich and Malenkov (potential rivals), 1957. Succeeded Bulganin as prime minister, 1958–64. Official visits to USA, 1959, India and China, 1960. Deposed, 1964, following economic failures.

Kolchak, Alexander Vasilyevich (1874–1920): Russian sailor. After Russo–Japanese War, 1904–5, reorganised Navy. Commanded Black Sea Fleet from 1916. After 1917 Revolution, led counter-revolutionary government in Siberia. Captured by Bolsheviks and executed.

Kornilov, Lavr Georgyevich (1870–1918): Russian soldier. Fought in Russo–Japanese War, 1904–5. Divisional commander in Galicia during First World War. Appointed commander-in-chief after Revolution, March 1917. Accused of planning military coup. Arrested, but managed to join anti-Bolshevik forces on Don. Killed in action.

Kosciuszko, Tadeusz Andrzej (1746–1817): Polish patriot. Fought in American War of Independence. Returned to Poland, 1786. Led abortive rising against Tsar, 1794, following second Partition of Poland, 1793. In France, rejected conciliatory moves by Napoleon. Present at Congress of Vienna, 1814. Failed to persuade Tsar of strength of Polish case.

Kossuth, Lajos (Louis) (1802–1894): Hungarian revolutionary and politician. Member of Hungarian Diet, 1825–27. As a journalist, wrote in support of Hungarian independence. Twice imprisoned. Insistence on Magyar supremacy within Hungary aroused suspicions of other nationalities. Returned to Diet, 1832–6, 1847–9. Speech in favour of independence, March 1848, signalled beginning of Revolution. Key role in enactment of 'March Laws', abolishing privileges of nobility and ending serfdom. Introduced responsible government. Served as minister of finance. Became provisional governor of Hungary, 1849, ruling in dictatorial style. Went into exile following Russian intervention in Hungary on behalf of Austria. Attempted to organise risings in Hungary against Austrian rule, 1859, 1861, 1866. Withdrew from politics following *Ausgleich*, 1867.

Kruger, (Stephanus Johannes) Paulus (1825–1904): Afrikaner politician. One of leaders of revolt against British, 1880, which restored independence of Transvaal. Elected President of Transvaal, 1883; re-elected 1888, 1893, 1898. Refused to grant political rights to incoming (non-Afrikaner) miners following discovery of gold on Rand. Resulting tensions contributed to Boer War, 1899–1902. Canvassed European support for Afrikaner cause, 1900.

Kun, Béla (1886–1937): Hungarian Communist leader. Following capture by Russians during First World War, established brief Soviet Republic in

Hungary, March–August 1919. Escaped to Vienna after counter-revolution, settled in USSR. Died in Stalinist purge.

Lafayette, Marquis de (1757–1834): French soldier and politician. Fought in American War of Independence, winning French support for America. Sat in Assembly of Notables, 1787. Elected to States General, 1789, remaining when Third Estate decided to become National Assembly. Commander of National Guard. Politically moderate, earned hatred of Jacobins. Sought to restrain popular violence and to protect Louis XVI. Obliged to relinquish post in Paris, becoming commander of army in the east. Military failure against Austrians, 1792, led to his impeachment by National Convention. Sought safety in Germany. Detained there until 1797. Entered Chamber of Deputies, 1818, becoming leader of left-wing opposition. Involved in 1830 Revolution, supporting Louis Philippe and commanding National Guard. Personified Revolutionary ties between USA and France.

Lamartine, Alphonse Marie Louis de (1790–1869): French poet and politician. Held diplomatic posts in Italy until 1828. Politically a moderate royalist. Elected deputy, 1833. Declined position of foreign minister under Polignac, 1829. Criticised 1830 Revolution. After fall of July Monarchy, 1848, became foreign minister, but refused to grant aid to other revolutionary movements. Stood for election as president, but was defeated by Louis Napoleon. Subsequently retired from political life. Political and religious ideas expressed in writings such as *Harmonies poétiques et religieuses*, and *La Chute d'un Ange*.

Laval, Pierre (1883–1945): French politician. Member of Chamber of Deputies, 1914–19, and from 1924 onwards. Originally a Socialist, became Independent after 1927, on elevation to Senate. Minister of public works, 1925. Minister of justice, 1926. Prime minister, 1931–2, 1935–6. Foreign minister, 1934–6. Negotiated Hoare–Laval Pact with Britain, 1935. Proponent of closer ties with Germany and Italy. After fall of France, 1940, played major role in creation of Pétain's Vichy regime. Prime minister, 1942–4. Collaborated with Germany, e.g. in supply of forced labour. Fled to Germany, then Spain, after liberation of France. Repatriated, tried and executed for treason.

Lenin, Vladimir Ilyich (V.I. Ulyanov) (1870–1924): Russian revolutionary leader and architect of Soviet State. After expulsion from Kazan University for political activity, absorbed writings of Marx. In St Petersburg, organised League for the Liberation of the Working Class. Exiled to Siberia, 1897. In London, 1903, when Russian Social Democratic Labour Party divided into Mensheviks and Bolsheviks. Led Bolshevik wing and published newspaper, *Iskra*, ('The Spark'). Involved in abortive Russian Revolution, 1905. Controlled revolutionary movement from exile in Switzerland. Smuggled into Russia by Germans, 1917. Overthrew Kerensky's provisional government and became head of Council of People's Commissars. Ended war with Germany and concluded treaty of Brest-Litovsk, March 1918. Civil war with 'White' armies continued until 1921. As chairman of Communist Party, established virtual dictatorship and dissolved Constituent Assembly. Created Communist International,

1919, to encourage world revolution. Introduced New Economic Policy, 1921, in diversion from planned communist transformation of economy. Recognised dangers implicit in rise of Stalin. Important both as theoretical writer on Marxism and as practical revolutionary organiser.

Litvinov, Maxim Maximovich (1876–1951): Soviet diplomat. Early recruit to Bolshevik Party. Diplomatic representative in Britain after November Revolution, 1917. Deported, 1918. Deputy foreign commissar, 1921–30, 1939–46. Foreign commissar, 1930–9. Sought to improve USSR's foreign relations. Took USSR into League of Nations, 1934. Advocate of collective security, supporting Franco–Russian Pact, 1935. Dismissed in favour of Molotov when Stalin required agreement with Hitler, 1939. Ambassador to Washington, 1941–2.

Lloyd George, David, 1st Earl Lloyd George of Dwyfor (1863–1945): British Liberal statesman. Member of parliament, 1890–1945. President of the Board of Trade, 1905–8. Chancellor of the exchequer, 1908–15. Introduced controversial People's Budget, 1909, proposing increased taxation to fund social reform and naval rearmament. Budget rejected by House of Lords, causing constitutional crisis leading to Parliament Act, 1911. Minister of munitions, 1915–16. Secretary for war, 1916. Prime minister, 1916–22. Leader of the Liberal Party, 1926–31. Created Earl Lloyd George, 1945. Dynamic and efficient wartime leader. Attended Paris Peace Conference, 1919. Opposed calls for draconian penalties on Germany. Faced economic problems at home in postwar period. Continuing violence in Ireland led to creation of Irish Free State, 1921, weakening Lloyd George's position, as did revelations of his sale of honours. Forced to resign, 1922, when Conservatives left coalition. Never held office again.

Louis XVI (1754–93): King of France, 1774–93. Grandson of Louis XV. In early years of reign, successive ministers (e.g. Turgot, Necker) attempted financial reforms, but nobility resisted proposals to include them in taxation net. Costly intervention in American War of Independence spread constitutional theories in France. Summoned States General, 1789, on advice of Necker (its first session since 1614). Third Estate's decision to meet separately as National Assembly constituted first act of French Revolution. With death of Mirabeau, 1791, Louis lost a valuable supporter. Sought refuge in Varennes, and appealed to fellow monarchs for help, while France was already at war with Prussia and Austria. Royal family subsequently imprisoned. Republican majority in Convention secured trial and execution of Louis, 1793.

Louis XVIII (1755–1824): King of France, 1814–24, but assumed royal title during Revolution in 1795. Younger brother of Louis XVI. Fled France during Revolution. Maintained links with groups of monarchist exiles. Returned to France on fall of Napoleon, 1814. Negotiated Charter (Constitution) with Talleyrand prior to return. Withdrew to Ghent during Napoleon's 'Hundred Days', resuming throne after battle of Waterloo. Sought national reconciliation by granting constitutional rule. Unable to prevent ascendancy of ultra-Royalists, e.g. in reactionary *Chambre Introuvable*. Former Republicans, Imperialists and Protestants suffered during 'White Terror'.

Louis Philippe (1773–1850): King of the French, 1830–48. Son of Philippe Égalité. Duke of Orléans. Supported Revolution, later lived abroad. Permitted to return to France, 1817, though avoided political involvement. Appointed Lieutenant-General after 1830 Revolution. Chosen to replace Charles X as king. Initial popularity waned as government became increasingly reactionary, e.g. under Guizot, who limited press freedom and interfered with judicial process. Reign saw growth of middle-class prosperity and of republicanism. Toppled by 1848 Revolution. Settled in England.

Ludendorff, Erich (1865–1937): German soldier. Entered army, 1882. Major-general by 1914. Planned deployment of German armies at outbreak of First World War. With Hindenburg, won victory at Tannenberg, 1914. Transferred to Western Front, 1916. Shared increasing control of government with Hindenburg after 1916. Conceived spring offensive, 1918. Involved in abortive Kapp Putsch, 1920. Took part in Hitler's Munich Putsch, 1923. Founded extreme nationalist party, 1925. Unsuccessful candidate for Reich presidency, 1925.

Luxemburg, Rosa (1870–1919): Polish-born German revolutionary leader. Major theoretician of Marxism. Imprisoned for opposition to First World War, 1915–18. Founded German Communist Party in 1918 with Karl Liebknecht, based on earlier Spartacist group. Opposed the nationalism of existing Socialist groups, as shown by their participation in War. Critical of German Social Democrats in government. Sought to restrain more violent colleagues, but unable to prevent Spartacist uprising, January 1919. Brutally murdered by counter-revolutionary troops.

MacMahon, Patrice (1808–93): French soldier and President. Military career began under Charles X. Served in Algeria. Chief successes came under Second Empire. Fought in Crimean War. Created Marshal of France, 1859. Duke of Magenta, 1859–70. Governor-General of Algeria, 1864–70. Fought in Franco-Prussian War. Crushed Paris Commune, 1871. President of Third Republic, 1873–9. Politically a royalist. Sought to make full use of president's executive authority. Dismissed prime minister, 1877. Hoped to appoint Orléanist nominee, Duc de Broglie. Dissolved Chamber of Deputies, held elections, but did not secure royalist majority. Resigned, 1879.

Mahmud II (1785–1839): Sultan of Turkey, 1808–39. Strong ruler, restored authority over Pashas, eliminated Janissaries from politics, 1826. Waged unsuccessful war with Russia, 1809–12. Implemented reforms in government, education and the army. Unable to maintain control of outlying territories, e.g. Serbia and Greece. Tried to crush Greek independence movement, 1821–9. Obliged to recognise Greek independence by treaty of Adrianople, 1829. Increasingly threatened by Mehemet Ali in Egypt, 1830s.

Mannerheim, Baron Carl Gustaf Emil (1867–1948): Finnish soldier and statesman. Served in Russian Imperial Army, 1889–1917. Became General during Russo–Japanese War, 1904–5. Commanded 'White' Guards, 1918, retaking Helsinki from Communists. Regent of Finland,

1918–19. Head of state, 1919–20. Led Finnish armies against Russia. Gained independence of Finland from USSR. Created field marshal, 1933. President of Defence Council, 1931–9. Active in defence of Finland following Russian attack, 1939. Made pact with Germany against Russia, 1941. Marshal of Finland, 1942. President, 1944–6. Declared war on Germany, March 1945.

Maria Theresa (1717–80): Archduchess of Austria, Queen of Hungary and Bohemia. Daughter of Charles VI. Succeeded to rule of Habsburg territories, 1740, as result of Pragmatic Sanction. Fought France, Spain and Prussia in War of Austrian Succession, 1740–8. Gained Imperial title for her husband Francis, 1745. Ceded Silesia and Italian territories, 1748. Suffered humiliating losses while allied to France in Seven Years' War, 1756–63. Ruled jointly with her son, Joseph II, 1765–80. Took part in Partition of Poland, 1772. Introduced economic reforms which strengthened Austrian resources.

Marx, Karl (1818–1883): German philosopher. Father of 'Scientific Socialism'. Editor of *Rheinische Zeitung*, 1842. Exile in Paris, 1843–5, and Brussels, 1845–8. Sympathised with early German socialists. Wrote *The Communist Manifesto*, 1848, with Engels. Returned to Cologne during 1848 Revolution. Founded *Neue Rheinische Zeitung*. Expelled from Prussia, settled in London, 1849. European correspondent for *New York Tribune*, 1851–62. Developed philosophy of 'class struggle', described economic laws of capitalism. Derived ideas from dialectic of Hegel, and from materialism of Feuerbach. First volume of *Capital* published 1867. Helped establish International Workingmen's Association in London, 1864. Conflicts with Bakunin led to disintegration of Association, 1876.

Masaryk, Tómaš (1850–1937). Czech philosopher and statesman. Became Professor of Philosophy at Prague, 1882. Represented Young Czech Party in Austrian parliament, 1891–3. Led 'Czech Realists', 1907–14. Critical of Austrian policies. Became chairman of Czech National Council in London, 1914. Described views on nationality question in *The New Europe* (periodical), from 1916 onwards. Organised Czech Legion in Russia, 1917. Won support of President Wilson. Accepted by USA as head of an allied government, 1918. Returned to Czechoslovakia as president-elect, 1918. Re-elected twice. Resigned, 1935.

Matteotti, Giacomo (1885–1924): Italian Socialist politician. Elected deputy, 1919. Became general secretary of Socialist party, 1924. Denounced Fascist violence in *The Fascisti Exposed*. Murdered by Fascists as a result. Death produced political crisis. Non-Fascist deputies blocked normal operation of parliament. Party meetings banned by Mussolini, censorship introduced. Incident cost Fascists foreign sympathy.

Maximilian, (Ferdinand Maximilian Joseph) (1832–67): Archduke of Austria. Emperor of Mexico, 1864–7. Brother of Emperor Francis Joseph. Commanded Austrian Navy, 1854. Governor of Lombardy-Venetia, 1857–9. Unable to withstand Piedmontese–French attack on Lombardy, 1859. Became Emperor of Mexico as nominee of Napoleon III, 1863.

Empire collapsed when French withdrew military backing under US pressure. Captured by Liberals under Juárez and executed.

Mazzini, Giuseppe (1805–72). Italian patriot. Member of Carbonari, 1830. Imprisoned and exiled to France. Founded 'Young Italy' revolutionary movement. Aimed to unify Italy under republican government. Proposed rising proved abortive, 1832. Movement became increasingly violent. Settled first in Marseilles, then London, 1837. Extended ideas by founding 'Young Europe' to foster concept of community of republican nations. Liberated Milan, 1848. Member of brief Roman Republican triumvirate, 1849. Lost prestige after fall of Rome, never returning to Italy. Prompted attempted risings in Mantua, 1852, Milan, 1853, and Genoa, 1857.

Mehemet Ali (1769–1849): Ruler of Egypt. Led Albanian troops against France on behalf of Turkey, 1799. Governor of Egypt, 1805. Granted supreme authority in Egypt by Sultan, 1811. Sponsored military and economic growth. Conquered Sudan, 1820–2. Founded Khartoum, 1823. Helped Turkey during Greek War of Independence, 1823–8. Appointed governor of Crete. War with Turkey, 1832–3, won him Syria and Adana. After second war, 1839–41, forced to give up earlier conquests by Great Powers, gaining status as hereditary ruler of Egypt in return.

Metternich, Klemens (1773–1859): Austrian statesman and diplomat. Created Prince, 1813. Represented Westphalia at Congress of Rastadt, 1797–9. Entered Austrian diplomatic service, holding posts in Dresden, 1801–3, Berlin, 1803–6, and Paris, 1806–9. Foreign minister, 1809–48. Chancellor, 1812–48. Led Austria into alliance with Russia against France, 1813. Presided at Congress of Vienna, 1814–15. Architect of 'Metternich System'. i.e. balance of power in Europe in interests of general peace. Politically conservative, aiming at resisting liberal demands and maintaining stability. Led Austria to focus attention on territories in Italy rather than on interests in Germany. Obliged to resign during 1848 Revolution. Returned to Austria, 1849, though no longer holding office.

Molotov, Vyacheslav Mikhailovich (1890–1986). Soviet politician. Emerged as prominent Bolshevik during November Revolution, 1917. Loyal colleague of Stalin, 1921 onwards. Member of Politburo, 1926–57. Helped implement Five Year Plan, 1928. Premier, 1930–41. Foreign minister, 1939–49. Negotiated Pact with Ribbentrop, August 1939. Deputy premier, 1941–57. Negotiated treaties with Eastern Bloc countries, 1945–9. Became member of ruling triumvirate following death of Stalin, 1953. Negotiated Austrian State Treaty, 1955. Minister of state control, 1956–7. Became foreign minister again, 1957. Influence declined with rise of Khrushchev. Ambassador to Mongolia, 1957–60. Retired, 1961–2.

Moltke, Helmuth von (1800–91): German soldier. Entered Prussian Army, 1822. Joined General Staff, 1832. Seconded as adviser to Turkish Army, 1835–9. Personal aide to Prince Henry, 1845–6, and to Frederick William, 1855–7. Appointed Chief of Prussian General Staff, 1857. Introduced major reorganisation of Army, 1858–88. Produced strategic planning which secured Prussian victories against Denmark, 1864, Austria, 1866, and France, 1870. Became chief of Imperial General Staff, 1870. Created field marshal, 1871.

Monnet, Jean (1888–1979): French politician, economist and diplomat. Member of Inter-Allied Maritime Commission, 1915–17. First deputy secretary-general of League of Nations, 1919–23. Chairman, Franco–British Economic Co-ordination Committee, 1939–40. Became minister of commerce, 1944. Fostered establishment of National Planning Council, becoming head of Council, 1945–47. Architect of European Community. Chairman, Action Committee for United States of Europe, 1955–75. Instrumental in foundation of European Coal and Steel Community. President of ECSC, 1952–5.

Montgomery, 1st Viscount, Sir Bernard Law Montgomery (1887–1976): British soldier. Lieutenant – colonel and battalion commander by end of First World War. Evacuated from Dunkirk with 3rd Division under his command, 1940. By December 1941, head of South-Eastern Command as lieutenant-general. Chosen to command 8th Army in North Africa, 1942. Halted Rommel's advance, defeating him at El Alamein. Led invasion of Sicily and Italy. Appointed land commander of Operation Overlord (Normandy landings), 1944. Uneasy relationship with American allies. Commander of occupation forces in Germany. After war, became chief of Imperial General Staff. Deputy commander of NATO, 1951–8.

Murat, Joachim (1767–1815): French soldier and King of Naples. French Cavalry Commander and colleague of Napoleon Bonaparte. Involved in suppression of Vendémiaire rising, 1795. Fought in first Italian campaign. Won military reputation during Egyptian expedition. Major role in Napoleon's Brumaire coup, 1799. Won victory at Marengo, 1800. Created marshal, 1804. Crushed rising in Madrid, 1808. Created King of Naples as Joachim I Napoléon. Active in Russian campaign. Fought at Leipzig. Attempted to keep throne by negotiations with Allies, 1813–14. Sought to rally Italian aid for Napoleon without success, 1815. Led abortive rising in Calabria, 1815. Tried and executed.

Mussolini, Benito (1883–1945): Dictator of Italy. Originally a Socialist. Imprisoned for political activities, 1908. Editor of Socialist national newspaper, *Avanti*, 1912–14. Resigned from party having been criticised for supporting war with Austria. Founded newspaper, *Il Popolo d'Italia*, Milan, 1914. Organised groups (*fasci*) of workers to campaign for social improvements. Amalgamated into Fascist Party, 1919. Elected to Chamber of Deputies, 1921. During period of civil unrest, led 'March on Rome', 1922. Appointed prime minister by King Victor Emmanuel III, 1922. Headed Fascist/nationalist coalition, as *Duce*. Acquired dictatorial powers, 1922. Dictatorship established, 1925. Single party, corporatist state instituted 1928–9. Large-scale public works introduced. Lateran Treaty settled Church/State relations, 1929. Expansionist foreign policy: Corfu incident, 1924; invasion of Abyssinia, 1935. Created 'Axis' with Hitler, 1936. Left League of Nations, 1937. Annexed Albania, 1939. Declared war on France and Britain, 1940. Invaded Greece, 1940. Military setbacks in East Africa and Libya. Heavily dependent on Germany by 1941. Forced to resign following coup by Victor Emmanuel III and Marshal

Badoglio, 1943. Detained, but freed by Germans. Established Republican Fascist government in German-controlled North Italy. Captured and executed by Italian partisans, April 1945.

Napoleon I, Bonaparte (1769–1821): Emperor of the French, 1804–15. Entered French army, 1785. Won recognition after campaigns in North Italy. Laid down peace terms to Austria at Campo Formio. Led unsuccessful expedition to Egypt. Overthrew Directory in 'Brumaire' coup, 1799. Created Consul for Life, 1802. Effective dictator of France, 1799–1814. During consulate, introduced legal reforms in *Code Napoléon*, and achieved Concordat with Church. After winning War of Second Coalition, crowned himself Emperor, 1804. Won victories at Austerlitz and Jena during War of Third Coalition, 1804–7. Obliged Russia to accept Peace of Tilsit, 1807. Power reduced after 1808 by failure of 'Continental System', and involvement in Peninsular War. Defeated Austrians at Wagram, 1809. Invaded Russia, 1812. Won victory at Borodino, but forced to retreat from Moscow. Defeated at Leipzig during War of Fourth Coalition. Abdicated, April 1814. Permitted by Allies to retain Imperial title and sovereignty over Elba. Escaped from Elba, February 1815. During 'Hundred Days' resumed rule as Emperor. Finally defeated at Waterloo, June 1815, and exiled to St Helena.

Napoleon III (Charles Louis Napoleon Bonaparte) (1808–1873): Emperor of the French, 1852–70. Nephew of Napoleon I. Made two unsuccessful attempts to mount Bonapartist risings against July Monarchy, 1836, 1840. Imprisoned after second attempt, but escaped, 1845, settling in London. Exploited 'Napoleonic Legend'. Elected president of Second Republic, 1848. Undertook coup d'état in order to widen his authority. Established Second Empire, 1852. Entered Crimean War as ally of Britain, and ensured Peace Congress was held at Paris, 1856. Planned joint campaign to achieve Italian independence after meeting with Cavour at Plombières. Made peace with Austria, 1859, without consulting Piedmont. Founded Catholic Empire in Mexico, 1861. Secured Imperial title of Mexico for Archduke Maximilian of Austria, 1864. Diplomatically outflanked by Bismarck during Austro–Prussian War, 1866. Faced Franco–Prussian War, 1870, without allies. After defeat at Sedan, detained in Germany. Exiled in England, 1871–3.

Nesselrode, Count Karl Robert (1780–1862): Russian statesman. Entered Russian Navy, 1797. Chief adviser to Tsar Alexander I in Paris, 1814. Prominent role in Congress of Vienna, 1815. Foreign minister, 1822–56. Chancellor, 1845–62. Pursued conservative policies. Sought to gain influence over Turkey by conciliation. Engineered treaty of Unkiar Skelessi, 1833. Claimed Crimean War conflicted with his policy and advised suing for peace. Concluded Treaty of Paris, 1856. Saw dangers in exploiting Balkan nationalism and in Russian territorial growth in Asia. Resisted Polish national claims and helped Austria crush Hungarian Revolt, 1849.

Ney, Michel (1769–1815): French soldier. Organised Army of the Rhine, 1799. Fought at Hohenlinden, 1800. Created Marshal of France, 1804. Designated the 'Bravest of the Brave' after Battle of Friedland. Created Prince of the Moscowa after Borodino, 1812. Given title Duc d'Elchingen,

1808. Remained in Army after Restoration of Louis XVIII. Reverted to support of Napoleon during 'Hundred Days'. Fought at Waterloo. Court-martialled by Chamber of Peers and executed.

Nicholas 1 (1796–1855): Tsar of Russia, 1825–55. Succeeded his brother, Alexander I. Repressed Decembrist plot. Pursued reactionary policies. Introduced codification of laws, 1833. Freed serfs on state lands, 1838. Strengthened autocratic government. Created secret police ('Third Section'), 1826. Through education minister, Uvarov, resisted development of higher education and schools. Crushed Polish Revolt, 1830–1. Helped Austria suppress Hungarian Revolt, 1849. Policy towards Turkey alarmed Britain, resulting in war with Turkey, 1853, and Crimean War, 1854–6.

Nicholas II (1868–1918): Tsar of Russia, 1894–1917. Son of Alexander III. Reluctant to introduce political reforms. Influential in achievement of International Peace Conference in The Hague, 1898. Encouraged building of Trans-Siberian Railway. Forced by revolutionary mood of 1905 (stemming from industrial unrest, poor harvests and disastrous Russo–Japanese War) to summon elected *Duma*. Made gestures of reform under prime minister Stolypin. Fell under influence of Rasputin after 1906. Undertook Supreme Command of Russian Armies, 1915. Accused of maintaining communications with Germany during First World War. Abdicated after Revolution, March 1917. Murdered by local Bolsheviks at Ekaterinburg, 1918, together with family.

Nietzsche, Friedrich Wilhelm (1844–1900): German philosopher. Developed ideas of need for social elite of realists, led by a 'superman' unhindered by conventional morality. Later association of his writings with political developments (especially National Socialism and Fascism) has been questioned. Essentially an individualist, suspicious of extreme nationalism. Writings edited posthumously by fanatically nationalistic sister. Insane in later life.

O'Connell, Daniel (1775–1847): Irish nationalist; known as 'The Liberator'. Born in County Kerry, he founded the Catholic Association in 1823 as a mass movement to campaign for Catholic emancipation. Elected for County Clare in 1828, but as a Catholic not allowed to take his seat. His efforts helped to secure the passing of the Roman Catholic Relief Act, 1829. Subsequently, took seat as MP for County Clare, 1830, and for Waterford, 1832. Organised mass meeting in 1842 and 1843 to secure repeal of the 1800 Act of Union. His cancellation of the Clontarf meeting in October 1843 discredited him with many Irish extremists. He died at Genoa.

Orlando, Vittorio Emmanuele (1860–1952): Italian statesman. Professor of constitutional law at Palermo. Elected to parliament, 1897. Minister of justice, 1916. Prime minister, 1917–19, in aftermath of military defeat at Caporetto. President of Chamber of Deputies, 1919. Led Italian delegation at Paris Peace Conference, 1919–20. Disagreed with President Wilson over Italy's territorial aspirations. Influence declined thereafter. Resigned presidency of Chamber of Deputies in protest at Fascist electoral malpractice, 1925. President, Constituent Assembly, 1946–7.

Orsini, Felice (1819–1858): Italian nationalist conspirator. Joined Mazzini's 'Young Italy' movement. After several plots against Papacy, attempted to assassinate Napoleon III and Empress Eugénie, believing Napoleon had betrayed Italy. After his execution, press published a letter in which he appealed to Napoleon to assist Italian cause. Ironically contributed to Napoleon's meeting with Cavour at Plombières.

Palmerston, 3rd Viscount, Henry John Temple (1784–1865): British statesman. Tory MP, 1807–31. Whig MP, 1831–65. Succeeded as Viscount Palmerston, 1802. Lord of the Admiralty, 1807–9. Secretary for War, 1809–28. Foreign secretary, 1830–4, 1835–41, 1846–51. Home secretary, 1852–5. Prime minister, 1855–8, 1859–65. As foreign secretary, supported British interests aggressively. Supported liberal causes abroad. Instrumental in securing Belgian independence, 1830–1. Formed Quadruple Alliance in defence of Spanish and Portuguese monarchs. Lent support to Turkey against Egyptian and Russian threats. Declared war on China ('Opium War'), 1840. Conflicted with Cabinet colleagues. Dismissed after recognising Louis Napoleon's coup against Second Republic. As home secretary, encouraged prison and factory reforms. As prime minister, concluded Crimean War. Suppressed Indian Mutiny, 1857. Recognised new Kingdom of Italy. Achieved return of Ionian islands to Greece. During American Civil War, kept Britain neutral.

Parnell, Charles Stewart (1846–91): Irish nationalist leader. Son of Anglican gentry family, educated at Cambridge. Nationalist MP for Co. Meath, 1875–80, Cork 1880–91, leading Irish Nationalist Party in parliament from 1880. Led agitation for Home Rule, skilfully coordinating political bargaining at Westminster with more radical movements in Ireland. Career ruined when cited in O'Shea divorce case of 1890.

Pasic, Nikola (1845–1926): Serbian/Yugoslavian politician. One of founders of Radical Party, 1881. Became member of legislature, 1878. Exiled, 1883–9. Chief minister of Serbia, 1891–2. Ambassador to Russia, 1893–4. Exiled, 1899–1903. Helped engineer establishment of Karadjordjevic dynasty in Serbia, 1903. Chief minister, 1904–8. Minister of foreign affairs, 1904. Chief minister, 1910–18. Faced opposition from militant Serbian 'Black Hand' organisation, which he suppressed in 1917. Led joint delegation of Serbs, Croats and Slovenes at Paris Peace Conference, 1919. Chief minister of Yugoslavia, 1921–6, giving priority to Serbian interests.

Paul I (1754–1801): Tsar of Russia, 1796–1801. Succeeded his mother, Catherine the Great. Led Russia into War of Second Coalition, 1798–9. Switched to support of France, 1800. Introduced law of royal succession through male line. Liberalised laws on serfdom, 1797. Aroused opposition among nobility and army. Killed in palace coup, 1801.

Pétain, Henri Philippe (1856–1951): French soldier and politician. Entered army, 1876. Lectured at *Ecole de Guerre*, 1906 onwards. Became colonel, 1912. Commanded an army corps, 1914. National renown followed defence of Verdun, 1916. Commander-in-chief of French armies in the field, 1917. Created Marshal of France, 1918. Vice-president, Higher Council of War, 1920–30. Led joint French–Spanish campaign against insurgents in Morocco, 1925–6. Inspector–general of army, 1929. Became minister of war, 1934. Ambassador to Spain, 1939. Became prime minister, June 1940. Secured Armistice with Germany. Given powers by National Assembly to rule by authoritarian means, July 1940. Became head of state in unoccupied ('Vichy') France, 1942. Obliged to flee France with retreating Germans, 1944. Sentenced to death for treason, 1945, but sentence commuted to life imprisonment by de Gaulle.

Pilsudski, Josef (1867–1935): Polish soldier and statesman. Exiled to Siberia for political activities, 1887–92. Founded Polish Socialist Party, 1892. Became editor of Polish underground Socialist newspaper, *Robotnik*. Increasingly nationalist in outlook. Sought Japanese support for Polish rising during Russo–Japanese War, 1904. Recruited by Austria to lead Polish legion against Russia, 1914. Interned by Germans, 1917. On release, became commander of all Polish armies. Elected chief of state, 1918. Remained dictator until Constitution established, 1922. Led Polish campaign against Bolsheviks, 1919–20. Created field marshal, 1920. Commanded army until retirement, 1923. Executed military coup 1926. Served as prime minister, 1926–8, 1930. Retained dictatorial powers until death, 1935. Unable to convince France of threat from Nazi Germany. Concluded Non-Aggression Pact with Germany, 1934.

Pitt, William, 'The Younger' (1759–1806): British politician. Son of Pitt 'The Elder'. MP, 1781–1806. Chancellor of the exchequer, 1782–3. Prime minister and chancellor of the exchequer, 1783–1801, 1804–6. Youngest ever prime minister. Undertook major administrative reforms in 1780s. Initially sympathetic to parliamentary reform. Led Britain in wars against Revolutionary France after 1793. Negotiated European coalitions against France, 1793, 1798, 1805. Took stern line with radical opposition at home. Secured Bill for union of Great Britain and Ireland, 1800. Introduced income tax. Resigned, 1801, when George III vetoed Catholic Emancipation.

Pius IX, Pope (1792–1878): Pontiff, 1846–78. Regarded as a progressive cardinal. Seen by Italian nationalists as the 'Liberal Pope' they had sought. Declared political amnesty, 1846. Refused to take part in war against Austria, thereby precipitating revolt in Rome, 1848. Obliged to flee Rome, but restored with French military backing, 1850, relying on this support until 1870. Following restoration, became reactionary in outlook. Failed to restore liberal constitution of 1848. Re-established Catholic hierarchy in Britain, 1850, and Holland, 1853. Established Concordats with Spain, 1851, and Austria, 1855. Stated doctrine of Immaculate Conception, 1854. Issued *Syllabus Errarum*, criticising liberalism, 1864. Convoked First Vatican Council, 1869–70, which issued declaration of Papal Infallibility, provoking opposition, e.g., in Germany, leading to '*Kulturkampf*'. Rome occupied by Italian troops, 1870. Pius thereafter felt himself to be a prisoner.

Pius XII (Eugenio Pacelli) (1876–1958): Elected pope 1939. Prior to this, he had been papal nuncio in Germany and papal secretary of state. Much controversy surrounds his conduct during World War II, in particular his failure to condemn the Nazi régime.

Pobedonostsev, Konstantin Petrovich (1827–1907): Professor of Constitutional Law, Moscow University, 1860–5. Tutor to both Alexander III and Nicholas II. Became member of Council of the Empire, 1872. Appointed Procurator of Holy Synod (i.e. lay administrator of Russian Orthodox Church), 1880. Used his influential position to resist parliamentary government, and to bolster *status quo*. Approved of oppression of non-Russian nationalities within Empire.

Poincaré, Raymond (1860–1934): French statesman. Elected deputy, 1887. Education minister, 1893–4. Finance minister, 1894–5. Senator and finance minister, 1906. Became prime minister, 1912. Strengthened Dual Alliance with Prussia. Supported Entente with Britain. President, 1913–20, influential on legislation. Prime minister, 1924–6, simultaneously foreign minister. Pursued nationalistic policy, disagreeing with Britain over reparations question. Authorised French occupation of Ruhr, 1923. Prime minister and finance minister of Government of National Union, 1926–9, imposing rigorous economies and achieving currency stabilisation.

Pompidou, George (1911–1974): French politician. Member of Resistance during Second World War. Aide to General de Gaulle, 1944–6. Member of Council of State, 1946–54. Deputy director-general of tourism, 1946–9. Director-general of Rothschild's (banking house), 1954–8. Chief of de Gaulle's personal staff, 1958–9. Involved in drafting of Constitution of Fifth Republic. Negotiated ceasefire agreement with Algerian nationalists, 1961. Prime minister, 1962–8. President, 1969–74. Pursued policies similar to those of de Gaulle.

Primo de Rivera, Miguel (1870–1930): Spanish dictator, 1923–30. Entered Spanish army, 1888. Served in Morocco, Cuba and Philippines. Became major-general, 1910. Military governor of Cadiz, 1915–19, Valencia, 1919–22, Barcelona, 1922–3. Assumed power with support of King Alfonso XIII, 1923. Dissolved Spanish parliament, suspended trial by jury, imposed censorship of press. Political opponents imprisoned. Intended to establish Fascist regime. Faced growing opposition, e.g. over failure to implement agricultural reforms. Ended Moroccan War, 1927. Continued in office as prime minister, but obliged to resign when he lost support of army, 1930. Actions and policies contributed to collapse of monarchy.

Proudhon, Pierre Joseph (1809–1865): Influential French socialist propagandist and theorist. His publications included *Qu'est-ce que la propriété* (1840) and the weighty *Système des contradictions economiques* (1846).

Quisling, Vidkun (1887–1945): Norwegian soldier, politician and traitor. Military attaché in Petrograd, 1918–19, Helsinki, 1919–21. Minister of war, 1931–3. Expanded right wing National Unity Party. Visited Germany, 1939. Advised Hitler on creation of sympathetic regime in Norway. Headed puppet regime following German occupation, 1940. Tried and executed, 1945.

Radetzky, Josef (1766–1858): Austrian soldier. Fought Turks, 1788–89. Served in all major campaigns against France during Napoleonic wars.

Chief of staff, 1809. Appointed commander-in-chief in Lombardy, 1831. Created field marshal, 1836. After rising in Milan, obliged to retreat to 'Quadrilateral', 1848. Secured victory over Piedmontese at Custozza, 1848. Regained Venice, 1849. Continued as Governor–General in Lombardy–Venetia until 1857.

Ranke, Leopold von (1795–1886): German historian. Professor of history at Berlin, 1825–72. Established modern critical methods of historiography, stressing need for thorough examination of sources and objective analysis. Made use of documents previously unavailable. Wrote many major works, including *History of the Roman and German Peoples, 1494–1514*, 1824, and a history of the Papacy in the sixteen and seventeenth centuries, 1834–7.

Rasputin, Gregori (1871–1916): Russian mystic. Used hypnotic talents over ailing Tsarevich Alexei (1904–18) to gain influence at court. Interference in politics damaged position of monarchy and provoked opposition among court. Suspected of working on behalf of Germany during First World War. Murdered by aristocrats.

Rathenau, Walther (1867–1922): German statesman. Director of giant AEG electrical combine. Made responsible for organising war economy, 1916. Founded (liberal) Democratic Party, 1918. Became minister of reconstruction, 1921, and minister of foreign affairs, 1922. Represented Germany at Cannes Conference, 1922. Engineered reduction of Germany's reparations commitment for 1922. Played leading role in achieving Treaty of Rapallo with Russia, 1922. Assassinated by anti-Semitic nationalists.

Ribbentrop, Joachim von (1893–1946): German Nazi diplomat. Involved in negotiations between Hitler and German government. Helped organise Nazi government, 1933. Ambassador at large, 1935. Concluded Anglo–German Naval Treaty, 1935, and Anti-Comintern Pact, 1936. Ambassador in London, 1936–8. Foreign minister, 1938–45. Responsible for giving German foreign policy a distinctly 'Nazi' character. Negotiated Molotov–Ribbentrop Pact, 1939, and Pact with Italy and Japan, 1940. Tried as war criminal at Nuremberg. Hanged, 1946.

Robespierre, Maximilien de (1758–1794): French Revolutionary leader. Dubbed 'The Incorruptible'. Lawyer, 1781–9. Represented Third Estate of Artois in States General, 1789. Emerged as radical in National Assembly, subsequently Constituent Assembly, 1789–91. Drew political inspiration from works of Rousseau. Believed himself to be embodiment of 'General Will'. Leader of radical Montagnard party. Elected to Committee of Public Safety, acquiring dominant position. Called for death of Louis XVI, 1793. Removed political opponents, e.g. Danton and Hébert, 1793–4. Created political dictatorship and attempted to transform society, involving 'Reign of Terror'. Provoked opposition among majority of National Convention. Deposed in 'Thermidorean Reaction', 1794, and executed.

Rommel, Erwin (1891–1944): German soldier. Served on Romanian and Italian fronts during First World War. Lectured at War Academy. Joined Nazi Party, 1933. Commanded 7th Panzer Division, penetrated Ardennes,

May 1940. Became commander of 'Afrika Corps', 1941, earning nickname 'The Desert Fox'. Defeated by campaigns of Alexander and Montgomery, 1942–3. Given task of strengthening defences in France, 1944. Active in resistance to Allied landings in Normandy, June 1944. Implicated in plot to assassinate Hitler. Apparently forced to commit suicide, October 1944.

Rousseau, Jacques (1712–1778): Swiss-born philosopher. Attracted interest through his writings which criticised existing social order. *Du Contrat social*, 1762, described his political views, *Emile*, 1762, his theories on education. *Du Contrat social* became extremely influential, especially during and after French Revolution. Saw society itself as source of contemporary ills. Claimed political rulers derived power from popular mandate.

Salazar, Antonio de Oliveira (1889–1970): Portuguese dictator. Professor of economics at Coimbra University, 1916. Minister of finance, 1926, 1928–32. Prime minister, 1932–68. Also minister of war, 1936–44, foreign minister, 1936–7. Principal architect of authoritarian constitution introduced in 1933. Implemented fascist-type government on virtually dictatorial lines, stifling political opposition. Restored public finances and modernised transport system. Organised public works schemes. Maintained Portuguese neutrality during Second World War.

Salisbury, 3rd Marquess of, Robert Arthur Talbot Gascoyne-Cecil (1830–1903): Cecil was Conservative MP for Stamford, 1853–68. In 1865 he became Viscount Cranbourne. He served as secretary for India in 1866, resigning in protest at the 1867 Reform Bill. In 1868 he succeeded as Marquess of Salisbury. He returned as secretary for India, 1874–6, and as foreign secretary, 1878–80. He was leader of the opposition in the House of Lords and joint leader of the Conservative Party, 1881–5. In 1885 he became prime minister and sole party leader. He acted as prime minister and foreign secretary, 1887–92 and 1895–1900. He was prime minister and lord privy seal, 1900–2. Salisbury was a remarkably able diplomat, while in the domestic sphere he had an incisive knowledge of the Conservative Party. As a Tory and a High Church Anglican he was able to control an unruly party, and by moderate social reform and opposition to Home Rule he succeeded in forging the Unionist alliance which dominated British politics between 1886 and 1906.

Scharnhorst, Gerhard Johann von (1755–1813): Prussian soldier. Served in Hanoverian Army, 1793–5. Entered Prussian army, 1801. Selected to train fresh armies. Fought in campaigns, 1806–7. Head of Army Reform Commission, 1807. Reorganised Prussian army. Chief of staff to Blucher.

Schlieffen, Alfred, Count von (1833–1913): German soldier. Chief of German General Staff, 1891–1905. Prepared strategic planning for war with France ('Schlieffen Plan'). In modified form, plan was used in German attack on France, 1914. Believed rapid defeat of France was essential to German success. Plan provided for violation of neutrality of Holland, Belgium and Luxembourg, by-passing France's defences.

Schwarzenberg, Prince Felix (1800–52): Austrian statesman. Protégé of Metternich. Engaged in diplomatic service in Italy. Appointed adviser to

Radetzky in Lombardy, 1848. Through influence of army, became prime minister and foreign minister of Austria, 1848–52. Secured abdication of Emperor Ferdinand and succession of Francis Joseph. Took firm line with Hungarian rebels, 1849. Temporary 'concessions' granted providing for representative and responsible government, 1849. (Withdrawn 1851). Created highly centralised state administration. Achieved Prussian recognition of Austrian primacy in Germany, 1850.

Seeckt, Hans von (1866–1936): German soldier. Chief of staff to Mackensen on Eastern Front during First World War. Won victory at Gorlice, 1915. Served in Balkans and Turkey. Appointed Head of *Truppenamt*, 1919. Supervised Germany's secret rearmament, 1919–26, especially through co-operation with Russia. Head of *Reichswehr*, 1920–6. Resigned in response to President Hindenburg's hostility, 1926. Member of Reichstag, 1930–2. Created an army capable of rapid expansion after 1933.

Sieyès, Emmanuel Joseph ('Abbé Sieyès') (1748–1836): French Catholic priest and Revolutionary leader. Attracted interest of reformers by publishing *Essai sur les privileges* and *Qu'est-ce que le Tiers État?* Suggested Third Estate should meet as National Assembly, 1789. Involved in composing Constitution, 1791. Refused offer of Archbishopric of Paris, 1791. Member of Council of Five Hundred, 1795–9. Entered Directory, 1799. Supported Napoleon Bonaparte in Brumaire coup. Architect of Consulate system. Created Count and Senator under Empire. Lived in exile in Belgium, 1814–30. Returned to France under July Monarchy.

Smith, Adam (1723–1790): Scottish economist. Professor of logic at Glasgow, 1751, and of moral philosophy, 1752. Friend of Hume. Greatest work, *An Enquiry into the Nature and Causes of the Wealth of Nations*, 1776. Criticised mercantilist economic thought. Proponent of free-market, laissez-faire system. Placed great stress on individual freedom. Devised theory of division of labour, money, prices, wages and distribution.

Sorel, Georges (1847–1922): French syndicalist philosopher. Studied Marxism after engineering career. Saw need for violent revolution under trade union control. Had little influence on French trade unions. Criticised both Socialist and Radical parties. Lent support to monarchist movement, 1909, and to Bolsheviks, 1917. Ideas on manipulating popular opinion impressed Hitler and Mussolini.

Speransky, Michael (1772–1839): Russian political reformer. Advised Alexander I on constitutional reforms. Instrumental in establishment of Council of State, 1810. Introduced state budgetary system. Earned hostility of reactionary elements by proposing creation of local and central representative bodies. Exiled, 1812. Returned to Russia under Nicholas I. Completed codification of Russian law, 1832.

Stalin, Josef Visarionovitch (J. V. Djugashvili) (1879–1953): Soviet leader. Expelled from seminary for political activities, 1899. Exiled to Siberia twice. Attended conferences of Russian Social Democrats in

Stockholm, 1906, and London, 1907. Expert on racial minorities in Bolshevik Central Committee, 1912. Became editor of *Pravda*, 1917. Worked with Lenin in Petrograd during Revolution, 1917. Member of Revolutionary Military Council, 1920–3. People's Commissar for nationalities, 1921–3. General Secretary of Central Committee of Communist Party, 1922–53. During Civil War, supervised defence of Petrograd. Co-operated with Kamenev and Zinoviev to exclude Trotsky from office, 1923. (Secured Trotsky's exile, 1929.) Gained control of Party at Fifteenth Congress, 1927. Embarked on policy of 'Socialism in One Country' through Five Year Plans, 1928. Achieved rapid economic development. Eliminated political opponents in series of 'show trials', 1936–8. Chairman of Council of Ministers, 1941–53. During Second World War, as Commissar of Defence and Marshal of the Soviet Union, took over direction of war effort. Present at Teheran, Yalta and Potsdam conferences. Established firm control of Eastern European Communist 'satellites', with exception of Yugoslavia, during postwar period. 'Personality cult' of Stalin officially condemned by Khrushchev at Party Congress, 1956.

Stambolisky, Alexander (1879–1923): Bulgarian politician. Involved in peasant agitation, 1897. As member of Agrarian Union, won fame as popular orator, 1908–15. Imprisoned for opposing entry into First World War. Instrumental in forcing King Ferdinand to abdicate, 1918. Proclaimed Republic, 1918. Prime minister, 1919–23. Wielded almost dictatorial power. Concluded treaty of Neuilly, 1919. Introduced land reforms and revised taxation in favour of peasants. Deposed and murdered in coup, 1923, having sought to help Yugoslav government crush Macedonian revolutionaries.

Stambulov, Stefan (1854–1895): Bulgarian statesman. Active in revolutionary movement, 1875. Emerged as national leader following Bulgarian union with Eastern Roumelia, 1886. Appointed Regent, September 1886. Lent support to Prince Ferdinand of Saxe-Coburg. Hoped to conciliate Turkey. Dismissed by Ferdinand, 1894. Murdered, 1895.

Stavisky, Serge (d. 1934): Central figure in 'Stavisky Case', 1934. Russian–Jewish financier, living in France. Sold valueless bonds. Took own life before charges could be made. Revelations of his involvement in other questionable activities and protection by public figures caused outcry. Murder of member of Public Prosecutor's staff attributed to attempted cover-up. Case had political repercussions, providing ammunition for extremes of right and left against corruption in Third Republic. Rioting and general strike, February 1934, led to formation of broad coalition government.

Stein, Baron Heinrich Friedrich Karl vom und zum (1757–1831): Prussian statesman. Entered Prussian Civil Service, 1780. Appointed chief minister, 1807. Implemented social transformation. Serfs freed, 1810. Land reforms introduced. Administrative changes at central and local levels. After flight from Prussia, 1808, entered service of Alexander I. Administrator of liberated German territories, 1813–14. Proposals for German unification vetoed by Metternich.

Stolypin, Peter (1862–1911): Russian statesman. Governor of Saratov Province. Subdued agrarian disturbances, 1905. Became minister of interior, 1906. Prime minister, 1906–11. Advocated moderate political reforms. Sought to create class of independent middle-sized farmers (Kulaks) as counterweight to liberals in *Duma*. Introduced property qualification for candidates for *Duma*. Took repressive line with rioters. Renewed anti-Semitic policies. Planned improvements in education, local government and system of social insurance. Assassinated, 1911.

Stresemann, Gustav (1878–1929): German statesman. Elected to *Reichstag*, 1907–12, 1914–29. Leader of National Liberals, 1917. Took nationalistic position during First World War, supporting High Command. Became more moderate after war. Founded People's Party (DVP), 1919. Advocated meeting Germany's commitments under treaty of Versailles, thereby gaining confidence of Allies. Became Chancellor during crisis year, 1923. Foreign minister, 1923–9. Restored Germany's diplomatic position. Concluded Locarno Pact, 1925. Achieved German entry into League of Nations, 1926. Secured reduction of reparations demands. Negotiated terms for Allied evacuation of Rhineland. Supported Dawes Plan, 1924, and Young Plan, 1929. Awarded Nobel Peace Prize, 1926.

Strossmayer, Josef (1815–1905). Croatian priest. Bishop of Djakovo, 1849–1905. Supporter of Yugoslav nationalism. Influential in curbing repressive policies of Hungarian authorities. Established South Slav Academy at Zagreb, 1867, and Zagreb University, 1874. As a 'Liberal Catholic', opposed doctrine of Papal Infallibility. In close contact with Gladstone. Fostered interest of western liberals in possibilities of union of southern Slavs.

Suvorov, Alexander (1729–1800): Russian soldier. Active in campaigns against Sweden, Prussia and Turkey. Popular with Catherine the Great. Renowned for severity of his actions in Bessarabia, 1790, and against Polish rebels, 1795. Commanded Russian Army against French in North Italy. In joint effort with Austrians, expelled French armies from Milan and Turin, 1799. Recalled to St Petersburg having been obliged to retreat. Fell into disfavour.

Talleyrand, Charles Maurice de (1754–1838). French cleric and politician. Bishop of Autun, 1789. Supported Revolutionaries in States General, though retained see until 1791. Suggested confiscation of Church property to increase government revenue. Excommunicated, 1791. Sent to London as envoy, 1792. Left France for USA after death of Louis XVI, not returning until establishment of Directory. Foreign minister, 1797–9. Supported Napoleon during Brumaire coup. Foreign Minister, 1799–1807. Played major role in creation of Confederation of the Rhine. Created Prince of Benevento, 1806. Attended Erfurt Conference, 1808. Opportunistically established contact with Allies, 1814. Obtained Louis XVIII's agreement to issue constitution following Restoration. Represented France at Congress of Vienna, securing recognition of France as a Great Power. Drove diplomatic wedge between former Allies. Retired, 1815, but active in creation of July Monarchy, 1830. Ambassador to London, 1830–4. Eventually reconciled with Catholic Church.

Thiers, Adolphe (1797–1877): French politician and journalist. Among group which persuaded Louis Philippe to accept throne in 1830. Politically an Orléanist throughout career. Minister of interior, 1832, 1834–6. Suppressed rioting in Paris and Lyons. Prime minister and foreign minister, 1836, 1840. During 1848 Revolution, advised King to leave Paris, and reassert authority with provincial help. Detained during Louis Napoleon's coup, 1851. Re-elected Deputy, 1863. Prominent among liberal opposition. Elected 'Head of the Executive Power' of Third Republic, Bordeaux, 1871. Negotiated Peace Treaty with Bismarck following Franco–Prussian War. Raised loans to pay war indemnity. President of Third Republic, 1871–3.

Tirpitz, Alfred von (1849–1930): German Grand Admiral. Entered Prussian Navy, 1865. Won support of Kaiser after stressing importance of battle fleet, 1891. Minister of marine, 1897–1916. Expanded High Seas Fleet. Proponent of unrestricted submarine warfare. Resigned when suggestions not acted upon.

Tisza, István (1861–1918): Son of Kálmán Tisza. Prime minister, 1904–5, 1913–17. Took strong line in quelling political disputes. Linked Hungary's policy closely with that of Austria during crisis, 1914. Engineered succession of Charles after abdication of Francis Joseph. Murdered during violence in Hungary in last stage of war.

Tisza, Kálmán (1830–1902): Founded Hungarian Liberal Party, 1875. Prime minister, 1875–90. Implemented policy of 'magyarisation' of subject national groups.

Tito, Josip Broz (1892–1980): Yugoslav statesman. Member of Yugoslav Communist party since early 1920s, becoming its secretary-general, 1937. Led Yugoslav partisan forces during Second World War. Became marshal 1943. After war, secured independence from USSR, 1948. First president of Yugoslav Republic, 1953–80. Pursued independent foreign policy, encouraging co-operation among non-aligned nations.

Tocqueville, Alexis de (1805–1859): French politician and historian. Studied American penal system during 1820s. Published *Democracy in America*, 1835. Profoundly interested in question of liberal society. Elected deputy, 1839–48. Elected deputy to National Assembly after 1848 Revolution. Involved in formulation of Constitution of Second Republic. Became foreign minister, 1849. Disillusioned by Louis Napoleon's retreat from liberalism. Wrote *The Ancien Regime and the Revolution*, 1856, and *Recollections of 1848*, published 1889.

Trotsky, Lev Davidovich (L. D. Bronstein) (1879–1940): Russian revolutionary of Ukrainian–Jewish descent. Exiled to Siberia, 1898. Joined Lenin in London, 1902. Became an independent socialist, 1902. Hoped to achieve reconciliation between Bolsheviks and Mensheviks. Returned to Russia, 1905, and organised first soviet in St Petersburg. Exiled to Siberia again. Returned to St Petersburg from New York, May 1917. Chairman of Petrograd Soviet, November 1917. First Commissar for Foreign Affairs. Delayed conclusion of Treaty of Brest–Litovsk, 1918.

Commissar for War during Civil War, creating Red Army. After death of Lenin, and disagreements with Stalin, excluded from office. Theory of 'Permanent Revolution' condemned by Communist Party. Lost influence over Party policy, 1925. Expelled from Communist Party, 1927. Deported, 1929. Wrote *History of the Revolution* while in France. Murdered by Stalinist agent in Mexico, 1940.

Turgot, Anne-Robert-Jacques (1727–1781): French administrator and economist. *Intendant* of Limoges, 1761–74. Became minister of marine, 1774. Controller-general of finance, 1774–6. One of central figures of Physiocrat school of economics. Abolished *corvée* (forced labour on roads). Encouraged building of roads and bridges. Reformed interest rates and imposed taxes more equitably. Ended some feudal privileges. Tried to re-establish free trade in grain between provinces.

Venizelos, Eleutherios (1864–1936): Greek statesman. Involved in rising against Turkey, 1896. President of Cretan Assembly. Declared union of Crete with Greece, 1905. Became prime minister of Greece, 1910. Introduced financial, military and constitutional reforms. Took Greece into Balkan War. Gained Macedonia from peace settlement. Attempted to enter First World War on Allied side, 1915. Removed from office by King Constantine. Formed rebel government in Crete, 1916, later moved to Salonika. Declared war on Germany and Bulgaria. Secured abdication of Constantine and became legitimate prime minister in Athens, 1917. Attended Paris Peace Conference. In seeking to gain Anatolia for Greece, provoked war with Turkey which produced electoral defeat, 1920. Briefly in office, 1924. Prime minister, 1928–32, again, 1933. Supporters staged uprising, 1935, leading to short civil war. Fled to France.

Victor Emmanuel II (1820–78): King of Piedmont-Sardinia, 1849–78; King of Italy, 1861–78. Son of Charles Albert of Savoy. Succeeded to throne when Charles Albert abdicated after Radetsky expelled Piedmontese from Lombardy. Supported moves for Italian unity. Remained a constitutional monarch, upholding liberal Piedmontese constitution, 1849.

Victoria, Queen (1819–1901): Queen of United Kingdom, 1837–1901; Empress of India, 1876–1901. Longest reigning British monarch. Symbol of period of British expansion. Last reigning Hanoverian. Married her cousin, Albert, 1840. Reign saw limitations on power of monarchy in relation to ministers. Victoria long claimed special supervision of foreign affairs, leading to disputes with Palmerston and Lord John Russell. Lived in seclusion for ten years after death of Albert, 1861. Popularity demonstrated by Golden Jubilee, 1887, and Diamond Jubilee, 1897. Disliked Gladstone, favouring Disraeli. Related to most of European royal houses through marriages of her children.

Voltaire (François Marie Arouet) (1694–1778): French philosopher. Imprisoned in Bastille, 1717–18, 1726. In *Lettres philosophiques*, 1734, contrasted French and English institutions. Lived briefly in Potsdam under patronage of Frederick II. Corresponded with Catherine the Great. Philosophical works include *Dictionnaire philosophique*, 1764. Criticised dogmatic religions, especially Catholicism. Consistent theme in his writings is a lack of respect for authority and institutions, therefore preparing intellectual climate for French Revolution. Campaigned on behalf of victims of religious and political persecution.

Walesa, Lech (1943–   ): Polish trade unionist. Former Gdansk shipyard worker. Emerged as leader of independent 'Solidarity' trade union. Solidarity comprised some 40 per cent of Polish workers by late 1980. Mounted outspoken opposition to economic and social policies of government. Detained following imposition of martial law, December 1981. Released 11 months later. During his detention, Solidarity was banned. Continued to hold prominent position. Granted audience with Pope John Paul II, 1983. Awarded Nobel Peace Prize, 1983.

Weizmann, Chaim (1874–1952): Zionist leader. Headed British Zionist movement before First World War. Advised Foreign Office during planning of Balfour Declaration, 1917. Head of World Zionist Movement after 1920. Became head of Jewish Agency for Palestine, 1929. Elected first president of Israel, 1948.

Wellington, 1st Duke of, Arthur Wellesley (1769–1852): British soldier and politician. Outstanding military leader during Napoleonic Wars. MP, 1790–95, 1806, 1807, 1807–9. Commanded British force in Portugal, 1808. Created Earl Wellington, then Marquess, 1812. Campaigns in Peninsular War culminated in invasion of southern France, 1813. Created Duke of Wellington, 1814. British ambassador to Paris, 1814. Chief secretary for Ireland, 1807–9. Won decisive victory over Napoleon at Waterloo, June 1815. Commander of British occupying forces in France, 1815–18. Helped ensure moderate treatment of France by Allies. Master-General of the Ordnance, 1819–27. Prime minister, 1828–30. Achieved Catholic Emancipation, 1829. Reluctant to introduce electoral reform, 1830, consequently lost office. Prime minister and secretary of state for all Departments, November–December, 1834. Foreign secretary, 1834–5. Minister without portfolio, 1841–6. Commander-in-Chief, 1842–52.

William II, (1859–1941). German Emperor, King of Prussia, 1888–1918. Son of Emperor Frederick III. Dismissed Bismarck from Chancellorship, 1890. Implemented 'New Course' in policy, aiming to assert German claims to world leadership. Increasingly under control of German High Command. Obliged by them to abdicate following Germany's military defeat, 1918. Went into exile in Holland.

Witte, Serge (1849–1915). Russian statesman. Minister of communications during 1880s. Minister of Finance, 1892–1903, with supervisory role over commerce, industry and labour relations. Principal achievement was construction of Trans-Siberian Railway. Able to stimulate industry with loans from France. Dismissed as result of military opposition, 1903. Returned to office to negotiate peace at Portsmouth following Russo-Japanese War. Became prime minister after 1905 Revolution. Substantial loans from Britain and France allowed him to by-pass *Duma*. Dismissed after six-month term of office. Strong critic of First World War.

Zimmermann, Arthur (1864–1940): German foreign minister. Sent telegram to German diplomat in Mexico, 1917, proposing alliance between Germany and Mexico, on understanding that Mexico would invade USA if USA entered war against Germany. In return, Mexico would receive lost territory in Texas, Arizona and New Mexico. Telegram intercepted by Britain and contents revealed to Washington. Instrumental in winning approval of Congress for US entry into war, 1917.

Zinoviev, Gregori (1883–1936): Russian Bolshevik leader. Returned to Russia from exile with Lenin, April 1917. Held prominent office in Third International, 1920–26. Alleged to have written to British Communists calling on them to cultivate revolution ('Red Letter Scare', 1924). Disagreed with Stalin, 1926. Discredited as ally of Trotsky and deposed from Politburo. Tried and sentenced to imprisonment for treason, 1935. Executed after second trial, 1936.

Section VI
Glossary of terms

Action Française   French right-wing political movement founded by Charles Maurras in 1899 based on a royalist, nationalist and antisemitic programme. Although nominally supporting the Roman Catholic Church, the movement's other policies led to a papal ban in 1926. During the Second World War, the movement actively supported the Vichy regime an action which resulted in its being banned after the war.

Agadir Crisis   Diplomatic and military crisis in 1911 caused by arrival of German warship 'Panther' in Moroccan port of Agadir. Although supposedly sent to protect German residents, the main aim was to gain colonial concessions from the French elsewhere in Africa in exchange for recognition of the French interest in Morocco.

Ancien Regime   (Fr. lit. 'old order')   Describes the structure of government and society prevailing in Europe prior to the French Revolution of 1789. Its chief characteristics were absolute or despotic monarchy, and the division of society into three 'orders', viz. aristocracy, clergy and the Third Estate (*i.e.* the ordinary people) (*q.v.* Tiers Etat).

Anglo-French Entente, *see* Entente Cordiale

Anschluss   The idea of union between Austria and Germany, current after the collapse of the Hapsburg Monarchy in 1918 and given further impetus after Hitler became German Chancellor in 1933. The deliberate destabilisation of the Austrian government by the Nazis in 1938 led to the resignation of Chancellor Schuschnigg and his replacement by Arthur Seyss-Inquart, a Nazi nominee who invited the Germans to occupy Austria. The union of Austria with Germany was proclaimed on 13 March 1938.

Anti-Clericalism   Term applied to the opposition to organised religion, and largely directed against the power of the Roman Catholic Church. Anti-clericalism prevalent during the revolutionary period in France and throughout the nineteenth century. Also apparent in Spain, especially during the Second Republic, 1931–9, in Germany as a result of the Kulturkampf (*q.v.*) and sporadically in Italy.

Anti-Comintern Pact   The agreement between Germany and Japan signed on 25 November 1936 which stated both countries' hostility to international communism. The pact also signed by Italy in 1937 and, in addition to being a commitment to oppose the Soviet Union, the pact also recognised the Japanese regime which had ruled Manchuria since 1931.

Anti-Semitism   Term used to describe animosity towards the Jews, either on a religious or a racial basis. Originally coined by racial theorists of the later nineteenth century, anti-semitism can take a number of different political, economic or racial forms. A number of political parties in Germany and Austria were based on anti-semitism, and it also appears in France via Action Française (*q.v.*). Economic and political anti-semitism was also a feature of Tsarist Russia with frequent pogroms (*q.v.*) against Jewish communities, a form of activity which seems to have recurred in the Soviet Union in 1958–9 and 1962–3. Anti-semitism was one of the central planks of Nazi ideology and the major theme in Hitler's thinking, with the Jews epitomised as all that was wrong with German society. The ideas of making Germany 'Jew-free' given practical form in anti-semitic legislation and the 'final solution' put into operation during the Second World War.

Armed Neutrality   Declaration of policy by a state in times of war or international crisis that, while not wishing to become involved, it will nevertheless defend its interest and territorial integrity from incursions by any belligerent power.

Armenian Massacres   The systematic destruction of the monophysite Christian Armenian people in the Ottoman Empire by Moslem Turks in 1894–5. This action signalled the end of British support for the Empire and was followed by the extermination or deportation of the entire Armenian people by the Turkish government in 1914 and 1915.

Assignats   (Fr.)   Interest-bearing Treasury bonds introduced by the French Constitutional Assembly in December 1789 to facilitate the purchase of nationalised Church lands. In September 1790 they became paper currency, but over-issue as a means of financing the revolutionary wars led to depreciation and the inflationary crisis in 1793.

Atlantic Charter   A statement of principles agreed by Churchill and Roosevelt on behalf of Britain and the United States in August 1941, on the conduct of international policy in the postwar world. These included no territorial or other expansion; no wish for territorial changes other than those agreed by the peoples concerned; respect for the rights of all peoples to choose their form of government; desire for general economic development and collaboration; the need to disarm aggressor nations and the wish to construct a general system of international security. Although mainly a propaganda exercise, the US refused to acknowledge any future international obligations in spite of British pressure. The charter was endorsed by the Soviet Union and fourteen other states at war with the Axis powers in September 1941.

Ausgleich   (Ger. compromise)   Agreement reached between the Austrian government and moderate Hungarian politicians in 1867 which transformed the Austrian Empire into the Dual Monarchy of Austria–Hungary. The system remained in operation until 1918, despite tensions resulting from commercial union and the resentment of other nationalities within the Empire at the privileged position of the Hungarians.

Axis   A term first used by Mussolini on 1 November 1936 to describe Fascist Italy's relationship with Nazi Germany established by the October protocols of 1936. He referred to the Rome–Berlin Axis, a term which was reinforced by a formal treaty in May 1939, the Pact of Steel. In September 1940, Germany, Italy and Japan signed a tripartite agreement which led to the term 'Axis Powers' being used to describe all three, as well as their Eastern European allies.

Balance of power   A theory of international relations which aimed to secure peace by preventing any one state or group of states from attaining political or military strength sufficient to threaten the independence and liberty of others. The policy was based on the maintenance of a counterforce equal to that of the potential adversaries, and was the central theme of British policy in Europe against the French, and from 1904 to 1914, the Germans. This was epitomised by the creation of the Entente Cordiale (*q.v.*) with France to counter the threat from Germany, and later the Triple Entente (*q.v.*) of Britain, France and Russia to balance the Triple Alliance (*q.v.*) of Germany, Austria–Hungary and Italy. In the inter-war period, Britain again attempted to create a balance against French power by encouraging the rapid recovery of Germany. The policy was abandoned in the 1930s as Germany and Japan began to pursue more aggressive foreign policies which could not be countered by the League of Nations' security system, nor by further alliances.

Bastille   Royal fortress commanding the eastern side of Paris. A radical pamphlet campaign on the eve of the Revolution gave it exaggerated notoriety as a state prison. Its destruction on 14 July 1789 by the workers of the Faubourg St Antoine has been commemorated ever since as a symbol of the fall of Royal despotism and the beginning of the French Revolution.

Black Hand   Popular name of the Serbian secret society (*Ujedinjenje ili Smrt*) formed in Belgrade in May 1911. Led by Col. Dragutin Dimitrievič and consisting mainly of army officers, the society's main aim was the unifying of Serb minorities in Austria–Hungary and the Ottoman Empire with the independent state of Serbia. They were responsible for the training of Gavrilo Princip who assassinated the Austrian Archduke Francis Ferdinand in Sarajevo on 28 June 1914. The society was in conflict with the Serbian government throughout the First World War culminating in the arrest and execution of Dimitrievič with two others, and the banning of the organisation. These sentences were later quashed by the supreme court of Serbia in 1953 when the country had been incorporated into Yugoslavia.

Blitzkrieg   (Ger. lightning war)   A theory of warfare which involved a rapid attack on a very narrow front to create penetration in depth. The technique involved prior aerial bombing to reduce enemy resistance and then the deployment of highly mobile armoured columns. Used extensively by the German army in the Second World War and especially by General Guderian in the campaign against France in 1940. Also abbreviated to 'Blitz' in English to describe the heavy bombing and night attacks on British cities by the German air force during the Second World War.

Bloody Sunday   A term used to describe a number of events as follows:
(1) In Britain, Sunday, 13 November 1887   A meeting held by the Social Democratic Federation in London to demand the release of the nationalist Irish MP William O'Brien was dispersed by police and Lifeguards resulting in the deaths of two people and injuries to over a hundred.
(2) In Britain, Sunday, 30 January 1972   Thirteen civilians were killed in

Londonderry after a demonstration in favour of a united Ireland was broken up by British paratroopers.

(3) In Russia, Sunday, 22 January 1905 A procession of workers and their families led by Fr. George Gapon was fired on by troops guarding the Winter Palace in St Petersburg. The procession had intended to present a petition to the Tsar calling for an eight hour day, a constituent assembly and an amnesty for political prisoners. Over one hundred people were killed and several hundred wounded, an event which helped to spark off the 1905 Russian Revolution.

Bolshevik (Russ. lit. member of the majority) A term applied to the radical faction of the Russian Social Democratic Party which split in 1903. Lenin led the Bolsheviks in opposition to the more moderate Mensheviks (*q.v.*). The Bolsheviks came to power in Russia after the October Revolution of 1917, and the name was retained by the Soviet Communist Party until 1952.

Boulangist A supporter of General George Boulanger (1837–91) who in 1888 began a campaign for the revision of the French constitution and the establishment of a more authoritarian government. He fled France in April 1889 and was condemned in absentia for treason. The Boulangist movement did not survive his flight.

Boxers The popular name for the Society of Harmonious Fists, a movement active in China at the turn of the twentieth century. Its main targets were European commercial interests in the Chinese Empire and, with the tacit approval of the government, they carried out a series of attacks against missionaries and the foreign-owned railways culminating in the siege of the foreign legations in Peking in the summer of 1900. The siege was finally lifted by an international expeditionary force in August of that year.

Brissotins The followers of Jacques-Pierre Brissot, the dominant group of left-wing deputies in the French Legislative Assembly and subsequently known as the Girondins. Fervent advocates of the Revolutionary Wars. By October 1793, most had been imprisoned and guillotined.

Brumaire (Fr. lit. foggy month) Month in the French revolutionary calendar from 21 October to 20 November. Napoleon's coup d'état of 18 Brumaire (9 November 1799) replaced the Directory (*q.v.*) with government by Consulate.

Bundestag Federal Diet of the German Confederation (1815–66). Now one of the two legislative chambers of the Federal Republic of Germany. Elected by direct universal suffrage for four years, it in turn elects the Chancellor who is head of the government.

Bundeswehr The West German Armed Forces.

Cahiers de doléances Lists of grievances drawn up by each of three estates in towns, villages and guilds for presentation at the meeting of the French Estates General in 1789.

Carbonari   (It. lit. charcoal burners)   Italian secret society aiming to overthrow governments established by Versailles settlement of 1815, and establishing national unity. Instigated unsuccessful revolts in Naples (1820) and Piedmont (1821) as well as wider series of risings in 1831. Eventually absorbed into Mazzini's 'Young Italy' movement.

Carlists   Supporters of Don Carlos (1788–1855) and his descendants for their claim to the Spanish throne following Ferdinand VII's ending of the Salic Law in Spain to allow the succession of Queen Isabella in 1833. The resultant Carlist civil war lasted from 1834 until 1837 but disorder lasted until the end of the reign in 1868. Open war was resumed in 1870 and unrest continued throughout the nineteenth century. The Carlist movement also became prominent in opposition to the Second Spanish Republic 1931–6 and as supporters of the Nationalist cause in the Spanish Civil War 1936–9.

Caudillo, El   (Sp. lit. the leader)   Title assumed by Francisco Franco in 1937 as head of the insurgent nationalist forces in the Spanish Civil War, and of the so-called Burgos Government. His authority was reinforced in July 1947 with the declaration that he should remain 'Caudillo' or head of state for life, pending the restoration of the monarchy.

Central Powers   Initially members of the Triple Alliance created by Bismarck in 1882, namely Germany, Austria–Hungary and Italy. As Italy remained neutral in the First World War, the term was applied to Germany, Austria–Hungary, their ally Turkey and later also Bulgaria.

Cheka   (Russ.)   Extraordinary commission, or secret political police force established by the Bolsheviks (*q.v.*) in post-revolutionary Russia to defend the regime against internal enemies.

Chetniks   Originally Serbian guerrillas seeking liberation from the Ottoman Empire. Active against German supply lines in occupied Balkan states during the First World War. They also opposed German occupation in the Second World War and were aided by the British until 1944. Some commanders collaborated with the Germans and Italians against Tito's partisans.

Christian Democracy   Anti-communist, moderate political movement formed in many European countries with the development of a mass electorate in the late nineteenth and twentieth centuries. Amongst the largest was the Italian Christian Democrat Party founded in 1943 as the successor to the pre-Fascist Popular Party, formed in 1919, and the major representative of Catholic, moderate opinion. The German National People's Party, formed in 1918, and the German Centre Party, formed in 1870, also represent this tradition, latterly taken up by Adenauer's Christian-Democratic Union, formed in 1945. Many other European countries have political parties with this or similar labels.

Citoyen   (Fr. lit. citizen)   Used during the French Revolution to indicate loyalty to the Republic or revolutionary cause. Refusal to be called by the title 'citoyen' often resulted in arrest and execution.

Code Napoleon   The French Civil Law code, enacted on 21 March 1804 and renamed in honour of the Emperor in 1807. The need for a uniform civil law stemmed from the chaotic system which had emerged in the eighteenth century with Roman law in the south and custom law in the north, a situation further complicated by local laws and innumerable exemptions. The Code finally contained 2281 articles and remains the basis of French law. In addition, it has also formed the basis for legal codes in other states.

Cold War   Protracted state of tension between countries falling short of actual war. The term was first used in a US Congress debate on 12 March 1947 on the doctrine expounded by Harry S. Truman (1894–1972) promising aid to 'free peoples who are resisting attempted subjugation by armed minorities or by outside pressures'. A direct product of the civil war in Greece (1946–9), the doctrine bore the wider implication that the US would actively respond anywhere in the world to what it saw as direct encroachment by the USSR. The practical division of Europe occurred as a result of the Eastern European states' rejection of US Marshall Aid, often under pressure from the Soviet Union, and their subsequent membership of Comecon (q.v.). This division into two hostile camps was completed by the creation of NATO (1949–50) (q.v.) and the Warsaw Pact (1955) (q.v.). The Cold War between the Soviet Union and the USA continued into the 1970s before being superceded by a period of détente. The main crises within the Cold War period were the Russian invasion of Hungary in 1956; of Czechoslovakia in 1968; the Berlin Blockade of 1948 and the Cuban Missile Crisis of 1962. Western outrage at these supposed manifestations of Soviet expansion was tempered by the British and French involvement in Suez in 1956 and the US involvement in Vietnam during the 1960s and early 1970s.

Collectivisation   The process of transferring land from private to state or collective ownership. Extensively operated in the Soviet Union during the early 1930s when peasants' individual holdings were combined to form agricultural collectives (Kolkhoz) or in some cases state-owned farms (Sovkhoz) which were run by state employees.

Comecon   Council for Mutual Economic Assistance. Organisation established in Moscow in January 1949 to improve trade between the Soviet Union and other Eastern European States. Regarded by Stalin as an instrument to enforce an economic boycott on Yugoslavia, and also used as a Soviet response to growing Western European economic interdependence.

Comintern   Abbreviated title of the Third International established in March 1919 to promote revolutionary Marxism. By 1928 it had become a vehicle for Stalin's ideas. Finally dissolved in May 1943 as a goodwill gesture to the Soviet Union's western allies.

Communard   A member of the Paris Commune which was formed on 26 March 1871 after the withdrawal of troops from the city by the Thiers government in response to rioting. MacMahon's forces eventually retook the city after bitter street fighting and the Commune was suppressed.

The Commune was inspired by democratic and socialist ideas of the time although the rioting which led to the government's withdrawal of troops had been against the peace settlement with Germany and the conservatism of the newly formed Third Republic.

Concert of Europe   The term used to describe the workings of the Congress System (*q.v.*) whereby treaties were made and guaranteed by the European Powers meeting together. The idea of the 'summit' meeting extended to the settlement of the Eastern Question (*q.v.*) and colonial disputes in the later nineteenth centuries.

Concordat   An agreement between the Pope, as head of the Roman Catholic Church, and the secular authorities of individual states on the rights, privileges and obligations of the Church within those states.

Congress system   A system of settling international disputes and maintaining peace in Europe through the use of regular diplomatic conferences. Initiated by the Congress of Vienna in 1815 between the victorious powers in the Napoleonic Wars (Britain, Russia, Austria and Prussia), further congresses were held at Aix-la-Chapelle (1818), Troppau (1820), Laibach (1821), Verona (1822) and St Petersburg (1825). System was weakened by British withdrawal before the 1825 congress when it was realised that the other powers were anxious to use the power of the congress to interfere in the affairs of other states and to prevent the spread of liberalism.

Consulate   The system of government used in France from the overthrow of the Directory (*q.v.*) in November 1799 until Napoleon declared himself Emperor in 1804. The government consisted of three legislative chambers and an executive headed by three consuls. In practice, Napoleon as First Consul dominated the proceedings of the government throughout its life.

Continental system   Policy of economic warfare conducted by Napoleon Bonaparte in an attempt to bring Britain to her knees during the Napoleonic Wars. The Berlin Decree of 21 November 1806 sought to close continental ports to British trade and the Milan Decree of December 1807 attempted to extend the policy to neutral ships trading with Britain. In 1807 the policy was extended to Russian ports after Tilsit, (*see* pp. 56–7) and to the Iberian peninsula in 1808. The policy proved only partially effective through the British retaliatory Orders in Council, blockading French trade, the diversion of British trade elsewhere, widespread smuggling, and the non-compliance of many states.

Cortes   Spanish Parliament. Originally a medieval institution, the Cortes has served as a representative body during periods of democratic rule in the nineteenth and twentieth centuries. Suppressed in 1923 by the dictatorship of Primo de Rivera, it was restructured by the Second Republic as a democratically elected institution, only to be swept away by the civil war (1936–9). Restored again in 1942 as a cypher for Franco's dictatorship, the institution was again restructured in 1978 when the monarchy was restored and free elections took place to the Cortes General. This body has two houses, a congress of deputies with 350 members elected every four years by universal suffrage, and an upper house (Senate) with four representatives from each of Spain's provinces and autonomous communities.

Dauphin   Eldest son and heir to the French king. The last Dauphin was prevented from succeeding to his father's throne (Louis XVI) by the French Revolution and the establishment of the Republic after 1789.

Decembrists   Members of an abortive conspiracy of army officers in St Petersburg and of gentry in southern Russia who aimed to overthrow Tsarist autocracy and replace it with a more liberal regime at the death of Alexander I in December 1825. The rising was severely put down by the new Tsar Nicholas I. It is sometimes known as the first Russian Revolution.

Directory   The Directory was established in France after the fall of Robespierre in August 1794 and Thermidor (*q.v.*). As the executive power in France it consisted of five directors and a council of 500, together with a Council of Ancients. The period of the Directory was characterised by a period of chaos in provincial administration, and defeat in the wars of the Second Coalition coupled with the revolt in the Vendée made the government unpopular. It was finally overthrown by Napoleon on 9 November 1799 and replaced by the Consulate (*q.v.*).

Dreikaiserbund   (Ger. League of the Three Emperors)   An informal alliance created in 1872 between the states of Germany, Russia and Austria as a result of the meeting of their respective Emperors. The alliance was already a dead letter before the creation of the Triple Alliance (*q.v.*) in 1882.

Dreyfus Affair   Scandal in France between 1894 and 1899 involving Alfred Dreyfus (1859–1935), a Jewish army officer who was accused, tried and convicted of passing information to the Germans. Having been sentenced to life imprisonment on Devil's Island, he was found innocent and later exonerated by a second trial in 1899 which proved that many of the documents used to convict him had been forgeries. It became apparent that the authorities had used Dreyfus as a scapegoat to cover up the activities of a Major Esterhazy. During the time taken to convince the authorities of the need for a second trial, many accusations were made, including Zola's letter 'J'accuse', that anti-Semitism of the authorities and the army had ensured Dreyfus' conviction and delayed his retrial. The 'Dreyfusard' and 'Anti-Dreyfusard' camps displayed many of the characteristic cleavages in the Third Republic.

Dual Alliance   Also known as the Dual Entente. An alliance between Russia and France which lasted from 1893 until the Bolshevik Revolution of October 1917.

Duce   (It. lit. leader)   Title assumed by Benito Mussolini (*see* pp. 286–7).

Duma   Russian parliament established by the Tsar in 1905 in response to demands which emanated from the abortive revolution of 1905. Free elections to the first two Dumas led to radical demands and rapid dissolution by the government. Third Duma elected with much greater government interference did produce some limited administrative and land reform instigated by premier Stolypin. In spite of government disapproval, the Duma remained a platform for protest and in November 1916 warned the government of impending revolution. As a result of its criticisms of the government, the Duma was suspended for much of the war period.

Eastern Question   The title given to the various problems of international and especially European, relations created by the gradual decline of the Ottoman Empire in the late nineteenth and early twentieth centuries. A number of European powers vied for territorial concessions. Austria–Hungary looked to expand into the Balkans, Russia to gain access to the Mediterranean Sea for her Black Sea fleet. Until 1897, the fear of the Russians led Britain to support the Ottoman Empire, but most of this support disappeared after the Armenian Massacres (*q.v.*). Germany began to play an increasing role in Turkish affairs after a personal visit by the Kaiser in 1898 gave valuable commercial and railway concessions in exchange for a German military mission. The independence of the Balkan states further complicated the issue, especially when Serbia and Romania combined against the Ottoman Empire during the Balkan Wars of 1912. The Empire's alliance with Germany led to its destruction in 1918 and the creation of a Turkish national state.

Emancipation   Term used to denote the freeing of religious groups such as Jews or Roman Catholics from institutionalised legislative or judicial disadvantage. Both Catholic and Jewish emancipation were important issues in western European states during the eighteenth and nineteenth centuries.

Emigrés   (Fr. lit. emigrants)   Term used originally to describe opponents of the French Revolution who chose, or were forced to leave the country. Many were members of the nobility and some were active in trying to promote a coalition of European sovereigns against the Revolutionary government. The Revolutionaries enacted various punitive decrees against émigrés. More recently, the term has been applied to many types of refugee who have fled from political, religious or racial persecution.

Ems telegram   Telegram sent by the King of Prussia to Bismarck from the German spa town of Ems in July 1870, reporting on his conversations with the French ambassador over the Hohenzollern candidature to the Spanish throne. The telegram was doctored by Bismarck in such a way that it appeared that the French ambassador had been insulted and vice-versa and was thereby calculated to inflame French opinion when released to the press. Its publication duly excited French national pride and led to their declaration of war against Prussia on 19 July, four days after the telegram had been sent.

Enlightened despotism   Used to describe a form of government prevalent in the eighteenth century in which absolute rulers acted for the general welfare of their subjects rather than for their own benefit under the influence of the enlightenment. Characterised by an interest in administrative reform, the reduction of feudal privilege, including serfdom, religious toleration, and economic development, a number of rulers, notably Catherine the Great, Frederick the Great, Leopold II of Tuscany, and Joseph II, have usually been grouped under this term, although a number of others display certain of its features.

Enlightenment A widespread movement in Europe in the seventeenth and eighteenth centuries based on the conviction that through reason, man could achieve true knowledge. The philosophical base of the movement was extended by other thinkers into the realms of political and economic theory (e.g. Rousseau, Voltaire etc.).

Entente Cordiale (Fr. cordial agreement) Term first used in the 1840s to describe the special relationship between Britain and France. Revived in the Anglo-French Entente of 8 April 1904 and a similar agreement with Russia in August 1907. These three were known as the Entente Powers until 1917, the agreements being converted to military alliances in September 1911. The basis of the Anglo-French agreement had been the settlement of colonial differences and it survived the First World War but was strained by the French occupation of the Ruhr in 1923 and the British attack on the French fleet in 1940. Attempts were made after the Second World War to revive the entente by the treaty of Dunkirk (1947).

Falange The only political party permitted in Franco's Spain. Founded by José Antonio Primo de Rivera in 1933 as a right-wing movement opposed to the Republic. José Antonio was assassinated in November 1936 in the early months of the Spanish Civil War. The movement survived his death to be used by Franco when the Grand Council of the Falange replaced the Cortes as the legislative body in Spain between June 1939 and July 1942.

Fascist An Italian nationalist, authoritarian, anti-communist movement developed by Mussolini after 1919 which became the only authorised political party in Italy after the 'March on Rome' in 1922. The movement derived its name from the 'fasces' (bundle of sticks), the symbol of state power in ancient Rome. More generally applied to authoritarian and National Socialist movements in Europe and elsewhere (q.v. Nazi).

Fashoda Incident Crisis in Anglo-French relations as a result of rival claims to Sudan. A French detachment under Marchand had marched to the town of Fashoda on the Upper Nile from French West Africa, reaching it in July 1898, just before the arrival of General Kitchener, fresh from his defeat of the Mahdi's forces at Omdurman, with a large Anglo-Egyptian army. France's claim to the area by right of prior conquest was hotly disputed by Britain who wished to retain control of the Nile Valley. A 'war scare' was fanned in both countries by the popular press, but France's distraction by the Dreyfus affair (q.v.) and lack of support from Russia forced her to back down. Marchand withdrew from Fashoda in November 1898 and France agreed in March 1899 to renounce all claims to the Nile Valley.

Final Solution Translation of the German 'entlösung' used to describe the destruction of European Jewry carried out by Nazi Germany in occupied countries between 1941 and 1945.

First International   The first International Working-men's Association (IWMA) was formed by Marx (*q.v.*) in London in 1864. It aimed to establish socialism by coordinating the efforts of the working class in different countries. Riddled with disputes between Marx and the anarchists under Bakunin (*q.v.*), it moved headquarters to New York and was finally dissolved in 1876.

Five Year Plan   System of economic planning first adopted in the Soviet Union between 1928 and 1933. The plan laid down short term aims and targets for the development of heavy industry and the collectivisation of agriculture. The second plan, 1933–37 aimed at increased production of consumer goods but the third, 1938–42 returned to the primacy of heavy industry, largely directed towards rearmament. The five year plan has since been adopted as a method of planning by other socialist countries.

Fourteen Points   A peace programme put forward by President Woodrow Wilson to the US Congress on 8 January 1918 and accepted as the basis for an armistice by Germany and Austria-Hungary. Later it was alleged that the allied powers had violated the principles embodied in the Fourteen Points, especially in relation to the prohibition of Anschluss (*q.v.*), the union of Germany with Austria. The original points were: the renunciation of secret diplomacy; freedom of the seas; the removal of economic barriers between states; arms reductions; impartial settlement of colonial disputes; evacuation of Russia by Germany and her allies; restoration of Belgium; German withdrawal from France and the return of Alsace-Lorraine; readjustment of the Italian frontiers; autonomous development of nationalities in Austria-Hungary; evacuation of Romania, Serbia and Montenegro and guarantees of Serbian access to the sea; free passage through the Dardanelles and the self-determination of minorities in the Ottoman Empire; creation of an independant Poland with access to the sea; and the creation of a general association of states.

Free French   The *Forces Françaises Libres* made up of French troops and naval units who continued the fight against Nazi Germany after the fall of France in the summer of 1940. In opposition to the Vichy regime in France, Gen. de Gaulle established a 'Council for the Defence of the Empire', and later the *Comité National Français*. The Free French were active against Vichy forces in Syria and Miquelon and St Pierre in 1941. On 19 July 1942 the Free French were renamed the *Forces Françaises Combatantes* (Fighting French Forces) FFC. The FFC represented de Gaulle's main claim as the true representative of French liberation. As the Allied forces liberated France in the summer of 1944, the FFC were able to provide the first allied troops to enter Paris after an uprising organised by the *Forces Françaises de L'Interieur*.

Führer   (Ger. lit. leader)   Title first coined in 1921 to describe Hitler as head of the Nazi party. After his appointment as Chancellor in 1933, the term was used more widely to describe him as 'führer' of Germany.

Gauleiter (Ger.) Regional chief of the NSDAP. The party had divided Germany into areas for the purposes of administration. Each 'Gau' was the basis of the party in Germany and the Gauleiter retained their positions of power even after the Nazi takeover of Germany through their access to Hitler, and the parallel operation of party and state organisations at national and local level. The more prominent Gauleiter were able to impose their authority locally and during the war gained control over political and economic policy as well as labour allocation and civil defence.

Gestapo (Ger. abbreviation of *Geheime Staatspolizei*) Originally the political police force of the Prussian State Police, the Gestapo was developed as an instrument of internal control in Germany during the Nazi period by Heinrich Himmler as head of the German police. The Gestapo was used extensively to control and suppress opposition to Nazi rule, both inside Germany and later also in occupied territories.

Girondins Middle-class republican group in the French Legislative Assembly of 1791 and the Convention of 1792. Many of the group's members came from the Gironde region in south-west France. Led by Brissot, Roland, Petion and Vergniaud, they supported the French involvement in war but opposed the Jabobins as to its conduct. The Girondins were overthrown and their leaders executed in 1793.

Great Fear Name given to wave of peasant revolt, riot and chateau-burning which began in France towards the end of 1788 and gathered pace during 1789, especially after news of the fall of the Bastille (*q.v.*). The disturbances were fuelled by rumours of an aristocratic plot to starve the people and of bands of brigands pillaging the countryside, arising out of distress and confused reports coming from Paris.

Great Purge *see* Yezhovshchina.

Guillotine Instrument of execution first used in revolutionary France. Named after physician Joseph Ignace Guillotine, an advocate of capital punishment. Victims were decapitated by a falling blade.

Habsburgs The house of Habsburg–Lorraine, an Austrian royal dynasty which ruled from 1282 to 1918. The family held the title of Holy Roman Emperor from 1438 to 1740 and from 1745 to 1806. The dissolution of the Empire meant that they adopted the title Emperor of Austria but their acquisition of territory had been based on a series of marriages in the fifteenth and early sixteenth century culminating in the reign of the Emperor Charles V. After this, the Empire was divided between the Austrian and Spanish Habsburg families. The murder of the heir to the Austrian Habsburg throne in 1914, Francis Ferdinand, led to the outbreak of the First World War, and the last Emperor, Charles I, was forced to abdicate in 1918. Attempts to place his son Otto on the Austrian throne in the 1920s and 1930s were ended by the Anschluss (*q.v.*) with Germany in 1938.

Helsinki Agreement Product of the Helsinki Conference, 1975, between thirty-five nations concerning European security, proposals for economic collaboration between Eastern and Western blocs, and a reaffirmation of human rights. The last has been consistently utilised to raise the cases of dissidents suffering ill-treatment in the Soviet Union.

Herrenvolk   (Ger. lit. master race)   A doctrine expounded by the Nazis who used the supposed superiority of the 'aryan' race as a justification for German territorial expansion and the enslavement of 'inferior races'.

Hohenzollern   German royal dynasty which provided the three German Emperors, 1871–1918. Originally the Prussian royal house, the monarchy was finally brought to an end by the abdication of Kaiser Wilhelm II in November 1918.

Holocaust, the   Name given to the death of around six million Jews at the hands of the Nazis during the Second World War.

Holy Alliance   Alliance agreed by Russia, Prussia and Austria in September 1815 and eventually by most of the rulers of Europe at the instigation of Alexander I of Russia, promising to conduct their policies on Christian principles. Dismissed by many statesmen as an irrelevance, the alliance came to be used by the conservative powers as a justification for repressing liberal and national movements.

Hundred Days, the   Period of Napoleon's escape from Elba in February 1815 until his defeat at Waterloo (18 June 1815) and exile to St Helena. Technically, the hundred days cover the period from 20 March to 22 June 1815 when Napoleon again ruled as Emperor from Paris.

Intendants   The chief agents of Louis XVI's government who were centrally appointed to control the social and economic administration of the '*départements*'. They had considerable authority in the 'Pays d'Etat' but their power was checked by permanent officials and commissions of local estates. They disappeared with the end of royal authority.

International Brigades   Volunteer brigades formed to support the Republican cause in Spain during the Spanish Civil War. Composed mainly of left-wing and communist sympathisers from all parts of Europe and the United States, the volunteers saw the fight against Franco's Nationalist insurgents as part of the wider struggle against European fascism.

Internationals   *See under* First International; Second International etc.

Irredentists   Italian political party founded about 1878, committed to the incorporation of territories neighbouring the kingdom of Italy (*see* Italia Irredenta).

Italia Irredenta   Term applied to the territories of Trentino, Istria and South Tyrol which were acquired by Italy after the Treaty of St Germain (1919). Sometimes regarded as the completion of the *Risorgimento* (*q.v.*), the term irredentism has been used to describe any movement committed to the restoration of territory formerly held.

Jacobins   Name originally derived from a political club in 1789, the Jacobins became the most radical French revolutionary group. They were particularly associated with Robespierre and dominated the Montagnards (*q.v.*) and the Committees of Public Safety and General Security which effectively governed France until the coup of 9 Thermidor 1795.

Jacquerie   French peasant rising of 1358 named after 'Jacques Bonhomme', the popular name for a French peasant. The rebels murdered all those who refused to support them and burned over 22 chateaux. Their suppression was followed by equally severe reprisals. Sometimes applied to peasant movements of the modern period.

July Conspiracy   Otherwise known as the Hitler Bomb Plot, this was an attempt by disaffected sections of the German officer corps to assassinate Hitler and end Nazi rule in order that negotiations could take place with the Western Allies. The plot involved a bomb placed in Hitler's East Prussian headquarters by Col. von Stauffenberg on 20 July 1944 and was assumed to have succeeded by accomplices in Berlin who thus committed themselves to a new government. Hitler's almost miraculous survival signalled the failure of the plotters and the attempt was used as an excuse by Hitler to purge the army and other high ranking officials known to oppose the regime.

July Monarchy   Term used to describe the rule of Louis Philippe in France from his inauguration after the revolution of 1830 until his abdication on 24 February 1848. His attempts to create an Orléanist dynasty by naming his grandson as successor were ignored by the revolutionaries and a republic was established.

Junkers   Prussian aristocrats whose power rested on their large estates, predominantly east of the River Elbe, and their accepted role as army officers and civil servants. Considered as the bastions against liberalism they found it consistently harder to defend their agrarian interests from the industrialisation of the German Empire.

Kaiser   (Ger. Caesar, *i.e.* Emperor)   Title assumed by the Prussian King William I following the unification of Germany and the creation of the German Empire. William accepted the crown of a united Germany in December 1870.

Kremlin   (Russ. citadel)   Refers to the citadel in Moscow occupied by former Imperial Palace. Now the administrative headquarters of, and synonomous with, the government of the USSR.

Kruger Telegram   Telegram sent by Kaiser William II to Paul Kruger, President of the Transvaal, on 3 January 1896 congratulating him on the defeat of the Jameson Raid. As an attempt to assert German prestige in Africa, the telegram led to a worsening of Anglo–German relations.

Kulaks   (Russ. tight-fisted person)   Term used to describe Russian peasants who were able to become landowners as a result of the agrarian reforms of 1906 and were encouraged by Lenin's NEP (*q.v.*).Their resistance to collectivisation under the Five Year Plan (*q.v.*) led to Stalin's order for the liquidation of the kulak class. As a result, large numbers were deported to Siberia or executed in their villages. In August 1942, Stalin confessed to Churchill that the numbers killed amounted to some ten million people.

Kulturkampf (Ger. culture struggle)   The term used to describe the period between 1873 and 1887 when Bismarck as Chancellor of Germany came into conflict with the Roman Catholic Church. Ostensibly the result of alarm at the Vatican decrees which implied that the Church rather than the State had prior claim on the citizen's obedience, the Falk Laws were designed to subordinate the Church to State control after May 1873. In addition, it allowed an attack on the anti-Prussian Catholic Centre Party and enabled the creation of a political alliance of diverse interests based on anti-Catholicism. This means of creating a political alliance was superceded by the attack on the socialists after 1878 and negotiations with Pope Leo XIII led to the restoration of Catholic rights by 1887.

League of Nations International organisation set up as an integral part of the Versailles Settlement in 1920 to preserve the peace and settle disputes by negotiation. Although the United States refused to participate, it comprised 53 members by 1923. Based in Geneva, the League relied upon non-military means to coerce states, such as 'sanctions' (*q.v.*), but found itself virtually powerless in the face of the Japanese invasion of Manchuria and the Italian invasion of Abyssinia. The League was discredited by 1939 and was dissolved in April 1946 with the formation of the United Nations.

League of the Three Emperors,   *see* Dreikaiserbund.

Lebensraum (Ger. lit. living space)   Slogan adopted by German nationalists and especially the Nazi party in the 1920s and 1930s to justify the need for Germany to expand territorially in the East. The theory was based on the alleged overpopulation of Germany and the need for more territory to ensure their food supplies. Interpreted by some Germans as the desire for a return to the frontiers of 1914, the attack on the Soviet Union suggests that Hitler's interpretation of the concept was much wider.

Levée en Masse (Fr.)   French Committee of Public Safety's enactment of compulsory enlistment for military service in August 1793. It was applied to all men between the ages of 18 and 25. Its introduction established the principle of total mobilisation of the country's resources for defence purposes.

Liberum Veto The right of the Polish nobility to dissent from or veto measures in the national assembly. Used as a means of obstruction, often against Poland's perceived national interests, the right was abolished by the Constitution of 1791.

Loi Falloux Law introduced by Frederic Alfred Pierre Falloux, minister of education and public worship in Louis Napoleon's first government

(1848–9). Promulgated in 1850, the law greatly increased the power of the Roman Catholic Church in French education.

Loi le Chapelier   Law named after Jean le Chapelier, a French revolutionary leader. The law, introduced on 14 June 1791 prohibited the formation of employer or worker associations. In fact, the law only really operated against worker associations as employer meetings were impossible to monitor. The law survived the revolutionary period and was not repealed until 1884.

Los von Rom   (Ger. away from Rome)   Movement in German areas of the Austro-Hungarian Empire after 1897 which gave rise to Old Catholic (*q.v.*) groups in those areas. The main aim was to make those areas more acceptable as constituent parts of the German Empire if the Dual Monarchy collapsed.

Luftwäffe   German Air Force.

Maginot Line   French defensive fortifications stretching from Longwy to the Swiss border. Named after French minister of defence, André Maginot, the line was constructed between 1929 and 1934 as a means of countering a German attack. Due to the Belgians' refusal to extend the line along their frontier with Germany and French reluctance to appear to 'abandon' Belgium and build the line along the Franco–Belgian border to the sea, the defensive strategy relied on the Germans' inability to penetrate the Ardennes forest. This hope was seen as misguided when the Germans were able to turn the French flank by an advance through Belgium and the Maginot Line was still virtually intact when France surrendered on 22 July 1940.

Magyar   Native name for Hungarians but also a class term meaning one who owned land and was exempt from land tax, attended county assemblies and took part in elections to the Diet. The Austrian Habsburgs attempted to Germanise the Magyars on their territories but Hungarian nationalism provided sufficient pressure to ensure the creation of the Dual Monarchy after 1867 and independence for the state of Hungary after 1918.

Mandates   Rights granted to certain states at the end of the First World War by the League of Nations to administer the colonies and dependencies of Germany and the Ottoman Empire. The Mandates came in three forms. Some territories were only under a limited term mandate while they prepared for independence; the British control over Iraq, Palestine and Transjordan, and the French control of Lebanon and Syria came into this category. Others were to be administered indefinitely because of their lack of development. This included all the German colonies in Africa except for South West Africa. The third category were also to be administered indefinitely but could be treated as part of the mandate powers' territory. South West Africa, New Guinea and Samoa were included in these.

Maquis   Name derived from Corsican resistance movements which liberated Corsica in 1943. Maquis groups in mainland France increased greatly in 1943 and 1944, and those in Brittany were particularly effective in hampering German movements prior to D-Day on 6 June 1944.

Mare Nostrum   (Lat. our sea)   Mediterranean Sea.

Marseillaise   Rouget de Lisle's marching song of the army of the Rhine, it was popularised by the Fédérés from Marseilles who arrived in Paris shortly after the publication of the Brunswick manifesto. The song was made the French national anthem after the Franco–Prussian War of 1870.

Marshall Plan   United States Plan for the economic reconstruction of Europe, named after secretary of state General George C. Marshall. The Organisation for European Economic Cooperation was established to administer the aid in April 1948 but the Soviet rejection of the Plan meant that most of the monetary aid went to Western Europe. Between 1948 and 1952 the US provided some $17,000 million dollars which was a crucial element in European postwar recovery.

Mediterranean Agreements   Agreements between Britain, Austria–Hungary and Italy signed in March 1887. Essentially a mutual aid pact against a fourth power and mainly directed against Russia and France.

Mensheviks   (Russ. lit. member of the minority)   Moderate faction in Russian Social Democratic Party after the split of 1903. Operated in opposition to the more radical Bolsheviks (*q.v.*). Formally suppressed in 1922.

Metayage   A system of share-cropping which operated in more than two-thirds of pre-revolutionary France, especially in wine growing areas. The exploitative nature and harshness of the system were important peasant grievances.

Mitteleuropa   (Ger.) The idea of a German speaking supra-national state in Central Europe which was pioneered by Austrian Minister Schwarzenberg in 1848. The idea was later rejected by Bismarck when it was used to support German domination of south-eastern Europe and the Balkans. In spite of this, the idea was revived in 1915 with the publication of Friedrich Naumann's book *Mitteleuropa*.

Montagnards   (Fr. lit. members of the mountain)   Extremist political party in the French Legislative Assembly and National Convention during the revolution. The name was derived from their placement on the highest part of the left side in the Legislative Assembly. They developed the idea of the expediency of the Revolutionary War. The two constituent groups were the Cordeliers and the Jacobins (*q.v.*). The power of the Montagnards came to an end with the fall of Robespierre on 9 Thermidor 1794.

Moroccan Crisis   A European crisis precipitated by German attempts to break up the Anglo–French Entente of 1904. Wilhelm II's landing at Tangier and his expression of German support for Moroccan independence led to acrimonious relations between Germany and France and succeeded only in strengthening the bond between France and Britain. The Algeciras Conference of Jan.–Apr. 1906 recognised French predominance in Morocco and represented a defeat for the German stand.

Mountain, The, *see* Montagnards

Narodniki   (Russ.)   Members of a secret Russian revolutionary movement in 1873–4 and 1876. Its first supporters were university students who attempted to convert villagers to socialism. They were savagely suppressed by the government in 1877.

NATO   The North Atlantic Treaty Organisation, created by the North Atlantic Treaty of 4 April 1949. The organisation represented the first US commitment to European defence in peacetime. NATO came in response to Western fears about the power of the Soviet Union and the failure of the UN Security Council to operate in the face of the Soviet veto. The treaty states are obliged to take such action as they deem necessary to assist a fellow signatory subjected to aggression although there is no obligation to fight. The treaty states are Belgium, Luxembourg, The Netherlands, Britain, the United States, Canada, Italy, Norway, Denmark, Iceland, and Portugal who were original signatories plus Greece and Turkey (1952) and West Germany (1955). France was also an original signatory but withdrew from the organisation in 1966.

Nazi   Popular contraction of 'National Socialist' and used to describe both the NSDAP as a party and its individual members. The party was ideologically attached to right-wing authoritarianism (c.f. Italian Fascism *q.v.*) but also included strong anti-Semitism and a belief in the racial supremacy of the 'aryan' race. The party was led by Adolf Hitler from 1921 until his death in 1945. It was initially based in Munich and was given a setback by its involvement in the Beer Hall Putsch of November 1923. Nevertheless, the party under Hitler's guidance underwent a resurgence in the late 1920s and achieved a major electoral breakthrough when they captured 107 seats in the Reichstag. Their electoral success continued into 1932 and in an attempt to provide some form of consensus government, Hitler was offered the Chancellorship in 1933. After the 'seizure of power' Nazi party organisations such as the SS came to dominate many facets of life in Germany. The party organisation collapsed at the end of the Second World War and was made illegal after the German surrender.

New Economic Policy   Often shortened to NEP, the New Economic Policy was introduced in Russia by Lenin at the tenth Party Congress in March 1921. Disturbances and food shortages had made it impossible to impose communism and some amelioration was introduced. Private commerce was permitted and state banks reintroduced. The incentives this provided helped to improve food production and created a more contented peasantry. The NEP was finally abandoned in January 1929 in favour of the Five Year Plan and the collectivisation of agriculture.

'New Imperialism'   Term used to describe the more aggressive colonial policies of western European states in the later nineteenth century. This was epitomised by the 'scramble for Africa' in the 1880s which has been variously attributed to the need for secure markets for domestic manufactures, the need for investment opportunities, the need to assert international standing through the acquisition of colonies, or the need to introduce a foreign policy adventure as a unifying measure in domestic politics.

North German Federation   A union of north German states created by Bismarck after the Prussian defeat of Austria in 1866. The federation was an attempt to allay south German fears about Prussia's ambitions to create a unitary German state. The constitution did allow for the rights of individual states but was in practice dominated by Prussia. Four years later, it became the constitution of the German Empire, almost without amendment. The constitution was adopted by the North German Reichstag on 17 April 1867.

Octobrist   A section of the Russian liberal constitutional movement. The movement had been divided by the October Manifesto of 1905 into Octobrists and Kadets. The former were right-wing and prepared to cooperate with the government in the Duma. The party was supported by the right-wing of the Zemstvo Movement (q.v.) and business classes.

Octroi   Tax levied by French local authorities such as communes or municipalities on certain categories of goods entering the area.

OGPU   Soviet security police agency, established in 1922 as the GPU and retitled OGPU after the formation of the USSR in 1923. Founded to suppress counter-revolution and enemies of the system, it was used by the leadership to uncover political dissidents and, after 1928, in enforcing the collectivisation of agriculture. After 1930 it monopolised police activities in the Soviet Union before being absorbed by the NKVD in 1934.

Old Catholics   Name given to groups of western Christians who believe themselves to maintain the true doctrines and traditions of the undivided church, but who separated from the see of Rome after the first Vatican Council of 1869–70.

Ostpolitik   Eastern policy developed in the German Federal Republic by Kurt Kiesinger to normalise relations with those communist countries, other than the Soviet Union, which recognised the German Democratic Republic. It led to the conclusion of peace treaties with the USSR and Poland (1972) and border agreements over traffic and communication between East and West Berlin.

Panama Scandal   A corruption scandal involving the French Chamber of Deputies, which came to light in 1892. A lottery loan voted on behalf of the French Panama Canal Co. in 1888 was rumoured to have involved the 'support' of over 150 deputies. The resultant scandal which emerged in 1892 after the company had folded led to the resignation of the Loubet government and the imprisonment of a former government minister.

Panslavism   The name given to the various movements for closer union of peoples speaking slavic languages in the nineteenth and early twentieth centuries.

Papal Infallability   Doctrine of the Roman Catholic Church proclaimed at the Vatican Council of 1870 which holds that papal pronouncements on matters of faith and morals are not open to question. The basis of the doctrine is that not all questions are answered by the Bible and that further guidance has to be provided in an authoritative way. It has also been argued that the extension of the Pope's spiritual power was in response to the loss of temporal power over the previous five hundred years.

Papal States   Central Italian territory under papal authority until 1870. The area was dominated by Napoleon's army in the 1790s and again in 1808–9. Revolts against clerical rule took place 1830–1 and in 1849. The states remained an obstacle to Italian unification until French troops were withdrawn from Rome in 1870.

Pays d'Election   Central core of the French kingdom where the authority of the crown and its intendants (q.v.) tended to go unchallenged.

Pays d'Etat   Areas originally annexed to France where the relationship to the French crown was on a contractual basis. Provincial assemblies or estates functioned effectively in Brittany and Languedoc where they had fiscal privileges and shared authority with the crown.

People's Will, *see* Narodniki

Philosophes   Leading French thinkers of the pre-revolutionary period who included Montesquieu, Voltaire, Rousseau, Condorcet and Diderot. The main theme of their thinking was marked by faith in the power of human reason. They were critical of irrational privileges and many other aspects of the ancien regime. Conservatives alleged that the writings of the philosophes influenced the Revolution.

Physiocrats   Coterie of philosophes (*q.v.*) concerned with economic problems. Quesnay and Mirabeau were among the most prominent. They held that agriculture was the true source of national wealth and advocated fiscal equality through a universal land tax and other economic reforms, including free trade.

Plain, The   Independent and moderate members of the French Convention. They were led by Danton who was the chief intermediary between the Paris Commune and the Convention. Its members conspired with the Right to overthrow Robespierre.

Pogrom   (Russ. destruction)   Used to describe the physical persecution of Jews in Tsarist Russia. This form of anti-Semitic violence was especially marked in the Ukraine and in the 1880s and in 1905 the authorities unofficially encouraged these attacks to divert popular discontent.

Polish Corridor   The Treaty of Versailles decided that the new Polish state should have direct access to the sea. In order to provide this a large area of West Prussia and Posen, containing many Germans, was assigned to Poland. The 'Corridor' also had the effect of cutting East Prussia off from the rest of Germany. Danzig, standing at the mouth of the Vistula and the natural artery of Polish trade, but a German city and formerly part of Germany was placed under League of Nations control, Poland remaining responsible for her foreign relations. The creation of the 'Corridor' was bitterly resented by German nationalists and Hitler's demands for the return of Danzig and parts of the 'Corridor' formed part of the crisis which brought about war in September 1939.

Popular Front   Name used to describe the alliance of communists, socialists and liberal democrats which was designed to combat Fascism in Europe between 1935 and 1939. Alliances under this name gained power in Spain and in France under Léon Blum.

Poujadism   A right-wing political movement in France between 1954 and 1958 named after Pierre Poujade, a bookseller. The *Union de Défense des Commercants et Artisands* was anti-socialist, anti-intellectual and anti-European and drew its membership from small shopkeepers and the petit-bourgeoisie. The party won 52 seats in the National Assembly in 1956 but the return of de Gaulle led to their rapid decline.

'Prague Spring'   Name given to the period of attempted liberalisation in Czechoslovakia under Dubcek as Secretary to the Communist Party in spring 1968. The attempt was brought to an end by the intervention of Warsaw Pact troops in August 1968 and Dubcek's replacement by Husak.

Prairial   (Fr.) A law forced through the Convention in France by Robespierre on 10 June 1794 which allowed the Tribunal to dispense with evidence for the defence. Thus trial became a question of immediate acquittal or death, a process which greatly increased the Terror. Robespierre was deposed by his opponents before he could bring them to trial.

Provisional government   The government of Russia between March and October 1917. Brought to power after the deposition of the monarchy, the Provisional government was made up of members of the Duma (*q.v.*) but had to share power in Petrograd with the Workers' and Soldiers' Soviet. Rule ended by the Bolshevik Revolution and the creation of a Soviet government.

Purges, *see* Yezhovshchina

Putsch   (Ger.)   A term used to describe a right-wing *coup d'état* in Germany. Most notable were the Kapp Putsch in 1920 when a journalist Wolfgang Kapp and a number of disaffected army officers attempted to overthrow the government in Berlin. The plot was foiled by the indifference of the regular army and the opposition of the trade unions. Also notorious was the ill-fated Beer Hall Putsch involving Hitler and General Ludendorff in Munich on 9 November 1923.

Quadrilateral   Four fortified towns in northern Italy (Peschiera, Verona, Mantua and Legnano) which formed the strong point of the Austrian defence of Venetia in 1848, and in 1859 during the struggle for Italian unification.

Quai d'Orsay   Embankment of the River Seine in Paris where the French Foreign Office is situated. Term synonymous with the conduct of French foreign affairs.

Quisling   Eponym for leader of an enemy-sponsored regime, deriving from Vidkun Quisling (1887–1945) (*q.v.*).

Ralliement   A policy which attempted to end the estrangement of French Catholics from the Republic. It was initiated by an encyclical of Pope Leo XIII in 1892, but most Catholics and Monarchists remained hostile to the Republic and the conservative-monarchist right-wing continued to have a disruptive influence on French politics.

Realpolitik   Word coined by the liberal journalist and historian Rochau in 1859 and used to describe Bismarck's attitude to politics as a naked struggle for power, with ruthless pursuit of self-interest being the only possible policy for a great state.

Reich   (Ger.) The term used to describe the German Empire. The First Reich was considered to have been the Holy Roman Empire and thus the unified Germany after 1870 was known as the Second or *Kaiserreich*. This enabled Hitler's ideas of an enlarged Germany to be known as the Third Reich, although this name was officially dropped in the 1930s.

Reichstag   The German parliament (building) in Berlin created by the Constitution of 1871. Representatives were elected by universal suffrage and represented a concession to democracy although the Reichstag could not initiate legislation and could only block certain measures. Moreover, government ministers were not appointed by, nor responsible to, the Reichstag. Nevertheless, it became the focal point of politics (if not decision making) in the 1890s during the reign of Wilhelm II. The building was destroyed by fire on 28 February 1933; its destruction was used by the Nazis for propaganda purposes against the left and to pass a number of restrictive decrees.

Reinsurance treaty   Treaty signed between Germany and Russia on 18 June 1887 which gave the Russians guarantees of support for their policies in Bulgaria and the Bosphorus as well as a German agreement to stay neutral unless Austria–Hungary was attacked.

Reparations   Payments imposed on powers defeated in war to recompence the costs to the victors. Most commonly associated with the payments inflicted on Germany at the end of the First World War although the actual amount was not fixed until April 1921 when the sum was set at £6,600 million plus interest. The Dawes and Young Plans later reduced the repayments until the effects of the Depression caused reparations payments to be abandoned after Lausanne in 1932. Apart from their international ramifications, reparations payments played an important part in the domestic politics of the Weimar Republic.

Resistance   The popular term for the opposition to the Nazi regime, both inside Germany and in the occupied countries, 1940–5. From January 1942, the Free French began to organise resistance groups and in May 1943, the Maquis (*q.v.*) liberated Corsica. By 1945 resistance groups were active throughout Europe but were often divided amongst themselves on ideological grounds, providing the basis for postwar political conflicts.

Revisionist   Term applied by orthodox Marxists to one who attempts to reassess the basic tenets of revolutionary socialism. Originating in Germany in the 1890s and 1900s, its chief exponents were Edouard Bernstein and Karl Kautsky. Regarded as heresy in the Soviet Union, the Cuban, Chinese and Albanian Communists have since used the same term to describe the Moscow line.

Risorgimento   (It. resurrection)   The movement for the unification of Italy in the nineteenth century, the name was first used by Cavour in 1847 although the origins of the movement date from the post-Napoleonic period. The success of the movement culminated in the proclamation of the Kingdom of Italy in March 1861 and the later acquisition of Venetia (1866) and Rome (1870).

Romanov   The family name of the Russian royal house whose dynasty was ended by the deposition of Tsar Nicholas II in 1917 after the Russian Revolution.

SA   Abbreviation of the German *Sturmabteilung* or Storm Battalion, sometimes known as 'Brownshirts' from their uniform. Groups of ex-soldiers organised in quasi-military formations from 1923 to support the Nazis. Under their leader, Röhm, the force grew rapidly to an estimated four and a half million men by June 1934, when both Hitler's and the army's fear of its power prompted Hitler's murder of Röhm and the leaders of the SA in the 'Night of the Long Knives' (30 June 1934). Although it remained in existence, the power of the SA as a political force was broken.

Sanctions   Term usually applied to economic boycott of one country by another. Sanctions were the chief weapon of the League of Nations (*q.v.*) on countries who were not thought to be fulfilling their international obligations. An economic boycott was imposed on Italy in October 1935, following the invasion of Abyssinia, but its terms were limited and largely ineffective. These were finally lifted in July 1936. Similar sanctions were imposed on Rhodesia in 1965 by Britain and the UN but proved ineffective.

Sansculottes   (Fr. lit. without breeches)   A name used by Parisian militants to signify that they were manual workers wearing trousers, and not the knee-breeches of polite society. Between 1792 and 1794, the name referred to a specific group of political activists attempting to put pressure on the Convention through clubs and assemblies.

Schlieffen Plan   German military plan for offensive action named after Chief of German General Staff, Count Alfred von Schlieffen, and first produced in 1905. In spite of constant revision, the plan was the basis for the German attack in the west in August 1914. The basic features of the plan were based upon the premise that Germany would have to fight both France and Russia in any future war. The plan therefore provided for a swift 'knock-out' blow against France, while remaining on the defensive against Russia. Crucially, the plan involved an attack through the neutral countries of Holland, Belgium, and Luxembourg to avoid the strong defences on the Franco–German border, aiming to encircle Paris and force French surrender. Although modified subsequently, the plan to invade France via Belgium was used in 1914, bringing Great Britain into the war.

Scramble for Africa   Period of rapid colonisation of Africa in the last quarter of the nineteenth century, especially in the period following the British occupation of Egypt in 1882. By 1914 only Liberia and Ethiopia remained as independent African states.

Scrutins d'arrondissement   (Fr.)   Single member electoral constituencies. Following the formation of the Léon Gambetta government in 1881, he campaigned for the replacement of these by *scrutin de liste*, or voting on a departemental basis. Gambetta resigned after his proposals were rejected by the Chamber. Nevertheless, the 1885 elections were conducted on the system of *scrutins de liste*.

Second Empire   Created in France on 2 December 1852 when Louis Napoleon, then President of the Second Republic (*q.v.*) held a plebiscite and was elected Emperor and assumed the title Napoleon III. The Empire came to an end with the German invasion of France and Napoleon III's capture at Sedan in 1870.

Second International   Formed in Paris in 1889 and based on membership of national parties and trade unions, the Second International was a loose federation which held periodic international congresses. It stood for Parliamentary democracy and thus rejected anarchist ideas, but also reaffirmed the commitment to Marxist ideas of the class struggle. Thus there was no question of co-operation with non-socialist parties in power. A main aim was to try and avert war, but the International effectively ended in 1914 although attempts to revive it were made in 1919.

Second Reich   The German Empire 1871–1918 also known as the *Kaiserreich*; the period after German unification when William I, king of Prussia was offered the throne of the Empire. The last Kaiser, William II was forced to abdicate after the German army refused to support him at the end of the First World War.

Second Republic   Republic set up in France after the 1848 revolution. Under the presidency of Louis Napoleon (*see* Second Empire) the Republic had a legislative assembly with a monarchist majority. Unable to agree amongst themselves, the monarchists were able to obstruct the workings of the republic and prevent the re-election of president and legislature in 1852. In order to protect his position, Louis Napoleon organised a coup d'état on 1–2 December and had himself elected Emperor as Napoleon III.

Sinn Fein   Gaelic for 'Ourselves alone'. Irish Nationalist party founded in 1902 by Arthur Griffiths (1872–1922) and formed into the Sinn Fein League in 1907–8 when it absorbed other nationalist groups. The group rose to prominence in the 1913–14 Home Rule crisis when many Sinn Feiners joined the Irish Volunteers and many Dublin workers joined the organisation. Sinn Fein members were involved in the Easter Rising in 1916.

Slavophiles   A small group of Russian intellectuals in the 1840s and 1850s. Deeply nationalistic, they rejected the Westernisers' belief that Russia must follow western paths of development. They aimed to introduce reforms to restore an idealised pre-Petrine (Peter the Great) form of society. They also believed that the Tsar's authority should be personal and patriarchal.

Social Democracy   Non-doctrinaire, socialist or socialist-inclined political movement of the nineteenth and twentieth centuries, combining concern for greater equality with acceptance of a mixed economy and representing a non-communist left-wing tradition, often drawing support from organised labour. Notable examples include the Social Democratic Party of Germany, founded in 1875, and the Swedish Social Democratic Labour Party, formed in 1880.

Socialism in One Country   Doctrine expounded by Lenin in Russia after it became clear that the Revolution of 1917 was not going to affect the other states of Europe. The main task was to create a socialist society without help from outside, either political or economic.

Solidarity   Polish trade union and reform movement formed in the 1970s to demand liberalisation of the Polish communist regime and the formation of free trade unions. Under its leader, Lech Walesa, the movement won important concessions from the government before the threat of Soviet invasion and the assumption of power by the Polish army led to the banning of the organisation and the imprisonment of its leaders. It survives as a clandestine organisation.

Sonderbund   A League formed by seven Catholic Swiss Cantons in December 1845 to protect their interests against Liberal attempts to strengthen the control of the Federal government. The Federal Diet condemned the League as a secessionist movement and a brief civil car in 1847 led to its dissolution.

'Splendid Isolation'   Phrase used to describe Britain's diplomatic position in the latter part of the nineteenth century and, more generally, during the nineteenth century as a whole when Britain stood aside from entanglement in European alliances. The phrase was used in *The Times* in January 1896 and subsequently (9 November) by Lord Salisbury. The 'isolation' is customarily seen as being ended by the Anglo–Japanese treaty of 1902.

SS   Abbreviation of German *Schutzstaffel* or Guard Detachment. Hitler's personal bodyguard of dedicated Nazis founded in 1923 as a rival to Röhm's SA (*q.v.*). Placed under the command of Heinrich Himmler in 1929, the SS carried out the liquidation of the SA leadership in June 1934 and in July became an independent organisation with its own armed units. *SS-Verfugunstruppe* (Special Task Troops), organised as regular soldiers, were formed from 1935 and as the Waffen-SS comprised a group of élite regiments, separate from army control. Other sections of the SS provided concentration camp guards – the *SS-Totenkopfverbande* – and police squads in occupied territory.

States General   The national assembly in France where the three 'estates' were represented (nobility, clergy and commons). It met only rarely as the power of the monarchy increased, and not at all between 1614 and 1789. Louis XVI finally called the States General to try and quieten the growing discontent in the country but it declared itself a National Assembly, an act which marked the beginning of the French Revolution. The term is also used to describe the present Dutch parliament.

Straits Question   The issue of rights of passage through the Dardanelles and the Bosphorus which was disputed between the Great Powers and Turkey at several points in the nineteenth and twentieth centuries. A series of conventions have laid down restrictions on the classes of warships permitted to use the waterway.

Succession states   The states formed after the First World War from the territory of the former Austro–Hungarian Empire, or incorporating parts of it. These included Poland, Czechoslovakia, Yugoslavia, Romania, Hungary and Austria.

Sudetenland   German – speaking area of northern Bohemia assigned to Czechoslovakia in 1919. Claimed by Hitler for the Reich, the Sudetenland became the centre of an international crisis in 1938 over Germany's attempt to revise the Versailles Treaty by force. The threat of general European war was temporarily averted by the Munich Agreement in which Czechoslovakia was forced to cede the Sudetenland to Germany.

Sûreté   French criminal investigation department.

Swastika   Ancient religious symbol in the shape of a hooked cross. In European mythology it became linked with the revival of Germanic legends at the end of the nineteenth century. Adopted by a number of extreme right-wing groups in Germany after the First World War, including the Erhardt Brigade, a *Freikorps* unit active in the Kapp Putsch. It was also adopted by Hitler as the symbol of National Socialism and in September 1935 became Nazi Germany's national emblem.

Syndicalism   Theory which advocates the ownership and organisation of industry by workers and their organisations – usually trade unions. This is in contrast to the socialist theory of ownership by the state. Syndicalism is also associated with the belief in the power of trade unionism and the use of the general strike as a weapon to bring about major social and political change. Although often associated with anarchists, many of the syndicalists in the 1920s joined the communist or fascist parties.

Syndicat   (Fr. trade union)   The basic form of syndicalist activity.

Tennis Court Oath   Oath taken by the deputies of the French National Assembly on 20 June 1789, binding them to work together for the creation of a French constitution.

Terror, the   In April 1793 the National Convention delegated powers to a Committee of Public Safety in order to preserve the Republic in the face of its enemies, internal and external. Robespierre and the Jacobins established a virtual dictatorship, known as the 'Reign of Terror', especially after the Law of Prairial (*q.v.*) in June 1793. Leading opponents, such as Danton and Hébert, aristocrats, and suspected counter-revolutionaries were executed, usually by guillotine, both in Paris and the provinces. As many as 13,000 people are said to have died, the majority of humble background. The terror came to an end with Robespierre's arrest and execution in Thermidor.

Thermidor   (Fr.)   The 'hot weather' month of the French Revolutionary Calendar, 19 July–17 August. The period of Jacobin dictatorship ended on 9 Thermidor (27 July) 1794 when the Convention secured the proscription of Robespierre.

Third Estate   *See under* Tiers Etat.

Third International   Otherwise known as the Communist International or the Comintern. Founded by Lenin in March 1919 to unite revolutionary socialists. Finally disbanded by Stalin in May 1943 as a concession to his western allies.

Third Reich   Term used to describe the Nazi dictatorship in Germany, 1933–45. Originally coined by the Nazis to describe the expanded Germany of their theories, the term was dropped from official usage in the 1930s.

Third Republic   The term used to describe the government of France from the Franco–Prussian War in 1871 to the fall of France in 1940 and the establishment of the Vichy regime (*q.v.*).

Tiers Etat   The Third Estate, denotes all social classes in pre-revolutionary France other than the aristocracy, high-ranking clergy and privileged magistracy. Thus it included the bourgeoisie and 'sansculottes' (*q.v*).

Tricolour   Popular name for the French national flag since 17 July 1789, it was made up of the red and blue colours of the city of Paris and the white Bourbon emblem. It signifies the victory of the people of Paris on 14 July 1789.

Triple Alliance   Alliance formed between Germany, Austria–Hungary and Italy in 1882.

Triple Entente   Agreement between Britain, France and Russia to resolve their outstanding colonial differences; it became a military alliance in 1914.

Ultramontanism   Belief in the ultimate authority of the Catholic Church and that it supercedes loyalty to the state. Particularly evident in nineteenth-century France, it was encouraged by the Vatican decrees of 1870. It also contributed to the *Kulturkampf* (*q.v.*). Its long-term result was to free the papacy from dependence on civil powers and gave the Church new freedom of action.

United Nations, the   International peace-keeping organisation set up in 1945 to replace the League of Nations (*q.v.*). From the 50 states who signed the Charter of the UN in 1945, numbers had more than doubled by 1970 with the rise of independent ex-colonial states. All states have one vote in the General Assembly and its executive, the Security Council, can call on member states to supply armed forces. UN troops have been involved in peace-keeping duties in many parts of the world since 1945, notably in the Middle East, Africa, and Cyprus.

Vichy   French provincial spa town where the interim autocratic French government was established between July 1940 and July 1944. The Vichy regime was anti-republican, and collaborated extensively with the Germans who occupied the areas it controlled in November 1942. After the liberation of France in 1944, Pétain and the Vichy ministers established a headquarters in Germany.

Warsaw Pact   Military alliance of the USSR and Eastern European satellites formed when the Eastern European Mutual Assistance Treaty was signed in 1955 by the communist states in Europe (except Albania and Yugoslavia). The treaty made joint provision for mutual defence for twenty years and represented the communist, especially Russian, response to the formation of NATO (*q.v.*) in 1949 and the rearming of the Federal Republic of Germany. The Pact permits the USSR to keep forces in the satellite states and has a united command structure, reinforced by regular exercises and manoeuvres.

Weimar   Town where the German National Constituent Assembly met in February 1919. It gave its name to the German Republic of 1918–33. The town was chosen to allay fears of the allied powers and the other German states about Prussian domination in Berlin, and also to escape from the associations attached to the former capital city. The economic problems which beset the Weimar Republic and the concomitant unemployment, facilitated the rise of Hitler, and in March 1933 he suspended the Weimar Constitution of July 1919 to make way for the Third Reich (*q.v.*).

Weltpolitik   (Ger. lit. world politics)   A new trend in German foreign policy at the end of the nineteenth century. The Kaiser Wilhelm II determined to transform Germany into a first-rank global power. Ultra-nationalistic pressure combined with social and economic forces to support new interest in colonial expansion, the scramble for territory in China and Africa, and the establishment of a powerful navy.

White Russians   Term for Russians living on western border of Soviet Union, but used generally to describe counter-revolutionary forces in the aftermath of the Bolshevik Revolution of 1917.

Yezhovshchina   (Russ.)   A word used to describe the Stalinist purges of the 1920s and 1930s. The name derives from the head of the Soviet secret police, N. I. Yezhov.

Young Italy   Italian nationalist movement founded in 1832 by Giuseppe Mazzini, its main aim being the establishment of a free, independent and republican Italian nation. Acted as a pressure group Cavour in the 1850s which speeded the creation of an independent Italian state.

Young Turks   Liberal reform movement among young army officers in the Ottoman Empire, active between 1903 and 1909. The rebellion of 1908 led to the creation of a 'Committee of Union and Progress', headed by Enver Bey, Ahmed Djemel and Mehmed Talaat. They persuaded the Sultan to re-establish constitutional rule and convene a parliament. Splits arose between the three leaders (who went on to achieve prominence in the Balkan Wars and through their encouragement of the German alliance), and other radicals. Their influence lasted throughout the First World War.

Zemstvo   Russian provincial or district council first established by Tsar Alexander II in January 1864. The councils were dominated by the local gentry and were especially active in 1865–6 and 1917 in areas such as public health, agricultural development, road building, and primary education. In many areas the zemstvo became a genuine force for liberalism and a means of arousing political awareness at local level.

Zimmermann Telegram   Coded message of 19 January 1917 from the German foreign minister, Arthur Zimmermann, to the German minister in Mexico, urging the conclusion of a German–Mexican alliance in the event of a declaration of war on Germany by America when Germany resumed unrestricted submarine warfare against shipping on 1 February. Mexico would be offered the recapture of her 'lost territories' in New Mexico, Arizona and Texas. Intercepted by British Naval Intelligence, the telegram was released to the American press on 1 March, greatly inflaming feeling against Germany, and helping to precipitate the American Declaration of War against Germany on 6 April 1917.

Zollverein   (Ger.) The customs union established within the Prussian state after 1815 which gradually came to include most of the German states by 1833. The abolition of customs and the development of free trade helped to encourage industrialisation in the German states and to make Prussia, rather than Austria, the focus of German nationalism.

Topic Bibliography

Topics

1. The Ancien Regime.
2. The Coming of the French Revolution.
3. The French Revolution.
4. Napoleon.
5. The Revolutionary and Napoleonic Wars.
6. The Congress of Vienna and the Congress System.
7. France, 1815–51.
8. Russia, 1801–56.
9. Liberalism, nationalism and socialism in the nineteenth century.
10. The Revolutions of 1848.
11. The economic development of Europe, 1760–1914.
12. The Risorgimento and Italian Unification.
13. France, 1848–71.
14. European expansion overseas.
15. The unification of Germany.
16. Germany, 1871–1914.
17. France, 1871–1914.
18. Austria–Hungary, 1867–1918.
19. Russia, 1856–1917.
20. European diplomacy, 1871–1914.
21. The First World War, 1914–18.
22. The Russian Revolution and Lenin, 1917–24.
23. Italy from Unification to Mussolini, 1871–1943.
24. The Weimar Republic, 1919–33.
25. Nazi Germany, 1933–45.
26. Stalin's Russia, 1923–53.
27. Eastern Europe between the Wars, 1918–39.
28. The Spanish Civil War, 1936–9.
29. France, 1918–44.
30. Inter-war Diplomacy, 1919–39.
31. The Second World War, 1939–45.

List of abbreviations

A.H.R.	*American Historical Review*
C.E.H.	*Central European History*
C.H.J.	*Cambridge Historical Journal* (later, *Historical Journal*)
Econ.H.R.	*Economic History Review*
E.H.R.	*English Historical Review*
E.H.Q.	*European History Quarterly*
E.S.R.	*European Studies Review* (later, *European History Quarterly*)
H.	*History*
H.J.	*Historical Journal*
H.T.	*History Today*
H.W.J.	*History Workshop Journal*
I.R.H.S.	*International Review of Social History*
J.C.H.	*Journal of Contemporary History*
J.H.I.	*Journal of the History of Ideas*
J.M.H.	*Journal of Modern History*
P.P.	*Past and Present*
R.P.	*Review of Politics*
S.R.	*Slavic Review*

Introductory note

This bibliography is arranged in rough chronological order and is intended to represent many of the major topics and themes in modern European history. The essay titles are intended to focus attention on some of the most commonly raised issues, but should not be regarded as exhausting the range of possibilities on each subject. The reading is deliberately greater than would be required for an average essay, but does reflect the wealth of bibliographical material now available for most of these topics and allows a degree of specialisation on particular aspects of a subject. Similarly, the article literature mentioned, while not an exhaustive list, is intended as a guide to some of the most important material available in academic journals. A selection of source material is also provided for each topic.

General Texts

For the first part of this period, E. N. Williams, *The Ancien Régime in Europe* (1970) is valuable; the latter sections of W. Doyle, *The Old European Order, 1660–1800* (1978) and many parts of R. R. Palmer, *The Age of the Democratic Revolution* (2 vols, 1959–64) are also relevant. J. M. Roberts, *Revolution and Improvement: the Western World 1775–1847* (1976) is a vigorous analysis going up to the mid-nineteenth century; covering a shorter period, but valuable, is I. Collins, *The Age of Progress, 1789–1848* (1964). E. J. Hobsbawm, *The Age of Revolution, 1789–1848* (1962) is especially strong on social and intellectual movements. A. J. Grant and H. Temperley, *Europe in the Nineteenth and Twentieth Centuries* (7th edn, rev. A. Ramm, 2 vols, 1984) remains a valuable overview, as does D. Thompson, *Europe since Napoleon* (rev. edn, 1966). See also, on the later period, J. Joll, *Europe since 1870* (1973). *The New Cambridge Modern History*, Vols VIII–XII (1960–5) are relevant to this period. The earlier *Cambridge Modern History*, Vol. XII (1910) has bibliographical material which the more recent series lacks, though inevitably rather dated. 'The Rise of Modern Europe' series, edited by W. L. Langer, contains several volumes for this period, although some are rather dated: C. Brinton, *A Decade of Revolution, 1789–99* (1934), G. Brunn, *Europe and the French Imperium, 1799–1814* (1938), F. B. Artz, *Reaction and Revolution, 1814–1832* (1953), R. C. Brinkley, *Realism and Nationalism, 1852–1871* (1951) and C. J. H. Hayes, *A Generation of Materialism, 1871–1900* (1951). In the Fontana series, see O. Hufton, *Europe: Privilege and Protest, 1730–1789* (1980), G. Rudé, *Revolutionary Europe, 1789–1815* (1964), and J. Droz, *Europe between Revolutions, 1815–1848* (1967), J. A. S. Grenville, *Europe Reshaped, 1848–1878* (1976) and N. Stone, *Europe Transformed, 1878–1919* (1983). In the Longman series, *see* M. S. Anderson, *Europe in the Eighteenth Century* (2nd edn, 1976), F. L. Ford, *Europe 1780–1830* (1970), H. Hearder, *Europe in the Nineteenth Century* (1966) and J. M. Roberts, *Europe 1880–1945* (1967).

Amidst a large selection of national histories, a number of general works or series can be consulted. For France, A. Cobban, *A History of Modern France 1715–1945* (3 vols, 1961–5) is readily accessible, while the older J. P. T. Bury, *France 1815–1940* (1949) remains a useful single volume treatment. The three volume Fontana History of Modern France is a more recent addition, comprising D. M. G. Sutherland, *France 1789–1815; Revolution and Counterrevolution* (1985), R. Magraw, *France 1815–1914: The Bourgeois Century* (1984), and D. Johnson, *France 1914–1983; The Twentieth Century* (1986). See, too, the volumes in the Cambridge History of Modern France; A. Jardin and A-J. Tudesq, *Restoration and Reaction 1815–1848* (1984), M. Agulhon, *The Republican Experiment, 1848–1852* (1983); A. Plessis, *The Rise and Fall of the Second Empire, 1852–1871* (1985); J-M. Mayeur and M. Reberioux, *The Third Republic from its Origins to The Great War, 1871–1914*; P. Bernard and H. Dubief, *The Decline of the Third Republic, 1914–1938* (1985); and J-P. Azema, *From Munich to the Liberation, 1938–1944* (1985). For the twentieth century J. F. McMillan, *Dreyfus to de Gaulle: Politics and Society in France, 1898–1968* (1985) is an up-to-date study. Also of general importance are G. Dupeaux, *French Society, 1789–1970* (1976) and T. Zeldin, *France, 1848–1945* (1973–7). On Spain, the standard work available in English is now R. Carr, *Spain, 1808–1975* (rev. edn, 1980), replacing the older A. R. Oliveira, *Politics, Economics and Men of Modern Spain, 1808–1946* (1946) and R. Altamara, *A History of Spanish Civilisation* (1930). For Italy, R. Albrecht-Carrié, *Italy from Napoleon to Mussolini* (1950) and D. Mack Smith, *Italy* (1959) remain useful. More recent are the two volumes in the Longman History of Italy, H. Hearder, *Italy in the Age of the Risorgimento, 1790–1870* (1983) and M. Clark, *Modern Italy, 1871–1982* (1984).

Germany has received treatment in a number of general texts, amongst the most accessible are W. Carr, *A History of Germany, 1815–1945* (rev. edn, 1979); A. Ramm, *Germany, 1789–1919* (1967), and *A History of Modern Germany* (3 vols, 1959–69), R. Flenley, *Modern German History* (1959) and K. S. Pinson, *Modern Germany: Its History and Civilisation* (1954). The Low Countries are not well-served in English, but see G. Edmunson, *A History of Holland* (1922); P. J. Blok, *History of the People of The Netherlands* (1898–1912); B. H. M. Vlekke, *Evolution of the Dutch Nation* (1951) and G. J. Renier, *The Dutch Nation* (1944). On Belgium see A. de Meeus, *History of the Belgians* (1962). On Scandinavia, see T. K. Derry, *A Short History of Norway* (1957), B. J. Hovde, *The Scandinavian Countries, 1720–1865* (1948), M. Cole and C. Smith (eds), *Democratic Sweden* (1938), I. Anderson, *A History of Sweden* (1965) and S. Oakley, *The Story of Sweden* (1966).

For Russia, M. T. Florinski, *Russia: A History and Interpretation* (2 vols, 1953–4) and B. Pares, *A History of Russia* (3rd edn, 1955) are old, but still useful. See also G. V. Vernadsky, *A History of Russia* (rev. edn, 1961). H. Seton-Watson, *Imperial Russia, 1801–1917* (1967) covers a major part of this period. B. H. Sumner, *A Survey of Russian History* (1944) is thematically arranged but covers a long-sweep of Russian history, as does R. Pipes, *Russia Under the Old Régime* (1974). In the Longman History of Russia, the relevant published volumes are P. Dukes, *The Making of Russian Absolutism, 1613–1801* (1982), H. Rogger, *Russia in the Age of Modernisation and Revolution, 1881–1917* (1983) and M. McCauley, *The Soviet Union since 1917* (1981). On the twentieth century, see also G. Hosking, *A History of the Soviet Union* (1985). J. Blum, *Lord and Peasant in Russia* (1961) tackles a perennial theme of Russian history and on the less Europeanised dimension of Russian history see P. Longworth, *The Cossacks* (1969) and W. E. D. Allen, *The Ukraine: A History* (1940).

Polish history is covered generally in O. Halecki, *The History of Poland* (1942), H. Frankel, *Poland, The Struggle for Power, 1772–1939* (1946) and W. H. Reddaway *et al.* (eds), *The Cambridge History of Poland, 1697–1935* (1941). For the Habsburg lands, see C. A. Macartney, *The Habsburg Empire, 1790–1918* (1968), A. J. P. Taylor, *The Habsburg Monarchy, 1815–1918* (2nd edn, 1949), R. A. Kann, *The Multi-National Empire: Nationalism and National Reform in the Habsburg Monarchy, 1848–1918* (2 vols, 1950), and C. A. Macartney, *Hungary* (1934).

For the British Isles, R. K. Webb, *Modern England: From the Eighteenth Century to the Present* (1969) presents the most succinct overview, but for a comprehensive further account of the general texts now available on British history see the *Longman Handbook of Modern British History, 1714–1980*, p. 302. On Ireland, see J. C. Beckett, *The Making of Modern Ireland, 1603–1923* (1966), F. S. L. Lyons, *Ireland since the Famine* (rev. edn, 1973) and R. Dudley Edwards, *An Atlas of Irish History* (2nd edn, 1981).

European economic development is discussed in B. H. Slicher van Bath, *The Agrarian History of Western Europe* (1983), A. Milward and S. B. Saul, *The Economic Development of Continental Europe, 1780–1870* (1973), C. Trebilcock, *The Industrialisation of the Continental Powers, 1780–1914* (1981), W. W. Rostow, *The Stages of Economic Growth* (1960), W. O. Henderson, *The Industrial Revolution on the Continent* (1961), H. Feis, *Europe the World's Banker* (1930) and W. Ashworth, *A Short History of the International Economy since 1850* (1952). See also the last four volumes of C. M. Cipolla (ed.), *The Fontana Economic History of Europe* (1973) which contains articles on individual countries and more general themes. The economic and social development of Europe can be traced in the later sections of F. Braudel, *Capitalism and Material Life, 1500–1800* (1967) also available in a recent three-volume edition, *Civilisation and Capitalism, 15th–18th Century* (1985). Also useful is H. Kamen, *Social History of Europe, 1500–1800* (1984). For the later period, see D. Geary, *A Social History of Western Europe, 1848–1945* (1985), P. N. Stearns, *European Society in Upheaval* (1967) and G. Mosse, *The Culture of Western Europe: The Nineteenth and Twentieth Centuries* (1961).

For Europe's relationship with the wider world consult the later sections of two excellent histories of the world, W. H. McNeill, *A World History* (1967) and J. M. Roberts, *A History of the World* (1967). The latter's *The Triumph of the West* (1985) elevates Europeanisation into a major theme of world history. R. Davis, *The Rise of the Atlantic Economies* (1973) deals with the earlier phases of European involvement overseas, while D. K. Fieldhouse, *The Colonial Empires* (1966) and V. Kiernan, *European Empires from Conquest to Collapse, 1815–1960* (1982) present them in maturity and after. Europe's place in the twentieth-century world is covered by J. A. S. Grenville, *A World History of the Twentieth Century, 1900–84* (2 vols, 1980–5).

For reference purposes, there is a wealth of statistical information in B. R. Mitchell, *European Historical Statistics, 1750–1975* (2nd edn, 1980). See also P. Flora (ed.) *State, Economy and Society in Western Europe, 1815–1975* (2 vols, 1983–4). For detailed reference works on a wide variety of political topics, see J. Babuscio and R. Dunn, *European Political Facts, 1648–1789,* (1984), C. Cook and J. Paxton, *European Political Facts, 1789–1848* (1980), C. Cook and J. Paxton, *European Political Facts,*

1848–1918 (1978) and C. Cook and J. Paxton, *European Political Facts, 1918–1984* (rev. edn, 1985). S. H. Steinberg, *Historical Tables (58 BC–AD 1978)* (10th edn., 1979) is an invaluable chronological reference work.

1. The Ancien Regime

The latter half of the eighteenth century is inevitably overshadowed by the events of the Revolutionary and Napoleonic era, but deserves study in its own right. The age of 'enlightenment' witnessed a ferment of social, economic and intellectual changes, but ones which still seemed, prior to 1789, to permit the old order to adapt and maintain itself. The degree to which 'enlightened despotism' can be regarded as a coherent and serious influence on the attitude and behaviour of rulers is one aspect of the period which has received attention; another is the relationship between monarchs and their nobility; while the wider intellectual critique of the old order and its allies, notably the church, should also be considered.

Essay topics

How much substance was there to the claim of some ancien regime rulers to be 'enlightened'?

Where and why did European aristocracies find themselves in conflict with their rulers in the latter part of the eighteenth century?

Why did the Church find itself the target of so much criticism in late eighteenth-century Europe?

Sources and documents

T. C. W. Blanning, *Joseph II and Enlightened Despotism* (1970) is readily accessible and ranges beyond Joseph II in its coverage. For the *philosophes'* critique of the *ancien regime* there is little substitute for reading some of the great classics of enlightenment literature, such as Jean-Jacques Rousseau, *Du contrat social* (1762, trans. as *The Social Contract*); C. L. Montesquieu, *De l'esprit des lois* (1748) and *Persian Letters* (1721) and Voltaire's *Candide* (1759) and *Philosophical Dictionary* (1764). See also J. F. Lively, *The Enlightenment* (1966). R. R. Palmer, *The Age of the Democratic Revolution, vol. i; The Challenge* (1959) also has some documents of value in the appendices.

Secondary works

There are excellent broad surveys in E. N. Williams, *The Ancien Regime in Europe* (1970); M. S. Anderson, *Europe in the Eighteenth Century* (1961); R. R. Palmer, *The Age of the Democratic Revolution, vol. i: The Challenge* (1959). See also the latter sections of W. Doyle, *The Old European Order, 1660–1800* (1978).

For the ideas behind the enlightenment, see A. Cobban, *In Search of Humanity: The Enlightenment in Modern History* (1960) and N. Hampson, *The Enlightenment* (1968). P. Gay, *The Enlightenment: an*

Interpretation (1967) and *The Party of Humanity* (1964). Also useful is
P. Hazard, *European Thought in the Eighteenth Century* (1963) and C.
Becker, *The Heavenly City of the Eighteenth Century Philosophers* (1932).

On enlightened despotism in general, T. C. W. Blanning, *Joseph II and
Enlightened Despotism* (1970) is a good short introduction; see too the
older F. Hartung, *Enlightened Despotism* (1957) J. G. Gagliardo,
Enlightened Despotism (1968) and S. Andrews, *Enlightened Despotism*
(1967). R. Porter and M. Teich, *The Enlightenment in National Context*
(1981) is an excellent modern study. See also A. R. Myers, *Parliaments
and Estates in Europe to 1789* (1975); F. Venturi, *Utopia and Reform in
the Enlightenment* (1971) and A. Goodwin, *The European Nobility in the
Eighteenth Century* (1953).

Individual rulers are examined in C. A. Macartney, *The Habsburg and
Hohenzollern Dynasties* (1970); A. C. Johnson, *Frederick the Great and
his Officials* (1976); D. B. Horn, *Frederick the Great* (1964); G. Ritter,
Frederick the Great (1968) and W. Hubstsch, *Frederick the Great* (1975).
On the general history of Prussia and Frederick's part in it, see
H. Holborn, *History of Modern Germany*, vol. II (1964), S. B. Fay and
K. Epstein, *The Rise of Brandenburg–Prussia to 1786* (rev. edn, 1964)
and F. L. Carsten, *The Origins of Prussia* (1954). On the role of the army,
see G. A. Craig, *The Politics of the Prussian Army, 1640–1945* (1955)
and C. Duffy, *The Army of Frederick the Great* (1974). For economic
developments see W. O. Henderson, *The State and the Industrial
Revolution in Prussia, 1740–1870* (1958) and his *Studies in the Economic
Policy of Frederick the Great* (1963).

On Catherine and Russia, see M. Raeff, *Imperial Russia, 1682–1825*
(1971), P. Dukes, *Catherine the Great and the Russian Nobility* (1967) and
P. Dukes (ed.), *Russia under Catherine the Great* (1977–8). M. Raeff (ed.),
Catherine the Great (1972) has views on Catherine. See too
W. F. Reddaway (ed.), *Documents of Catherine the Great: the
correspondence with Voltaire and the instruction of 1767 in the English
text of 1768* (1931). I. de Madariaga, *Russia in the Age of Catherine the
Great* (1981) is a recent addition to the literature. On the Pugachev rising,
see P. Avrich, *Russian Rebels* (1973), M. Raeff, 'Pugachev's rebellion', in
R. Forster and J. P. Greene (eds), *Pre-Conditions of Revolution in Early
Modern Europe* (1970), and P. Longworth, 'The Pugachev Revolt: the last
great Cossack peasant rising', in H. Landsberger (ed.), *Rural Protest:
Peasant Movements and Social Change* (1974). For Russian expansion
see G. S. Thompson, *Catherine the Great and the Expansion of Russia*
(1947) and A. W. Fisher, *The Russian Annexation of the Crimea,
1772–1783* (1970).

For Joseph II, apart from T. C. W. Blanning's short guide, see
S. K. Padover, *The Revolutionary Emperor – Joseph II* (1967); E.
Wangermann, *The Austrian Achievement, 1700–1800* (1973) and *From
Joseph II to the Jacobin Trials* (1959). The early part of C. A. Macartney,
Hapsburg Empire, 1790–1918 (1968) and H. Holborn, *History of Modern
Germany*, Vol. II (1964) are useful; see too, H. Strakosch, *State
Absolutism and the Rule of Law* (1967) and K. Roider, *Austria's Eastern
Question, 1700–90* (1982).

On the other eighteenth-century states, see R. Herr, *Eighteenth Century
Revolution in Spain* (1958); A. Hull, *Charles III and the Revival of Spain*
(1980). Scandinavia is less well-served for the period after 1760 than
earlier, but for Gustavus III, see I. Anderson, *A History of Sweden* (1956)

and S. Oakley, *The Story of Sweden* (1966), ch. 13. The impact of
enlightened ideas on Italy is discussed in F. Venturi (ed.), *Italy and the
Enlightenment* (1972), while Britain's experience is traced in R. Pares,
Limited Monarchy in Great Britain (Historical Association, 1957) and
J. Brooke, *George III* (1973).

Specifically on the churches, see G. R. Cragg, *The Church and the Age
of Reason* (1960) and R. R. Palmer, *Catholics and Unbelievers in
Eighteenth Century France* (rev. edn, 1961), F. E. Manuel, *The Eighteenth
Century Confronts the Gods* (1959), and R. Wollheim (ed.), *Hume on
Religion* (1963). Of importance too are J. Delumeau, *Catholicism between
Luther and Voltaire* (1977), H. Kamen, *The Spanish Inquisition* (1965), and
T. Tackett, *Priest and Parish in Eighteenth Century France* (1977).

Articles

A useful starting point on the literature on 'enlightened despotism' is
H. Scott, 'Whatever happened to the Enlightened Despots?', *H.* (1983);
see also B. Behrens, 'Enlightened despotism', *H.J.* (1975), G. Parry,
'Enlightened government and its critics in eighteenth century Germany',
H.J. (1963) and M. Raeff, 'The well-ordered police state and the
development of modernity in seventeenth and eighteenth century
Europe', *A.H.R.* (1975). Useful too are V. G. Kiernan, 'Foreign mercenaries
and absolute monarchy', *P.P.* (1957) and 'State and nation in Western
Europe', *P.P.* (1965).

On individual countries see also W. L. Dorn, 'The Prussian bureaucracy
in the eighteenth century', *Political Science Quarterly* (1931 and 1932);
D. E. D. Beales, 'The false Joseph II', *H.J.* (1975); I. de Madariaga,
'Catherine II and the serfs', *S.R.* (1974); A. H. Kamen, 'The decline of
Spain: a historical myth?', *P.P.* (1978); E. J. Hamilton, 'Money and
economic recovery in Spain under the first Bourbon', *J.M.H.* (1943);
W. J. Callahan, 'Crown, nobility and industry in eighteenth century
Spain', *International Review of Social History* (1966); and L. Rodriguez,
'The Spanish riots of 1766', *P.P.* (1973).

For the influence of the enlightenment in general, see P. Gay, 'The
Enlightenment in the history of political theory', *Political Science
Quarterly*, (1954); T. Besterman, 'Reason and progress', *Studies on
Voltaire and the Eighteenth Century* (1963); G. Iggers, 'The idea of
progress: a critical reassessment', *A.H.R.* (1965).

2. The Coming of the French Revolution

A huge topic which draws upon a great variety of explanations as to why
and how the revolution occurred. These range from the fundamentally
Marxist accounts which find the roots of the revolution in economic,
social and intellectual changes to the more contingent and 'accidental'
views of the coming of the revolution. The literature is still dominated by
the historians who see long-term processes at work which culminated in
the revolution, although there have been distinguished attempts by
scholars of all perspectives to free the period from too much intellectual
abstraction and to engage in detailed discussion of the nature of the
ancien regime in France.

Essay topics

How intractable were the problems facing the French government in the twenty years prior to the French Revolution?

Discuss the influence of the *philosophes* upon the outbreak of the French Revolution.

Account for the calling of the Estates General in 1789.

Sources and documents

J. Hardman, *The French Revolution: the Fall of the Ancien Regime to the Thermidorian Reaction, 1785–1795* (1981) is comprehensive, but see also R. C. Cobb, J. Hardman, and J. M. Roberts, *French Revolution Documents* (1966–73). A. Young, *Travels in France During the Years 1787, 1788, 1789* (ed. C. Maxwell, 1929) is a valuable eye-witness account of the pre-revolutionary regime.

Secondary works

Of the general studies, A. Cobban, *A History of Modern France, vol. I, 1715–1799* (rev. edn, 1965) remains a good starting point, but see also C. A. B. Behrens, *The Ancien Regime* (1967) and L. Gershoy, *From Despotism to Revolution, 1763–1789* (1944). W. Doyle, *Origins of the French Revolution* (1980) is an excellent fresh interpretation. J. M. Roberts, *The French Revolution* (1978), ch. 1 and J. Godechot, *France and the Atlantic Revolution of the Eighteenth Century* (1965) are also valuable on the combination of long-term and short-term processes at work. Detailed studies of the last years of the French monarchy are also part of the canvas of the standard accounts of the French Revolution by G. Lefebvre, *The French Revolution: from its origins to 1793* (1962) and A. Soboul, *The French Revolution, 1787–99* (1974). M. Vovelle, *The Fall of the French Monarchy, 1787–1792* (1984) is a modern view of the collapse of the French government, for which see also J. Godechot, *The Taking of the Bastille* (1970) and G. Lefebvre, *The Great Fear of 1789* (1973). The historiographical issues were taken up in A. Cobban, *Historians and the Causes of the French Revolution* (Historical Association pamphlet, 1958).

For the general social and economic background to the French Revolution see G. Lefebvre, *The Coming of the French Revolution* (1939) and the collection in D. Johnson (ed.), *French Society and the Revolution* (1976). P. Goubert, *The Ancien Regime* (1973) and H. See, *Economic and Social Conditions in France during the Eighteenth Century* (1927). Individual social groups are discussed in O. H. Hufton, *The Poor of Eighteenth Century France* (1974); F. L. Ford, *Robe and Sword: the Regrouping of the French Aristocracy after Louis XIV* (1953); R. Forster, *The Nobility of Toulouse in the Eighteenth Century: A Social and Economic Study* (1960); E. Barber, *The Bourgeoisie in Eighteenth Century France* (1955) and useful case studies in O. H. Hufton, *Bayeux in the Eighteenth Century* (1967) and 'Life and death among the very poor', in A. Cobban (ed.), *The Eighteenth Century* (1969); C. Jones, *Charity and Bienfaisance: the treatment of the Poor in the Montpellier region, 1740–1815* (1983), and J. K. J. Thompson, *Charmont-de-Lodeve, 1633–1789: Fluctuations in the Prosperity of a Cloth Making Town* (1982).

For population see L. Henry, 'The population of France in the eighteenth century', in D. V. Glass and D. E. C. Eversley, *Population in History* (1965).

Serious discussion of the economic features of France under the ancien regime can be found in the early parts of R. Price, *The Economic Modernisation of France* (1975) and T. Kemp, *Economic Forces in French History* (1971). See also the selection of articles in R. Greenlaw (ed.), *The Economic Origins of the French Revolution: Poverty or Prosperity* (1958). There is an important comparative essay on British and French economic development by F. Crouzet, 'England and France in the eighteenth century: a comparative analysis of two economic growths', in R. M. Hartwell (ed.), *The Causes of the Industrial Revolution in England* (1967). The definitive study of French finances is J. F. Bosher, *French Finances, 1770–1795* (1970) and on the influence of Turgot on economic policy, see D. Dakin, *Turgot and the Ancien Regime in France* (1939). An important case-study of the impasse faced by reformers of the fiscal system is J. F. Bosher, *The Single Duty Project: A Study of the Movement for a French Customs Union* (1964).

On the place of the Church see J. McManners, *French Ecclesiastical Society under the Old Regime* (1961) and R. R. Palmer, *Catholics and Unbelievers in Eighteenth Century France* (1939). For the role of the *philosophes* in preparing the ground for the revolution, see N. Hampson, *The Enlightenment* (1968), W. F. Church (ed.), *The Influence of the Enlightenment on the French Revolution: Creative, Disastrous, or Non-existent* (1964) and A. Cobban, *Aspects of the French Revolution* (1968), ch. 1. On the activities of the parlements, see J. H. Shennan, *The Parlement of Paris* (1968).

Articles

For the continuing debate about the origins of the French Revolution and their interpretation see G. Ellis, 'The "Marxist interpretation" of the French Revolution', *E.H.R.* (1978) and G. C. Cavanaugh, 'The present state of French revolutionary historiography: Alfred Cobban and beyond', *French Historical Studies* (1972).

On the social and economic background, see C. Lucas, 'Nobles, bourgeois and the origins of the French Revolution', *P.P.* (1973), A. Davies, 'The origins of the French Peasant Revolution of 1789', *H.* (1964), N. Temple, 'The control and exploitation of French towns during the Ancien Regime', *H.* (1966), and R. Forster, 'The provincial noble: a re-appraisal', *A.H.R.* (1962–3). Other aspects are discussed in A. Woyd Moote, 'The French Crown *versus* its judicial and financial officials', *J.M.H.* (1962), W. Doyle, 'The parlements of France and the breakdown of the old Regime, 1770–1778', *French Historical Studies* (1970) and A. Cobban, 'The Parlements of France in the eighteenth century', *H.* (1950). On the influence of the philosophes, see H. Peyre, 'The influence of eighteenth century ideas on the French Revolution', *Journal of the History of Ideas* (1949) and R. S. Tate, 'Voltaire and the parlements', *Studies on Voltaire and the Eighteenth Century* (1972).

For the immediate events leading up to the revolution, see A. Goodwin, 'Calonne, the assembly of French notables of 1787 and the origins of the Révolte nobilaire', *E.H.R.* (1946).

3.   The French Revolution

There are many and varied interpretations of the French Revolution.
Almost all, however, confront certain basic issues, such as why it proved
impossible to create a stable constitutional monarchy after 1789, the
nature and character of the Jacobin 'Terror', and the establishment of a
more moderate government after the fall of Robespierre. As well as the
continuing debate on the interpretation of the revolution and its
personalities, there has been a considerable widening of the literature to
examine the social context of the revolution with analyses of the 'crowd'
and of social groups such as artisans and women. A good deal of
research in recent years has been devoted to the French Revolution as
experienced in the provinces. This provides some useful perspectives on
the extent to which change or continuity were the most significant
aspects of the French Revolution.

Essay topics

Why was France unable to evolve a stable system of constitutional
monarchy in the period 1789 to 1793?
    What was the significance of the Terror?
    To what extent should the French Revolution be seen as an essentially
Parisian phenomenon?

Sources and documents

Several collections of documents are available; see J. Hardman, *The
French Revolution: the Fall of the Ancien Regime to the Thermidorian
Reaction, 1785–1795* (1981), a one volume set; R. C. Cobb, J. Hardman,
and J. M. Roberts, *French Revolution Documents* (1966–73);
D. G. Wright, *Revolution and Terror in France, 1789–1795* (1974);
P. H. Beik, *The French Revolution: selected documents* (1970); and J. Hall
Stewart, *A Documentary Survey of the French Revolution* (1951).

Secondary works

For an outline, see A. Cobban, *A History of Modern France I, 1715–1799*
(rev. edn, 1965). The most comprehensive work is G. Lefebvre, *The
French Revolution: From its Origins to 1793* (1962) and *The French
Revolution: from 1793 to 1799* (1964). For another French scholar
working in the Marxist tradition see A. Soboul, *The French Revolution,
1787–1799* (1974). J. M. Thompson, *The French Revolution* (1944) is now
rather dated but still valuable, as is the lucid brief account by
A. Goodwin, *The French Revolution* (1953). More recent are
M. J. Sydenham, *The French Revolution* (1965), and *The First French
Republic, 1792–1804* (1974) and D. M. G. Sutherland, *France, 1789–1815:
Revolution and Counter Revolution* (1985). N. Hampson, *A Social History
of the French Revolution* (1963) gives particular prominence to social
factors rather than the conventional political narrative. Recent additions
in English translation are M. Vovelle, *The Fall of the French Monarchy,*

1787–1792 (1984); M. Bouloiseau, *The Jacobin Republic, 1792–1794* (1983), and D. Woronoff, *The Thermidorean Regime and the Directory, 1794–1799* (1984).

For a major attack on the Marxist interpretation of the French Revolution, see A. Cobban, *The Social Interpretation of the French Revolution* (1964); see also his *Aspects of the French Revolution* (1968), especially the essay 'Myth of the French Revolution'. A more recent and wide-ranging survey of the field is J. M. Roberts, *The French Revolution* (1978). See also G. Rudé, *Interpretations of the French Revolution* (1961) and J. McManners, 'The historiography of the French Revolution', in Volume VIII of the *The New Cambridge Modern History* (1957–9).

The personalities involved in the revolution can be examined through R. R. Palmer, *Twelve who Ruled* (1941), M. J. Sydenham, *The Girondins* (1961), and J. M. Thompson, *Leaders of the French Revolution* (1929). On Robespierre, see J. M. Thompson, *Robespierre* (1939) and N. Hampson, *The Life and Opinions of Maximilien Robespierre* (1974). On other figures see L. Gottschalk's, *Jean Paul Marat: a study in radicalism* (1967), L. Gershoy, *Bertrand Barere, A Reluctant Terrorist* (1962); R. B. Rose, *Gracchus Babeuf* (1978); L. Gottschalk and M. Maddox, *Lafayette in the French Revolution, through the October Days* (1969) and *Lafayette in the French Revolution, from the October Days through the Federation* (1973). See also E. N. Curtis, *Saint Just, Colleague of Robespierre* (1935), O. J. G. Welch, *Mirabeau* (1951), and J. H. Clapham, *The Abbe Sieyès* (1912).

On the role of Paris see G. Rudé, *The Crowd in the French Revolution* (1959) and *Paris and London in the Eighteenth Century: Studies in Popular Protest* (1970). J. Godechot, *The Taking of the Bastille* (1970) also looks at Paris. A. Soboul, *The Parisian Sans-Culottes and the French Revolution, 1793–4* (1964) deals with a significant group, as does G. A. Williams, *Artisans and Sans-culottes* (1968). The wider perspective is offered by R. Cobb, *Paris and its Provinces* (1975). For regional studies, see W. Scott, *Terror and Repression in Revolutionary Marseilles* (1973), C. Lucas, *The Structure of the Terror: the example of Javogues and the Loire* (1973), C. Tilly, *The Vendée* (1964), A. Forrest, *Society and Politics in Revolutionary Bordeaux* (1975), and C. Lewis and C. Lucas. *Beyond the Terror: Essays on French Regional and Social History, 1794–1815* (1984).

On particular themes, see R. Cobb, *The Police and the People: French Popular Protest 1789–1820* (1970), J. McManners, *The French Revolution and the Church* (1969) and S. G. Harris, *The Assignats* (1930). On the 'Terror' see N. Hampson, *The Terror in the French Revolution* (Historical Association pamphlet, 1981), D. Greer, *The Incidence of the Terror during the French Revolution* (1935) and *The Incidence of the Emigration during the French Revolution* (1951). For the transition to the latter 1790s, see I. Woloch, *Jacobin Legacy* (1970), M. Lyons, *France under the Directory* (1975), and C. H. Church, 'In search of the Directory', in *French Government and Society* (1973).

Articles

For general interpretations, see G. Ellis, 'The "Marxist Interpretation" of the French Revolution', *E.H.R.* (1978); G. C. Cavanaugh, 'The present state of French revolutionary historiography: Alfred Cobban and beyond', *French Historical Studies* (1972); and C. B. A. Behrens, 'Professor Cobban and his critics', *H.J.* (1966). On the experience of the revolution, see R. Cobb, 'The revolutionary mentality in France, 1793–4', *H.* (1957) and J. Le Goff and D. M. G. Sutherland, 'The Revolution and the rural community in eighteenth-century Brittany', *P.P.* (1974) and R. B. Rose, 'Tax revolt and popular organisation in Picardy, 1789–1791', *P.P.* (1969). For the later period see A. Goodwin, 'The French Executive Directory: a revaluation', *H.* (1937) and C. Lucas, 'The first Directory and the rule of law', *French Historical Studies* (1977). Also useful are C. H. Church, 'The social basis of the French Central Bureaucracy under the Directory', *P.P.* (1967) and R. Forster, 'The survival of the nobility during the French Revolution', *P.P.* (1967).

4. Napoleon

As one of the most titanic figures of modern European history, Napoleon can be looked at in a number of ways. How he came to achieve such power and how he held onto it is one line of enquiry. Another is the extent to which he exemplified or consolidated the revolutionary ideals of the 1790s. Some have even seen him as the last of the 'enlightened despots'. Considerably more information is now available about the regional and social history of France throughout the Revolutionary and Napoleonic periods and permits closer assessment of the impact of Napoleon on France. The European dimension of the Napoleonic Empire is discussed in the next topic.

Essay topics

What factors enabled Napoleon to become Emperor of France?
    Was Napoleon the last of the Enlightened Despots?
    Who lost and who gained from Napoleon's exercise of power in France?

Sources and documents

J. M. Thompson, *Napoleon's Letters* (1934) is an edited collection of his correspondence; see too C. Harold, *The Mind of Napoleon* (1959).

Secondary works

Many of the general histories of the French Revolution cited in the last topic carry their analyses up to and beyond the Napoleonic coup d'état. But for detailed assessment of both Napoleon and the Napoleonic era G. Lefebvre, *Napoleon* (1935) remains the essential starting point, but F. Markham, *Napoleon I* (1957) and *Napoleon and the Awakening of Europe* (1954) and J. M. Thompson, *Napoleon Bonaparte: His Rise and Fall* (1952) are all valuable. P. Geyl, *Napoleon, For and Against* (1949) is a stimulating comparison of views; see also the two chapters in his *Debates with Historians* (1962). More recent biographies include

V. Cronin, *Napoleon* (1971), J. Tulard, *Napoleon: the Myth of the Saviour* (1977) and C. Barnett, *Bonaparte* (1978).

On internal affairs in France under Napoleon, see I. Collins, *Napoleon and his Parliaments* (1979); G. Lewis and C. Lucas (eds), *Beyond the Terror: Essays on French Regional and Social History, 1794–1815* (1984); R. Cobb, *The Police and the People: French Popular Protest, 1789–1820* (1970). For relations with the Church see E. E. Y. Hales, *Revolution and the Papacy, 1769–1846* (1960) and *Napoleon and the Pope* (1972), as well as the older H. H. Welsh, *The Concordat of 1801* (1934). L. Bergeron, *France under Napoleon* (1972) is a recent study of French national life under Napoleon; see also M. Guerrini, *Napoleon and Paris* (1970). On the servants of the Napoleonic empire, see E. A. Whitcombe, *Napoleon's Diplomatic Service* (1979) and P. Young, *Napoleon's Marshals* (1972). On its leading personalities, see J. Orieux, *Talleyrand* (1974) and J. F. Bernard, *Talleyrand* (1977), H. Cole, *Fouché* (1971), and J. H. Clapham, *The Abbé Sieyès* (1912). The last phase of Napoleon's career is covered in B. Norman, *Napoleon and Talleyrand, the Last Two Weeks* (1977). See also N. I. Mackenzie, *The Escape from Elba* (1982).

Articles

R. Forster, 'The survival of the nobility during the French Revolution', *P.P.* (1967).

5.   The Revolutionary and Napoleonic Wars

The French Revolution developed into a large-scale European conflict which lasted almost a quarter of a century. Early attempts by the established powers to subvert and crush the revolution failed, whilst significant minorities in many European countries showed enthusiasm for the ideals of the French Revolution. French expansionism and the rise of Napoleon gradually alienated many who had once welcomed the Revolution and began to arouse strong patriotic and national feelings. The early years of the conflict are less well covered than the Napoleonic period. The nature and fate of Napoleon's bid for European mastery inevitably occupies a central place, but the effects of the struggle upon individual countries is a major aspect. Napoleon's military abilities and the changing nature of warfare are also important themes.

Essay topics

Why were the major European powers unable to defeat revolutionary France during the decade after 1789?

To what extent was Napoleon defeated by the same forces he claimed to represent?

To what extent did the conduct of warfare change in the course of the Revolutionary and Napoleonic Wars?

Sources and documents

J. M. Thompson, *Napoleon's Letters* (1934) are a useful insight into his actions and thoughts. For reference purposes, A. Palmer, *An*

Encyclopaedia of Napoleon's Europe (1984) is an extremely valuable guide to events and personalities; on military matters, see D. Chandler, *Dictionary of the Napoleonic Wars* (1979).

Secondary works

The general texts (see the introductory bibliography) provide the most accessible accounts of the general European situation in 1789 and the following decade. The elderly study by J. H. Clapham, *The Cause of the War of 1792* (Cambridge, 1899) has now been superceded by T. C. W. Blanning, *The Origins of the French Revolutionary Wars* (London, 1986), discussing both the causes and impact of the wars of the 1790s. On the survival of the Republic see J. M. Roberts, *The French Revolution* (1978), ch. 3 for a recent overview; also H. Mitchell, *The Underground War against Revolutionary France* (1965) and W. R. Fryer, *Republic or Restoration in France, 1794–7* (1965). On the Napoleonic empire, F. H. M. Markham, *Napoleon and the Awakening of Europe* (1954) remains standard; see too O. Connelly, *Napoleon's Satellite Kingdoms* (1965).

As far as individual countries are concerned; for Britain, see H. T. Dickinson, *British Radicalism and the French Revolution, 1789–1815* (1985); C. Emsley, *British Society and the French Wars, 1792–1815* (1979); A. Goodwin, *The Friends of Liberty* (1979); E. P. Thompson, *The Making of the English Working Class* (rev. edn, 1968) and G. A. Williams, *Artisans and Sans Culottes* (1968). The Irish connection with revolutionary France has received definitive treatment in M. Elliott, *Partners in Revolution: the United Irishmen and France* (1982).

For Germany, T. C. W. Blanning, *The French Revolution in Germany: Occupation and Resistance in the Rhineland, 1792–1802* (1983) is a recent work dealing with the sections of Germany; see also O. Connelly, *Napoleon's Satellite Kingdoms* (1965) (on Westphalia). G. S. Ford, *Stein and the Era of Reform in Prussia, 1807–15* (1922) remains the authoritative account, while the old H. A. L. Fisher, *Studies in Napoleonic Statesmanship: Germany* (1903) still has its uses. The relevant chapters of G. A. Craig, *The Politics of the Prussian Army, 1648–1948* (1955) are a very succinct view of the military and political reforms brought about by the defeats at Jena and Auerstadt.

For Austria–Hungary: the opening sections of C. A. Macartney, *Habsburg Empire, 1790–1918* (1969) are a good introduction, but see too the important E. Wangermann, *From Joseph II to the Jacobin Trials* (1959) and the latter section of his *The Austrian Achievement, 1700–1800* (1973), as well as the older W. C. Langsam, *Napoleonic Wars and German Nationalism in Austria* (1930); for Hungary, see C. A. Macartney, *Hungary* (1934) and B. M. Kiraly, *Hungary in the late eighteenth century* (1969). See also E. M. Link, *The Emancipation of the Austrian Peasant, 1740–1798* (1949).

For the Low Countries: Simon Schama, *Patriots and Liberators: revolution in The Netherlands, 1780–1830* (1977) is now the standard work, replacing the massive older P. J. Blok, *History of the People of the Netherlands* (1898–1912); see also E. H. Kossman, *The Low Countries, 1780–1940* (1978) and his 'The crisis of the Dutch State, 1780–1813: nationalism, federalism, uniystidm' in J. S. Bromley and E. H. Kossman (eds), *Britain and the Netherlands, IV* (1971). See also A. C. Carter, *Neutrality or Commitment: the Evolution of Dutch Foreign Policy* (1975).

For Italy, H. Hearder, *Italy in the Age of the Risorgimento, 1790–1870* (1983) is a modern overview; there is also J. Rath, *The Fall of the Napoleonic Kingdom of Italy* (1941) and the old R. M. Johnston, *The Napoleonic Empire in Southern Italy and the Rise of Secret Societies* (1904). O'Connelly, *Napoleon's Satellite Kingdoms* (1965) is also relevant. H. Cole, *The Betrayers* (1972) has material on the end of the Kingdom of Naples, while E. E. Y. Hales, *Napoleon and the Pope* (1962) details the relationship of Napoleon with Pius VII.

For Spain, R. Herr, *The Eighteenth Century Revolution in Spain* (1958) provides the background to Spanish development and for the later period of Napoleonic Spain, R. Carr, *Spain, 1808–1939* (1975) is the standard work. G. H. Lovett, *Napoleon and the Birth of Modern Spain* (1965) is important, but see too O'Connelly, *Napoleon's Satellite Kingdoms* (1965).

For Russia, see the relevant chapters of B. Pares, *A History of Russia* (1955), the early section of H. Seton-Watson, *The Russian Empire, 1801–1917* (1967) and the latter parts of M. Raeff, *Imperial Russia, 1682–1825* (1971). On Alexander I, see A. Palmer, *Alexander I, Tsar of War and Peace* (1974) and A. McConnell, *Alexander I* (1970). On diplomatic relations between France and Russia, see H. A. Ragsdale, *Detente in the Napoleonic Era; Bonaparte and the Russians* (1980). For Poland, see *The Cambridge History of Poland, 1697–1935* (1941), N. Davies, *God's Playground: A History of Poland, vol. 1* (1981) and B. Grochulska, 'The place of the Enlightenment in Polish social history', in J. K. Fedorowicz, *A Republic of Nobles: Studies in Polish History to 1864* (1982).

On Napoleon's continental system see E. F. Heckcher, *The Continental System: an economic interpretation* (1922) and the important article by Crouzet listed below. G. Ellis, *Napoleon's Continental Blockade* (1981) is an important recent study focusing on the effects of the system on Alsace. The wider effects upon the continent are considered in W. O. Henderson, *The Industrialisation of Europe, 1780–1914* (1969), R. E. Cameron, *France and the Economic Development of Europe 1800–1914* (1961) and A. S. Milward and S. B. Saul, *The Economic Development of Continental Europe, vol. i* (1973). The effects of the system on Britain are discussed in Emsley, above, and W. F. Galpin, *The Grain Supply of England during the Napoleonic Wars* (1925).

There is a vast literature on the military aspects of the Napoleonic period. Serious studies of the development of warfare are G. Best, *War and Society in Revolutionary Europe, 1770–1870* (1982), G. Rothenberg, *The Art of Warfare in the Age of Napoleon* (1977) and D. Chandler, *The Campaigns of Napoleon* (1966). See also J. Marshall-Cornwall, *Napoleon as Military Commander* (1967) and H. C. B. Rogers, *Napoleon's Army* (1974).

The naval war against Napoleon by Britain is discussed comprehensively in G. J. Marcus, *A Naval History of England*, 2 (1971); see also the classic Admiral Mahan, *The Influence of Sea Power upon the French Revolution and Empire* (1882) and P. Mackesy, 'Problems of an amphibious power: Britain against France, 1793–1815', *Naval War College Review* (1978). Britain's vital role in maintaining the wars by financial aid is discussed in J. M. Sherwig, *Guineas and Gunpowder: British Foreign Aid in the Wars with France, 1793–1815* (1969) and

K. F. Helleiner, *The Imperial Loans, A Study in Financial and Diplomatic History* (1969).

Articles

R. R. Palmer, 'Much in little: the Dutch revolution of 1795', *J.M.H.* (1954) examines one particular context of revolutionary influence; for others, see P. F. Sugar, 'The influence of the Enlightenment and the French Revolution in eighteenth century Hungary', *Journal of Central European Affairs* (1958) and P. Body, 'The Hungarian Jacobin conspiracy of 1794–5', *Journal of Central European Affairs* (1962). On Russia, see H. A. Ragsdale, 'A continental system in 1801; Paul I and Bonaparte', *J.M.H.* (1970), and, on the continental system, F. Crouzet, 'Wars, blockades, and economic change in Europe, 1792–1815', *J.M.H.* (1964).

6.   The Congress of Vienna and the Congress system

The peace settlement at the end of the Napoleonic Wars represents one of the major arbitrations of European affairs in the modern period. The aims and objectives of the peacemakers and how they were fulfilled is an important theme. Traditionally, the peacemakers are condemned for failing to give sufficient weight to the forces of nationalism and liberalism, which produced major revisions of the settlement in the course of the nineteenth century, while still in some respects remaining the framework of European international relations until the First World War.

Essay topics

What was attempted and on what principles by the framers of the peace treaties of 1814 and 1815?
    'The strange thing is, not that the Congress System was finally abandoned, but that it and its work lasted for so long.' Discuss.
    What were Metternich's objectives?

Sources and documents

On one particular development, see R. Clogg (ed.), *The Movement for Greek Independence, 1770–1821* (1976).

Secondary works

C. K. Webster, *The Congress of Vienna* (1934) and *The European Alliance, 1815–1825* (1929) are good starting points. H. Kissinger, *A World Restored: Metternich, Castlereagh and the Problems of Peace, 1815–22* (1957) is more recent. The workings of the Congress are discussed in H. Nicolson, *The Congress of Vienna* (1946) while a longer-term perspective is offered by E. V. Gulick, *Europe's Classical Balance of Power* (1955), L .C .B. Seaman, *From Vienna to Versailles* (1955),

H. G. Schenk, *The Aftermath of the Napoleonic Wars* (1947), and
F. R. Bridge and R. Bullen, *The Great Powers and the European States System, 1815–1914* (1981).

For the personalities involved, see C. K. Webster, *The Foreign Policy of Castlereagh, 1815–22* (1925); G. Ferraro, *Talleyrand and the Congress of Vienna* (1941), G. Mann, *Secretary of Europe: the life of Friedrich Gentz* (1946). On Metternich see A. Herman, *Metternich* (1932), A. Cecil, *Metternich, 1773–1859* (1947), Constantin de Grunwald, *Metternich* (1953), A. Palmer, *Metternich* (1972) and the older, standard biography, H. von Srbik, *Metternich* (1921–6), and, on Alexander I, A. Palmer, *Alexander I* (1974).

Detailed studies of individual crises can be found in R. Carr, *Spain, 1808–1939* (1975) for the Spanish Revolution of 1820–2; E. H. Kossmann, *The Low Countries, 1780–1940* (1978), for the Belgian crisis of 1830 and H. Hearder, *Italy in the Age of the Risorgimento, 1790–1870* (1983) for Italian revolts in the period.

Poland has attracted much attention; see the well-established *The Cambridge History of Poland, 1697–1935* (1941), H. Frankel, *Poland, the Struggle for Power, 1772–1939* (1946) and O. Halecki, *The History of Poland* (1942). More recent are P. S. Wandyck, *The Lands of Partitioned Poland, 1795–1910* (1975), R. F. Leslie, *Polish Politics and the Revolution of November 1830* (1956), and N. Davies, *God's Playground*, Vol. 2 (1981). J. A. Betley, *Belgium and Poland in International Relations, 1830–1* (1960) links up the two crises of those years. Austro–German relations are discussed in P. J. Katzenstein, *Disjoined Partners: Austria and Germany since 1815* (1976). For Greece, see the old C. W. Crawley, *The Question of Greek Independence, 1821–33* (1930) and D. Dakin, *The Greek Struggle for Independence, 1821–33* (1973).

Articles

On Metternich see R. W. Seton-Watson, 'Metternich and Internal Austrian Policy', *S.R.* (1939), P. Viereck, 'New views on Metternich', *Review of Politics* (1951), and R. A. Kann, 'Metternich: a reappraisal of his impact on international relations', *J.M.H.* (1960).

On Poland see R. F. Leslie, 'Politics and economics in Congress Poland, 1815–64', *P.P.* (1955); on the Balkans, G. H. Bolsover, 'Nicholas I and the partition of Turkey', *The Slavonic and East European Review* (1948).

7.   France, 1815–51

The Restored Monarchy in France proved a more successful regime in the short term than might have been expected. But the divisions which remained from the revolutionary era and were to develop during the post-1815 period produced an unstable and difficult political situation. The accession of Charles X and his more reactionary policies provoked the revolution of 1830. A change of dynasty led to another period of seeming calm, only to be shattered by the revolutions of 1848. The nature of France's 'instability' and the role of the various political groupings within it raise important questions, particularly as France can be regarded as being in the forefront of many political developments.

The underlying conservatism of the middle classes and the peasantry serve as a contrast to the ferment of ideas and the critical role of Paris in revolutionary politics. For France in 1848, see the topic bibliography on 1848.

Essay topics

Was the restoration of the Bourbon monarchy doomed to failure?
Who benefited from the French Revolution of 1830?
Has the instability of France between 1815 and 1848 been exaggerated?

Sources and documents

Reactionary thought can be sampled in the writings of de Maistre in J. S. McClelland (ed.), *The French Right: from de Maistre to Maurras* (1970). A. de Tocqueville, *Recollections* (London edn, 1970) presents a compelling view of France in 1848 and on the last phase of this period see also R. Price, *1848 in France* (1975).

Secondary works

A. Cobban, *A History of Modern France, vol. II* (1962–5) remains a very useful introduction, but the more modern and detailed study is I. Collins (ed.), *Government and Society in France, 1814–1848* (1970). An even more recent contribution is A. Jardin and A. J. Tudesq, *Restoration and Reaction, 1815–1848* (1984). M. R. D. Leys, *Between Two Empires* (1955) remains useful, as does B. de Sauvigny, *The Bourbon Restoration* (1955) and F. B. Artz, *France under the Bourbon Restoration* (1931). On the ferment of ideas in post-revolutionary France, see R. H. Soltau, *French Political Thought in the Nineteenth Century* (1931), J. P. Mayer, *Political Thought in France from the Revolution to the Fourth Republic* (1949) and J. Plamenatz, *The Revolutionary Movement in France, 1815–1871* (1952). On particular institutions, see D. Porch, *Army and Revolution: France, 1815–48* (1974) and C. H. Church, *Revolution and Red Tape: the French Ministerial Bureaucracy, 1770–1850* (1983). For 1830 see D. Pinkney, *The French Revolution of 1830* (1973) and on popular disorder in general C. Tilly, L. Tilly and R. Tilly, *The Rebellious Century* (1975).

Economic changes are discussed in W. O. Henderson, *The Industrialisation of Europe, 1780–1914* (1969), R. C. Cameron, *France and the Economic Development of Europe* (1961), A. S. Milward and S. B. Saul, *The Economic Development of Continental Europe* (1973), and R. Price, *The Economic Development of France* (1975).

On 1848 in France, see the commentary in R. Price, cited above, and his *The Second French Republic* (1972); also P. N. Stearns, *The Revolutions of 1848* (1974).

Articles

On post-Restoration conditions see D. Higgs, 'Politics and landownership

among the French nobility after the Revolution', *European Studies
Review* (1971), N. G. Hudson, 'The circulation of the Ultra-Royalist press
under the French Restoration', *E. H. R.* (1974) and L. O'Boyle, 'The
problem of an excess of educated men in Western Europe, 1800–1850',
J. M. H. (1970). On the 1830 revolution see R. D. Price, 'The French army
and the Revolution of 1830', *European Studies Review* (1973),
D. H. Pinkney, 'The crowd in the French Revolution of 1830', *American
Historical Review* (1964), E. L. Newman, 'The blouse and the frock coat',
J. M. H. (1974) and R. D. Price, 'Legitimist opposition to the Revolution of
1830 in the French provinces', *H. J.* (1974). For the fall of the Orléanist
monarchy, see P. L. R. Higonnet and T. B. Higonnet, 'Class corruption
and politics in the French Chamber of Deputies, 1846–48', *French
Historical Studies* (1967), G. Fasel, 'Urban workers in provincial France,
February–June 1848', *I. R. S.H.* (1972) and 'The wrong revolution: French
Republicanism in 1848', *French Historical Studies* (1974).

8.   Russia, 1801–1856

The French Revolution and the death of Catherine the Great marked a
new era in Russian history. The troubled reign of Paul I was followed by
the accession of Alexander I, a Tsar whose contradictions have
fascinated historians. Ostensibly liberal, he led Russia through the
Napoleonic conflict and earned her a major place as an arbiter of
European politics.

His increasing conservatism, however, combined with the rise of an
intelligentsia and the continuing backwardness of Russian society,
produced conflict. The 'Decembrist' Revolt of 1825 marked the beginning
of a long campaign against autocracy by intellectuals and others. The
reign of Nicholas I marked an attempt to entrench Russia's own
distinctive conservatism against the intellectual and social currents
which were at work in the rest of Europe. The exposure of Russia's
weaknesses in the Crimean War and the death of Nicholas I set the scene
for new developments under Alexander II.

Essay topics

Why did Alexander I fail to liberalise Russia?
What was the significance of the Decembrist revolt for the
development of a revolutionary movement in Russia?
Did Nicholas I bequeath more problems to Russia than he inherited?

Sources and documents

See A. Herzen, *My Past and Thoughts; the Memoirs of Alexander Herzen*
(6 vols, 1924–8). In a great age of Russian literature, M. Lermentov, *A
Hero of our Times* (1840) and N. Gogol's *The Government Inspector*
(1836) and *Dead Souls* (1842) give something of the flavour of the period.

Secondary sources

Consult the general histories by B. Pares, *A History of Russia* (3rd edn,

1955) and H. Seton-Watson, *The Russian Empire, 1801–1917* (1967). The more thematic treatments by B. H. Sumner, *A Survey of Russian History* (1948) and R. Pipes, *Russia under the Old Regime* (1974) are also important.

For Alexander I, see A. Palmer, *Alexander I, Tsar of War and Peace* (1974); N. K. Schilder, *Emperor Alexander I* (1904); and A. McConnell, *Tsar Alexander I* (1970). M. Raeff, *M. Speransky: Statesman of Imperial Russia, 1772–1839* (1957) deals with one of the most important figures of the period, while S. Monas, *The Third Section: Police and Society in Russia under Alexander I* (1961) looks at the repressive side of the regime. For Nicholas I, see W. Bruce Lincoln, *Nicholas I* (1978).

On the serf question see J. Blum, *Lord and Peasant in Imperial Russia* (1961) and G. T. Robinson, *Rural Russia under the Old Regime* (1932).

For the opposition to the autocracy, see A. G. Mazour, *The First Russian Revolution, 1825* (1937), M. Zetlin, *The Decembrists* (1958) and M. Raeff, *The Decembrist Movement* (1966). For a wider perspective, see F. Venturi, *Roots of Revolution* (1960), J. Walkin, *The Rise of Democracy in Pre-revolutionary Russia* (1963) and M. Raeff, *The Growth of the Russian Intelligentsia* (1966). E. H. Carr, *The Romantic Exiles* (new ed, London, 1949) describes various revolutionaries in exile. On individuals, see E. H. Carr, *Michael Bakunin* (1937) and E. Acton, *Alexander Herzen and the Role of the Intellectual Revolutionary* (1979).

Russia's involvement with other nationalities is discussed in P. S. Wandycz, *The Lands of Partitioned Poland, 1793–1910* (1974) and there is useful material in R. Pearson, *National Minorities in Eastern Europe, 1848–1944* (1983). Foreign policy is examined in G. H. Bolsover, 'Aspects of Russian policy, 1815–1914', in R. Pares and A. J. P. Taylor (eds), *Essays Presented to Sir Lewis Namier* (1956).

Articles

G. Vernadsky, 'Alexander I's reforms', *Review of Politics* (1947), W. M. Pinter, 'The social characteristics of the early nineteenth century Russian bureaucracy', *S. R.* (1970) and R. Pipes, 'The Russian military colonies 1810–31', *J. M. H.* (1950).

9. Liberalism, nationalism and socialism in the nineteenth century

Many of the political developments of the nineteenth century are only comprehensible in terms of the ferment of ideas released by the French Revolution and the Napoleonic struggle. Generally, these are best comprehended in terms of the three main themes of liberalism, nationalism, and socialism which were often simultaneously represented in some of the great upheavals of the period. The relative importance of the different forces and the way in which they inter-related and developed during the nineteenth century and into the twentieth centuries require examination. Liberalism and nationalism are not easy to define with precision whilst socialist, including communist, ideas took many different forms.

Essay topics

Assess the strength of liberalism and nationalism in Europe by 1848.
Had liberalism or nationalism proved the stronger force in Europe by 1900?
To what extent did socialism represent a coherent body of principles and practice by 1900?

Sources and documents

The major texts of the principal intellectual figures should obviously play an important part. For liberalism see J. Stuart Mill, *On Liberty* (1859); A. de Tocqueville, *Democracy in America* (1835), F. Guizot, *On Democracy in France* (1849) and H. S. Reiss, *Political Thought of the German Romantics* (1955). Also useful are the readings in E. K. Bramsted and K. J. Melhuish, *Western Liberalism: A History in Documents from Locke to Croce* (1978).

For different socialist movements see R. Owen, *Report to the County of Lanark* (1817); K. Marx and F. Engels, *The Communist Manifesto* (1848) and P.A. Kropotkin, *Fields, Factories, Workshops* (1899).

Secondary works

Of the general works E. J. Hobsbawm, *The Age of Revolution, 1789–1848* (1962) gives considerable space to the intellectual movements. See also J. Bowle, *Politics and Opinion in the Nineteenth Century* (1954).

On liberalism, there is a useful short introduction in I. Collins, *Liberalism in Nineteenth Century Europe* (Historical Association pamphlet, 1971) and see her *Revolutionaries in Europe, 1815–48* (Historical Association pamphlet, 1974). The older H. J. Laski, *The Rise of European Liberalism*, (2nd edn, London, 1947) and Guido de Ruggiero, *The History of European Liberalism* (translated, 1927) can now be supplemented by J. J. Sheehan, *German Liberalism in the Nineteenth Century* (1982), a useful case study. Particular studies of relevance are J. Plamenatz, *The Revolutionary Movement in France, 1813–71* (1952), M. Raeff, *The Rise of the Russian Intelligentsia* (1966) and Sir Lewis Namier, *1848: The Revolution of the Intellectuals* (1944).

On nationalism see E. Gellner, *Nations and Nationalism* (1983), C. J. Hayes, *Nationalism* (1966), E. Kedourie, *Nationalism* (1960) and H. Kohn, *Nationalism: its meaning and history* (1971). Liberalism's relationship with nationalism is discussed in one context in R. Hinton Thomas, *Liberalism, Nationalism, and the German Intellectuals, 1822–47* (1952). On Eastern European nationalism see P. Sugar and I. Lederer, *Nationalism in Eastern Europe* (1969), R. Pearson, *National Minorities in Eastern Europe, 1848–1944* (1983) and R. F. Leslie, *Polish Politics and the Revolution of 1830* (1974).

On the socialist movements in general see G. D. H. Cole, *A History of Socialist Thought* (1953–60), D. McClelland, *Marx* (1974), G. Woodcock, *Anarchism* (1963) and J. Joll, *The Anarchists* (1969). On labour movements, see H. Pelling, *A History of British Trade Unionism* (rev. edn, 1986) and H. Grebing, *A History of the German Labour Movement* (1969).

10.   The Revolutions of 1848

1848 was a year of widespread protest, rebellion and revolution in
Europe, probably more widespread than at any time in the modern
period. The varying causes of these revolts, economic, social, political
and intellectual need to be considered. The causes and background to
the unrest in the different parts of Europe form one major theme, as well
as the actual course of events. The reasons why the revolts largely failed
in the short-term and their contribution to later events form another. The
revolutions can be studied as a whole or through the experience of
individual countries.

Essay topics

Why was 1848 a year of revolutions in Europe?
   To what extent could the events of 1848 be described as a 'revolution
of the intellectuals'?
   Did the revolutions of 1848 fail?

Documents and sources

On events in France over the period 1848–51, see R. Price (ed.), *1848 in
France* (1975) for a wide selection of documents. Also invaluable is A. de
Tocqueville's *Recollections* (translated edn, 1970). For a short general
collection see P. Jones, *1848 Revolutions* (1982).

Secondary works

For the broad context of the revolutions of 1848 it is wise to consult the
general texts cited in the introduction; see especially I. Collins, *The Age
of Progress 1789–1870* (1964), E. J. Hobsbawm, *The Age of Revolution,
1789–1848* (1962) and J. Roberts, *Revolution and Improvement* (1976).
   General histories of the revolts include P. N. Stearns, *The Revolutions
of 1848* (1974), J. Sigmann, *1848, the Romantic and Democratic
Revolutions in Europe* (1973), F. Fejto, *The Opening of an Era: 1848*
(1948), P. Robertson, *Revolution of 1848: A Social History* (1952), A.
Whitridge, *Men in Crisis: the Revolutions of 1848* (1949), and L. B.
Namier, *1848: the Revolution of the Intellectuals* (1944).
   On the background to the revolts see I. Collins, *Revolutionaries in
Europe, 1815–48* (Historical Association, 1974), C. Morazé, *The Triumph
of the Middle Classes* (1968), J. Plamenatz, *The Revolutionary Movement
in France, 1815–71* (1952), R. Hinton Thomas, *Liberalism, Nationalism
and the German Intellectuals, 1822–47* (1952) and E. Kamenka and F. B.
Smith (ed.), *Intellectuals and Revolution* (1979). C. Tilly, L. Tilly and R.
Tilly, *The Rebellious Century, 1830–1930* (1975) is an attempt to trace the
pattern of collective violence in France, Germany and Italy in this period.
   For the events of the revolutions see the main national histories for
France, notably A. Cobban, *A History of Modern France* (Vol. II, 1962–5)
and A. Jardin and A. J. Tundesq, *Restoration and Reaction, 1815–1848*
(1984) and M. Agulhon, *The Republican Experiment, 1848–1852* (1983);

also R. Price, *The Second French Republic* (1972) and G. Rudé, *The Crowd in History* (1964), ch. 11. For Germany, see W. Carr, *A History of Germany, 1815–1945* (rev. edn, 1979), L. B. Namier (1944, above), E. Eyck, *The Frankfurt Parliament 1848–1849* (1968), V. Valentin, *1848: Chapters in German History* (1940), P. Noyes, *Organisations and Revolt* (1966), H. Grebing, *History of the German Labour Movement* (1969) and J. Kucynski, *A Short History of Labour Conditions, 1800–1945* (1942–6). On Austria–Hungary, see R. A. Kann, *The Multi-National Empire: Nationalism and National Reform in the Habsburg Monarchy, 1848–1918* (1950), C. A. Macartney, *Hungary* (1934), J. Blum, *Noble Landowners and Agriculture in Austria, 1815–1848* (1948), R. J. Rath, *The Viennese Revolution of 1848* (1969), P. J. Katzenstein, *Disjoined Partners: Austria and Germany since 1815* (1976) and A. Sked, *The survival of the Habsburg Empire: Radetsky, the imperial army and the class war, 1848* (1979), and I. Deak, *The Lawful Revolution: Kossuth and the Hungarian Revolution 1848–49* (1979). On Italy, see D. Mack Smith, *The Making of Italy, 1796–1866* (1969) and the more recent H. Hearder, *Italy in the Age of the Risorgimento, 1790–1870* (1983). The older G. F. H. Berkeley and J. Berkeley, *Italy in the Making, 1846–1848* (1936) and *Italy in the Making, 1848* (1940) are still useful, but see also A. Sked (above), and P. Ginsborg, *Daniele Manin and the Venetian Revolution of 1848–9* (1979).

For the survival of the European order after 1848, see W. E. Mosse, *Liberal Europe: the age of bourgeois realism, 1848–75* (1974), E. J. Hobsbawm, *The Age of Capital, 1848–75* (1975) and J. Blum, *The End of the Old Order in Rural Europe* (1978).

Articles

For central Europe see C. A. Macartney, '1848 in the Habsburg Monarchy', *European Studies Review* (1977) and R. J. Rath, 'Public opinion during the Viennese Revolution of 1848', *Journal of Central European Affairs* (1948–9). On Italy, see P. Ginsborg, 'Peasants and revolutionaries in Venice and the Veneto, 1848', *H. J.* (1974), L. Jennings, 'Lamartine's Italian policy in 1848', *J. M. H.* (1970) and R. J. Rath, 'The Carbonari: their origins, initiation rites and aims', *A. H. R.* (1964).

11.   The economic development of Europe, 1760–1914

As with the intellectual developments examined earlier, much of European history in this period can only be understood against the background of the development of agriculture, commerce and industry from the late eighteenth century. The reasons why some countries enjoyed economic advance while others stagnated is an important question, often focussed around the issue of why other countries were not able to industrialise at the same time as Britain. Such questions imply a knowledge of how economic growth and industrialisation occur, by no means a matter of agreement amongst economic historians (see Kemp, below). Some knowledge of the experience of Great Britain is inevitably useful in this context as the yardstick by which other economies are measured, though Britain's particular version of economic growth should not be allowed to dominate analysis of why, how, and in what forms, economic development occurred. The character of industrial development in continental Europe by 1914 and its social and political repercussions is another aspect to be explored.

Essay topics

'For most Europeans in the century after 1760 by far the most important economic developments lay in trade and agriculture.' Discuss.

Why was Great Britain able to become the leading industrial power in Europe by 1850?

Who had gained and who had lost by the industrial development of Europe by 1914?

Sources and documents

There are useful documents in S. Pollard and C. Holmes (eds) *Documents of European Economic History* (3 vols, 1968–73) and B. Supple, *The Experience of Economic Growth* (1963). Vital works for the spread of ideas about economic development see A. Smith, *The Wealth of Nations* (1776) and F. Engels, *The Condition of the English Working Class in 1844* (1892). Amidst a wealth of 'social' literature, see especially, E. Zola, *Germinal* (1885).

Secondary works

C. M. Cipolla (ed.), *The Fontana Economic History of Europe*, vols 3 and 4 (1973) offers a wide-ranging analysis of economic development both in individual countries and for European-wide themes. For the commercial development of the period see R. C. Davies, *The Rise of the Atlantic Economies* (1973) and P. Curtin, *The Atlantic Slave Trade (1969)*. For agriculture, see B. H. Slicher van Bath, *The Agrarian History of Western Europe* (1963) and M. Tracey, *Agriculture in Western Europe* (1964).

The industrialisation of Europe and the questions it raises are admirably discussed in T. Kemp, *Industrialisation in Nineteenth-century Europe* (1969), but see also A. Milward and S. B. Saul, *The Economic Development of Continental Europe, 1780–1870* (1973), C. Trebilcock, *The Industrialisation of the Continental Powers, 1780–1914* (1981), H. J. Habakkuk and M. Postan (eds), *The Cambridge Economic History of Europe, The Industrial Revolution and After, Vol. vi, pt. II* (1965), W. O. Henderson, *The Industrial Revolution on the Continent* (1961) and J. H. Clapham, *The Economic Development of France and Germany* (4th edn, 1936). The financial aspects of the industrial revolution are also considered in W. O. Henderson, *Britain and Industrial Europe, 1750–1870* (2nd edn, 1966), H. Feis, *Europe the World's Banker* (1930) and W. Ashworth, *A Short History of the International Economy since 1850* (1962).

On individual countries see for Great Britain as an introduction, R. M. Hartwell, *The Industrial Revolution in England* (Historical Association, rev. edn, 1966) and M. W. Flinn, *The Origins of the Industrial*

Revolution (1966). The standard modern works are P. Mathias, *The First Industrial Nation, an Economic History of Britain, 1700–1914* (1969) and P. Deane, *The First Industrial Revolution* (1965). The older treatments, P. Mantoux, *The Industrial Revolution in the Eighteenth Century* (1928) and T. S. Ashton, *The Industrial Revolution, 1760–1830* (1948) are also still valuable.

For France, see R. Price, *The Economic Modernisation of France* (1975) and J. H. Clapham (1936, above). The most useful comparison of France and England appears in P. Crouzet, 'England and France in the eighteenth century, a comparative analysis of two economic growths', in R. M. Hartwell (ed.), *The Causes of the Industrial Revolution in England* (1967). See also A. L. Dunham, *The Industrial Revolution in France, 1815–1848* (1955). For Germany, see Clapham (1936, above) and T. S. Hamerow, *Restoration, Revolution, Reaction* (1966).

For other countries, see M. Falkus, *The Industrialisation of Russia* (1972) and J. Blum, *Lord and Peasant in Imperial Russia* (1961), G. T. Robinson, *Rural Russia under the Old Regime* (1932) and R. Pipes, *Russia under the Old Regime* (1974). For southern Europe see S. B. Clough, *Economic History of Modern Italy* (1964), J. Vicens Vives, *Economic History of Spain* (1969), A. R. Oliveira, *Politics, Economics and Men of Modern Spain, 1808–1946* (1946) and C. la Force, *The Development of the Spanish Textile Industry, 1750–1850* (1965).

The broader consequences of industrialisation can be traced in E. J. Hobsbawm, *The Age of Revolution* (1962), C. Morazé, *The Triumph of the Middle Classes* (1966) and M. D. Biddiss. *The Age of the Masses* (1977). The survival of the old order is discussed in J. Blum, *The End of the Old Order in Rural Europe* (1978) and A. Mayer, *The Persistence of the Old Regime* (1981).

Urban and social consequences are discussed in A. Weber, *The Growth of Cities in the Nineteenth Century* (1899), H. J. Dyos and M. Wolff (eds), *The Victorian City: Images and Realities* (1973) and A. Briggs, *Victorian Cities* (1965) and L. Chevalier, *Labouring Classes and Dangerous Classes in Paris during the first half of the Nineteenth Century* (1973). For urban protest, see C. Tilly, L. Tilly and R. Tilly, *The Rebellious Century, 1830–1930* (1975) and G. Rudé, *The Crowd in History* (1964).

Articles

On French industrial performance see S. B. Clough, 'Retardative factors in French economic growth', *J. Econ. H.* (1949), R. C. Cameron, 'Economic growth and stagnation in France', *J. M. H.* (1958), and T. Kemp, 'Structural factors in the retardation of French economic growth', *Kylos (1962)*; for Belgium, see S. Clark, 'Nobility, bourgeoisie and the industrial revolution in Belgium', *P. P.* (1984) and on Russia, A. Baykov, 'The economic development of Russia', *Ec. H. R.* (1954–5) and H. J. Ellison, 'Economic modernisation in Imperial Russia', *J. Ec. H* (1965). For southern Europe see S. B. Clough and C. Livi, 'Economic growth in Italy', *J. Ec. H.* (1956).

12. The Risorgimento and Italian Unification

The Italian struggle for independence from foreign control and for a
united, liberal state was one of the major alterations to the settlement of
Europe reached in 1815. Failed revolts, principally in 1820 and 1848, did
eventually make way for the successful unification of Italy. The role of
the leading personalities and of the differing ideologies at work in the
movement have to be considered, as well as the reasons why unification
actually occurred when previous attempts had failed. The place of the
movement in contemporary European diplomacy must be considered, as
well as the weaknesses which the new Italian state inherited.

Essay topics

What was the Risorgimento?
 Why was Italian unification not achieved earlier?
 What weaknesses were inherited by united Italy?

Sources and documents

J. Mazzini, *Duties of Man* (1877) is an example of some of the forces at
work in Italy during this period; see too the documents in D. Beales, *The
Risorgimento and the Unification of Italy* (1982).

Secondary sources

There are good introductions to the subject in the opening section of
D. Beales, *The Risorgimento and the Unification of Italy* (1982),
S. J. Woolf, *The Italian Risorgimento* (1969) and A. Ramm, *The
Risorgimento* (Historical Association pamphlet, 1972). The standard
histories by D. Mack Smith, *Italy: a modern History* (1959) and *The
Making of Italy, 1796–1870* (1968) should be consulted; see too D. Mack
Smith, 'Italy', in the *New Cambridge Modern History*, vol. x (1960) and
R. Albrecht-Carrié, *Italy from Napoleon to Mussolini* (1950). A more
recent addition is H. Hearder, *Italy in the Age of the Risorgimento,
1790–1870* (1983). On the leading personalities, see D. Mack Smith,
Cavour and Garibaldi in 1860 (1954), *Garibaldi* (1957) and his *Victor
Emmanuel, Cavour and the Risorgimento* (1971). Older, but still useful
are A. J. Whyte, *The Early Life and Letters of Cavour, 1810–1848* (1925)
and *The Political Life and Letters of Cavour, 1848–1861* (1930).
G. M. Trevelyan's trilogy, *Garibaldi's Defence of the Roman Republic*
(1908), *Garibaldi and the Thousand* (1909), and *Garibaldi and the Making
of Italy* (1911) remain useful. There is a brief account of Cavour's career
in H. Hearder, *Cavour* (Historical Association pamphlet, 1972). For
Mazzini, see G. O. Griffith, *Mazzini, Prophet of Modern Europe* (1932),
G. Salvemini, *Mazzini* (1985), and E. E. Y. Hales, *Mazzini and the Secret
Societies* (1956). For the role of the church see E. E. Y. Hales, *Pio Nono*
(1954) and A. C. Jemolo, *Church and State in Italy, 1850–1950* (1960). R.
Grew, *A Sterner Plan for Italian Unity* (1963) examines the part played by
the liberal pressure group, the National Society.

The economic context is examined in L. Cafagna 'Italy, 1830–1914', in C. M. Cipolla (ed.), *The Fontana Economic History of Europe*, Vol. 4 (1973), S. B. Clough, *Economic History of Modern Italy* (1964) and the southern problem in G. Schacter, *The Italian South* (1965).

Articles

D. Mack Smith, 'Cavour's attitude to Garibaldi's expedition to Sicily', *C. H. J.* (1949), H. M. Smyth, 'The armistice of Novara: a legend of a liberal king', *J. M. H.* (1935) and R. Grew, 'How success spoiled the Risorgimento', *J. M. H.* (1962) are useful.

13.   France, 1848–71

The events of 1848 provoked a period of governmental instability in France in which a second French Republic was founded only to fall with the coup d'état of Louis Napoleon. Napoleon III's 'Second Empire' represents an enigmatic era in which initial dictatorship and repression gradually gave way to a more liberal regime. Napoleon's achievements, such as the rebuilding of Paris, his genuinely philanthropic impulses, and the glittering façade of Parisian society in this period, were overshadowed by disasters abroad, as in Mexico, internal disagreement about the status and legitimacy of the regime, and humiliating defeat by Prussia. Whether Napoleon's regime could have transformed itself into a constitutional monarchy had the Franco–Prussian war not intervened and how far the Commune was a representative verdict on the epoch are frequent questions. In spite of a commonly perceived chronic political instability, French society and administration had many strengths, paving the way for the era of the Third Republic.

Essay topics

Was the Second French Republic doomed to failure?
   Could the Liberal Empire have succeeded in uniting France under Napoleon III?

Sources and documents

For 1848 and its aftermath see R. Price, *1848 in France* (1975). S. Osgood, *Napoleon III and the Second Empire* (1973) is also useful. For some contemporary comment see W. Bagehot, 'Letters on the French coup d'état of 1851' and 'Caesarism as it existed in 1865', in *Collected Letters and Essays* (1971)

Secondary works

The standard histories such as A. Cobban, *History of Modern France*, Vol. 2 (1965) and J. P. T. Bury, *France, 1815–1940* (1949) give reasonably balanced coverage. R. Price, *The Second French Republic* (1972) and

M. Agulhon, *The Republican Experiment 1848–1852* (1983) deal with the confused events following the 1848 revolution. An addition to the coverage of the period that followed is A. Plessis, *The Rise and Fall of the Second Empire, 1852–1871* (1985). On a more specific theme, see D. McKay, *The National Workshops* (1933). Napoleon's rise to power is examined in great detail in F. A. Simpson, *The Rise of Louis Napoleon* (1909) and *Louis Napoleon and the Recovery of France, 1848–56* (1923). Also still valuable is J. M. Thompson, *Louis Napoleon and the Second Empire* (1954) and H. A. L. Fisher, *Bonapartism* (1908). T. Zeldin, *The Political System of Napoleon III* (1958) is an invaluable insight into political life under Louis Napoleon, while his *Emile Ollivier and the Liberal Empire* (1963) deals with the latter part of his reign.
T. A. B. Corley, *Democratic Despot* (1961) is a useful biography. On the political undercurrents in French society, see J. Plamenatz, *The Revolutionary Movement in France, 1815–1871* (1952), J.P. Mayer, *Political Thought in France from the Revolution to the Fourth Republic* (1949) and R. H. Soltau, *French Political Thought in the Nineteenth Century* (1931). On Napoleon's foreign policy, see A. J. P. Taylor, *The Struggle for Mastery in Europe, 1848–1918* (1954) and, more specifically, D. Dawson, *The Mexican Adventure* (1935).

    For Paris under the Empire, see D. H. Pickney, *Napoleon III and the Rebuilding of Paris* (1958) and H. Sealman, *Paris Transformed* (1971). Much of the texture of French society in the period is conveyed by T. Zeldin's multi-volumed work, *France, 1848–1945* (1973–78), while his *Conflicts in French Society* (1970) also contains important essays. M. Howard, *The Franco–Prussian War* (1981) examines the conduct of the war which ended the Second Empire.

Articles
T. Zeldin, 'The myth of Napoleon III', *H. T.* (1958).

14. European expansion overseas

A huge topic, which can be broken down into three main phases. The first European empires of the late eighteenth and the first half of the nineteenth centuries were often the legacy of even earlier colonial conquest and have an important bearing upon the economic expansion of Europe. The reasons for the 'new imperialism' of the late nineteenth and early twentieth centuries which saw a vast extension of European (and North American) influence over the rest of the world is a source of major debate, especially the question of the extent to which European colonisation was the result of political, economic or social pressures from within Europe. The process of decolonisation and its repercussions for European states is now much more fully covered.

Essay topics
'Millstones around our necks.' To what extent did Europe's colonies bear out this description between 1760 and 1870?

Why was there a 'scramble' for colonies by the European powers in the latter part of the nineteenth century?
Was imperialism the 'highest stage of capitalism'?
Why did the European powers decolonise so rapidly after 1945?

Sources and documents

For the earliest phase of colonial dispute, see J. R. Pole (ed.), *The Revolution in America, 1754–1788* (1970). M. M. Wright (ed.), *The New Imperialism* (1961) and P. W. Winks (ed.), *British Imperialism: Gold, God, Glory* (1966) look at the later period. J. A. Hobson, *Imperialism: a study* (1902) and V. I. Lenin, *Imperialism, the Highest Stage of Capitalism* (1917) are two important texts emphasising the economic theory of imperialism. D. K. Fieldhouse, *The Theory of Capitalist Imperialism* (1967) has texts with introductions.

Secondary sources

For the earlier phase of empire, see R. Davies, *The Rise of the Atlantic Economies* (1973), P. Curtin, *The Atlantic Slave Trade* (1969), V. T. Harlow, *The Founding of the Second British Empire, 1763–93* (1952) and the *Cambridge History of the British Empire* (1929–59). For other countries, see H. I. Priestley, *France Overseas through the Ancien Regime* (1939), *France Overseas, a Study of Modern Imperialism* (1966), W. A. Roberts, *The French in the West Indies* (1942), G. M. Wrong, *The Rise and Fall of New France* (1928), G. S. Graham, *Empire of the North Atlantic* (1950), H. H. Dodwell, *Dupleix and Clive* (1920), J. H. Parry, *Trade and Dominion* (1971), G. Williams, *The Expansion of Europe in the Eighteenth Century* (1966), J. H. Parry, *The Spanish Seaborne Empire* (2nd edn, 1967), C. R. Boxer, *The Portuguese Seaborne Empire* (1969) and C. R. Boxer, *The Dutch Seaborne Empire* (1965).

For the earliest 'independence' struggles, see I. R. Christie, *Crisis of Empire: Great Britain and the American Colonies, 1754–1783* (1966) as a brief introduction to Britain's American crisis. Spain's is discussed in W. S. Robertson, *Rise of the Latin American Republics* (1965), J. H. Lynch, *The Spanish American Revolution* (1973), T. Anna, *Spain and the Loss of America* (1983) and more generally R. Carr, *Spain, 1808–1939* (1975) and A. R. Oliveira, *Politics, Economics and Men of Modern Spain, 1808–1946* (1946). The economic background is discussed in J. H. Imlah, *Economic Elements of the Pax Britannica* (1958) and the mid-Victorian view of Empire is discussed in C. A. Bodelsen, *Studies in Mid-Victorian Imperialism* (1924).

M. E. Chamberlain, *The New Imperialism* (Historical Association pamphlet, 1967) is a good survey, see too D. K. Fieldhouse, *Colonialism, 1870–1945* (1983), *The Colonial Empires* (1966) and *Economics and Empire* (1976). See also R. Koebner, *Empire* (1961) and R. Koebner and H. D. Schmitt, *Imperialism . . . a political word, 1840–1960* (1964), B. Porter, *The Lion's Share: a short history of British imperialism, 1850–1970* (1975) provides a comprehensive account of the British imperial experience. See too R. Hyam, *Britain's Imperial Century, 1815–1914: a study of empire and expansion* (1976) and J. Bowle, *The Imperial Achievement: the rise and transformation of the British Empire*

(1977). J. Gallagher and R. Robinson, *Africa and the Victorians: the official mind of imperialism* (1961) examines how European conquest actually occurred. For other countries, see H. Brunschwig, *French Colonialism, 1871–1914; myths and realities* (1966) and W. O. Henderson, *Studies in German Colonial History* (1962). Particular areas are discussed in J. D. Hargreaves, *Prelude to the Partition of West Africa* (1963), W. D. McIntyre, *The Imperial Frontier in the Tropics, 1865–75* (1967) and W. P. Morrell, *The Great Powers in the Pacific* (Historical Association pamphlet, 1965).

The economics of imperialism are discussed in D. C. M. Platt, *Finance, Trade and Politics in British Foreign Policy, 1815–1914* (1968), H. Feis, *Europe, the World's Banker, 1870–1914* (1930), A. R. Hall (ed.), *The Export of Capital from Britain, 1870–1914* (1968), A. K. Cairncross, *Home and Foreign Investment, 1870–1913* (1953) and S. B. Saul, *Studies in British Overseas Trade, 1870–1914* (1960). B. Semmel, *Imperialism and Social Reform* (1960) examines the domestic aspects of imperialism. The diplomatic repercussions of the late nineteenth-century expansion are discussed in W. Langer, *The Diplomacy of Imperialism, 1890–1902* (1935).

For the early twentieth century, see M. Beloff, *Imperial Sunset, Volume 1: Britain's Liberal Empire, 1897–1921* (1969) and for the later period M. E. Chamberlain, *Decolonization: the fall of the European Empires* (1985) and C. Cross, *The Fall of the British Empire* (1968). Recent publications include R. Betts, *France and Decolonisation* (1982); D. Judd, *The Evolution of the Modern Commonwealth* (1982); and N. Mansergh, *The Commonwealth Experience* (1982).

Articles

See J. Gallagher and R. Robinson, 'The imperialism of free trade', *Econ. H. R.* (1953), D. C. Platt, 'Economic factors in British policy during the "New Imperialism" *H.* (1968), also R. Koebner, 'The concept of economic imperialism', *Econ. H. R.* (1949), D. K. Fieldhouse, '"Imperialism": an historiographical revision', *Econ. H. R.* (1961), E. Stokes, 'Great Britain and Africa: the myth of imperialism', *H. T.* (1960) and E. Stokes, 'Late nineteenth century colonial expansion and the attack on the theory of economic imperialism', *H. J.* (1969). German expansion is discussed in H. Pogge van Strandmann, 'Domestic origins of Germany's colonial expansion under Bismarck', *P. P.* (1969).

15.   The unification of Germany

The notion of a united Germany had received considerable stimulus during the Napoleonic Wars and the period after 1815 was marked by the growth of national sentiment. Although the revolutions of 1848 failed to bring about the liberal, united Germany dreamt of by some, they showed the crucial importance of Prussia to any future plan for German unification. The rise of Prussia to a position of dominance in central Europe, both politically and economically, and its influence upon the timing and character of German unification is a major topic. Bismarck's role in the process and the details of the conflicts with the other European powers are covered in a wide variety of studies. The creation of the most powerful European state by 1871 in military terms should not

be allowed to distract from the weaknesses which the newly unified
Empire carried into the later nineteenth and early twentieth centuries.

Essay topics

Why was the unification of Germany not achieved before 1871?
   How far did militarism triumph over liberalism in the creation of the
German Empire?

Sources and documents

For 1848 in Germany see the short collection by P. Jones, *1848
Revolutions* (1982), while W. M. Simon, *Germany in the Age of Bismarck*
(1968) covers the later Bismarckian period. R. H. Lord, *Origins of the War
of 1870* (1924) and G. Bonnin, *Bismarck and the Hohenzollern
Candidature for the Spanish Throne* (1957) are detailed treatments of the
last phase of German unification.

Secondary sources

For the general history of Germany in this period see W. Carr, *A History
of Germany, 1815–1945* (rev. edn, 1979), H. Holborn, *A History of Modern
Germany, Vol. III* (1969) and the early part of G. A. Craig, *Germany,
1866–1945* (Oxford, 1978). M. Kitchen, *The Political Economy of
Germany, 1815–1914* (1978) examines the economic and social
background to German unification. For the era of nationalism prior to
Bismarck, see R. Hinton Thomas, *Liberalism, Nationalism and the
German Intellectuals, 1822–47* (1952), E. Eyck, *The Frankfurt Parliament,
1848–1849* (1968), V. Valentin, *1848: Chapters in German History* (1940)
and L. B. Namier, *1848: the Revolution of the Intellectuals* (1944). On
Bismarck, see B. Waller, *Bismarck* (1985), W. N. Medlicott, *Bismarck and
Modern Germany* (1965) and W. Richter, *Bismarck* (1964). E. Eyck,
Bismarck and the German Empire (1950) is still a valuable older account,
as is the lively and accessible A. J. P. Taylor, *Bismarck* (1955).
H. -U. Wehler, *The German Empire, 1871–1914* (trans. Leamington Spa,
1984) argues that Bismarck unified Germany 'from above' to frustrate
liberalism, a view discussed in the opening chapter of R. Evans (ed.).
Society and Politics in Wilhelmine Germany (1978) and criticised in
G. Eley and D. Blackbourn, *The Peculiarities of German History:
Bourgeois Society and Politics in Nineteenth-Century Germany* (1984).
J. Sheehan, *German Liberalism in the Nineteenth Century* (Chicago,
1978) is a modern treatment of an important strand of German politics.
   Detailed discussion of the diplomatic context of German unification
can be found in A. J. P. Taylor's *The Struggle for Mastery in Europe,
1848–1918* (1954) and H. Kohn (ed.), *German History: Some New
German Views* (1954) contains revaluations of Bismarck's policy and
diplomacy in the period before 1870. Also of value are F. Darmstaedter,
Bismarck and the Creation of the Second Reich (1948), H. Friedjung, *The
Struggle for Supremacy in Germany, 1859–1866* (1935) and L. D. Steefel,
The Schleswig–Holstein Question (1932).

For economic developments which assisted German unification see
W. O. Henderson, *The Zollverein* (Cambridge, 1939), J. H. Clapham, *The Economic Development of France and Germany* (4th edn, 1936),
W. O. Henderson, *The Industrialisation of Europe, 1780–1914* (1969),
T. Kemp, *Industrialisation in Nineteenth-century Europe* (1969),
C. Trebilcock. *The Industrialisation of the Continental Powers, 1780–1914* (1981) and A. Milward and S. B. Saul, *The Economic Development of Continental Europe, 1780–1870* (1973).

On military matters, see G. Best, *War and Society in Revolutionary Europe, 1770–1870* (1982), M. Howard, *The Franco–Prussian War* (1981) and on the wider influence of the army, G. A. Graig, *The Politics of the Prussian Army, 1648–1945* (1955).

16.   Germany, 1871–1914

The declaration of the German Empire in Germany, 1871, brought onto the world stage a major new power with a large and growing population and a rapidly expanding industry. Following victories over Austria and France, her size and industrial development made her the most powerful state in continental Europe. Under Bismarck Germany was given the formal apparatus of democratic institutions – the *Reichstag*, or parliament, and universal suffrage, but power remained substantially vested in the Kaiser, the Chancellor, and the military. Bismarck enforced strict controls on any groups such as the Catholics and the Socialists, whom he saw as threatening the Empire, and used foreign diversions, such as colonial expansion, to distract attention from domestic conflicts. The nature of Bismarck's political system and its long-term effects on Germany, at a time when democratic and social developments throughout Europe were causing unrest, needs to be considered.

After Bismarck's removal by the new Kaiser, William II, in 1890, social conflicts came increasingly to the fore in which both liberals and a growing labour movement found themselves at odds with a government dominated by junkers, industrialists and the military. By 1914, Germany faced deep political divisions which were to surface after the declaration of war.

Essay topics

In what ways were the interests of Germany served by Bismarck after 1871?

How united and stable was Germany on the eve of war in 1914?

Sources and documents

L. Snyder, *Documents of German History* (1958) has material on this period, but more accessible is W. N. Medlicott and D. Coveney, *Bismarck and Europe* (1971). Heinrich Mann's novel, *Man of Straw* (1918, trans. 1947) is a liberal critique of Imperial Germany.

Secondary works

There are several works which place this period in the wider context of modern German history: W. Carr, *A History of Germany, 1815–1945* (rev. edn, 1979), A. Ramm, *Germany, 1789–1919* (1967), G. A. Craig, *Germany, 1866–1945* (1978) and J. C. G. Rohl, *From Bismarck to Hitler* (1970). Of recent work which provides an analysis of German politics in terms of its social and economic structure see M. Kitchen, *The Political Economy of Germany, 1815–1914* (1978) and on the Imperial period as a whole H.-U. Wehler, *The German Empire, 1871–1914* (trans. Leamington Spa, 1984) and G. Eley and D. Blackbourn, *The Peculiarities of German History: Bourgeois Society and Politics in Nineteenth Century Germany* (Oxford, 1984). See also J. Sheehan (ed.), *Imperial Germany* (New York, 1976). Analyses of Bismarck's character and importance can be found in B. Waller, *Bismarck* (1985), as well as the older studies such as A. J. P. Taylor, *Bismarck* (1955), W. Richter, *Bismarck* (1964), W. N. Medlicott, *Bismarck and Modern Germany* (1965) and E. Eyck, *Bismarck and the German Empire* (1950). E. Eyck, *Bismarck after Fifty Years* (Historical Association, 1965) examines historians' changing views of Bismarck.

For the Wilhelmine era, see M. Balfour, *The Kaiser and His Times* (1964) and the essay collection by R. Evans (ed.), *Society and Politics in Wilhelmine Germany* (1978). Dealing with the immediate aftermath of Bismarck's resignation see J. A. Nichols, *Germany after Bismarck* (1958), concentrating on Caprivi, and J. C. G. Rohl, *Germany without Bismarck* (1967) which ends in 1900. On the pre-war decade, see V. R. Berghann, *Germany and the Approach of War in 1914* (1973) and B. Heckart, *From Basserman to Bebel* (New Haven, 1974). On personalities, see J. C. G. Rohl and N. Sombart (eds), *Kaiser Wilhelm II: New Interpretations* (Cambridge, 1982) and K. Jarausch, *The Enigmatic Chancellor: Bethmann-Hollweg and the Hubris of Imperial Germany* (London, 1973).

On the role of the right, see G. Eley, *Reshaping the Right: Radical Nationalism and Political Change after Bismarck* (1980) and on the military, M. Kitchen, *The German Officer Corps: 1870–1914* (1968) and G. A. Craig, *The Politics of the Prussian Army, 1640–1945* (1945). On the left, see C. E. Schorske, *German Social Democracy, 1905–17* (1955) and P. Gay, *The Dilemma of Democratic Socialism* (New York, 1952). R. Evans (ed.), *The German Working Class, 1888–1933* (1982), D. Geary, *European Labour Protest, 1848–1939* (1981) and H. Grebing, *The German Labour Movement* (1969) all have useful material on this period; see also D. Crew, *Town in the Ruhr: A Social History of Bochum* (New York, 1979) for the relationship of social conditions and political allegiance. On industrial development see the chapter in C. M. Cipolla (ed.), *The Fontana Economic History of Europe, vol. iv* (1973); G. Stolper, *German Economy, 1870 to the Present* (2nd. edn, 1967); and W. O. Henderson, *The Industrialisation of Europe, 1780–1914* (1969). On social conditions, see Ashok V. Desai, *Real Wages in Germany, 1871–1913* (1968).

A good general survey of foreign policy throughout the period is I. Geiss, *German Foreign Policy, 1871–1914* (1976). Geiss's views are influenced by F. Fischer, *Germany's Aims in the First World War* (1967), a controversial critique of German foreign policy under the Kaiser, which Fischer followed up in *War of Illusion* (1972); see also A. J. P. Taylor, *The Struggle for Mastery in Europe, 1848–1914* (1954). J. Steinberg,

Yesterday's Deterrent: Tirpitz and the birth of the German battle fleet (1965) is important on the creation of a German navy to rival that of Britain; see also P. A. Kennedy, *The Rise of the Anglo–German Antagonism, 1860–1914* (1980).

Articles

On politics, see J. C. Rohl, 'The Politics of Bismarck's Fall', *H.J.* (1966), and H. J. Pogge von Strandemann, 'The domestic origins of Germany's colonial expansion', *P.P.* (1969). On the Centre Party, see D. Blackbourn, 'The political alignment of the Centre Party in Wilhelmine Germany: a study of the party's emergence in nineteenth-century Wurttemberg', *H.J.* (1975) and also his 'Peasants and politics in Germany, 1871–1914', *E.H.Q.* (1984). J. P. Nettl, 'The German Social Democratic Party 1890–1914 as a political model', *P.P.* (1965), and D. Geary, 'The German labour movement', *E.S.R.* (1976) are useful on the left.

17. France, 1871–1914

On the surface France in this period presented a picture of political instability. The Third Republic was only established by a one-vote majority in 1875 and was characterised by short-lived governments and a series of scandals. Beneath the surface however, France possessed certain strengths. The bulk of the population were conservative-minded peasants; the existence of a meritocratic system ensured the loyalty of professional groups, such as lawyers and teachers; whilst the low rates of population growth and of industrialisation were such as to make social problems less pressing than elsewhere in Europe. Even in the political sphere there were signs of stability: the monarchist right was discredited, pressures from the left were channelled into anti-clericalism, and the same ministers kept returning to power. The Third Republic became the longest-lived post-revolutionary regime, and survived the First World War triumphant.

Essay topics

'The regime that divided Frenchmen least.' Discuss this view of the Third Republic.
    Assess the significance of the Dreyfus Affair for French politics and society.

Sources and documents

A wonderful period for French literature and culture with Zola's *Germinal* (1885) and *La Débâcle* (1892) of most direct historical relevance.
    For the French right see the writings of Drumont and Barres in J. S. McClelland (ed.), *The French Right: from de Maistre to Maurras* (1970).

Secondary works

There are numerous general introductions to French history in this period. D. W. Brogan, *The Development of Modern France, 1870–1940* (1940), J. P. T. Bury, *France, 1814–1940* (1949), A. Cobban, *A History of Modern France, vol. III* (1965) and G. Wright, *France in Modern Times* (1960) still all have some use, although the best specific introductions to this period are J-M. Mayeur and J. Reberioux, *The Third Republic, 1871–1914* (1984), R. D. Anderson, *France, 1870–1914*, (1983), R. Magraw, *France 1815–1914* (1984), and J. F. McMillan, *Dreyfus to de Gaulle: Politics and Society in France, 1898–1969* (1985). T. Zeldin, *France, 1848–1945* (2 vols, 1973) provides a full discussion of social, intellectual and political life, whilst E. Weber, *Peasants into Frenchmen, 1870–1914* (1979) concentrates on social change.

On the beginning of the period A. Horne, *The Fall of Paris* (1983) includes a discussion of the Commune, whilst the same author's *The French Army in Politics* (1984) covers the army's role over both the Commune and the Dreyfus Affair. On the Commune see also E. Schulkind, *The Paris Commune of 1871* (Historical Association, 1971), F. Jellinek, *The Paris Commune of 1871* (1937 and 1971), R. L. Williams, *The French Revolution of 1870–1871* (1969), S. Edwards, *The Paris Commune, 1871* (1971) and R. Tombs, *The War against Paris, 1871* (1981). The Dreyfus Affair is the subject of G. Chapman, *The Dreyfus Case* (1955) and D. Johnson, *France and the Dreyfus Affair* (1966); M. Marrus, *The Politics of Assimilation: a Study of the French Jewish Community at the Time of the Dreyfus Affair* (1971) treats the same subject from the Jewish viewpoint. H. Holdberg, *The Life of Jean Jaurès* (1962) and J. P. T. Bury, *Gambetta and the Making of the Third Republic* (1973) look at two leading figures on the left in the period.

French foreign policy is discussed in C. Andrew, *Théophile Delcassé and the Making of the Entente Cordiale* (1968) and J. Keiger, *France and the Origins of the First World War* (1983).

Articles

R. Tombs, 'The Thiers government and the outbreak of civil war in France, 1871', *H.J.* (1980) emphasises the existence of political moderation even in 1871; see also P. H. Hutton, 'Boulangism and the rise of mass politics', *J.C.H.* (1976).

18.   Austria–Hungary, 1867–1918

Despite the triumph of the Habsburg monarchy over the liberal and national movements of 1848, pressures on the imperial position soon revived. By 1867 Austrian influence in both Italy and Germany had been defeated and the Emperor Franz Josef was forced to agree to an *Ausgleich* (compromise) with the largest national majority in his Empire, the Hungarians. From 1867 to 1918 Austria and Hungary had separate governments, though with a single army, foreign policy and ruler. The *Ausgleich* did not end the pressures from other nationalities for equality and independence however. Within Austria, the Czechs especially wanted reform; whilst in Hungary the Yugoslav movement was strengthened by the existence of an independent Slav state, Serbia. Austria–Hungary was not without some strengths, including loyalty to the monarchy, a multinational army, and a reasonably stable economy. Vienna also happened to be amongst the foremost centres of cultural and intellectual life in pre-1914 Europe. Although widely thought of as the sick man of Europe, the real questions lie in whether the collapse of the Empire was inevitable or primarily the result of the strain of war.

Essay topics

Which nationality represented the greatest threat to the unity of Austria–Hungary, 1867–1914?

Was it war or more deep-seated causes which explained the breakup of the Habsburg monarchy?

Sources and documents

R. W. Seton-Watson, *Racial Problems in Hungary* (1908) and H. Wickham Steed, *The Habsburg Monarchy* (1913) are 'on the eve' accounts. Consult a good historical atlas for the national and ethnic complexities of central Europe.

Secondary works

The period is placed in context by A. J. P. Taylor, *The Habsburg Monarchy, 1809–1918* (1964) and C. A. Macartney, *The Habsburg Monarchy, 1790–1918* (1968). R. Kann, *The Multinational Empire: nationalism and national reform in the Habsburg Monarchy, 1848–1914* (1950) provides a full coverage, though A. J. May, *The Habsburg Monarchy, 1867–1914* (1951) is shorter. On Austrian foreign policy, see F. R. Bridge, *From Sadowa to Sarajevo* (1972).

On the nationalist problem see R. Pearson, *National Minorities in Eastern Europe, 1848–1944* (1983) and V. Dedijer, *The Road to Sarajevo* (1967). Also useful are C. Regal, *The Slovenes and Yugoslavia* (1977) and C. A. Macartney, *Hungary: a short history* (1968).

N. Stone, *The Eastern Front* is a brilliant discussion of the fighting which throws considerable light on the Austrian state at war.

Z. A. B. Zeman, *The Break-up of the Habsburg Empire, 1914–18* (1961) discusses the war years and the end of the empire, as does O. Jaszi, *The Destruction of the Habsburg Monarchy* (1929) and A. J. May, *The Passing of the Habsburg Monarchy, 1914–18* (1966). A. J. P. Taylor, 'Allied war aims' in R. Pares and L. S. Sutherland (eds), *Essays Presented to Sir Lewis Namier* (1956) provides a critical link between the outcome of the war and the nationality question. F. L. Carsten, *Revolution in Central Europe, 1918–19* (1972) deals with events in Austria itself at the end of the war.

Articles

See K. R. Stadler, 'The disintegration of the Austrian Empire', *J.C.H.* (1968); N. Stone, 'Hungary and World War I', *J.C.H.* (1966).

19. Russia 1856–1917

Russian history in this period is inevitably coloured by the revolution
which occurred in 1917 and the unrest which preceded it. Following
defeat in the Crimean War and faced by peasant discontent and a
disaffected intelligentsia, Tsar Alexander II emancipated the serfs in 1861
and carried out a series of major institutional reforms. His assassination
in 1881 brought to a halt further attempts at liberalisation and the
autocratic political system was maintained by Alexander III and Nicholas
II. Russia's huge area, her backwardness and varied national make-up
continued to present serious problems and drove many opponents into
exile or terrorism.

There was, however, considerable industrial development under Count
Witte in the 1890s and effective land reform under Stolypin. In 1905,
following defeat by Japan, the regime faced a major crisis with
widespread unrest and the emergence of workers-soldiers 'soviets'.
Short-lived hopes for reform were frustrated and there was a growing
divergence between moderate reformers and a militant bolshevik
minority. Conservative forces remained strong, however, and on the eve
of the Great War it was still possible that Russia might have evolved
without revolutionary upheaval. The huge losses and strain of the
conflict finally brought revolution.

Essay topics

To what extent did the reforms of Alexander II mark a turning point in
Russian history?
    Was Tsarist autocracy doomed in Russia by 1914?

Sources and documents

Memoirs of revolutionary leaders include J. D. Duff (ed.), *Memoirs of
Alexander Herzen* (1923), M. Gorky, *Autobiography* (trns. 1953) and
Prince Kropotkin, *Memoirs of a Revolutionist* (1899). L. Trotsky, *1905*
(1971) describes the thwarted revolution of that year by a leading
participant. Of Lenin's writings, *What is to be done?* (1902) was the
seminal document outlining Bolshevik strategy. A great age of Russian
literature, much of it political in tone, is perhaps best represented by Ivan
Turgenev's, *On the Eve* (1860) and *Fathers and Children* (1862) and
Maxim Gorky's, *The Lower Depths* (1902).

Secondary works

M. Kochan and R. Abraham, *The Making of Modern Russia* (1983) and
H. Seton-Watson, *The Russian Empire* (1967) are valuable for placing
the period in the context of Russian history in general, as are J. N.
Westwood, *Endurance and Endeavour: Russian History, 1812–1971* (1973)
and E. Crankshaw, *The Shadow of the Winter Palace* (1978). R. Pipes,
Russia under the Old Regime (1977) takes a long, thematic perspective
and is better on the period before 1900. Still valuable are B. Pares, *The
Fall of the Russian Monarchy* (1955) and M. T. Florinsky, *Russia: a history*

and an interpretation (1947). L. Kochan, *Russia in Revolution, 1890–1918* (1966) is a more recent analysis.

On Alexander II, W. E. Mosse, *Alexander II and the Modernisation of Russia* (1959) provides a useful survey. For the problems of rural Russia see J. Blum, *Lord and Peasant in Russia* (1965); G. T. Robinson, *Rural Russia under the Old Regime* (1949) and W. S. Vucinich, The *Peasant in Nineteenth Century Russia* (1968). On Witte, see T. H. von Laue, *Sergei Witte and the Industrialisation of Russia* (1963). On the Dumas, G. A. Hosking, *The Russian Constitutional Experiment: Government and Duma, 1907–1914* (Cambridge, 1973) and R. B. McKean, *The Russian Constitutional Monarchy, 1907–1917* (Historical Association, 1977) are valuable.

On economic development in general see E. Falkus, *The Industrialisation of Russia, 1700–1914* (1972); A. Nove, *An Economic History of the U.S.S.R.* (1969); and W. O. Henderson, *The Industrial Revolution on the Continent, Germany, France and Russia, 1800–1914* (1961).

K. Fitzlyon and T. Browning, *Before the Revolution* (1977) surveys Russia under Nicholas II, and on the 1905 revolution see H. Harcave, *First Blood: the Russian Revolution of 1905* (1965), while G. Katkov (ed.), *Russia Enters the Twentieth Century* (1972) has valuable essays.

Specific works dealing with the opposition to the old order are F. Venturi, *The Roots of Revolution: a history of the Populist and Socialist movements in nineteenth century Russia* (1960); P. Avrich, *The Russian Anarchists* (1967); J. L. H. Keep, *The Rise of Social Democracy in Russia* (1963); and A. B. Ulam, *Lenin and the Bolsheviks* (1965).

On foreign policy see D. Lieves, *Russia and the Origins of the First World War* (1983), while on the effects of the war see M. T. Florinsky, *The End of the Russian Empire* (1931), R. Pearson, *The Russian Moderates and the Crisis of Tsarism, 1914–17* (1977) and N. Stone, *The Eastern Front, 1914–17* (1978). J. Dunn, *Modern Revolutions* (1972) ch. 1, has a useful short account of the revolutionary crisis.

Articles

On unrest, see M. Perrie, 'The Russian peasant movement, 1905–7', *P.P.* (1972) and L. H. Harrison, 'Problems of social stability in urban Russia', *S.R.* (1964 and 1965); and A. P. Mendel, 'Peasant and worker on the eve of the First World War', *S.R.* (1965). On other aspects see T. H. von Laue, 'The chances for liberal constitutionalism', *S.R.* (1965) and G. L. Yaney, 'The concept of the Stolypin land reform', *S.R.* (1964).

20. European diplomacy, 1871–1914

The European diplomatic scene after the Franco–Prussian War was dominated by Bismarck's attempts to ensure the lasting security of the new German Empire. At first he tried to achieve this through the 'Dreikaiserbund', a conservative alliance with Austria–Hungary and Russia in the 1870s, but this was increasingly undermined by Austrian and Russian ambitions in the Balkans, where the decline of the Ottoman

Empire created a power vacuum. In 1879 Bismarck decided to ally with Austria–Hungary alone in the Dual Alliance, whilst in 1894 Russia made an alliance with France. Tension between the two blocs grew, notably over the Bosnian Crisis in 1908, whilst Britain too became suspicious of German ambitions. In 1914 another crisis in the Balkans brought the two sides to war. Various interpretations of the origins of the war have been put forward; from early anti-Germanism, there was a swing towards blaming the alliance systems in general. More recently Fischer has revived interest in Germany's responsibility for the war and the wider factors affecting Europeans' readiness to go to war have to be considered.

Essay topics

How stable was the European diplomatic system created by Bismarck?
   Why did a crisis in the Balkans lead to a general European war in 1914?

Sources and documents

M. Hurst (ed.), *Key Treaties for the Great Powers, vol. II, 1870–1914* (1972) covers the whole period, though mere treaty texts are rather unexciting sources. To be preferred perhaps is I. Geiss, *July, 1914: Selected Documents* (1967) which concentrates on the pre-war crisis.

Secondary sources

A. J. P. Taylor, *The Struggle for Mastery in Europe, 1848–1918* (1954) remains a remarkably thorough analysis of the diplomatic struggles, whilst R. Albrecht-Carrié, *A Diplomatic History of Europe from the Congress of Vienna* (1961) provides the wider background. Another well-established, but essential account, is W. L. Langer, *European Alliances and Alignments, 1871–90* (1956), which he followed with *The Diplomacy of Imperialism, 1890–1902* (1951). On individual countries see C. Andrew, *Théophile Delcassé and the Making of the Entente Cordiale* (1968) and P. V. Rolo, *Entente Cordiale* (1969).
   The origins of the First World War have attracted a vast literature. J. Joll, *The Origins of the First World War* (1985) is a recent modern overview. B. Schmitt, *The Outbreak of War in 1914* (Historical Association pamphlet, 1964) is a brief account of the traditional interpretation that the alliance system was to blame for the outbreak of the war and see also his longer study, *The Coming of the War* (2 vols, 1930). The great classic of this school of thinking is L. Albertini, *The Origins of the War of 1914* (3 vols, 1952–7). Shorter and more recent accounts are L. C. F. Turner, *The Origins of the First World War* (1970) and H. W. Koch, *The Origins of the First World War* (1984 edn). Also useful is the short account of the break-up of the nineteenth-century international system, R. Langhorne, *The Collapse of the Concert of Europe, 1890–1914* (1981), while M. S. Anderson, *The Eastern Question, 1774–1923* (1966) provides a wider perspective on that particular problem. Amongst the most important recent interpretations has been F. Fischer, *Germany's War Aims in the First World War* (1967) which sees the war as a result of Germany's pre-war expansionism. See also his *War of Illusion* (1972). On Germany see

also I. Geiss, *German Foreign Policy, 1871–1914* (1976) and G. Ritter, *The Schlieffen Plan* (1958). On France see J. Keiger, *France and the Origins of the First World War* (1983) and on Russia D. Lieves, *Russia and the Origins of the First World War* (1983). Z. S. Steiner, *Britain and the Origins of the First World War* (1977) is the most detailed account of British involvement. The classic study of Anglo–German naval rivalry is E. L. Woodward, *Great Britain and the German Navy* (1935), but now updated on the naval side by A. J. Marder, *From the Dreadnought to Scapa Flow, vol. i: The road to war, 1904–14* (1961) and on the political by P. Kennedy, *The Rise of the Anglo–German Antagonism, 1860–1914* (1980).

Broader interpretations of the social and psychological factors have gained some currency in recent years; see for example M. Howard, 'Reflections on the First World War' in his *Studies in War and Peace* (1970).

Articles

Two articles which take up the theme of the relationship between domestic and foreign policy are W. J. Mommsen, 'Domestic factors in German foreign policy before 1914', *C.E.H.* (1973), reprinted in J. Sheehan (ed.), *Imperial Germany* (New York, 1976) and M. R. Gordon, 'Domestic conflict and the origins of the First World War: the British and German cases', *J.M.H.* (1974).

21.   The First World War, 1914–18

When war broke out in August 1914 it was widely expected to be 'over by Christmas'. Instead, in the West at least, the situation soon became one of trench warfare and deadlock. Modern weapons, especially the machine gun, barbed wire and heavy artillery, ensured huge casualties, concentrated among men aged between about twenty and forty. Armies numbering millions of men were mobilised, whilst behind them 'home fronts' were established: economies were geared to war production, women went to work in factories, propaganda machines ensured loyalty to the war effort and hatred of the enemy. The strain on European society was enormous. Governments were changed in France and Britain, revolutions broke out in Russia and Germany, and the Austro–Hungarian and Turkish Empires were finally shattered. The world would never be the same again.

Essay topics

Why did the First World War not end until November 1918?

Why did western democratic regimes tend to survive the war more successfully than the eastern autocracies?

Sources and documents

P. Vansittart, *Voices from the Great War* (1983) draws together eye witness evidence on the war from all levels of society. Of the memoirs, see D. Lloyd George, *War Memoirs* (2 vols, 1928) and W. S. Churchill, *The World Crisis* (1928). Of the literature produced by the war, H. Barbusse's *Le Feu (Under Fire)* (1917), E. Junger, *The Storm of Steel* (1929), R. Graves, *Goodbye to All That* (1929), and E. M. Remarque, *All Quiet on the Western Front* (1929) are outstanding.

Secondary works

There are numerous general histories of the war but among the most approachable are A. J. P. Taylor, *The First World War: an illustrated history* (1966), invaluable because of its illustrations, C. Falls, *The First World War* (1960) and B. H. Liddell-Hart, *History of the First World War* (1970). M. Ferro, *The Great War* (1963) is another short, readable introduction. See also, J. Terraine, *The Western Front, 1914–18* (1964). For works which place the military aspects of the war in a broader context see K. Robbins, *The First World War* (Oxford, 1984), B. Bond, *War and Society in Europe, 1870–1970* (1984) and G. Hardach, *The First World War* (1977).

The nature of the new warfare is discussed in J. Ellis, *Eye-Deep in Hell* (1976) and A. E. Ashworth, *The Trench Warfare* (1980), while A. Horne, *The Price of Glory: Verdun, 1916* (1964), L. Macdonald, *They Called it Passchendaele* (1983) and M. Middlebrook, *The First Day on the Somme* (1971) and *The Kaiser's Battle* (1983) (on Germany's 1918 offensive) give full treatment of individual battles, as does J. Keegan, *The Face of Battle* (1979).

The effect of the war on individual societies can be traced in J. Kocka, *Facing Total War: German Society, 1914–1918* (1985), A. Rosenberg, *Imperial Germany: the birth of the German Republic* (1931), A. Marwick, *The Deluge: British Society and the First World War* (1965), A. J. May, *The Passing of the Habsburg Monarchy* (2 vols, 1966), L. Kochan, *Russia in Revolution, 1890–1918* (1966), J. J. Becker, *The Great War and the French People* (1983), and N. Stone, *The Eastern Front* (1978). General coverage of such issues is provided by A. Marwick, *War and Social Change in the Twentieth Century* (1974).

The revolutionary effects of the war are discussed in C. L. Bertrand (ed.) *Revolutionary Situations in Europe, 1917–1922* (Montreal, 1977) and F. L. Carsten, *Revolution in Central Europe, 1918–1919* (1972). For Germany, see A. J. Ryder, *The German Revolution* (1966) and D. Geary, 'Radicalism and the worker: metalworkers and revolution, 1914–1923', in R. J. Evans (ed.), *Society and Politics in Wilhelmine Germany* (1978).

War aims and the failure of early peace attempts are discussed in F. Fischer, *Germany's War Aims in the First World War* (1967), V. Rothwell, *British War Aims and Peace Diplomacy* (1971), C. Andrew and A. Kanya-Forstner, *France Overseas* (1981), as well as A. J. P. Taylor, *The Struggle for Mastery in Europe, 1848–1918* (1954). See also, M. Kitchen, *The Silent Dictatorship* (1976), on the growing role of the German General Staff.

Articles

The thesis that sections of the German lower middle classes were radicalised by the war is raised in J. Kocka, 'The First World War and the

"Mittelstand": German artisans and white-collar workers', *J.C.H.* (1973); and for a review of these views, see W. J. Mommsen, 'Society and war: two new analyses of the First World War', *J.M.H.* (1977). D. Geary, 'The German labour movement, 1848–1918', *E.S.R.* (1976) is also useful for German reactions.

22.   The Russian Revolution and Lenin, 1917–24

Under the pressures of war the Tsarist autocracy finally collapsed early in 1917 and power was given to a more democratic regime of elected representatives. The change of government unleashed forces that were difficult to control however: soldiers deserted from the army, factory workers adopted militant political views, and the peasants began to seize land for themselves from the great estates. In the 'October Revolution' the communist 'Bolsheviks' seized power under Lenin, and established a radically reformist but authoritarian regime. They made peace with Germany, overcame their conservative opponents and defeated the attempts of the western powers to overthrow them. Historians debate about the kind of regime Lenin might have created had he not become increasingly ill and died in 1924.

Essay topics

Was the Bolshevik seizure of power in 1917 primarily the result of their own strengths and abilities?

What were the main achievements and failings of Lenin in power, 1917–24?

Sources and documents

M. McCauley, ed., *The Russian Revolution and the Soviet State, 1917–21* (1980) provides a full set of documents, whilst L. Trotsky, *The History of the Russian Revolution* (1977) is an account by a leading revolutionary. J. Bunyan and H. Fisher, *The Bolshevik Revolution, 1917–18* (1934) gives documents on the early period. There are memoirs by N. Sukhanov, *The Russian Revolution, 1917* (1955), J. Reed, *Ten Days that Shook the World* (1961) (the latter an American observer of the October Revolution), and A. Kerensky, *The Kerensky Memoirs* (1966).

Secondary works

Some of the national histories are good starting points for the breakdown of the regime; see H. Seton-Watson, *The Russian Empire, 1801–1917* (1967), J. N. Westwood, *Endurance and Endeavour: Russian History, 1812–1971* (1973) and L. Kochan and P. Abraham, *The Making of Modern Russia* (1983). R. B. McKean, *The Russian Constitutional Monarchy, 1907–1917* (Historical Association, 1977) synthesises much recent research. There are also useful essays in R. Pipes (ed.), *Revolutionary Russia* (1968) and a useful, short interpretative essay in J. Dunn, *Modern Revolutions* (1972), ch. 1.

E. H. Carr, *A History of Soviet Russia: The Bolshevik Revolution* (3 vols, 1966) provides the standard account of these years, although his *The Russian Revolution from Lenin to Stalin* (1980) is shorter. See also G. Hosking, *A History of the Soviet Union* (1985), and other accounts on aspects of this period are provided by G. Katkov, *Russia, 1917: the February Revolution* (1967), R. Pipes, *The Formation of the Soviet Union* (1954) and M. Ferro, *October 1917: a social history of the Russian Revolution* (1980). M. Wood, *The Russian Revolution* (1979) provides a short analysis and some documents.

Several works approach the period from a biographical viewpoint including B. Wolfe, *Three Who Made a Revolution* (1966), on Lenin, Trotsky and Stalin, D. Shub, *Lenin* (1966), C. Hill, *Lenin and the Russian Revolution* (1971), A. B. Ulam, *Lenin and the Bolsheviks* (1965), I. Deutscher, *Stalin* (1966) and I. Deutscher, *The Prophet Armed: Trotsky, 1879–1921* (1963). On the Marxist background to Bolshevik thinking see E. Wilson, *To the Finland Station* (1947).

The civil war period and allied intervention are discussed in J. Bradley, *Allied Intervention in Russia* (1968), R. Ullman, *Intervention and the War: Anglo–Soviet Relations, 1917–21* (1961), whilst R. Service, *The Bolshevik Party in Revolution, 1917–23* (1979) and T. Rigby, *Lenin's Government* (1979) look at Soviet institutions in this period.

A work looking beyond 1924, and rather general, is S. Fitzpatrick, *The Russian Revolution, 1917–32* (1982). The long-term development of foreign policy is considered in A. B. Ulam, *Expansion and Coexistence, Soviet Foreign Policy, 1917–72* (1968).

23.   Italy From Unification to Mussolini, 1871–1943

The final unification of Italy in 1871 failed to fulfil the great hopes of the 'risorgimento' period. Deep economic and social divisions between north and south, the alienation of the Catholic Church from the new Italian monarchy, and the narrow electoral franchise, left a picture of division and weakness in the late nineteenth century. Around 1900 there was increasing violence in the countryside and factories. The 'Giolitti era' marked a return to relative calm but the strains of the First World War and the effects of electoral reform, created the conditions for Mussolini's rise to power in the 1920s. His Fascist regime was characterised by authoritarian rule and bold foreign adventures, but it failed to tackle Italy's deeper social problems and brought defeat, and Mussolini's overthrow, in the Second World War. The weaknesses of Italian democracy and the nature of Mussolini's brand of fascism are common areas of interest.

Essay topics

Why was Mussolini able to overthrow Italian democracy?

What were the main successes and failings of Mussolini in office, 1922–43?

Sources and documents

Ciano's Diaries, 1937–8 (1952) and *1939–43* (1947) cover the later Fascist period from within the government whilst the views of opponents can be found in G. Salvemini, *The Fascist Dictatorship in Italy* (1928) and *Under the Axe of Fascism* (1936)

Secondary works

For a general background to Italian history see D. Mack Smith *Italy: a modern history* (1959), which is superior to R. Albrecht-Carrié, *Italy from Napoleon to Mussolini* (New York, 1950). M.Clark, *Modern Italy, 1871–1982* (1984) is a substantial modern study. A helpful short introduction to the Fascist era is M. Blinkhorn, *Mussolini and Fascist Italy* (1984); see also A. Lyttleton, *The Seizure of Power, 1919–29* (1973).

On the pre-Fascist period C. Seton-Watson, *Italy from Liberalism to Fascism* (1967) is the standard work, but R. Busworth, *Italy and the Approach of the First World War* (1983) looks at internal factors troubling the country before 1915, as well as foreign policy issues, and J. A. Davis, *Conflict of Control: Law and Order in the Making of Modern Italy* (1984) is good, on internal disorders; J. Meisel (ed.), *Pareto and Mosca* (1965) looks at two critics of democracy.

The development of fascism is discussed in A. Lyttlton, *Italian Fascism from Pareto to Gentile* (1973). On the Fascist period F. Chabod, *A History of Italian Fascism* (1961) provides a general political survey, whilst E. R. Tannenbaum, *Fascism in Italy, 1922–45* (1972) looks at social and cultural aspects. Also useful is E. Wiskemann, *Fascism in Italy* (1969). Church-state relations are covered in A. Jemolo, *Church and State in Italy, 1850–1950* (1960) and R. A. Webster, *The Cross and the Fasces: Christian Democracy in Italy, 1860–1960* (1960).

Of the biographies of Mussolini, C. Hibbert, *Benito Mussolini* (1962) is accessible, see also L. Fermi, *Mussolini* (1961). D. Mack Smith, *Mussolini's Roman Empire* (1977) and E. M. Robertson, *Mussolini as Empire Builder* (1977), which concentrates on 1932–6, survey foreign policy, whilst E. Wiskemann, *The Rome–Berlin Axis* (1949) concentrates on the German alliance, as does F. W. Deakin, *The Brutal Friendship* (2 vols, 1966). The economic performance of Fascist Italy is examined in W. G. Welk, *Fascist Economic Policy: An Analysis of Italy's Economic Experiment* (1938) and R. Sarti, *Fascism and Industrial Leadership in Italy, 1919–1940* (1971).

Articles

A. Albertoz, 'The crisis of the corporative state', *J.C.H.* (1969) and S. Woolf, 'Mussolini as revolutionary', *J.C.H.* (1966) are useful.

24.   The Weimar Republic, 1919–33

The Weimar Republic was established in the wake of military defeat in the First World War and the overthrow of the Kaiser, and soon faced even greater problems – the harsh peace of Versailles, enforced by the Allies, and the massive inflation of the early 1920s. It was in this difficult period that the Nazi party, under Adolf Hitler, came into being and attempted to overthrow the government in the Munich putsch of 1923. In the years after this the Republic staged something of a recovery, achieving economic growth, political stability and even, thanks to Stresemann, international standing. Historians argue whether, but for the effects of the 'slump' after 1929, and the bankruptcies and political extremism which it created, Weimar could have survived. The appeal of Nazism and the role of army, business and churches under Weimar have all received attention.

Essay topics

Did the possession of 'the most democratic constitution in the world' tend to help or hinder the Weimar Republic in its search for political stability?
   Assess the contribution of Hitler to the Nazi rise to power.

Sources and documents

For excellent selections of documents on Weimar and the rise of Nazism, see J. Noakes and G. Pridham (eds), *Documents on Nazism, 1919–1945* (1974) and J. Noakes and G. Pridham (eds), *Nazism, 1919–1945. Vol. I. The Rise to Power, 1919–1934* (1983). J. Hiden, *The Weimar Republic* (1974) has useful material specifically on Weimar. Hitler's *Mein Kampf* (1925–6) is available in translation (ed. D. C. Watt, 1969); see also N. H. Baynes, *The Speeches of Adolf Hitler, April 1922–August 1939* (1942).

Secondary sources

E. Eyck, *History of the Weimar Republic* (2 vols, 1962, 1963) is a full and useful introduction to the period. A. J. Nicholls, *Weimar and the Rise of Hitler* (1968) is shorter and more analytical, whilst R. J. Bessel and E. J. Feuchtwanger (eds), *Social Change and Political Development in the Weimar Republic* (1981) is an important group of essays.
   The revolution of 1918–19 and the birth of Weimar has received quite full treatment. A. Rosenberg, *Imperial Germany: the birth of the German Republic* (1931) remains a useful, if old, account; A. J. Ryder, *The German Revolution* (1967) concentrates on the Socialists (see also the shorter account in his Historical Association pamphlet of the same title, published in 1959). F. L. Carsten, *Revolution in Central Europe, 1918–19* (1971) is excellent on the 'grass roots' establishment of workers' and soldiers' councils, and J. P. Nettl, *Rosa Luxemburg* (2 vols) provides a biography of a leading revolutionary. R. Cooper, *Failure of a Revolution: Germany in 1918–19* (1955) criticises the Social Democrats, for whom see also R. N. Hunt, *German Social Democracy, 1918–1933* (Chicago, 1970) and W. L. Guttsman, *The German Social Democratic Party, 1875–1933* (1981). E. J. Hobsbawm, 'Confronting defeat: the German Communist Party' in *Revolutionaries* (1977) looks at the KPD.
   Two leading characters in the Republic are discussed in H. A. Turner, *Stresemann and the Politics of the Weimar Republic* (1963), H. W. Gatzke,

Stresemann and the Rearmament of Germany (1954) and A. Dorpalen, *Hindenburg and the Weimar Republic* (1964).

J. W. Wheeler-Bennett, *The Nemesis of Power: the German army in politics, 1918–45* (1980 edn) is critical of the military under Weimar. The same theme is covered by F. L. Carsten, *The Reichswehr and German Politics, 1918–33* (1966) and the older and more general, G. Craig, *The Politics of the Prussian Army, 1640–1945* (1955). The political rise of the Nazis at 'grass roots' level can be traced in M. Kater, *The Nazi Party, 1919–45* (1984), W. S. Allen, *The Nazi Seizure of Power* (1966) and J. Noakes, *The Nazi Party in Lower Saxony* (1971). There is a useful set of essays in E. Matthias and A. J. Nicholls (eds), *German Democracy and the Triumph of Hitler* (1971) and P. D. Stachura (ed.), *The Nazi Machtergreifung* (1983).

Articles

On the role of the KPD in assisting the Nazi's rise, see C. Fischer, 'Class enemies or class brothers? Communist–Nazi relations in Germany, 1929–33' and D. Geary, 'Nazis and workers, a response to Conan Fischer's "Class enemies or class brothers"', *E.H.Q.* (1985). On the role of business in the rise of the Nazis, see H. Ashby Turner, 'Big business and the rise of Hitler', *A.H.R.* (1969), G. D. Fieldman, 'The social and economic policies of German big business, 1918–1929', *A.H.R.* (1969); and E. Nolte, 'Big business and German politics', *A.H.R.* (1969). More generally on Nazi support see T. Childers, 'The social bases of the National Socialist vote', *J.C.H.* (1976), J. Noakes, 'Nazi voters', *H.T.* (1980) and K. O'Lessker, 'Who voted for Hitler: a new look at the class basis of Nazism', *American Journal of Sociology* (1969).

25. Nazi Germany, 1933–45

Having obtained power by what, on the surface, could be portrayed as 'constitutional' means, Hitler overthrew the Weimar Republic and enforced authoritarian government, with himself as Führer and the Nazi party as the only legitimate political force. At first, despite rigged elections, the imprisonment of opponents, and the enforcement of strict controls on the people, he had successes, reducing unemployment and increasing Germany's international standing. But in 1939 his expansionist foreign policy brought conflict with Britain and France. Already Hitler had inspired anti-Semitic outrages, blaming the Jews for Germany's past misfortunes, and during the war the 'Final Solution' involving the slaughter of millions of Jews was adopted. Meanwhile however the strain of 'total war' proved too much for Germany. Hitler himself, increasingly deranged, committed suicide in the midst of defeat in 1945. Exactly how such a man could gain and wield such power has concerned historians ever since.

Essay topics

Why did the German people not overthrow Hitler?
What were the main facets of Nazi political ideology?

Sources and documents

J. Noakes and G. Pridham (eds), *Documents on Nazism, 1919–1945* (1974) presents a good selection of documents on the whole era, and on the Hitlerite period see their *Nazism, 1919–1945: Vol. II. State, economy and society, 1933–1939* (1984). Hitler's *Mein Kampf* (1925–6, ed. D. C. Watt, 1969) and Goebbel's *Diaries* (1948) provide a valuable insight into the Nazi mind. More accessible and compelling on the war period is A. Speer, *Inside the Third Reich* (1970), though it should be approached with care, while H. Rauschning, *Germany's Revolution of Destruction* (1939) is remarkably perceptive on the revolutionary strand in Hitler's make-up. D. G. Williamson, *The Third Reich* (1982) is a short modern selection of documents with introductory chapters.

Secondary works

There is an enormous amount of work on Hitler and the Nazis. H. R. Trevor-Roper's introduction to *The Last Days of Hitler* (1978 edn) remains impressively perceptive. Of the biographies of Hitler, A. Bullock, *Hitler* (1962) remains a readable but full account; J. C. Fest, *Hitler* (1974) and J. Toland, *Adolf Hitler* (1976) are long and detailed; whilst N. Stone, *Hitler* (1980) is short but stimulating. J. C. Fest, *The Face of the Third Reich* (1970) looks at Hitler's deputies, one of whom receives full coverage in E. K. Bramstedt, *Goebbels and National Socialist Propaganda* (1965). Two interesting attempts at 'psychohistory' can be found in W. Langer, *The Mind of Adolf Hitler* (1972) and W. Carr, *Hitler: A Study in Personality and Politics* (1978).

A good general history of the Nazi rise and impact is K. Bracher, *The German Dictatorship* (1973), itself written by a German; see too, I. Kershaw, *The Nazi Dictatorship* (1985) and K. Hilderbrand, *The Third Reich* (1984). D. Orlow, *A History of the Nazi Party, 1933–45* (1973), R. Gruenberger, *A Social History of the Third Reich* (1974) and J. P. Stern, *The Führer and the People* (1975) cover various aspects of the Third Reich, while J. Hiden and J. Farquharson, *Explaining Hitler's Germany* (1983) looks at historical views of the Nazi regime. J. Noakes (ed.), *Government, Party and People in Nazi Germany* (Exeter, 1980) has several good essays and a bibliography of recent writing. On other aspects of German society, see A. Schweitzer, *Big Business in the Third Reich* (1964), D. Guerin, *Fascism and Big Business* (1979), R. J. O'Neill, *The German Army and the Nazi Party, 1933–1939* (1966), Z. A. B. Zeman, *Nazi Propaganda* (1964), E. K. Bramsted, *Goebbels and Nationalist Socialist Propaganda, 1925–1945* (1965), J. S. Conway, *The Nazi Persecution of the Churches* (1968), and G. Lewy, *The Catholic Church and Nazi Germany* (1964).

Hitler's opponents are considered in H. Graml *et al.*, *The German Resistance to Hitler* (1970) and I. Kershaw, *Popular Opinion and Political Dissent in the Third Reich: Bavaria, 1933–1945* (1986). Hitler's anti-Semitism is considered in Kershaw, *Nazi Dictatorship*, ch. 5 and H. Krausnick, 'The persecution of the Jews', in H. Krausnick *et al.*, *Anatomy of the SS State* (1968) but see also L. Dawidowicz, *The War against the Jews, 1933–45* (1975), H. Hohne, *The Order of the Death's Head* (1970) and K. Schleunes, *The Twisted Road to Auschwitz* (1970).

Foreign policy is considered in G. I. Weinberg, *The Foreign Policy of Hitler's Germany: Diplomatic Revolution in Europe, 1933–1936* (1970) and *The Foreign Policy of Hitler's Germany: Starting World War II* (1980). K. Hildebrand, *The Foreign Policy of the Third Reich* (1973) stresses Hitler's pragmatism, while W. Carr, *Arms, Autarky and Aggression: A Study in German Foreign Policy, 1933–1939* (1972) relates economic policy to foreign policy.

On Hitler's economic policies, see W. Carr, *Arms, Autarky and Aggression*, B. A. Carroll, *Design for Total War: Arms and Economics in the Third Reich* (1968), and B. H. Klein, *Germany's Economic Preparations for War* (1959). T. Mason, 'The primacy of politics: politics and economics in National Socialist Germany', in S. J. Woolf (ed.), *The Nature of Fascism* (1968) discusses the Nazi attitude to economics, a view taken up by A. Milward in W. Laqueur (ed.), *Fascism: A Readers' Guide* (1979). For the German economy at war, see A. Milward, *The Germany Economy at War* (1965) and his wider *War, Economy and Society, 1939–1945* (1977).

Articles

R. Bressel, 'Living with the Nazis: some recent writing on the social history of the Third Reich'. *E.H.Q.* (1984) comments on German domestic reactions. See also T. Mason, 'Labour in the Third Reich', *P.P.* (1966) and 'Women in Germany, 1925–40: family, welfare and work', *H.W.J.* (1974). L. D. Stokes, 'The German people and the destruction of the European Jews', *C.E.H.* (1973).

26. Stalin's Russia, 1923–53

In the aftermath of Lenin's death Joseph Stalin gradually asserted himself in power, defeating even the able Leon Trotsky. Stalin's concept of 'socialism in one country' by arguing that Russia could achieve communism herself, without the 'world revolution' predicted by other Marxists gave Russia new faith in herself. After 1928 the 'Stalinisation' programme was pursued to industrialise Russia, by strict control of agriculture and strong central direction, and a series of 'five year plans'. This was accompanied in the 1930s by increasingly totalitarian methods and the elimination of all possible opposition to Stalin. Nevertheless in 1941–5 the communist regime survived Hitler's invasion intact and Stalin's control remained secure down to his death in 1953. His totalitarian legacy has troubled his successors, but he had seen Russia become the world's second greatest power.

Essay topics

Was the 'Stalinisation' programme justified?

What factors helped Stalin to establish and maintain his personal authority in Russia?

Sources and documents

M. McCauley, *Stalin and Stalinism* (1983) has some useful documents, but M. Fainsod, *Smolensk under Soviet Rule* (1959) remains a vivid account from Soviet archives of the realities of the collectivisation process. On the purges see the experiences of V. Serge, *Memoirs of a Revolutionary* (1963) and E. Ginsberg, *Into the Whirlwind* (1968). M. Djilas, *Conversations with Stalin* (1969) shows the later Stalin; see also N. Khrushchev, *Khrushchev Remembers* (1970) and A. Solzhenitsyn, *The Gulag Archipelago 1918–56* (1974).

Secondary works

On Stalin himself there are excellent biographies by I. Deutscher, *Stalin* (1966) and A. B. Ulam, *Stalin* (1973).

The aftermath of Lenin's death is discussed in E. H. Carr, *The Interregnum, 1923–4* (1978), *Socialism in One Country, 1924–6* (1978) and his *The Russian Revolution from Lenin to Stalin, 1917–29* (1970), whilst the demise and exile of Trotsky are dealt with in I. Deutscher, *The Prophet Outcast* (1963) and R. Segal, *The Tragedy of Leon Trotsky* (1983). For the debates after Lenin's death, see A. Erlich, *The Soviet Industrialization Debate, 1924–1928* (1960).

On 'Stalinisation' in the 1930s see A. Nove, *An Economic History of the U.S.S.R.* (1972), as an introduction and the work by R. W. Davies, *The Socialist Offensive* (1980) on the collectivisation of agriculture. R. Conquest, *The Great Terror* (1968) concentrates on the purges, whilst L. L. Schapiro, *The Communist Party of the Soviet Union* (1970) is excellent. See also G. Hosking, *A History of the Soviet Union* (1985).

For the war period see A. Werth, *Russia at War* (1965) and A. Dallin, *German Rule in Russia, 1941–5* (1957), and, on the postwar years, A. Wath, *Russia: 1945–53* (1984).

Stalin's foreign policy is discussed in G. F. Kennan, *Russia and the West under Lenin and Stalin* (1961), A. B. Ulam, *Expansion and Co-existence* (1967) and J. Haslam, *Soviet Foreign Policy, 1930–3* (1983) and *The Soviet Union and the Struggle for Collective Security* (1984).

Articles

See D. R. Brower, 'Collectivised agriculture in Smolensk: the Party, the peasantry and the crisis of 1932', *The Russian Review* (1977); S. Cohen, 'Stalin's revolution reconsidered', *S.R.* (1973).

27.   Eastern Europe between the Wars, 1918–39

The break up of Austria–Hungary at the end of the First World War, together with the defeats of Russia, Germany and Turkey allowed the various nationalities of eastern Europe to assert their independence. Many, impressed by the victory of the western powers in 1918, established democratic regimes. Unfortunately these states soon faced enormous problems. Political inexperience, limited industry, illiteracy, and inflation all took their toll; certain nationalities (such as the Slovaks and Ukrainians) still sought independent rights, whilst the defeated powers, like Hungary, resented the victors, like Romania. In most states democracy simply collapsed from within and with the coming of the 'slump' eastern Europe fell prey to foreign domination, largely by Germany. In 1938 Hitler absorbed Austria and much of Czechoslovakia. In 1939 events in eastern Europe became the cause of a world war.

Essay topics

Why were the states of eastern Europe generally unable to establish stable, democratic regimes between the wars?
    Why was Czechoslovakia unable to resist Hitler's annexationist pressures in 1938?

Sources and documents

Eastern Europe was the stamping ground for many intellectuals and historians who sought to identify and, if possible, solve the problems of eastern Europe's kaleidoscope of cultures, nationalities and prejudices. Many of their contemporary writings are historical documents in themselves. See, for example, E. Wiskemann, *Czechs and Germans* (1938) and *The Europe I Saw* (1968); E. Beneš, *My War Memoirs* (1928); C. A. Macartney, *Hungary and her Successors* (1937) and R. W. Seton-Watson, *A History of the Czechs and Slovaks* (1943).

Secondary works

General introductions to the period are provided by H. Seton-Watson, *Eastern Europe between the Wars* (1962) and the more recent *East Central Europe between the Two World Wars* (1974) by J. Rothschild, whilst a wider perspective is given in A. Palmer, *The Lands Between: a history of east central Europe since the Congress of Vienna* (1970). C. A. Macartney and A. Palmer, *Independent Eastern Europe* (1962) and H. and C. Seton-Watson, *The Making of a New Europe* (1981) are also helpful.
    A. Polansky, *The Little Dictators* (1975) covers each east European state since 1918 in turn, and there are various individual works on east European states, notably R. Clogg, *A Short History of Modern Greece* (1979), M. Macdermott, *A History of Bulgaria* (1962), S. Pollo and A. Puto, *The History of Albania* (1981), S. Fischer-Galati, *Twentieth Century Rumania* (1970) and A. Polonsky, *Politics in Independent Poland 1921–39* (1972). With regard to German expansion in the 1930s, Austria is discussed in J. Gehl, *Austria, Germany and the Anschluss, 1931–9* (1963) and G. Brook-Shepherd, *Anschluss* (1963). On the more complex Czechoslovakian issue see J. W. Bruegel, *Czechoslovakia before Munich* (1973), E. M. Smelser, *The Sudeten Problem, 1933–8* (1975) and, for background, J. Korbel, *Twentieth Century Czechoslovakia* (1977).

28. The Spanish Civil War, 1936–9

In 1931 the Second Republic was established in Spain, following a period
of right-wing dictatorship and inept monarchical rule. But it soon fell
victim to the deep, historical divisions in Spanish politics, and in July
1936 an army uprising led by General Franco and General Mola began
the civil war. Internally, this represented a struggle between conservative
groups, such as the army, church, landowners and fascist elements,
against republicans, socialists, communists and anarchists. However, the
war soon gained a wider European significance, representing to many
the struggle against fascism by democratic and left-wing ideologies.
Foreign volunteers, as 'International Brigades', fought for the Republic
and it received important assistance from the Soviet Union. Franco
received support from Mussolini and Hitler, while the western
democracies pursued a controversial policy of 'non-intervention'. Franco
gradually conquered most of Spain and achieved victory in 1939,
establishing a personal dictatorship which was to last until the 1970s.
The origins of the war and the relative significance of historic as opposed
to short-term factors in its outbreak and character are major issues,
particularly in regard to the conduct of the Popular Front government
prior to the outbreak of the war. The extent to which the war was, in fact,
one between fascism and democracy, as opposed to one drawing on
primarily Spanish issues is important, as is the role of foreign
intervention and the influence of the war on international relations.

Essay topics

To what extent was the Spanish Republic established in 1931 the author
of its own downfall?

How important to the outcome of the Spanish Civil War were the
policies of the major European powers?

Was the Spanish Civil War primarily a war of rival ideologies?

Sources and documents

R. Fraser, *Blood of Spain* (1979) has eyewitness accounts of the conflict,
while George Orwell, *Homage to Catalonia* (1938) and J. Gurney,
Crusade in Spain (1974) are two accounts from British volunteers who
fought for the Republic. See too P. Toynbee, *The Distant Drum:
Reflections on the Spanish Civil War* (1976). Two contemporary novels
which breathe something of the atmosphere of the conflict are E.
Hemingway, *For Whom the Bell Tolls* (1940) and A. Malraux, *Days of
Hope* (1938). F. Borkenau, *The Spanish Cockpit* (1937) was an influential
tract for the times.

Secondary works

R. Carr, *Spain, 1808–1939* (1966; rev. ed, *Spain, 1808–1975*, 1982) is an
essential starting point, rooting the Civil War in Spanish development, as
does his *The Spanish Tragedy* (1977). G. Brenan, *The Spanish Labyrinth*
(1943) is widely recognised as a modern classic for its deep

understanding of the Spanish context. P. Preston (ed.), *Revolution and War in Spain, 1931–1939* (1984) has an extremely useful historiographical essay by the editor, as well as a number of essays reflecting modern scholarship on the origins and nature of the war.

H. Thomas, *The Spanish Civil War* (rev. edn, 1977) remains a well-balanced, narrative, but see also G. Jackson, *The Spanish Republic and the Civil War* (1965). On the origins of the war, P. Preston, *The Coming of the Spanish Civil War* (1978) gives emphasis to the land question, as does E. E. Malefakis, *Agrarian Reform and Peasant Revolution* (1970). R. Carr (ed.), *The Republic and the Civil War in Spain* (1971) is another useful collection of essays. On the right-wing forces, see R. Robinson, *The Origins of Franco's Spain* (1970), S. Payne, *Falange* (1961) and the biographies of Franco by J. Trythall, *Franco* (1970) and B. Crozier, *Franco* (1967). On the left, see S. Payne, *The Spanish Revolution* (1970) and P. Broué and E. Témime, *The Revolution and the Civil War in Spain* (1972), the latter critical of the communists' role. Two books sympathetic to the anarchists are V. Richards, *Lessons of the Spanish Revolution* (1957) and M. Bookchin, *The Spanish Anarchists* (1977). The role of the communists is also considered in D. T. Cattell, *Communism and the Spanish Civil War* (Berkeley, 1955) and B. Balloten, *The Grand Camouflage* (1961), reissued as *The Spanish Revolution: The Left and the Struggle for Power during the Civil War* (1979). A fascinating case study of a group which exemplify the complexities of Spanish politics is M. Blinkhorn, *Carlism and Crisis in Spain, 1931–1939* (1975).

Interventionism is discussed in D. Puzzo, *Spain and the Great Powers, 1936–41* (1962), V. Brome, *The International Brigades* (1965), J. F. Coverdale, *Italian Intervention in the Spanish Civil War* (1977), J. Edwards, *Britain and the Spanish Civil War* (1979), and E. H. Carr, *The Comintern and the Spanish Civil War* (1984). G. Weintraub, *The Last Great Cause* (1976) is an exposé of the war of propaganda carried out by both sides to enlist support and on the most famous episode – the bombing of Guernica – see G. Thomas and M. Witts, *Guernica* (1975) and H. R. Southworth, *Guernica! Guernica! A Study of Journalism, Diplomacy, Propaganda and History* (1977).

29. France, 1918–44

Although the Third Republic emerged victorious from the First World War, the inter-war period was one of increasing self-doubt and division for France. Unstable governments, industrial and demographic weaknesses, and economic problems (especially the 'slump') were compounded by increasing extremism on the left and right, with the emergence of the Communist party and Fascist groups. In the 1930s the Stavisky riots and failure of the 'Popular Front' government, alongside the growing Nazi menace, created grave disillusion. Even so, the Third Republic retained many of its pre-war strengths, including social stability and widespread sympathy for the regime, and historians question whether the Republic would have collapsed but for the overwhelming military defeat at German hands in 1940. In 1940 Marshal Pétain made peace with Germany and established a collaborationist regime at Vichy. France did not recover her independence for four years.

Essay topics

How close did France come to civil war in the inter-war period?
  Was France 'defeatist' in the face of war in 1939–40?

Sources and documents

J.-P. Sartre's novel, *Iron in the Soul* (1949, trans. 1950) represents one
view of the period of the Second World War; but see also P. Laval, *The
Unpublished Diary of Pierre Laval* (1948) and S. M. Osgood (ed.) *The Fall
of France, 1940* (1965).

Secondary works

J. F. McMillan, *Dreyfus to de Gaulle: Politics and Society in France,
1898–1969* (1985) is a recent study. The older studies are J. P. T. Bury,
France, 1870–1940 (1951), A. Cobban, *A History of Modern France, vol. 3*
(1965), and D. W. Brogan, *The Development of Modern France* (1940).
There is also a short account by P. Williams, 'From Dreyfus to Vichy' in
J. M. Wallace-Hadrill (ed.) *France, Government and Society* (1957).
    On the demise of the Republic see W. L. Shirer, *The Collapse of the
Third Republic* (1969) which gives a full and lively account of 1940,
together with the background, A. Adamthwaite, *France and the Coming
of the Second World War* (1977) and, specifically on 1940, A. Horne, *To
Lose a Battle: France, 1940* (1979). Also useful is R. Collier, *1940: The
World in Flames* (1980). Similar issues are tackled from the point of view
of one leading politician in G. Warner, *Pierre Laval and the Eclipse of
France* (1968) whilst A. Werth, *The Twilight of France, 1933–40* (1966)
remains valuable, though originally written in 1942. J. Coulton, *Leon
Blum* (1974) and P. Larmour, *The French Radical Party in the 1930s* (1964)
look at the left in this period, whilst W. D. Irvine, *French Conservatism in
Crisis* (1979) and C. A. Micaval, *The French Right and Nazi Germany,
1933–9* (1972), look at the right.
    Much has been written on Vichy, notably R. Aron, *The Vichy Regime,
1940–4* (1958) and R. Paxton, *Vichy France* (1972) on the regime in
general, R. Cobb, *French and Germans, Germans and French* (1983) for
the German occupation and on resistance see H. R. Kedward, *Resistance
in Vichy France* (1978), M. Dank, *The French against the French* (1978)
and M. R. D. Foot, *Resistance* (1976).

Articles

D. R. Watson, 'The politics of electoral reform in France during the Third
Republic, 1900–40', *P.P.* (1966); A. Sauvy, 'The economic crisis of the
1930s in France', *J. C. H.* (1969) and D. Johnson, 'Leon Blum and the
Popular Front', *H.* (1970) are all useful.

30. Inter-war Diplomacy, 1919–39

Despite the enormous casualties of the First World War the peacemakers
who gathered in Paris in 1919 failed to achieve a stable diplomatic

framework in Europe. The Treaty of Versailles with Germany seemed vindictive in retrospect and many powers came away from Paris determined to alter the settlement. The new international peace-keeping body, the League of Nations, proved weak and in the 1920s even Britain and France fell out over the treatment of Germany and colonial problems. In the 1930s Hitler's Germany and Mussolini's Italy adopted expansionist policies, which the western democracies at first tried to end by 'appeasement'. By September 1939, however, Hitler had already established domination over much of eastern Europe, and his invasion of Poland finally led to a European war.

Essay topics

To what extent should the Versailles Peace Conference be described as a failure?

Was there any point before 1939 when Hitler could have been more effectively opposed?

'The Second World War was Hitler's war.' Discuss.

Sources and documents

A. Adamthwaite, *The Lost Peace* (1980) provides an invaluable documentary source on the whole period. J. M. Keynes's *The Economic Consequences of the Peace* (1919) represents one of the most influential critiques of the peace. See also H. Nicholson, *Peacemaking, 1919* (1933). For the later period see on Germany foreign policy, N. H. Baynes, *The Speeches of Adolf Hitler, April 1922–August 1939* (1942) and on Italy, *Ciano's Diaries, 1937–8* (1952) and *1939–43* (1947). For Britain, see Lord Avon, *Facing the Dictators* (1962) and *The Reckoning* (1965) and W. S. Churchill, *The Second World War, Vol I, The Gathering Storm* (1949); and for Russia, see I. Maisky, *Who Helped Hitler?* (1964).

Secondary works

E. H. Carr, *The Twenty Years Crisis* (new edn, 1981) remains a stimulating account of the period. G. N. Gathorne-Hardy, *A Short History of International Affairs, 1920–39* (1950) has aged less well and, among general accounts, H. Gatzke, *European Diplomacy between the Two World Wars* (1972) is to be preferred, and once again R. Albrecht-Carrié, *A Diplomatic History of Europe from the Congress of Vienna* (1961) provides the wider background. R. A. C. Parker, *Europe, 1919–45* (1969) is also a good general introduction.

On 1919 and its immediate aftermath A. J. Mayer, *The Policy and Diplomacy of Peacemaking* (1968), G. Schulz, *Revolution and Peace Treaties* (1972) and S. Marks, *The Illusion of Peace* (1976) are useful, whilst F. P. Walters, *A History of the League of Nations* (1960) remains the most thorough account of that body.

On the origins of war in 1939, A. J. P. Taylor, *The Origins of the Second World War* (1963) is still exciting and very readable, though its arguments have been undermined. E. M. Robertson, *The Origins of the Second World War* (1976) is more recent but less challenging. On the 1930s especially, see also C. Thorne, *The Approach of War* (1967),

D. C. Watt, *Too Serious a Business* (1975), and A. Adamthwaite, *The Making of the Second World War* (1977). A recent overview is P. Bell, *The Origins of the Second World War in Europe* (1986).

On specific events and issues, N. Rostow, *Anglo–French Relations, 1934–6* (1984) analyses western policies at a key period, whilst K. Robbins, *Munich* (1968) and T. Taylor *Munich* (1979) look at the most criticised episode in 1930s diplomacy. S. Newman, *March, 1939* (1976) concentrates on the British guarantee to Poland, which was so vital in the outbreak of war. On French policy see especially A. Adamthwaite, *France and the Coming of the Second World War* (1977), and on Germany, G. L. Weinberg, *The Foreign Policy of Hitler's Germany* (1970) and W. Carr, *Arms, Autarky and Aggression* (1972). And on British appeasement in general see especially M. Gilbert, *The Roots of Appeasement* (1966), K. Middlemas, *Diplomacy of Illusion* (1972) and W. R. Rock, *British Appeasement in the 1930s* (1976). See also the essays by N. Medlicott and M. Howard in D. Dilks (ed.), *Retreat from Power: Studies of Britain's Foreign Policy of the Twentieth Century: Volume One, 1906–1939* (1981).

Articles

Among the numerous articles on the various crises of the 1930s, see especially R. A. C. Parker, 'Great Britain, France and the Ethiopian Crisis, 1935–6', *E.H.R.*, (1974); C. A. Macdonald, 'Britain, France and the April Crisis of 1939', *E.S.R.* (1972); and M. Newman, 'The origins of Munich', *H.J.* (1978).

31.   The Second World War, 1939–45

Although Hitler was able to overrun Poland, Norway, Denmark, the Low Countries and France in 1939–40, Britain survived and in 1941 was joined by Russia and America. In the air the Germans lost the 'Battle of Britain' and were soon faced with Anglo–American bombing of their own cities; at sea, the allied use of radar helped defeat the U-boat menace; whilst on land the German army proved unable to break Russian resistance. Economic factors, notably American industrial production, and manpower began to tell in the Allies' favour, and from 1943 Hitler's defeat was clearly inevitable. The use of German technology to produce the snorkel, jet aircraft and rockets came too late to affect the outcome. Nonetheless, many would argue that it was Hitler's own ambition which ultimately proved his greatest enemy. The social and political repercussions of 'total war' with mass civilian involvement have also become important areas of discussion.

Essay topics

To what extent did economic considerations dictate the course of the Second World War in Europe?

How far did European experience of 'total war' affect its conduct and its outcome?

Why were the the campaigns of the Second World War more mobile than those of the First?

Sources and documents

H. Jacobsen and A. Smith (eds), *World War II* (1980) has documents on military policy and strategy, and there are numerous collections of memoirs. W. S. Churchill, *The Second World War* (6 vols, 1948–54) and C. de Gaulle, *War Memoirs* (3 vols, 1955–9) are perhaps the best from European statesmen and, from the generals, D. Eisenhower, *Crusade in Europe* (1948) and Montgomery of Alamein, *Memoirs* (1958). A. Speer, *Inside the Third Reich* (1970) remains a telling account of the resilience of the German war machine. On the civilian side, see on Holland O. Frank, *The Diary of Anne Frank* (1947), on Britain R. Broad and S. Fleming (eds), *Nella Last's Diary* (1981), and on the concentration camps O. Lengyel, *Five Chimneys* (1959). Two English language accounts of life within Germany are C. Bielenberg, *The Past is Myself* (1985) and *The Berlin Diaries, 1940–1945, of Marie 'Missie' Vassiltchikov* (1985).

Secondary works

Of the general introductions, G. Wright, *The Ordeal of Total War* (1968), B. Liddell Hart, *The Second World War* (1970), P. Calvocoressi and G. Wint, *Total War* (1974) and A. J. P. Taylor, *The Second World War: an illustrated history* (1976) are all useful, whilst A. Marwick, *War and Social Change in the Twentieth Century* (1974) concentrates on the social effects. D. Irving, *Hitler's War* (2 vols, 1983) gives a controversial account from the German side; on Russia, see A. Werth, *Russia at War* (1965) and on Britain, A. Calder, *The People's War* (1969). A. S. Milward, *War, Economy and Society, 1939–1945* (1977) is a brilliant synthesis of the economic ramifications of 'total war'; see also his *The German Economy at War* (1965) and *The New Order and the French Economy* (1970).

The opening phase of the war is covered by B. Collier, *1940: the World in Flames* (1980) and *1941: Armageddon* (1982). The controversy over the effectiveness and morality of the bombing offensive against Germany is considered in N. Frankland. *The Bombing Offensive against Germany* (1965) and M. Hastings, *Bomber Command* (1979). For the German side of the air war, see D. Irving, *The Rise and Fall of the Luftwaffe* (1973). For the war at sea, see D. Macintyre, *The Battle of the Atlantic* (1961), J. Costello and T. Hughes, *The Battle of the Atlantic* (1977), and W. Frank, *The Sea Wolves* (1955). The decisive struggle on the eastern front is considered in A. Clark, *Barbarossa* (1965), and J. Erickson, *The Road to Stalingrad. Stalin's War with Germany* (1975) and *The Road to Berlin* (1983). For the final phase of the war see E. Belfield and H. Essame, *The Battle for Normandy* (1965) and C. Ryan, *The Last Battle*. Specifically on the new form of mobile warfare, see H. Guderian, *Panzer Leader* (1952) and F. W. von Mellenthin, *Panzer Battles* (1955). Technical developments affecting the conduct of the war are discussed in R. V. Jones, *Most Secret War* (1978) and B. Johnson, *The Secret War* (1978).

The fate of areas conquered by the Germans is considered in

W. Warmbrunn, *The Dutch under German Occupation* (1963), A. Dallin, *German Rule in Russia, 1941–5* (1957) and R. O. Paxton, *Vichy France* (1973), whilst the resistance movements are analysed in H. Michel, *The Shadow War: Resistance in Europe, 1939–45* (1972) and M. R. D. Foot, *Resistance* (1976).

On diplomacy during the war see H. Feis, *Churchill, Roosevelt, Stalin* (1957), W. H. McNeill, *America, Britain and Russia* (1953) and G. Kolko, *The Politics of War* (1968).

32. The Cold War

Despite their wartime alliance the Soviet Union and the western powers, America and Britain, soon differed over the shape of the postwar world. The Russian takeover in Eastern Europe, and enforcement of communist regimes, together with Soviet pressures in Germany and the Middle East, led to the Truman Doctrine, in 1947, by which the Americans undertook to resist communist pressure. America and the West Europeans joined together in NATO in 1949, and the following years were characterised by deep-seated tension, known as the Cold War, with notable crises over the Korean War, the future of Berlin and Cuba.

Essay topics

To what extent may Russia be blamed for beginning the Cold War?
   At what point, if any, did the Cold War end?

Sources and documents

A readily accessible selection can be found in M. McCauley, *The Origins of the Cold War* (1983), but the early period is well covered from the documentary side by W. Lafeber, *The Origins of the Cold War* (1977) and M. Carlyle, (ed.), *Documents on International Affairs, 1947–8* (1952) and *1949–50* (1953). There are numerous memoirs on the Cold War theme but among the best are H. S. Truman, *Year of Decisions, 1945* (1955) and *Years of Trial and Hope, 1946–53* (1956), and D. Acheson, *Present at the Creation* (1970).

Secondary works

For the background to the postwar period see W. H. McNeill, *America, Britain and Russia* (1953) and H. L. Feis, *Churchill, Roosevelt, Stalin* (1957).

There are several general works on the period, most being American. J. W. Spanier, *American Foreign Policy since the Second World War* (1980), is pro-American; S. E. Ambrose, *Rise to Globalism* (1983) and W. Lafeber, *America, Russia and the Cold War* (1982), are more questioning of US policy; whilst L. J. Halle, *The Cold War as History* (1967) is still a useful, balanced account on part of the period. On Britain see W. N. Medlicott, *British Foreign Policy since Versailles* (1940), and Soviet policy is the subject of A. B. Ulam, *Expansion and Coexistence*

(1968) and T. W. Wolfe, *Soviet Power and Europe, 1945–70* (1970).

The early years of the Cold War have received most coverage. Again there are conservative accounts, such as G. F. Hudson, *The Hard and Bitter Peace* (1966) and H. L. Feis, *From Trust to Terror* (1970), criticisms of America in G. and J. Kolko, *The Limits of Power* (1972) and D. Yergin, *Shattered Peace* (1977). J. L. Gaddis, *The United States and the Origins of the Cold War* (1973) is good, and on the British see V. Rothwell, *Britain and the Cold War, 1941–7* (1983).

Coverage of the continental states is slight, but on France see G. de Carmoy, *The Foreign Policies of France* (1970) and, on the early years, E. Furniss, *France, Troubled Ally* (1960).

Articles

R. Ovendale, 'Britain, the U.S.A. and the European Cold War, 1945–8', *H.* (1982) is a discussion of the major issues in the early post-war years, and G. Warner, 'The Truman Doctrine and the Marshall Plan', *International Affairs* (1974) discusses what was perhaps the key year. Of vital importance to the framing of America's anti-communist policy was G. F. Kennan, 'The sources of Soviet conduct', *Foreign Affairs* (1947), and A. Schlesinger, 'Origins of the Cold War', *Foreign Affairs* (1967) gives an intelligent, short discussion.

33.   Western European democracy since 1945

Western Europe in the aftermath of the Second World War proved far more stable and wealthy than after the First. Despite the reconstruction problems left by war, economic recovery, helped by the American Marshall Aid programme, was quite rapid, whilst democracy was re-established in France, Germany, Italy and elsewhere. The NATO alliance and extension of European unity created a feeling of security and solidarity, which helped make the 1950s and 1960s decades of relative calm. There were problems however. In France political instability and the difficulties of decolonisation brought the fall of the Fourth Republic in 1958. Italian political life was characterised by rapid government changes and extremist pressures, and, in the 1970s, despite the restoration of democracy in Spain, Portugal and Greece, all Europe was faced with the problems of inflation and unemployment.

Essay topics

Why has West Germany proved more politically stable than Italy as a postwar democracy?

To what extent can de Gaulle's period in office after 1958 be seen as a turning-point in French history?

Sources and documents

For a wide-ranging set of documents see P. Lane. *Europe Since 1945* (1985).

Secondary works

For general coverage of events see W. Laqueur, *Europe since Hitler* (1970), D. Urwin, *Western Europe since 1945* (1981) and P. Calvocoressi, *World Politics since 1945* (1982 edn). Also good are R. Mayne, *The Recovery of Europe* (1970), M. Crouzet, *The European Renaissance since 1945* (1970) and R. Morgan, *West European Politics since 1945* (1972). Rather narrower in interest is F. R. Willis, *France, Germany and the New Europe, 1945–67* (1969), whilst F. Fry and G. Raymond, *The Other Western Europe* (1980) looks at the smaller democracies.

On France in this period see P. M. Williams, *Crisis and Compromise: Politics in the Fourth Republic* (1964 edn); P. M. Williams and M. Harrison, *Politics and Compromise: Politics and Society in de Gaulle's Republic* (1971); J. Ardagh, *The New France* (1978), and M. Anderson, *Conservative Politics in France* (1974). See also the important recent study by J. F. McMillan, *Dreyfus to de Gaulle: Politics and Society in France, 1898–1969* (1985). On de Gaulle, see D. Cook, *Charles de Gaulle* (1984). For Germany, see A. Grosser, *Germany in Our Time* (1971), T. Prittie, *The Velvet Chancellors* (1979) and *Adenauer* (1971). On Italy, see M. Clark, *Modern Italy, 1871–1982* (1984) and E. Wiskemann, *Italy since 1945* (1971). Among other countries, Spain provides an interesting barometer of the spread of democracy in Western Europe; see R. Carr, *A History of Spain, 1808–1980* (rev. edn 1980), R. Carr and J. P. Fusi, *Spain: Dictatorship to Democracy* (1979) and D. Gilmour, *The Transformation of Spain* (1985).

34.   The movement for European unity

One of the most remarkable occurrences in Western Europe, in the aftermath of the Second World War, was the move towards some form of European unity. This was first seen in the Organisation for European Economic Co-operation (1948) and the Council of Europe (1949). Pressures far more far-reaching of a 'supranational' kind led to the Schuman Plan (1950) and eventually the European Economic Community or Common Market (1957). Originally these supranational bodies included only six states but after 1973 they were gradually extended. There were many strong reasons for such greater unity to come about, not least the experiences of war and Cold War and the dwarfing of Europe by the Superpowers: the doubts about 'supranationalism' from both Britain (down to the 1960s) and France's President de Gaulle (during the 1960s) were a major challenge to the European movement.

Essay topics

Account for the rise of the European unity movement in the postwar period.

To what extent was the move towards greater European unity shaped by French policy, 1950–69?

Sources and documents

Two very useful 'inside' accounts of the European unity movement can be found in the *Memoirs*, (1978) of Jean Monnet, the 'father of European unity' and P. H. Spaak, *The Continuing Battle* (1971). Relevant documents can be found in R. Vaughan, *Post-war Integration in Europe* (1976), and, on Britain and the Community, in U. Kitzinger, (ed.), *The Second Try: Labour and the E.E.C.* (1968).

Secondary works

There are general discussions of the European unity movement in W. Laqueur, *Europe since Hitler* (1970) and D. Urwin, *Western Europe since 1945* (1981 edn).

The fullest account of the early years of the unity movement can be found in W. Lipgens, *A History of European Integration, 1945–7* (1982), though this is very detailed. J. W. Young, *Britain, France and the Unity of Europe, 1945–51* (1984) is shorter and more analytical, whilst on the early 1950s see E. Fursdon, *The European Defence Community* (1981), on the vain bid to create a 'European Army'. On the Common Market itself see R. Pryce, *The Politics of the European Community* (1973).

American relations with the European unity movement are discussed by M. Beloff, *The United States and the Unity of Europe* (1963) and R. Manderson-Jones, *Special Relationship* (1972), while British relations are discussed in M. Camps, *Britain and the European Community, 1955–63* (1964) and U. Kitzinger, *Diplomacy and Persuasion* (1974).

For the development of the European Community in recent years see W. Feld, *The European Community in World Affairs* (1976). J. Fitzmaurice, *The European Parliament* (1978), V. Herman and J. Lodge, *The European Parliament and the European Community* (1978).

35. Eastern Europe since 1945

Although Britain and France went to war to liberate eastern Europe in 1939, the end of the Second World War largely saw German domination of the area replaced by that of Russia. Between 1944 and 1948 Communist parties established themselves in power, removed their democratic and rightist opponents and carried out Soviet-style reforms. But, although these states became linked to the USSR through the Warsaw Pact and COMECON, it became apparent that Russian control in the Eastern Bloc had limitations. Yugoslavia and Albania managed to escape the Soviet orbit, and although Moscow crushed opposition to her in East Germany, Hungary and Czechoslovakia, the communist states of the region managed to achieve differing degrees of independence in economic, social and even foreign policy by the 1970s.

Essay topics

How important was the presence of the Red Army as a factor in creating communist states in Eastern Europe, 1944–8?

Why did the Soviet Union intervene militarily in Hungary (1956) and Czechoslovakia (1968) but not in Yugoslavia (1948)?

Sources and documents

M. McCauley, *The Origins of the Cold War* (1983) has some relevant documents; see also V. Dedijer, *Tito Speaks* (1954).

Secondary works

F. Fejto, *A History of the People's Democracies* (1971), G. Ionescu, *The Break-up of the Soviet Empire in Eastern Europe* (1965); Z. Brzezinski, *The Soviet Bloc* (1974); L. Labedz (ed.), *Revisionism* (1962); and Hugh Seton-Watson, *Nationalism and Communism, Essays, 1946–63* (1964) are all useful, see also M. McCauley, *Communist Power in Europe, 1944–9* (1977). On important individuals see N. Bethell, *Gomulka* (1969) and P. Auty, *Tito* (1970). On East Germany see M. McCauley, *The German Democratic Republic* (1983) and J. P. Netti, *The Eastern Zone and Soviet Policy in Germany, 1945–50* (1951). On Hungary see D. Irving, *Uprising (1956)*. For Poland, see J. Coutouvidis and J. Reynolds, *Poland, 1939–1947* (1986) and N. Ascherson, *The Polish August* (1981).

Maps

1   Europe in the late eighteenth century

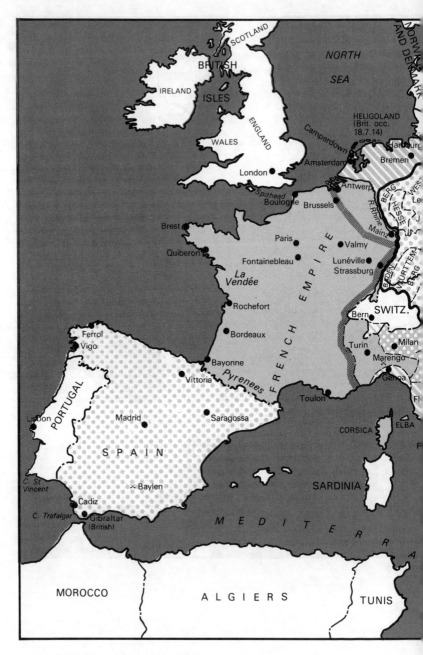

2   Europe at the height of Napoleon's power

France at the end of 1802

Acquisitions 1803–05

Acquisitions 1805–10

Kingdom of Italy, directly ruled by Napoleon

Dependent states

Boundary of France, 1792

Boundary of Confederation of the Rhine

0   300 mls

0   300 km

SWEDEN

BALTIC SEA

openhagen

BORNHOLM

PRUSSIA

Danzig (Rep.)   × Tilsit

Berlin   × Friedland

GRAND DUCHY OF WARSAW

Posen

Warsaw

SILESIA

R. Oder

Cracow

GALICIA

R. Elbe

EMIA

Austerlitz ×

AUSTRIA

Wagram ×

R. Danube

Pressburg

Vienna

Pesth

HUNGARY

EMPIRE

AUSTRIAN

RUSSIA

R. Dnieper

R. Dniester

MOLDAVIA

R. Pruth

TRANSYL-VANIA

WALLACHIA

BOSNIA

SERBIA

R. Danube

BLACK SEA

ADRIATIC SEA

PLES

MONTE-NEGRO

TURKISH

Bosphorus

Constantinople

ASIA MINOR

Dardanelles

ALBANIA

Janina

Maida

EMPIRE

Smyrna

IONIAN ISLANDS (French)

MOREA

Y

A

N

SEA

CRETE

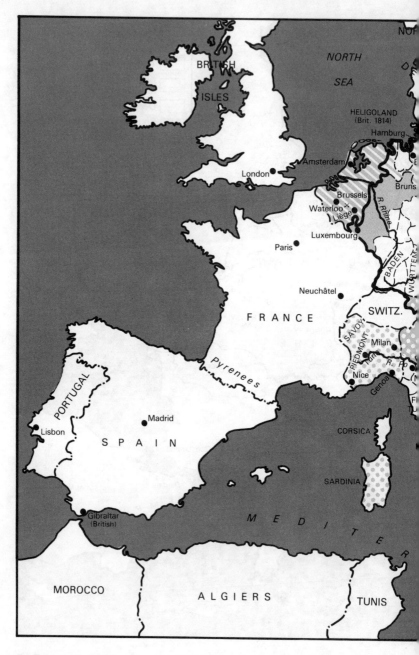

3   Europe in 1815

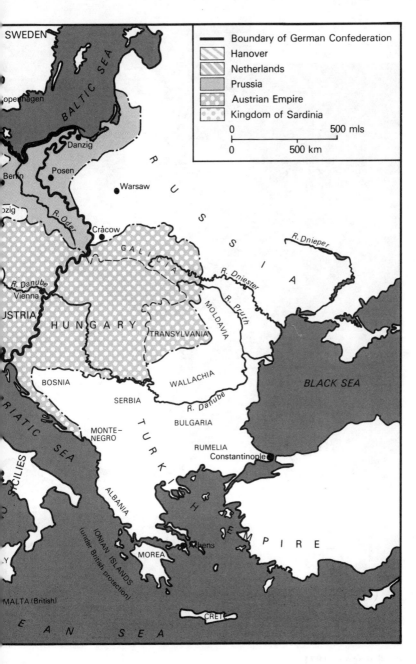

SWEDEN

BALTIC SEA

openhagen

Danzig

Berlin

Posen

ozig

R. Oder

Cràcow

Warsaw

R U S S I A

GALICIA

R. Dnieper

R. Dniester

R. Danube

Vienna

USTRIA

H U N G A R Y

MOLDAVIA

R. Pruth

TRANSYLVANIA

BOSNIA

WALLACHIA

SERBIA

R. Danube

MONTE-
NEGRO

BULGARIA

T U R K I S H

RUMELIA

Constantinople

BLACK SEA

RIATIC SEA

CILIES

ALBANIA

E M P I R E

IONIAN ISLANDS
(under British protection)

MOREA

Athens

Y

MALTA (British)

E A N   S E A

CRETE

Boundary of German Confederation
Hanover
Netherlands
Prussia
Austrian Empire
Kingdom of Sardinia

0   500 mls

0   500 km

4   Europe in 1871

SWEDEN
AND
NORWAY

FINLAND

St. Petersburg

Stockholm

BALTIC SEA

Copenhagen

RUSSIA

Danzig

Berlin

Warsaw

POLAND

GALICIA

R. Dnieper

BOHEMIA

R. Dniester

Vienna

Budapest

AUSTRIA-HUNGARY

R. Drave

CRIMEA

TRANSYLVANIA

R. Save

Belgrade

Bucharest

RUMANIA

*BLACK
SEA*

BOSNIA

SERBIA

R. Danube

ADRIATIC SEA

MONTE-
NEGRO

Sofia

Bosphorus

ALBANIA

T
U
R
K
E
Y

Constantinople

Dardanelles

SEA

GREECE

ASIA MINOR

Athens

5 European frontiers, 1919–37

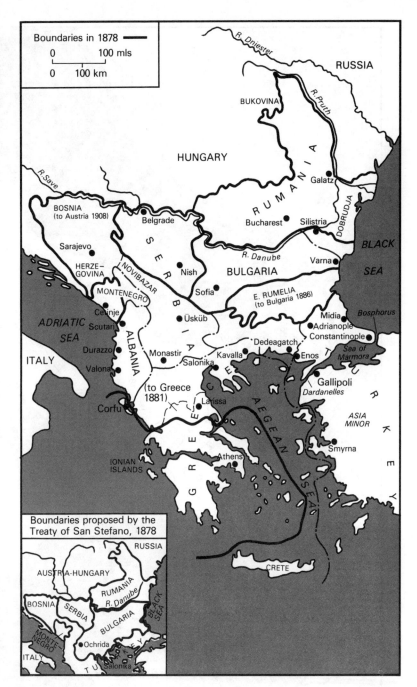

6   The Balkan peninsula, 1800–78

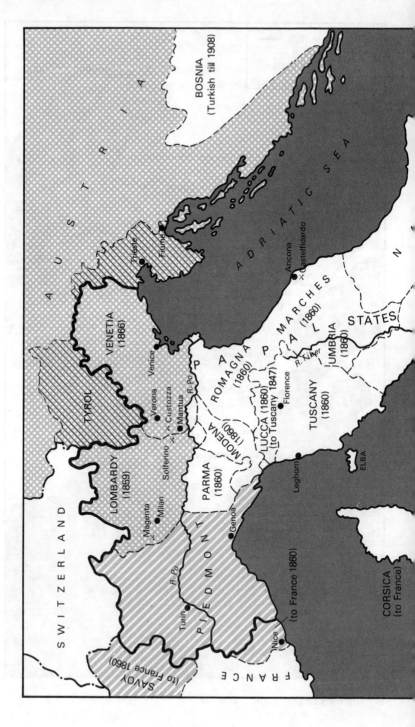

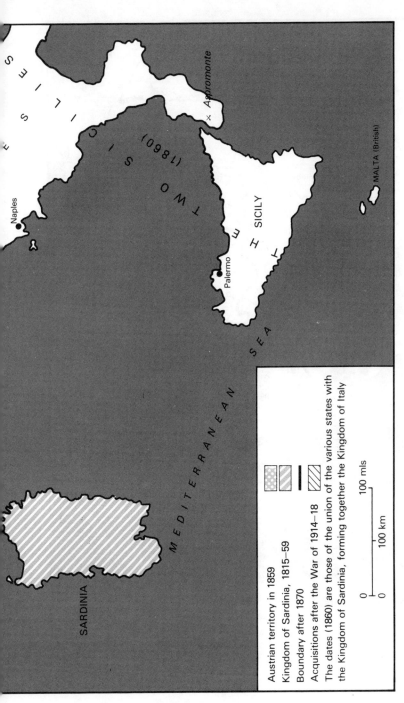

Austrian territory in 1859

Kingdom of Sardinia, 1815–59

Boundary after 1870

Acquisitions after the War of 1914–18

The dates (1860) are those of the union of the various states with
the Kingdom of Sardinia, forming together the Kingdom of Italy

0 _____ 100 mls

0 _____ 100 km

7   Italian unification

8   The Balkan states in 1913

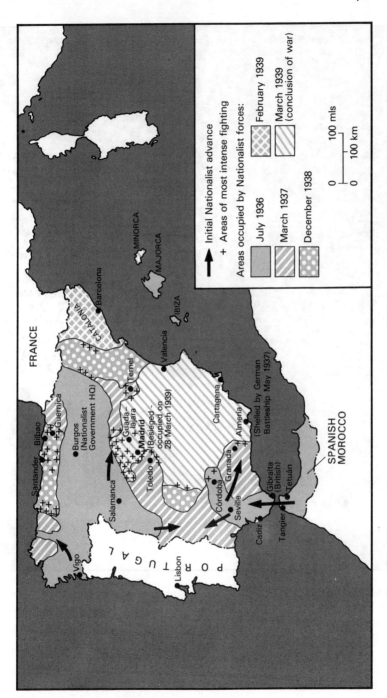

9   The Spanish Civil War

Initial Nationalist advance
+   Areas of most intense fighting

Areas occupied by Nationalist forces:

July 1936

March 1937

December 1938

February 1939

March 1939
(conclusion of war)

0   100 mls
0   100 km

FRANCE

CATALONIA

Barcelona

MINORCA

MAJORCA

IBIZA

Valencia

Cartagena

Almeria

(Shelled by German
Battleship May 1937)

Teruel

Guada-
lajara

Madrid
(Besieged-
occupied on
28 March 1939)

Guernica

Bilbao

Santander

Burgos
(Nationalist
Government HQ)

Salamanca

Toledo

Córdoba

Granada

Seville

Gibralta
(British)

Cadiz

Tangier

Tetuán

SPANISH
MOROCCO

Vigo

P O R T U G A L

Lisbon

10   Europe in 1945

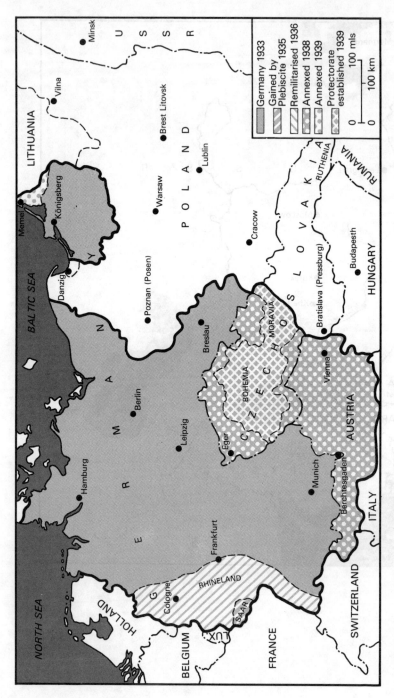

11 The expansion of Germany, 1935–39

Legend:
- Germany 1933
- Gained by Plebiscite 1935
- Remilitarised 1936
- Annexed 1938
- Annexed 1939
- Protectorate established 1939

Index

(*Note: numbers in bold refer to main subject entries*)